DOCUMENTARY OBJECTIVES

DOCUMENTARY OBJECTIVES

FILMING AFRICA FROM COLONIALISM TO INDEPENDENCE

RACHEL GABARA

INDIANA UNIVERSITY PRESS

This book is a publication of

Indiana University Press
Herman B Wells Library
1320 East 10th Street
Bloomington, Indiana 47405 USA

iupress.org

For customers in the European Union with safety or GPSR concerns, please contact Mare Nostrum Group B.V., Mauritskade 21D, 1091 GC Amsterdam, The Netherlands. Email: gpsr@mare-nostrum.co.uk

First Printing 2026

Cataloging information is available from the Library of Congress.

ISBN 978-0-253-07479-9 (hdbk.)
ISBN 978-0-253-07480-5 (pbk.)
ISBN 978-0-253-07482-9 (ebook)

CONTENTS

ACKNOWLEDGMENTS

I have been working on this book for a long time, and many organizations and individuals have supported my efforts. An African Regional Research Grant from the Fulbright Scholar Program enabled me to build groundwork while in Dakar, Senegal, and Ouagadougou, Burkina Faso, where staff at the West Africa Research Association and Center and the FESPACO film festival gave invaluable support. Research grants from Princeton University's Tuck Fund and Committee on Research in the Humanities and Social Sciences got me to archives in Dakar and Paris. A summer stipend from the National Endowment for the Humanities and a Franklin research grant from the American Philosophical Society allowed me to spend many hours in Salle P of the Bibliothèque Nationale de France. Research fellowships from the Willson Center for Humanities and Arts and the Office of the Vice President for Research at the University of Georgia made the development of a chronologically and geographically wide-ranging project possible. And a year-long fellowship from the National Endowment for the Humanities provided time and mental space to put everything together while the world was in lockdown.

My research builds on the work of scholars in multiple fields, whose names are cited in these pages. For important discussions and encouragement, I thank Moradewun Adejunmobi, Jude Akudinobi, Peter Bloom, Kelley Conway, Sam Di Iorio, Lindiwe Dovey, Frieda Ekotto, Rosalind Galt, Cajetan Iheka, Alessandro Jedlowski, Peter Limbrick, Sada Niang, Aboubakar Sanogo, Alexie Tcheuyap, Melissa Thackway, Subha Xavier, and Carina Yervasi. I am grateful for the support of Kenneth Harrow and Jonathan Kahana (may their memory be a blessing). When I first had coffee with Stéphane Vieyra in Paris, I did not imagine that our meeting would lead to Indiana University's acquisition of his father's archive, through a rewarding collaboration with Vincent Bouchard, Terri Francis, and Amadou Ouédraogo. A number of inspiring filmmakers have taken the time to speak and correspond with me, notably Jihan El-Tahri, Mahamat-Saleh Haroun, Osvalde Lewat, Cheikh Ndiaye, Mweze Ngangura, Raoul Peck, Abderrahmane Sissako, Jean-Marie Teno, and the late Samba Félix Ndiaye. Olivier Barlet, Mathieu Fournet, Amélie Garin-Davet, France Langlois, Catherine Ruelle, and Ninon Teissier provided invaluable help finding films. And I am indebted to a group of wonderful colleagues from the University of Georgia, particularly Dana Bultman, Stacey Casado, Cathy Jones, Rielle Navitski, Richard Neupert, Susan Rosenbaum, Betsy Wright, and, at the Willson Center, Nicholas Allen and Winnie Smith. Thanks also to Allison Chaplin, Sophia Hebert, and Nancy Lightfoot at Indiana University Press for bringing this book into the world.

The constant love and support of Uliana and Vlodek Gabara made everything possible. I treasure my walks and talks with Esther Gabara, sister extraordinaire and sounding board for professional opportunities and challenges. Claudio Saunt is the best of partners, a scholarly model who understands that the most important things in life are not work related. Leo and Milo grew into young adults while I was reading, watching, teaching, thinking, procrastinating, and writing, and they give joy and meaning to all of it.

DOCUMENTARY OBJECTIVES

INTRODUCTION

Paul Rotha's influential *Documentary Film*, originally published in 1935, was reissued in several updated versions, with a section added in the early 1950s to account for recent developments. A single page of this section was devoted to Africa, with Rotha's collaborator Sinclair Road noting that films shot in regions colonized by France and Belgium, like those produced by the Canadian National Film Board in South Africa and the British Colonial Film Unit in West, East, and central Africa, manifested a "shift away from travelogues toward the educational film."[1] A minor detail within a four-hundred-page book, this shift nonetheless gave Rotha his new frontispiece, which the list of illustrations titles "An African Audience." A dense crowd of Black children and adults sits around a projector, its light pointing toward a screen we cannot see. In a survey of nonfiction film production in the first half century of the cinema, Africans are featured as smiling consumers of moving images made by Europeans to facilitate the so-called civilizing mission.

As is often declared in introductions, this book is not about that. A great deal has been written about the work of Canada's National Film Board and Britain's Bantu Educational Experiment and Colonial Film Unit, the latter of which documented its activities just after World War II in a quarterly journal titled *Colonial Cinema*.[2] The book *Le cinéma pour africains* (Cinema for Africans) chronicled a comparable program established by Belgium's colonial government in Congo to make educational films for African audiences while training African technicians.[3] Somewhat paradoxically given the scholarly attention these efforts have received, they were chronologically quite limited, originating in the mid-1930s and concentrated during the fifteen years between the end of the war and African independence. Although French colonial filmmaking in West and central Africa did include an educational segment, its objective was not the education of Africans but the education of Europeans about Africa.[4] France's long tradition of shooting films in sub-Saharan Africa was built not by governmental film agencies but via private, commercial production, distribution, and exhibition—those companies and cameramen nonetheless subsidized and supported by colonial institutions and networks. Production of such films increased steadily from the early years of the twentieth century, their length, style, and focus changing over time and as technology evolved.

Although the details of the story are arguable, we usually say that the cinema was born in France in 1895 with the invention and marketing of the Lumière Brothers cinematograph. The same year saw both the French Colonial Ministry's creation of the Government General of French West Africa (AOF), a consolidation of smaller conquered territories, and the founding of the École Coloniale to train future administrators.[5] In his pivotal analysis of French colonial ideology, historian Raoul Girardet identified a wave of nationalist fervor for empire following France's 1871 defeat in the Franco-Prussian War and the resulting loss of Alsace-Lorraine. Between 1880 and 1895, both the area and population of France's overseas possessions expanded tenfold.[6] At its height, during the interwar period, the French empire extended over approximately 12 million square kilometers inhabited by 65 million people, while 40 million people occupied one-twentieth the space within hexagonal France. In sub-Saharan Africa, graduates of the École Coloniale were sent to French West Africa and French Equatorial Africa (AEF), a federation created in 1910, as well as to Cameroon and Togo, territories under mandate acquired from Germany after World War I. These regions now comprise fourteen independent nations with a combined population of nearly 200 million.

In *Documentary Objectives: Filming Africa from Colonialism to Independence*, I recount a film history in the spaces of what historian Gary Wilder has called the *imperial nation-state*: metropole and colonies together.[7] Rather than surveying moving images shot throughout Africa, the book zooms in on France's former colonies south of the Sahara, linked not just by empire but also by the development of a specific mode of filmmaking over the course of a century. The importance of comparative studies of French, Belgian, and British colonial filmmaking practices and of the wealth of independent filmmaking traditions across the African continent is undeniable. A limited geographical and linguistic focus, however, allows for a detailed study of the production, distribution, and reception of films in a wider chronological framework, spanning the colonial and postcolonial periods. Attention only to colonial cinema, even when it is denounced as such, repeats its foreclosure of African authorship, an authorship that in the case of film became possible only in the wake of six decades of European film history. And attention only to postcolonial cinema conversely ignores the context of its birth—the weight of six decades of European film history after which African filmmakers worked to create something new and their own. Doing so, director Jean-Marie Teno said of his first documentary feature, "I went to the colonial period to understand the present."[8]

In an analysis of colonial stereotyping that relies on Edward Said's characterization of orientalism as a "radical realism," postcolonial theorist Homi Bhabha argues that colonial discourse requires the creation of a colonized "other" that is "entirely knowable and visible."[9] Moving pictures did not invent a French discourse about sub-Saharan Africa but rather escalated claims made by other verbal and visual genres—adventure narratives, illustrated magazines, postcards, and a range of photographs—to provide an indexical representation of reality. On the shelves of what preeminent philosopher V. Y. Mudimbe called the *colonial library*, "a body of knowledge constructed with the explicit purpose of faithfully translating and deciphering the African object," these works are tethered both to each other and to colonial military and administrative power by their pretensions to objectivity and scientificity.[10] These same pretensions link them to ethnography such that, "in the first quarter of [the twentieth] century," Mudimbe notes, "it was clear that the traveler had become a colonizer and the anthropologist, his scientific advisor."[11] Within this network of nonfiction, films shot in Africa were fundamental to the development of French documentary cinema, forging a tradition to which African documentarists working after independence felt compelled to respond. In this book, I contend that any analysis of colonial-era French documentary is incomplete without a continuation of the story—the creations of those whose places, cultures, and stories were portrayed and narrated by outsiders. Understanding triumphalist French colonial documentary to constitute the prehistory of independent African nonfiction film, this study is structured to allow African filmmakers the last word while highlighting the substantial contribution of an African documentary corpus to both global documentary and African cinema as a whole.

Historian of early cinema Noël Burch describes the Lumière Brothers' project as "an experiment in the observation of reality: as we would put it today, it was a matter of 'catching' an action."[12] When French film scholar Alan Williams contrasted Lumière's "'documentary' impulse" with the vaudeville style of Edison films, however, he placed scare quotes around *documentary* to suggest that the professed accuracy of Lumière technology was more marketing ploy than scientific inquiry.[13] From its very beginnings, cinema advertised its documentaryness, and films shot outside of France and even Europe were an important component of Lumière publicity. The apparatus permitted world-traveling operators to project and shoot films, with pioneer Félix Mesguich playing on a linguistic ambiguity to announce of cinema that "its *objectif* is like the eye of the spectator, open to the world."[14] *Objectif* here signifies camera lens, evoking in French as in English the sense of a goal as well as of objectivity. The title of this book, *Documentary Objectives*, should be understood for this triple resonance: it announces an investigation of how cameramen and filmmakers shooting from varied perspectives with differing conceptions of documentary truth have been impelled by different motives toward various ends.

Cinema has always been a transnational enterprise but never an equal one. "Those who came to film us," renowned Malian director Souleymane Cissé explained in a 1991 interview with Franco-Cambodian documentarist Rithy Panh, "never showed the people here like human beings. . . . They came to show us like animals to their audiences." Colonial-era French filmmakers claimed to be shooting nonfiction, and their work was distributed and advertised as such. The duty of African filmmakers, Cissé continued, was therefore to make it clear that "those auteurs lied in their images. . . . They were liars."[15] The relationship between perspective and documentary truth lies at the heart of *Documentary Objectives*; my project arose from the supposition that when nonfiction films have lied about you and your world, you are unlikely to succumb to clichés about documentary objectivity and form. In 1965, legendary Senegalese director Ousmane Sembene accused legendary French director Jean Rouch of filming Africans as if they were insects. Pronounced five years after independence, this quote is itself legendary, whereas Sembene's clarification of its meaning is often forgotten. In response to Rouch's question of why Sembene did not like his "purely ethnographic films," Sembene answered that "they portray a reality, but without seeing its evolution."[16] Rejecting a European filmic gaze that echoed German philosopher G. W. F. Hegel's early nineteenth-century characterization of sub-Saharan Africa as "no historical part of the World," with "no movement or development to exhibit," Sembene insisted that, pinning traditions and rituals to the screen, Rouch and his colleagues ignored the essential aspect of documentary truth that is the transformation of African reality over time.[17]

Critical approaches to what some consider a genre and others a mode have varied, but, for over a century, dominant voices in filmmaking and media scholarship have agreed that documentary is dual, relying on both visual capture of reality and tools of fiction such as plotting, staging, and performance. The most frequently cited definition of documentary is "the creative treatment of actuality," a phrase attributed to British documentarist John Grierson's review of American Robert Flaherty's ethnographic film *Moana* (1926).[18] Flaherty's creatively performed and edited *Nanook of the North* (1922) is per this definition often listed in textbooks and film histories as the first documentary film. Soviet artists, writers, and filmmakers reflecting on the nature of documentary cinema in the same decade similarly invoked its narrativizing of nonfiction, with the "life caught unawares" of Dziga Vertov's kino-eye qualified by Sergey Tretyakov as "all a matter of montage." "Whether a film is fictional or nonfictional," Tretyakov continued, is "a question of the greater or lesser falsification of the material that is being filmed."[19]

If attempts to delineate documentary's boundaries are doomed to fail, it is the conventions delimiting those boundaries that restrict the category to works deemed either nonfictional enough or creative enough, leaving out crucial elements of documentary history in the parts of the world on which I focus. A century after *Nanook of the North* and Vertov's *Man with a Movie Camera* (1929), film scholar Bill Nichols has done more than perhaps anyone else to interrogate and expand our understanding of nonfiction filmmaking. In a series of articles and books, Nichols elaborates a complex taxonomy of documentary as made up of modes—expository, observational, performative, reflexive, and interactive. Yet his landmark study *Representing Reality: Issues and Concepts in Documentary* offers a simple and avowedly tautological definition: "Documentary is what those who regard themselves as documentarists produce." Its simplicity deceptive, this definition is necessarily "historically conditioned, unfolding, variable, and perpetually provisional," Nichols explains, based as much on easily classifiable films as on "test cases" that challenge and transform the category of documentary from its boundaries.[20]

If one corollary of the narrativization or falsification inherent to nonfiction film is that it is always partial, anchored in a particular vantage point, then the historical unfolding from colonial to postcolonial periods yields a privileged corpus for exploring how and why, as we are reminded by Cissé and Sembene, documentaries do not always show or tell the truth. Tracing a documentary history in sub-Saharan Africa, then, I account for what people who regarded themselves as documentarists produced as they developed first a colonial and then an independent mode of filmmaking, with both core and borderline cases from each period determining my understanding of epochal and generational shifts. If documentary does not necessarily accurately represent reality, it nonetheless relies on a certain claim to do so. Theoretical discussions of filmic realism often address attempts within feature fictions to self-consciously evoke and invoke the real, what French literary and cultural critic Roland Barthes called the "reality effect." Yet the work of Soviet semiotician Jurij Lotman reminds us that even in photographic and cinematographic art thought to produce copies of reality, realism is a question of style.[21] Like fiction filmmakers, documentarists exercise control as they shape a final product.

Critical explorations and evaluations of both fiction and nonfiction films have long been based solely on case studies from European and North American traditions. Just as scholar Lúcia Nagib has expanded the canon of global filmic realisms to include South America and East and South Asia, this study brings Africa into the discussion.[22] Six decades after the birth of sub-Saharan African cinema, it is past time to do so. Europe and Africa are inextricably linked in my nonfiction film history, which belongs to three fields—French and francophone studies, film and media studies, and African studies—each of which for its own reasons has barely acknowledged the documentaries I examine.

Film studies has been widely marked by what Charles Musser recognizes in scholarship of early cinema as "Anglo-American myopia."[23] Given colonial and neocolonial British film policies and practices, however, it is difficult to identify a documentary tradition in anglophone colonial or postcolonial cinema.[24] And cameramen and directors who traveled from the United States to film Africa, while certainly subject to similar stereotypes as those from Europe, were not traveling in colonies they identified as their own. The work I seek to accomplish can be done only by starting from a French colonial context, yet scholars of French film have for the most part ignored films shot in France's colonies.[25] Williams's history of the first century of French film, for example, devotes a single paragraph to 1920s costume dramas set in North Africa.[26] The few existing examinations of French colonial cinema are limited to these same interwar feature fictions. Even in an article that calls for a more complex analysis of the category, Martin O'Shaughnessy digs deeper into the 1930s rather than broadening his scope to either nonfiction or films shot in sub-Saharan Africa.[27] Extending our focus, we discover that French colonial-era films shot in West and central Africa were almost exclusively conceived of as nonfiction, as declared in the introduction to UNESCO's 1967 catalog of ethnographic films shot in sub-Saharan Africa: "Films about Africa are principally documentaries."[28]

Academic interest in documentary film began to flourish in the early 1990s, just as the first English-language studies of Black African cinema began to appear. But although a few regions of the Global South have been granted entry into a documentary canon that previously admitted only European and North American films, Africa has remained largely absent from studies of global documentary, whether wide-ranging overviews or monographs about specific regions. Proof of what Teno calls "a disdain for African documentary film," sub-Saharan African cinema is missing from almost every history of global documentary published in English, including Nichols's *Representing Reality*, *Blurred Boundaries: Questions of Meaning in Contemporary Culture* and *Introduction to Documentary*; Stella Bruzzi's *New Documentary: A Critical Introduction*; Michael Chanan's *The Politics of Documentary*; Brian Winston's *Claiming the Real II*; and Betsy McLane's *A New History of Documentary Film*.[29]

Just as documentary film studies has ignored Africa, African cinema scholarship, with a few exceptions, has ignored documentary.[30] In part a consequence of documentary's colonial history on the continent, this lack of engagement lays bare a tension between competing critical desires to establish the difference of African cinema and assert its place in world cinema. As a result, as we shall see, it is often said that sub-Saharan African documentary cinema did not exist before the 1990s, with earlier films exhibiting an ostensibly characteristic conflation of realist fiction and nonfiction. Allowing the relatively limited expository and observational modes of Nichols's taxonomy to define documentary, this approach has contributed to sidelining the innovations of African documentarists in the performative, reflexive, and interactive modes. Until very recently, in fact, the only sub-Saharan African film traditions to have been recognized for nonfiction were those of Mozambique and South Africa.[31] This book contends that in the spaces of former French colonies in West and central Africa, to quote the great Senegalese documentarist Samba Félix Ndiaye, "the African cinema began with documentary."[32] Ndiaye and his colleagues developed a difference for African documentary that I assess not in essentialist terms but rather as the result of specific cultural, political, historical, and film historical contexts. Framing reality, nonfiction filmmakers in Africa as elsewhere highlight and explore the stakes of visual representation.

Chronological but always recursive, *Documentary Objectives* moves forward while reading back, its interpretation of the past informed by the future. In the first half of the book, I address a history of French colonial documentary films shot in Africa that is from the outset informed by the second half, devoted to the history of African documentaries filmed in the same locations. The subtitle, *Filming Africa from Colonialism to Independence*, denotes a transformation simultaneously called for and studied by groundbreaking West African film critic, film historian, and filmmaker Paulin Soumanou Vieyra, whose *Le cinéma et l'Afrique* (Cinema and Africa) was both the first book to address sub-Saharan

African film and the first book of film history and criticism published by a Black African. Charting a path forward from a colonial past to an independent future with a focus on documentary film production, Vieyra titled his penultimate chapter "From Cinema and Africa to African Cinema."[33] Like Vieyra, I understand the French language throughout not as a Cartesian gift from France to its colonies but as a lingua franca used on both sides of the colonial divide, in a region that can be described in literary and cultural theorist Mary Louise Pratt's influential terminology as a *contact zone*.[34]

In an essay first delivered as a speech at the 1959 Congress of Black Writers and Artists in Rome, Frantz Fanon maintained on the eve of independence that colonialism "distorts, disfigures, and destroys" not just the present but also the past of colonized peoples.[35] Colonial cinema and documentary cinema specifically, Vieyra argued a decade and a half later, operated a parallel distortion, disfiguration, and destruction of African places, peoples, and inherited traditions. It was through colonial documentaries that Europeans learned about Africa and passed what they had learned on to their children, "before they, in turn, were conditioned by other films, whose technical qualities made them even more plausible even if, more often than people think, these images were manipulated during editing or faked during shooting."[36] Such films, moreover, were the only way Africans could see Africa and Africans on screen. Working after independence to represent their continent and its people differently, African documentarists would have to rethink and renew both filmic content and form.

Documentary Objectives is therefore structured around an abrupt shift at the time of independence from representation of the other to self-representation. For the colonial era, a period during which Africans were prevented from filming, I discuss moving images shot in colonized Africa by French cameramen and directors and screened in France. After independence, I no longer include documentaries shot by Europeans in Africa, not because such films no longer existed but because my interest lies in the development of an African documentary tradition. Neither is part 2 a mirror image of part 1; I do not move from Europeans filming Africans to Africans filming Europeans, although I do mention examples of this phenomenon. My documentary history is regional rather than national in both the colonial and postcolonial periods. Like most scholars of African filmmaking, I recognize the plurality and heterogeneity of independent African cinemas and their multiply transnational nature from the 1960s through the present.[37] My close readings of films attend to linguistic, cultural, and political differences among documentaries shot in different regions of West and central Africa while at the same time understanding historical, structural, and thematic reasons to bring them together.

All the works examined in this book stake claims to nonfictional status and merit examination on their own terms, as contributions to distinctive European and African traditions that participate in a global history of nonfiction film. I have opted to address documentaries that were shown in theaters, museums, and cultural centers as well as in festivals and, more recently, on television and online. These are for the most part works attributed to specific filmmakers rather than anonymous newsreels and educational films—works that were shot, edited, released, distributed, advertised, and reviewed rather than raw or amateur footage.[38] At the same time and in all of the book's chronological periods, I address a wide range of modes and styles, from expository travelogues and commissioned propaganda to avant-garde experiments. These choices, combined with a focus on films I have been able to watch, enable me to construct an argument anchored in close readings rather than a catalog or series of lists. This is not an industry history, although the development of French colonial and West and central African documentary cinemas proves impossible to understand without addressing questions of production funding and avenues for distribution and exhibition. Following Nichols's lead, my strategically expansive understanding of the category of documentary allows for a depth of analysis within the geographical range of two continents and a chronological scope that comes close to matching the age of cinema itself. Scholars of early cinema teach us that documentary cannot be limited to feature-length works. And if we account for early travel films and canonical shorts of the 1950s, considered documentaries at the time of their production, we must also consider the fifty-two-minute television documentaries of the 1990s through the present day.

Since the 1950s, both African filmmakers and scholars of African film have condemned what Sada Niang calls the "Manichean and degrading discourse of colonial documentary."[39] Part 1 of *Documentary Objectives* provides the details necessary to understand such assertions more fully, building the history within a single contact zone of a colonial documentary tradition that originated in the very first years of the twentieth century. Over the course of four decades, French cameramen and directors visited French colonies in Africa to shoot footage to be shown in Europe. These documentarists worked to highlight and promote French colonialism, their efforts greatly appreciated by viewing and critical publics. "It is good to make the French travel," regular contributor to *La nature* (Nature) R. Villers wrote in an abundantly illustrated 1922 cover story titled "Cinema in Africa," "if only to better use the cinema to make them know their own colonies, so rich in beautiful landscapes and diverse peoples." "In a few instants," Villers concluded, "thanks to the cinema, we can witness the most characteristic scenes of the lives of these primitive populations."[40] In moving images accompanied by descriptions and explanations—first in the form of omniscient intertitles and later, with the advent of sound, in voice-over commentaries—colonial documentary offered spectators in the metropole striking landscapes, wild animals, and exotic cultures without having to leave town or even their seats.

French literature has long exhibited a fascination with travel narratives featuring so-called explorers who venture far from the Hexagon, particularly to Africa. It is no surprise, then, that cameramen quickly set off for the northern part of the continent and then south of the Sahara. The films they shot in what they called *Black Africa* became so popular that Nobel Prize–winning novelist Roger Martin du Gard incorporated one into the third volume of his eight-part *Les Thibault* (The Thibaults), published in 1923 but set just over a decade earlier. His description details the content and aesthetic of these films as well as how they were seen. A young couple approaches a movie theater advertising screenings of *L'Afrique inconnue: Voyage chez les Ouoloffs, les Sérères, les Foulbés, les Moundangs, et les Baguirmiens* (Unknown Africa: Voyage to the lands of the Wolof, the Serer, the Fula, the Mundang, and the Bagirmi). Inside, we read, a newsreel precedes "the African film," for which the orchestra "struck up a Negro tune." Du Gard's account of the film includes its landscapes with giant trees, hippos, monkeys, and, in a grand conclusion, a village where Black Africans dance in a circle around two near-naked wrestlers, all to the beat of a "savage tam-tam."[41] In the same year, surrealist poet Robert Desnos wrote that devotees of documentary yearned to watch "long-distance voyages that permit them to talk about Dahomey as if they had been there."[42]

Chapter 1 of *Documentary Objectives* addresses the first dozen years of French documentary shot in sub-Saharan Africa, chapter 2 the 1920s and '30s, and chapter 3 the final decades before independence. Across these three periods, films offered spectators what renowned anthropologist James Clifford calls "the smooth ethnographic story of an access to Africa."[43] This access was inseparable from colonial propaganda; little more than a decade before the independence of France's African territories, an essay published in the journal of the French Maritime and Colonial League argued that only nonfiction films could fulfill cinema's colonizing mission. Author Pierre Laubriet mocked romantic melodramas set and filmed in North Africa, insisting that colonial cinema should be "an instrument of knowledge" and "a document" yet "leave room for dreams." He imagined that audiences would desire to "penetrate" and lose themselves in the world shown on screen. "You who see the high forests of Africa or the dances of Hindu priests," Laubriet asked his readers, "do you not feel both nostalgia for and curiosity about these lands and these peoples?"[44]

Part 1 of this book establishes a corpus of colonial documentary that began with travelogues and hunting films, evolved into longer expedition films, and culminated with ethnographic cinema, and part 2 charts the development of documentary in West and central Africa after independence. Cameroonian director Urbain Dia-Moukori wrote in 1967 that the African filmmaker could not compare his situation to that of his American or Italian colleagues. When the career became an option, cinema was already half a century old; it was "a moving train, which he had to catch on the fly."[45] In the just over sixty years since independence, African documentarists have caught and overhauled the train, producing a compelling body of work that demands sustained critical attention. Refuting colonial assertions about Africa and Africans and reclaiming their cinematic image from their former colonizers, they have developed new models for nonfiction filmmaking grounded in a sophisticated understanding of documentary realism. Their films constitute a revolution within a global tradition whose relationship with their continent had been one of either exoticization and oppression or neglect. Chapter 4 analyzes the emergence of African documentary in the 1960s and early '70s, chapter 5 its simultaneous consolidation and retreat in the '70s and '80s, and chapter 6 the revitalization of nonfiction filmmaking from the early '90s through the present day.

Documentary Objectives covers a large geographical area but also much chronological ground: part 1 the fifty-four years from 1906 to 1960 and part 2 the sixty-three years from 1960 to 2023. Each chapter of the book brings to light little-known aspects of world cinema. In chapter 1, I examine the earliest nonfiction films shot in sub-Saharan Africa, passed over when studies of documentary film and colonial cinema begin with the interwar period. Chapter 2 deals with the interwar period, addressing documentaries overlooked when studies of French colonial cinema acknowledge only feature fictions. Chapter 3, which explores the ascendancy of ethnographic documentary, details filmmakers and films that preceded and coincided with the widely celebrated works of Jean Rouch. The wealth and eclectic range of postindependence West and central African documentary cinema are revealed in chapter 4 and the innovations of African ethnographic documentary in chapter 5. Chapter 6 surveys a period during which African documentary at long last gained greater attention from audiences and critics, bringing together career documentarists who are taking multiple new directions. These individual chapters—each building on the work of scholars who have studied early travelogues, colonial expedition films, colonial propaganda films, ethnographic cinema, independent African cinema, and African documentary—are important contributions, I believe, but more important is the narrative created by their sequence. It is my contention that we should know the whole story.

Notes

1. Paul Rotha, *Documentary Film: The Use of the Film Medium to Interpret Creatively and in Social Terms the Life of the People as It Exists in Reality* (Hastings House, 1952), 304.

2. The founder and educational director of the Bantu Educational Cinema Experiment almost immediately published L. A. Notcutt and G. C. Latham, *The African and the Cinema* (Edinburgh House Press, 1937). For more recent accounts and analyses, see Rosaleen Smyth, "The Development of British Colonial Film Policy, 1927–1939, with Special Reference to East and Central Africa," *Journal of African History* 20, no. 3 (1979): 437–50; James Burns, "Watching Africans Watch Films: Theories of Spectatorship in British Colonial Africa," *Historical Journal of Film, Radio, and Television* 20, no. 2 (2000): 197–211; Aboubakar Sanogo, "Colonialism, Visuality and the Cinema: Revisiting the Bantu Educational Kinema Experiment," in *Empire and Film*, ed. Lee Grieveson and Colin MacCabe (Palgrave Macmillan, 2011), 227–246; and in most detail, Tom Rice, *Films for the Colonies: Cinema and the Preservation of the British Empire* (University of California Press, 2019). Glenn Reynolds's *Colonial Cinema in Africa: Origins, Images, Audiences* (McFarland, 2015) addresses both shooting and spectatorship across the continent, with chapters on British and Belgian colonial film policies, South Africa, and Hollywood productions.

3. L. Van Bever, *Le cinéma pour africains* (G. Van Campenhout, 1952). For a detailed and comprehensive overview of Belgian colonial cinema in Africa, see Francis Ramirez and Christian Rolot, *Histoire du cinéma colonial au Zaire, au Rwanda, et au Burundi* (Musée Royal de l'Afrique Centrale, 1985). On both British and Belgian colonial educational films, see Femi Okiremuete Shaka, *Modernity and the African Cinema* (Africa World Press, 2004), 155–212.

4. On French educational films shot in sub-Saharan Africa, see Peter Bloom, *French Colonial Documentary: Mythologies of Humanitarianism* (University of Minnesota Press, 2008); Alison Murray Levine, *Framing the Nation: Documentary Film in Interwar France* (Continuum, 2010).

5. For more details, see Alice Conklin, *A Mission to Civilize: The Republican Idea of Empire in France and West Africa, 1895–1930* (Stanford University Press, 1997), 23.

6. Raoul Girardet, *L'idée coloniale en France de 1871 à 1962* (La Table Ronde, 1972), 80.

7. Gary Wilder, *The French Imperial Nation-State: Negritude and Humanism Between the Two World Wars* (University of Chicago Press, 2020). See also articles

collected in Frederick Cooper and Ann Laura Stoler, eds., *Tensions of Empire: Colonial Cultures in a Bourgeois World* (University of California Press, 1997).

8. Frank Ukadike, *Questioning African Cinema: Conversations with Filmmakers* (University of Minnesota Press, 2002), 309.

9. Homi Bhabha, *The Location of Culture* (Routledge, 1994), 70–71.

10. V. Y. Mudimbe, *The Idea of Africa* (Indiana University Press, 1994), xii.

11. V. Y. Mudimbe, *The Invention of Africa: Gnosis, Philosophy, and the Order of Knowledge* (Indiana University Press, 1988), 44.

12. Noël Burch, *Life to Those Shadows*, trans. Ben Brewster (British Film Institute, 1990), 15.

13. Alan Williams, "The Lumière Organization and 'Documentary Realism,'" in *Film Before Griffith*, ed. John Fell (University of California Press, 1983), 158.

14. Félix Mesguich, *Tours de manivelle: Souvenirs d'un chasseur d'images* (Grasset, 1933), 37–38.

15. *Cinéma, de notre temps: Souleymane Cissé*, directed by Rithy Panh (ARTE, 1991, 53 min).

16. Albert Cervoni, "Une confrontation historique en 1965 entre Jean Rouch et Sembene Ousmane," *L'Afrique littéraire*, no. 61–62 (1981): 78.

17. Georg Wilhelm Friedrich Hegel, *The Philosophy of History* (Dover, 1956), 99.

18. Nothing resembling the phrase "creative treatment of actuality" appears in the review, which is also often cited as containing the first use of *documentary* as a noun in English despite the fact that the term appears only in adjectival form. John Grierson, "Flaherty's Poetic Moana," in *The Documentary Tradition*, 2nd ed., ed. Lewis Jacobs (W. W. Norton, 1979), 25–26.

19. "Symposium on Soviet Documentary: S. Tretyakov, V. Shklovsky, E. Shub, and O. Brik," in Jacobs, *Documentary Tradition*, 29.

20. Nichols introduces his classification of documentary cinema into expository, observational, interactive, and reflexive modes in Bill Nichols, *Representing Reality: Issues and Concepts in Documentary* (Indiana University Press, 1991), 32–75, adding the performative mode a few years later in Bill Nichols, *Blurred Boundaries: Questions of Meaning in Contemporary Culture* (Indiana University Press, 1994), 92–106. Nichols, *Representing Reality*, 32–75, 15.

21. Roland Barthes, "The Reality Effect," in *The Rustle of Language* (University of California Press, 1989), 141–48; Jurij Lotman, *Semiotics of Cinema* (Michigan Slavic Contributions, 1976), 10–22.

22. See Lúcia Nagib, *World Cinema and the Ethics of Realism* (Continuum, 2011). Two chapters of Nagib's *Realist Cinema as World Cinema: Non-cinema, Intermedial Passages, Total Cinema* (Amsterdam University Press, 2020) address documentary film.

23. Charles Musser, "Problems in Historiography: The Documentary Tradition Before *Nanook of the North*," in *The Documentary Film Book*, ed. Brian Winston (British Film Institute, 2013), 126n3.

24. Kenneth Cameron traces anglophone representations of sub-Saharan Africa as far back as early travel and hunting films, with one of thirteen chapters devoted to documentary. In the postindependence period, however, aside from white South African director Jamie Uys, Cameron includes only films made by non-African directors. Kenneth Cameron, *Africa on Film: Beyond Black and White* (Continuum, 1994).

25. For an exception that examines early French films shot in colonial Indochina, see Panivong Norindr, "Enlisting Early Cinema in the Service of 'La Plus Grande France,'" in *Early Cinema and the "National,"* ed. Richard Abel, Giorgio Bertellini, and Rob King (Indiana University Press, 2008), 109–17. In geographical proximity to the films discussed by Norindr, although not in French colonial spaces, see Ian Aitken and Camille Deprez, eds., *The Colonial Documentary in South and South-East Asia* (Edinburgh University Press, 2016); Sandeep Ray, *Celluloid Colony: Locating History and Ethnography in Early Dutch Colonial Films of Indonesia* (National University of Singapore Press, 2021); Nayoung Aimee Kwon, Takushi Odagiri, and Moonim Baek, eds., *Theorizing Colonial Cinema: Reframing Production, Circulation, and Consumption of Film in Asia* (Indiana University Press, 2022).

26. Alan Williams, *Republic of Images: A History of French Filmmaking* (Harvard University Press, 1992), 128.

27. Martin O'Shaughnessy, "Poor Propaganda: French Colonial Films of the 1930s," in *Empire and Culture: The French Experience, 1830–1940,* ed. Martin Evans (Palgrave Macmillan, 2004), 27–40.

28. UNESCO, *Premier catalogue sélectif international de films ethnographiques sur l'Afrique noire* (1967), 32.

29. Jean-Marie Teno, "Writing on Walls: Reflections on the Documentary Tradition in African Cinema," in *Through African Eyes: Conversations with the Directors,* ed. Mahen Bonetti and Morgan Seag (African Film Festival, 2010), 2:91; Bill Nichols, *Introduction to Documentary* (Indiana University Press, 2001); Stella Bruzzi, *New Documentary: A Critical Introduction* (Routledge, 2000); Michael Chanan, *The Politics of Documentary* (British Film Institute, 2007); Brian Winston, *Claiming the Real II* (Palgrave Macmillan, 2008); Betsy McLane, *A New History of Documentary Film* (Continuum, 2012). A list of anthologies and edited volumes on documentary that ignore African cinema would be too long. For an exception to this rule, see scholar of documentary Jonathan Kahana's monumental anthology *The Documentary Film Reader* (Oxford University Press, 2016), which includes Teno's "Writing on Walls," 938–42, and my "Mixing Impossible Genres: David Achkar and African AutoBiographical Documentary," 924–37.

30. For a critical overview in French, see Alexie Tcheuyap, "Documenter l'Afrique: Enjeux théoriques et politiques," *Nouvelles études francophones* 33, no. 1 (2018): 18–37. Tcheuyap's article is part of a special issue of the journal devoted to

francophone African and Afro-diasporic documentary, and his *African Documentary Cinema* (Routledge, 2024) is the first English-language monograph on the topic.

31. See Margarida Cardoso's film *Kuxa Kanema: The Birth of Cinema* (2003) as well as Maria Loftus, "*Kuxa Kanema*: The Rise and Fall of an Experimental Documentary Series in Mozambique," *Journal of African Cinemas* 3, no. 2 (2011): 161–71; Inês Cordeiro Dias, "Filming the Nation in Post-independence Mozambique," *Third Text* 34, no. 4–5 (2020): 538–50.

32. Baba Diop, "Il est parti Mister Doc . . . ," *Africiné*, 2009, http://www.africine.org/?menu=art&no=9003.

33. Paulin Soumanou Vieyra, *Le cinéma et l'Afrique* (Présence Africaine, 1969), 175, 187.

34. Mary Louise Pratt, *Imperial Eyes: Travel Writing and Transculturation* (Routledge, 1992), 4.

35. Frantz Fanon, "On National Culture," in *Wretched of the Earth* (Grove Press, 1961), 210.

36. Paulin Soumanou Vieyra, *Réflexions d'un cineaste africain* (OCIC, 1990), 62.

37. See, for example, Alexie Tcheuyap, *Postnationalist African Cinemas* (Manchester University Press, 2011), 11, 32.

38. For readings of amateur ethnographies, see Katherine Groo, *Bad Film Histories: Ethnography and the Early Archive* (University of Minnesota Press, 2019).

39. Sada Niang, "'Dead Man Walking', le voyage initiatique de Satché," in *Dix films d'Afrique*, ed. François Fronty (L'Harmattan, 2019), 97.

40. R. Villers, "Le cinéma en Afrique," *La Nature*, no. 2503 (1922): 183, 187.

41. David Steel, "Coïncidences africaines, *La belle saison* des *Thibault* et le *Voyage au Congo*: D'un film à l'autre," *Bulletin des Amis d'André Gide* 20, no. 94 (April 1992): 144–45.

42. Robert Desnos, "Documentaires," in *Cinéma* (Gallimard, 1966), 106. This essay originally appeared in *Paris-Journal* in 1923.

43. James Clifford, *The Predicament of Culture: Twentieth-Century Ethnography, Literature, and Art* (Harvard University Press, 1988), 173.

44. P. Laubriet, "L'outre-mer vu par le cinéma," *Mer outre-mer*, no. 1 (1947): 12.

45. Urbain Dia-Moukori, "Intuition d'un langage cinématographique africain," *Présence Africaine*, no. 61 (1967): 209n1.

PART 1

French Colonial Documentary,
1906–1960

In 1943, Vichy France's newly established newsreel production company France-Actualités released a short documentary that retraced the history of French newsreels. In the sentence from which the film's title is drawn, the voice-over describes *actualité* as "the machine that writes life, or better, the machine that writes history." In a montage of clips selected to highlight the range and power of film journalism, *La machine à écrire l'histoire* (The machine that writes history) begins with excerpts of famed 1895 Lumière Brothers shorts *Sortie de l'usine Lumière* (Workers leaving the Lumière Factory) and *L'arrivée d'un train en gare de La Ciotat* (The arrival of a train in La Ciotat) and continues with shots of early French aviators and scientific images of microbes and solar eclipses. An homage to world-traveling cameramen gives way to two clips that represent what these men film: an unidentified East Asian religious ceremony and several groups of men who are, according to the catalog text, "Black Africans, almost naked, at work." An aerial view of the Arc de Triomphe then immediately reasserts France's imperial domination. The film concludes with a lengthy and detailed advertisement for France-Actualités, with introductions of the men who shoot the footage and information about the distribution of completed newsreels to movie theaters around France.

In its triumphal narrative, *La machine à écrire l'histoire* places anonymous Africans, working under duress, at the heart of its celebration of the first half century of the cinematic medium. Concealing the truth about the forced labor legal in France's colonies until the passage of the Houphouët-Boigny law in 1946, the newsreel misrepresents the reality of the Africans it displays. Both documentary and documentary history, it exemplifies colonial distortion

France-Actualités, *La machine à écrire l'histoire*, 1943.

and manipulation of Africa's past and present, to return to the terminology of Fanon and Vieyra, while insisting on its objectivity and accuracy. In doing so, *La machine à écrire l'histoire* writes itself into a tradition as old as the Lumière films it invokes as ancestors, a tradition built on earlier genres of colonial-era literary and visual art.

Tracing the prehistory of documentary film in the United States, Charles Musser notes various technologies and light sources used since the seventeenth century to show images on some sort of screen. By the middle of the nineteenth century, collections of slides projected by magic lantern, stereoscope, or stereopticon accompanied lectures on world travel, combining information with entertainment.[1] A prehistory of French documentary in sub-Saharan Africa includes such illustrated lectures; a fuller genealogy, which I can only begin to sketch here, would encompass representations of Africa in drawings, engravings, photographs, postcards, illustrated magazines, and written expedition and travel narratives, both fictional and nonfictional. The technology of cinema inherited a colonial ideology that had been filtered through a range of representational practices, each in turn claiming to render like none before what art historian Annie Coombes has called "the spectacle of empire."[2]

French readers in the mid to late nineteenth century eagerly consumed the thrilling African voyages of René Caillié, Pierre Savorgnan de Brazza, David Livingstone, Henry Morton Stanley, and many others, who also served as models for innumerable fictional characters. Published prior to his stories of travels to the center of the earth and to the moon, Jules Verne's very first "extraordinary voyage," *Cinq semaines en ballon* (*Five Weeks in a Balloon*), bears the subtitle *A Journey of Discovery by Three Englishmen in Africa*.[3] In Picard's Colonial and Travel Library series, *Nos explorateurs en Afrique* (Our explorers in Africa) summarizes twenty-six expeditions undertaken over the course of the century, beginning with Caillié's journey to Timbuktu in the late 1820s. Author Jules Gros, member and former officer of the Society for Commercial Geography in Paris, asserted that "of all of the parts of the world still not completely known, Africa is without question the one that has in recent years most excited the curiosity and the investigations of the civilized world."[4]

As France conquered territory and built a more elaborate colonial administration, a network of colonial associations linking private companies to government initiatives grew as well. The French Colonial Union, the Committee for French Africa, and other, smaller organizations took propaganda as a primary goal. Founded in Paris in 1897, the Dupleix Committee collected and lent slides for use during seminars and conferences on the French empire.[5] By the turn of the twentieth century, then, strong documentary claims made by authors, lecturers, and visual artists, bound to explicit assertions of imperial power, heightened the mass appeal of exotic Africa. *Du Congo au Lac Tchad* (From Congo to Lake Chad), an expedition journal published in 1906 by physician, botanist, and member of the National Museum of Natural History Gaston-Jules Decorse, was subtitled "The bush as it is, the people as they are."[6]

This simple but powerful claim to represent Africa "as it is" was intensified by the advent of photography, which gradually replaced engravings in issues of French travel magazines such as *Le monde illustré* (The illustrated world), *Le tour du monde* (Around the world), and *Le journal des voyages* (The travel journal).[7] In photographs, announced *La dépêche colonial illustrée* (Illustrated colonial dispatch) in 1904, "natives live before our eyes in the reassuring sincerity of their physiognomy and their appearance. . . . All of this picturesqueness, all of this life, photography renders to us with the intensity of absolute truth."[8] Photographs were so prized as souvenirs and propaganda that a store in Paris's fifth arrondissement advertised cameras specifically "for the colonies," and specialty magazines like *La revue illustrée de photographie* (Illustrated photography magazine) dedicated sections to what they called "colonial photography."[9] Mass-produced photographs circulated in the form of postcards sent home by

L'illustration, 1908.

individual travelers: soldiers, administrators, and tourists. Before World War I, fifty-four French publishers produced seven thousand distinct postcards of sub-Saharan Africa and Africans.[10] A 1908 photograph of a French traveler-photographer in Africa encapsulated this representational ideology and practice for readers of *L'illustration* (Illustration). Wearing a pith helmet, known in French as a *casque colonial*, or colonial helmet, Alfred Machin leans to peer into the telephoto lens of his camera, which is balanced on the shoulder of a man wearing a caftan and turban. From a comfortable distance and with an African bearing the weight of his equipment, he captures an image of the continent.[11]

Serial photography, the most immediate precursor to film, also included Black Africans among its subjects. The archives of the Cinémathèque Française in Paris include images attributed to pioneer Étienne-Jules Marey titled "Homme en chaise à porteur en Afrique" (Man in sedan chair in Africa). Four Africans carry a bearded European, who waves at the camera.[12] Yet although Marey and his former student and assistant Félix Regnault used this technology to study human movement—more specifically, ostensible differences between Europeans and Africans and among different African ethnic groups—they did this work in France. "Homme en chaise à porteur en Afrique" in fact belongs to a series of chronophotographic films taken by Regnault and Charles Comte not in Africa but at the 1895 Ethnographic Exhibition on the Champ de Mars in Paris. The best known, "Wolof Potter" shows the traditional artisanry of a woman brought from Senegal. She was later taken to Marey's physiological station, where the images were reshot under more controlled circumstances, removed even from the simulacrum of the subject's home.[13]

Starting in the mid-nineteenth century, so-called Universal Exhibitions across Europe displayed objects and goods brought from colonies around the world. The organizers of the 1889 Universal Exhibition in Paris, however, also imported people from Gabon, Congo, Senegal, New Caledonia, and Tahiti to inhabit "native villages" constructed for the occasion.[14] These spectacles were so popular that newspapers reported exceptionally long lines, praising the accompanying illustrated brochures as "models of ethnographic exactitude."[15] Regnault was extremely impressed with such villages at the 1895 exhibition, where, he argued, "these Negroes live just like in their own countries, and their customs are faithfully respected and easy to see."[16] An enthusiastic tourist in this reconstructed and reenacted Africa, it is Regnault himself who waves from the sedan chair in "Homme en chaise à porteur en Afrique," carried by four Malagasy men.[17] French physical anthropologists shared his excitement, eagerly taking measurements of the residents of these "human zoos," as some scholars now call them.[18] A component of ethnographic, universal, and colonial exhibitions for decades, they would be the first production context for French colonial cinema featuring Black Africans.

Of the 1,428 films in the comprehensive Lumière Brothers catalog, eighty-six were shot in Africa. These were all likely the work of cameraman Alexandre Promio, who traveled to Algeria and Tunisia in 1896 and Egypt in 1897, while Marey and Regnault were working in Paris.[19] Promio's "authentic tableaux" of Algeria, wrote one journalist, "transport us to a few of the most delicious corners of our beautiful colony," while those of Egypt provide "a truly perfect idea of curious Muslim customs."[20] The several Lumière films that display Black Africans, however, like Regnault's chronophotographs were shot in France. In *Baignade de nègres* (Negroes bathing, 1896), European adults observe African boys diving into a lake against a background of African men in pirogues and traditionally constructed houses with thatched roofs. *Nègres en corvée* (Negroes doing chores, 1896) shows a large group of Africans, mostly women, sweeping and washing the ground in front of these houses. Under a minute each, both were shot in Paris at the Bois de Boulogne's botanical gardens, the site of numerous ethnographic exhibitions between 1877 and 1937. The fifteen films in Lumière's 1897 Ashanti Village series were filmed in Lyon at the Cours du Midi, where visitors could purchase tickets to see two hundred men and women brought from the Gold Coast, now Ghana. Seven films show these men and women dancing, and the rest their children eating, playing, and being bathed.

One of the main attractions of the 1900 Universal Exhibition in Paris was the Dahomey Village, set up alongside several others in the Trocadero Gardens. Walking through the various villages, musicologist Louis Laloy wrote in scientific journal *La nature* (Nature), "one can . . . get a fairly clear idea of the numerous populations that live in Africa."[21] And for the first time, along with the panoramas and dioramas that had long been a hallmark of such events, films joined exhibits of objects, photographs, and people to spotlight distant, exotic, newly acquired lands. Some were screened in combination with theatrical, dance, and musical performances; others were projected in dedicated cinematographic spaces. Detailing this imbrication with earlier arts and technologies, scholar Emmanuelle Toulet points to cinema's dual function at the exhibition, both entertainment and "documentary and scientific auxiliary in support of lectures and demonstrations."[22]

Five years after the integration of cinema into ethnographic exhibitions, French cameramen began traveling to sub-Saharan Africa to shoot footage destined for movie theaters in the metropole. Popular with both mass audiences and critics, their films were perceived as objective representations of a transparent and easily grasped African reality. The continent was presented as endlessly fascinating, with virtually every film shot there from 1906 to 1960 announced as either unprecedented or the most sensational of its kind. Over time, successive genres would claim to reveal for the first time more truth about Africa: hunting films as compared to views and travelogues, expedition films as compared to hunting films, ethnographic films as compared to expedition films. Yet in spite of these countless assertions of novelty, films reiterated and reinforced stereotypes about a region and its people. Spectators were repeatedly shown landscapes, wild animals, and tribes, types, habits, customs, and traditions, which were never dissociated from colonial propaganda.

These colonial films, shot in what cameramen and directors called *la plus grande France,* or greater France, have been largely forgotten. Although widely admired upon their commercial release, they are now tedious and quite painful to watch, should one manage to gain access to a decent print or digital copy. They are for the most part neither creatively constructed nor aesthetically interesting, significant rather for what they reveal about the political and cultural context in which they were produced. Valuable precisely for what is excruciating about them, they launched a cinematic tradition, shaping colonial documentary practices that would evolve and flourish over the course of half a century.

This forgetting has meant that, until recently, the study of French colonial cinema was limited to interwar dramas, and our conception of French documentary filmed in colonial-era Africa was limited to the postwar work of Jean Rouch. Colonial documentary as a whole remains uncharted, particularly the details of a tradition evolving in a single space over time. Katherine Groo uses the category of "expedition films," for example, to describe both the Lumière Ashanti series and footage shot by Lumière operators in North Africa and Mexico, eliding important differences resulting from disparate shooting contexts.[23] This lack of focus has had a marked impact on our understanding of films shot in Africa, especially outside of British territories and before World War II. It turns out that anthropologist Paul Stoller's designation of Marcel Griaule's *Sous les masques noirs* (Under the black masks, 1940) as both "one of the first documentary films about West Africa" and "one of the first French documentaries shot entirely in Africa" is far from accurate.[24] Griaule's work appeared in the wake of more than thirty years' worth of French documentaries shot in sub-Saharan Africa.

Eric Le Roy counts 820 French colonial documentary films produced between 1896 and 1955 and held in the collections of France's National Center for Cinema and the Moving Image (CNC). Just under half of these were shot in France's North African colonies—Algeria, Morocco, and Tunisia—and just over a quarter of them in the French colonies of West and Equatorial Africa.[25] I have not been able to consult all two hundred of the films in this last category, nor do they constitute the entirety of nonfiction film shot in France's sub-Saharan colonies, since at least as many have been lost. The next three chapters nonetheless provide an analytical overview of five and a half decades of French colonial documentaries, substantiated by archival research and close readings. Chapter 1 addresses the first dozen years of this tradition: actualities, travel films, and early propaganda pieces distributed between 1906 and 1918. Chapter 2 focuses on the interwar period, as expedition films became longer and more scripted and filmmakers and critics developed new ideas about exotic cinema and the importance of documentary. And chapter 3 investigates the last decades of colonial-era nonfiction from the late 1930s through the '40s and '50s via the rise of professional ethnographic cinema. Political contexts, technologies, and styles changed as one generation of filmmakers after another claimed to present the most exciting and authentic moving images of sub-Saharan Africa.

Notes

1. Musser, "Problems in Historiography," 120–23.

2. Annie Coombes, *Reinventing Africa: Museums, Material Culture and Popular Imagination in Late Victorian and Edwardian England* (Yale University Press, 1994), 63–108.

3. Jules Verne, *Cinq semaines en ballon: Voyages de découvertes en Afrique par trois anglais* (Paris: J. Hetzel, 1863).

4. Jules Gros, *Nos explorateurs en Afrique* (Paris: Alcide Picard et Kaan, 1893), 1.

5. Guido Convents, *À la recherche des images oubliées: Préhistoire du cinéma en Afrique, 1897–1918* (Éditions OCIC, 1986), 54.

6. J. Lecorse, *Du Congo au Lac Tchad: La brousse tel qu'elle est, les gens tels qu'ils sont* (Asselin et Houzeau, 1906).

7. Convents, *À la recherche*, 45; Girardet, *L'idée coloniale en France de 1871 à 1962*, 40. On representations of Africa in the French press of the period more generally, see William Schneider, *An Empire for the Masses: The French Popular Image of Africa, 1870–1900* (Greenwood Press, 1982).

8. Cited in Convents, *À la recherche*, 56.

9. Daniel Foliard, *Combattre, punir, photographier: Empires coloniaux, 1890–1914* (Éditions La Découverte, 2020), 132, 134. Foliard's deeply researched study focuses on the use of photography during the European colonial military campaigns of this period.

10. Jacques Marseille, "Les images de l'Afrique en France (des années 1880 aux années 1930)," *Canadian Journal of African Studies* 22, no. 1 (1988): 122.

11. Gustave Babin, "Les grandes chasses africaines," *L'illustration*, no. 3425 (October 17, 1908): 254.

12. Cinémathèque Française, P069-096.

13. On colonial and physiological ideology in the serial photography of Marey and Regnault, see Bloom, *French Colonial Documentary*, 17–24 and 153–56. For an extensive analysis of Regnault's chronophotography as ethnographic film, see Fatimah Tobing Rony, *The Third Eye: Race, Cinema, and Ethnographic Spectacle* (Duke University Press, 1996), chapters 1 and 2.

14. Jacques Thobie and Gilbert Meynier, *Histoire de la France colonial II: L'apogée* (Armand Colin, 1991), 129.

15. "Exposition universelle," *La cocarde*, August 26, 1889, 2.

16. Félix Regnault, "Exposition ethnographique de l'Afrique occidentale au Champ-de-Mars à Paris," *La nature*, no. 1159 (1895): 186.

17. Félix Regnault, "Le rôle du cinéma en ethnographie," *La nature*, no. 2866 (1931): 305.

18. Bloom, *French Colonial Documentary*, 154; Pascal Blanchard et al., eds., *Human Zoos: Science and Spectacle in the Age of Colonial Empires* (Liverpool University

Press, 2008). See also Catherine Hodeir, "Decentering the Gaze at French Colonial Exhibitions," in *Images and Empires: Visuality in Colonial and Postcolonial Africa*, ed. Paul Landau and Deborah Kaspin (University of California Press, 2002), 233–52.

19. Michelle Aubert and Jean-Claude Seguin, eds., *La production ciné-matographique des Frères Lumière* (Bibliothèque du Film, 1996). Promio eventually settled in Algiers, where in 1919 he created the photocinematographic service of the Government General of Algeria, tasked with establishing a library of colonial propaganda images. Jean-Claude Seguin, *Alexandre Promio ou les énigmes de la lumière* (L'Harmattan, 1999), 230, 236–37.

20. Aubert and Seguin, *Production cinématographique des Frères Lumière*, 34, 72.

21. Louis Laloy, "L'Afrique à l'Exposition universelle," *La nature*, no. 1410 (1900): 229.

22. Emmanuelle Toulet, "Le cinéma à l'Exposition universelle de 1900," *Revue d'histoire moderne et contemporaine* 33, no. 2 (1986): 183. On the transition in Paris from "panoramania" to early cinema, see Vanessa Schwartz, *Spectacular Realities: Early Mass Culture in* Fin-de-Siècle *Paris* (University of California Press, 1998), chapters 4 and 5.

23. Katherine Groo, "The Maison and Its Minor: Lumière(s), Film History, and the Early Archive," *Cinema Journal* 52, no. 4 (2013): 25–48.

24. Paul Stoller, "Regarding Rouch: The Recasting of West African Colonial Culture," in *Cinema, Colonialism, Postcolonialism*, ed. Dina Sherzer (University of Texas Press, 1996), 69.

25. Eric Le Roy, "Le fonds cinématographique colonial aux Archives du film et du dépôt légal du CNC," *Journal of Film Preservation*, no. 63 (October 2001): 55–57.

1

CONQUEST

Actualities to Propaganda

Discussing the 1931 Colonial Exhibition in Paris, industry journal *La critique cinématographique* (Film criticism) suggested that the conquest of Africa would have been more successful had France deployed cinema as a weapon of war:

> The most fearsome weapons can only spread death, cover the earth with ruins, and lead hearts to a hatred that in turn engenders new killings. The cinema, on the other hand, is an instrument of pacification. It allows us to instruct, shape minds, impose our culture, and make our civilization and its benefits known, without confrontation, while entertaining. . . . Who knows if the famous slogan of "peaceful penetration" would have been accomplished sooner if cinema had been better used, if it had been a part of our organizational plan, if the projector had followed the construction of roads and schools, if the cameraman had arrived in the same convoy as the schoolteacher responsible for instruction, for shaping young minds, and the doctor responsible for establishing the reign of hygiene?[1]

Per this argument, film—had the French chosen to use it to educate African spectators—could have subdued unruly subjects without inspiring resistance or revolt. Although there were Lumière shows at the turn of the twentieth century in Dakar (the capital of French West Africa) as well as farther north in Saint-Louis, these were accessible only to well-off French audiences, for the most part colonial administrators and their families.[2] France never followed the advice of Colonel Jean-Baptiste Marchand, late nineteenth-century leader of colonial troops in sub-Saharan Africa, who in 1914 wrote to *Le film* magazine that the screening of "carefully chosen" comic films in African colonies would "disarm the primitives."[3] Instead, early French colonial cinema consisted of moving images shot in Africa and screened in the metropole. Like the panoramas, dioramas, photographs, and novels that preceded them, these films entertained French audiences while serving as propaganda for the colonial enterprise.

A few years after Promio's tour of French North Africa in 1896 and 1897, European cameramen arrived in South Africa to shoot footage of the Anglo-Boer War.[4] By the second half of the new century's first decade, they were in West, central, and East Africa, eager to record images of colonial assets: exotic locales, animals, and peoples. There was little distinction between corporate and government propaganda, and many of the first filmed scenes were shot by itinerant cameramen for private trading companies seeking to highlight the sites of their extractive enterprises. In 1903, Charles Urban left the London-based Warwick Trading Company to found his own company specializing in scientific subjects and travel films. And in 1908, the Belgian company Le cinématographe des colonies (Cinematograph of the colonies) was created to fund the shooting of films in central Africa; a year later, the Cinéma colonial opened in Brussels to show audiences the results.[5] In France, commercial cinema companies took the lead in early colonial filmmaking, and Guido Convents contends that the French shot more films in Africa during this period than the British or the Belgians.[6]

The moving images of colonized Africa shown in France before World War I, however, have been left out of French film history. In the seventh edition of his landmark history of world cinema, published in 1963, Georges Sadoul mentions them in a single, tantalizing sentence: "since 1900 . . . numerous documentaries and feature films were shot in Black Africa, mostly by the English, the French, and the Americans." Sadoul's contemporaneous overview of French cinema contains not even this brief hint.[7] Written thirty years later, Richard Abel's lengthy examination of the first decade and a half of French cinema history similarly mentions only in a single sentence, and in parentheses, the existence of "travelogue footage of foreign countries (including the colonies)."[8] This lack of attention to early films shot in France's overseas possessions, particularly in sub-Saharan Africa, is but one aspect of a reciprocal sidelining of documentary film in early cinema studies and of early cinema in documentary studies.

Stephen Bottomore has argued that scholars of early cinema are primarily invested in the development of film as a narrative art form and therefore ignore "factual" films made before 1920.[9] Documentary is almost as absent from Abel's monumental study of early French cinema as is the continent of Africa, and Alan Williams's history of French film alludes only in passing to the presence of travelogues, newsreels, scientific films, and ethnographic films in early programs.[10] The filmography for the Georges Pompidou Center's glossy and weighty history of the Pathé Company, produced by a committee of prominent scholars and archivists that included Abel, Henri Bousquet, Jean-Pierre Jeancolas, Éric Le Roy, and Michel Marie, is prefaced with the caveat that "this filmography includes only fiction films."[11] And the Cinémathèque Française's history of Pathé rival Gaumont devotes just eight of its pages to nonfiction, with a filmography similarly limited to fiction films.[12] Scholars have been slow to follow the path blazed in the late 1990s by conferences on early nonfiction at the Netherlands Filmmuseum, now the EYE museum, and a special issue of the journal *1895* on nonfiction film in France through 1930.[13] Yet when *Cinémagazine* noted in 1921 the appearance of impressive "foreign documentaries," it was with the assertion that "for a long time, France was the only country producing documentary films."[14] If not the primary draw in a theater program, nonfiction films were popular with French audiences and critics in the cinema's first two decades; they were widely advertised, seen, and reviewed.

Just as scholarship of early cinema neglects documentary, documentary scholarship, according to Tom Gunning, has ignored the early cinema era to "skip blithely from Lumière to Flaherty."[15] In the 1980s, Gunning revolutionized the field of early cinema studies by rejecting what he deemed an anachronistic, backward-looking, teleological focus on narrativity. Early cinema was not an art of storytelling, he argued, but "a way of presenting a series of views to an audience" or "a cinema of attractions." Gunning drew this term from Soviet pioneer Sergei Eisenstein's theories of avant-garde theater, reminding readers that all early cinema—fictional or documentary—entertained the masses by "supplying pleasure through an exciting spectacle."[16] Maintaining that their "view aesthetic" is located in individual shots within which the camera "acts as a tourist, spectator, or investigator," Gunning later proposed to call pre–World War I nonfiction films *actualities*.[17] Other scholars have followed his lead, characterizing films made prior to the 1920s as nonfiction rather than documentary or returning to catalog and advertising labels used by companies such as Pathé and Gaumont: *actuality, plein-air, sports and acrobatics,* and *scientific scenes,* among others.

Actuality in this context is an anglicization of the French *actualité,* from *actuel,* meaning current rather than actual or real. Not synonymous with documentary, the term stressed the now-ness of what was being presented to the spectator; by World War I, it had come to designate what in English was called a newsreel. The use in French of the noun *documentaire* for a nonfiction film predated the comparable use of *documentary* in English by well over a decade.

André Robert traced its origin to Gaumont's 1911 catalog description of the scientific film *Souvenirs entomologiques d'Émile Fabre* (Entomological memories of Émile Fabre), and Roland Cosandey notes that *documentaire* was used instead of *plein-air* in catalogs and film programs as early as 1910.[18] Pathé-Frères, the leading film company in the world at the time, for example, characterized *En Russie, sur la Volga* (In Russia, on the Volga, 1910) as a "well-filmed travel documentary." *Documentaire* was also used as an adjective. *Fabrication des chapeaux de manille* (Production of manila hats, 1911), shot in the Philippines, was a "documentary view," as were *L'industrie de la soie au Cambodge* (The silk industry in Cambodia, 1912) and *Distillation de la fleur oranger en Tunisie* (Distilling orange blossom water in Tunisia, 1912). *Fabrication des chapeaux de paille à Fiesole (Italie)* (Fabrication of straw hats in Fiesola [Italy], 1912) and *Industrie du bois en Hongrie* (Lumber industry in Hungary, 1912) were each described as a "very interesting documentary scene." Industry film *Comment on obtient du plâtre* (How plaster is made, 1912) was an "interesting documentary reel," as was *La vie du mineur* (The life of a miner, 1914); *Dakar, principal port de commerce de l'Afrique Occidentale Française* (Dakar, the main commercial port in French West Africa, 1914) was an "interesting documentary view."[19]

Even if, as elucidated by Gunning, such films differ from our current conception of documentary, the category of *documentaire* existed in France before World War I, particularly for films shot outside of France and even Europe. In the earliest years of the cinema, actualities and travelogues figured on programs along with historical reenactments.[20] Pathé's catalogs did not distinguish between recorded and staged realities before the creation in 1908 of Pathé-Journal, France's first filmed newsreel.[21] Gaumont followed in 1910 with Gaumont-Actualités, and other studios in subsequent years created their own *journaux d'actualités*, or actuality periodicals, released biweekly or weekly. By 1913, Pathé-Journal appeared daily and was accompanied by a print publication of the same name, completing the circle from printed to filmed press and back again. Pathé claimed to be screening current events hour by hour and even minute by minute, announcing with punctuated emphasis that it would always be "the first to shoot the *document* as well as screen it, served up fully *alive* to the *masses*, who are hungry for *truth*."[22]

By World War I, then, the term *documentaire* had gained the sense of a recorded, exact, and objective copy of reality without any promise of narrative development. In 1914, *La science et la vie* (Science and life) featured a large photograph of a laboratory equipped by a major film studio to produce "documentary films"—in this case, to shoot close-up images of animals and plants. Outside of the studio and in contrast to dramas, which required sets, asserted

Pathé-Journal coeditor Armand Verhylle, "plein-air is authentic, and that is enough."[23] A lead essay in *Le film* the same year argued that, whereas the theater relies on illusion and convention, "at the cinema, what we look for is the photographic image of life." Audiences were most excited by "the documentary film that seems difficult to shoot," moreover, because a cameraman had confronted obstacles or dangers in pursuit of this image.[24] The desire for exactness through documentary underlay the 1913 creation of Gaumont's Encyclopedia Department, which included scientific laboratories but also sent cameramen to botanical gardens, zoos, and centers of industry. Critic Georges-Michel Coissac remarked that Gaumont's cameramen shot "views of the most remarkable sites and ethnographic and geographic documents, not only in France but in all regions."[25] Gaumont's project became a comprehensive one; its 1929 catalog included 1,200 documentary films released since 1907.[26] Almost half were plein-air and travel films, and Frédéric Delmeulle counts 68 shot in Africa, many fewer than in France (290) and the rest of Europe (218) but more than twice the number shot in Asia (30) and more than six times that shot in North America (11).[27]

This understanding of documentary as both objective and, over time, encyclopedic would pervade over a half century of French films shot beyond the Hexagon. Spectators in the metropole were promised a perfect match between reality and representation. According to *Hebdo-Film* (Film weekly), "the true interest of the cinema will have consisted in its exact and documentary views: the cataracts of Niagara, the sources of the Nile, tropical seas, ports of the Far West, hunting polar bears near the North Pole and lions in the center of Africa, etc. etc."[28] These films, their quantity hinted at by "etc. etc.," both reflected and supported French colonialism. France's claim to colonial mastery depended on what was widely called the *mise en valeur* of its conquered territories, including those in Africa.[29] This expression can be translated as valorization but also as calculated, successful exploitation; the forced labor witnessed by *La machine à écrire l'histoire* was not considered contradictory to France's "civilizing mission." In 1931, Coissac would assert that cinema, by contributing to "the *mise en valeur* of our possessions," had "most effectively served the work of initiating and expanding colonialism." By cinema, he meant films that represented, "in marvelous landscapes, the curious customs of tribes barely touched by our civilization."[30]

Around the same time Gunning deemed early cinema to be one of attractions, Charles Musser noted that scholars had neglected the genre of the travel film, one of the most popular in the early twentieth century.[31] And it is in work focusing on travelogues that early nonfiction films have gained attention. As a result of a dearth of extant films in often unpredictable archives, perhaps, such studies lump together films shot around the world by globe-trotting Euro-American cameramen, their efforts parallel to Albert Kahn's extraordinary, noncommercial "Archives of the Planet."[32] Alison Griffiths includes any on-site filming of "native peoples" in her extensively researched analysis of early travelogues as ethnography.[33] Yet this category of generic and interchangeable native—the *indigène* in French—was deployed by both cameramen and the companies that produced and distributed their films, reducing diverse populations to their nonwhite skin color and colonized status. And although Jennifer Peterson notes the dominance of French film companies in her innovative assessment of the spectatorial pleasure provided by early travelogues exhibited in the United States, she does not mention any films shot in sub-Saharan Africa.[34] Kevin Brownlow begins his forward to Neil Parsons's *Black and White Bioscope*, an overview of silent-era filmmaking in southern Africa, with a confession: "I have studied the silent film era for twice as long as it lasted, but until now I have hardly given a thought to early films made in Africa."[35] Convents's attention to the travels of early cameramen across the African continent is unique.[36]

The geographically specific early colonial cinema history that follows here, anchored by locations of both shooting and exhibition, reveals a colonial discourse about a particular space and the people who lived there, resisting the authority of the white cameraman (and film scholar) as omniscient world traveler. Just over a decade after Lumière operators filmed Black Africans on exhibit in France, the major French film companies began to send cameramen south of the Sahara to capture Africa and Africans on film, for display in the metropole. The result was a series of very short films called *panoramas*, *scenes*, and *views*, the earliest examples of which featured prominently at the 1906 Colonial Exhibition in Marseille, the first of its kind in France. The French West Africa exhibit displayed, for the region and then for each colony, sculptures, architectural details, paintings, photographs, railway maps, murals, plant and seed collections, and foodstuffs. Smaller buildings housed a "native village" like those of earlier ethnographic and universal exhibitions, as well as a "cinematographic pavilion" with a large screening room where "two hundred spectators can admire the curious and hitherto unseen scenes projected by the cinematograph."[37]

Pathé was awarded a grand prize as "cinematograph of the West Coast of Africa" for its films shown at the exhibition, one of which was Léo Lefebvre's *Panorama en Guinée* (Panorama in Guinea, 1906), a plein-air scene shot from the front of a moving train (CP, 944).[38] Other companies, most notably Éclipse, Raleigh et Robert, and Gaumont, soon joined Pathé to distribute films shot in sub-Saharan Africa. Between ninety and just over two hundred meters long, for a viewing time of four and a half to ten minutes, most consisted of a single shot from a fixed camera. Presenting views of new and exotic landscapes, the new moving pictures recalled painted panoramas and dioramas. As argued by Peterson, however, film provided a sense of "virtual mobility," creating "a new kind of tourist spectator."[39] "Thanks to the cinema," wrote a reviewer for *Cinémagazine* in the early 1920s, "a trip to Africa can be accomplished without fatigue."[40] To heighten the lure of exotic, faraway lands, many films were tinted or hand colored. The coloring added to each print could be monochrome, or, in an even more labor-intensive and expensive process, more than a single color could be added to a frame using brushes or stencils. Pathé's proprietary Pathé-color and Gaumont's Chronochrome and Gaumontcolor drew in viewers; since color was only worth adding to films that could attract large audiences, its use was a sign of the films' widespread appeal.

Lefebvre, best known for his 1906 films of Niagara Falls, famously traveled around the world for Pathé. In the wake of the Colonial Exhibition in Marseille, more of his African footage was released as *Vues de l'Afrique Française* (Views of French Africa, 1906), *Vues d'Afrique—En Guinée* (Views of Africa—In Guinea, 1906) and *Vues d'Afrique—Au Congo* (Views of Africa—In Congo, 1906). As these titles indicate, such films did not propose to tell a story. Fully a cinema of attractions, they showed an Africa that was both exotic and profitable. Among the tableaux that made up *Vues de l'Afrique Française*, "St. Louis Market" and "The Dakar Harbor" featured tourist sites; "Senegalese Trading Post," "Dynamite Mines in the Basalt Quarries of Cape Manuel," and "The Faidherbe Bridge" exploitable resources and colonial accomplishments; and "Native Customs" and "Crossing the Sandbar in Dahomey" the customs and occupations of colonized people. Some of this footage may also have been included in Lefebvre's *En Afrique occidentale* (In West Africa, 1907), which was shot, according to Pathé, in "regions thus far never explored by the cinematograph" (CP, 34–35). If few details remain about *En Guinée*, *Au Congo* began with images said to "parade before the eyes of spectators, initiating them into the very interesting life of a trading post in Congo." Spectators watched African workers, described in dehumanizing terms as "a swarm of natives," harvesting peanuts, fishing with nets, and constructing a traditional dwelling (CP, 933, 930). The film was still advertised for screenings at Pathé theaters two years later.

Renowned Lumière operator Félix Mesguich, who was born in Algeria, did not film on the African continent until 1906, several years after he left the Lumière organization.[41] Éclipse distributed footage he shot in Egypt and French Sudan as *Du Caire au centre d'Afrique* (From Cairo to the center of Africa, 1907) in the same year that Raleigh et Robert sent several cameramen to Africa, releasing a series of films titled *Du Cap au Caire, à travers l'Afrique centrale* (From the Cape to Cairo, across central Africa, 1907). The second of these, *Chasse à l'hippopotame* (Hippopotamus hunt), introduced wild African animals as a filmic attraction. The film played at a number of Paris theaters, including the Splendid-Cinéma and the Palace-Cinéma, and the Dufayel department store included it in a series of "extraordinary views" screened daily in celebration of the coming new year, accompanied by a buffet, a five o'clock tea service, and a symphony performance.[42] *Chasse à l'hippopotame* was proclaimed by an advertisement in *Phono-Ciné-Gazette* to be "the HIGHLIGHT of the 1906–1907 season." "The whole universe will talk about it," potential spectators learned, "as the most sensational, the most imposing, the most extraordinary, the most gripping, ever to appear. Nothing of the sort, nothing as beautiful, nothing as lively, has ever been seen." A review in the same publication described "views of a striking reality, filmed live [*sur le vif*]," that bring viewers "into the midst of these native tribes of little-known Africa."[43]

Used repeatedly to advertise African travelogues, the expression *sur le vif* is difficult to translate, signifying *on the spot* as well as *live* and *from life*. Compared to Lumière scenes shot in replica African villages in France, these films were sensational simply for having been shot in sub-Saharan Africa. But readers and spectators were to understand films such as *Chasse à l'hippopotame* as even more unprecedented and astonishing for having been filmed live and without staging. The *Du Cap au Caire* series was such a success that Raleigh et Robert released newly filmed images with the same title four years later. "A man dared place his camera several meters from!" began a full-page ad in *Ciné-Journal*, one of the most important industry publications of the period, subsequently reminding exhibitors of the financial success of the first version.[44] With the assurance that the new views were "truly sensational," Raleigh et Robert linked the film's documentary nature to its commercial viability and offered theater owners a forty-eight-page brochure along with "an enormous, American-style poster."

Following the success of its first films shot in sub-Saharan Africa, Pathé released just over a dozen more in the next four years, most classified as plein-air scenes. The same adjectives recurred endlessly in catalog text and periodicals: faraway, curious, mysterious, picturesque, savage, sensational, and never-before-seen. *Promenade au Soudan* (Promenade in Sudan, 1908) promised "a few typical scenes of life in French Sudan . . . a busy, swarming market, weavers making cloths . . . vendors of weapons and gold objects, traditional musicians, etc." (CP, 63). *Autour des grands lacs d'Afrique* (Around the great lakes of Africa, 1909) included "scenes of picturesque life, searching for a

Publicity for Raleigh et Robert, *Du Cap au Caire, à travers l'Afrique centrale*, 1907.

Pathé Frères postcard, 1907.

beehive, harvesting and tasting honey, a very primitive scene" (CP, 240). *Dans l'Afrique mystérieuse* (In mysterious Africa, 1909) was publicized as a conquest of African terrain by both cameraman and spectator, using quintessentially colonialist vocabulary: "We penetrate, with the explorer, into the Africa of unlimited deserts" (CP, 183). These films manifested a desire to capture flora and fauna on film, as well as an interest in the customs of people encountered along the way, stoked by three decades of ethnographic exhibitions staged in France. If not a large percentage of Pathé's catalog, they constituted an illustrious component, one the company used to advertise itself in a 1907 postcard. A woman and four men, three holding koras, look at the camera; the studio's name appears above the photograph, the iconic Pathé rooster at the upper left, and a caption below reads, "Excursion across the French colonies."

In some cases, companies attempted to profit by obscuring their shooting locations. Pathé's *Chez les Touaregs* (Tuaregs in their country, 1908), variously classified as educational, actuality, and travel film, opens with young women and children in traditional dress posing for the camera (CP, 53).[45] The film's subjects engage in daily activities, tying turbans and riding camels. A group of men performs sword and shield fighting and what an intertitle calls a "spear dance," after which a short narrative is integrated into the series of attractions. Spear-wielding Tuareg men on camels attack a European courier, who shoots; one of the men falls from his camel to the ground. From this moment of high drama, the film returns to showing Tuareg customs, as a group of men on horseback rides a fantasia while holding rifles. *Chez les Touaregs* concludes with a woman struggling to style her toddler's hair as the girl plays with a kitten, adding humor to ethnographic interest. A fence and chateau occasionally visible in the background are the only indications that the film was shot not in Tuareg country but at an ethnographic exhibition.

Gaumont, like Pathé, began to introduce spectators to African people as much as landscapes. A follow-up to *Au Sénégal* (In Senegal, 1910), *Femmes africaines travaillant au lavoir* (African women working at the wash house, 1910) shows, for a duration of one minute, women washing clothes. In *Dakar à Saint Louis du Sénégal* (Dakar to Saint-Louis in Senegal, 1910), after a couple of short pans across port and city landscapes, a series of Africans look directly at the camera, the first in an iris shot that catalog text calls a "locket" portrait.[46] Common in early French documentaries, such shots of African subjects looking into the camera recall colonial-era postcards like Pathé's above, which reflected prevailing European anthropological beliefs about the ethnic "types" found in different regions of the world.[47] Spectators were as well trained in physiognomic photographic portraiture as in the display of human beings in botanical gardens and fairgrounds. But *Dakar à Saint Louis du Sénégal* goes on to show African "habits and customs": women cook, a butcher cuts up meat at a market, a jeweler works at his anvil, a barber shaves a man's head, a kora player and a potter perform their arts. This evocation of daily activities and traditional "small" or "native" trades, of interest since Regnault's chronophotographic series, hints at an increasing ethnographic focus on filmed Africans beyond an illustration of types.

Short ethnographic scenes were added attractions within African travelogues, but it was with the hunting film, a combination of the plein-air and sports categories, that their popularity soared. In the wake of Raleigh et Robert's *Chasse à l'hippopotame*, Pathé released *Chasse aux vautours en Afrique* (Vulture hunt in Africa, 1908), an "attractive hunting tableau" showing the capture of a young vulture from its nest and the shooting of a group of vultures discovered eating the carcass of a gazelle (CP, 136). The chief Africanist of Pathé's pre–World War I years was Alfred Machin, and hunting films became his specialty. Machin is remembered primarily for his feature fictions, shot in France, Holland, and Belgium, and for his service in the Cinematographic Section of the French army (SCA) during the war.[48] Yet the footage he shot over the course of two expeditions across North and sub-Saharan Africa, accompanied by Swiss guide and hunting enthusiast Adam David, was used to create dozens of films.

Originally from northern France, Machin did his military service in North Africa in the very last years of the nineteenth century.[49] He worked as a photographer first for a friend, photographer and future filmmaker René Moreau, then for *L'illustration* magazine.[50] Inspired by a 1906 article titled "Adventures of a Hunter-Photographer in Africa" and the Raleigh et Robert and Éclipse films released the next year, Machin obtained financing from Pathé and left for Egypt in late 1907.[51] In a lengthy piece in *L'illustration*, Gustave Babin explained that Pathé had sent Machin to the center of Africa "to hunt great wild animals and record, on film, the major episodes of these exciting battles of man against savage animals." Babin traced Machin's travels, which repeated Mesguich's trip up the Nile and then continued into the Sudan region, his words accompanied by a number of photographs taken during the "cinematographic expedition." Detailing strategies for hunting and filming in Africa, he stressed that Machin did both.[52]

When Machin returned from his trip in August 1908, however, he discovered that most of his negatives were unusable. Only three films could be released from the salvaged footage: *La chasse à l'hippopotame dans le Nil bleu* (Hippopotamus hunt on the Blue Nile, 1908), *La chasse aux crocodiles* (Crocodile hunt, 1909), and *La chasse à la panthère* (Panther hunt, 1909) (CP, 146, 202).[53] *La chasse à la panthère* was hand colored, as would be many of Machin's subsequent films. Three European men hold rifles as they leave a hut, followed by four Africans, unarmed aside from a single machete. Intertitles explain that they set a trap and catch a leopard several hours later; spectators watch as the men torment the animal to show its ferocity off for the camera, then shoot it. A European hunter holds the dead animal's mouth open for the camera in a ritual display typical of such films, and the Africans carry it back to camp to be skinned and butchered.[54]

Machin began his second trip in late December 1909, during a period of intense global enthusiasm for hunting expeditions in Africa. Several months before leaving, he wrote in the pages of *Ciné-Journal* that French companies alone had twenty-seven "explorer-cameramen" filming in Africa.[55] Earlier that year, former president of the United States Theodore Roosevelt had begun a year-long expedition through British East Africa and Belgian Congo with the dual purpose of hunting and collecting for the Smithsonian Institution's new Natural History Museum in Washington. Roosevelt's highly publicized travels were recorded by Cherry Keaton in *Roosevelt in Africa* (1910), which sparked a trend of safari films in the United States.[56] *Paul J. Rainey's African Hunt* (1912) became a huge success in France as *Les chasses africaines*, with eighty-six screenings at the Casino de Paris alone.[57] Machin traveled from

Alfred Machin, *La chasse à la panthère*, 1909.

Alexandria to Khartoum to Fashoda, through French Sudan to Belgian Congo, French Congo, and Uganda, and then back to Khartoum, returning to France in August of 1910. He later recounted that he had met Roosevelt along the way, although no evidence confirms this. Better funded than for his first expedition, Machin had more cameras as well as a young assistant cameraman, Julien Doux.[58] Seventeen of the resulting films, released over a period of three years, were devoted to Africa south of the Sahara.

Much of Machin's footage features wildlife. Pathé's catalog reported that *Les oiseaux d'Afrique et leurs ennemis* (African birds and their enemies, 1911), shot along the lower Nile in French Sudan, shows roller birds and herons as well as their predators, genets and leopards (CP, 395). But most of Machin's films celebrate animals as victims of the sport of hunting; Pathé distributed them in at least five Great Hunts in Africa series. These were followed by a four-reel compilation titled *Voyages et grandes chasses en Afrique* (Travels and great hunts in Africa, 1913), which was long enough to be programmed on its own and prestigious enough to merit an accompanying orchestra of twenty musicians (CP, 702).[59] Beyond the thrill of the hunt, French spectators were encouraged to appreciate African wildlife as a resource from which they could personally benefit. In *Chasse à l'aigrette en Afrique* (Egret hunt in Africa, 1911), shots of an egret colony give way to views of European men shooting and African men retrieving dead birds. The last of the film's intertitles describes the monetary value of the feathers, announcing, in a moment of brutal honesty not quite disguised by light humor, that "every year, ladies, thousands of these pretty birds are massacred to adorn your hats" (CP, 454).

Machin's *Chasse aux singes* (Monkey hunt, 1912) begins with two European hunters in *casques coloniaux* pushing through underbrush accompanied by an African guide. A shot of a hunter taking out his binoculars is followed by one of a monkey climbing and sitting in a tree, framed as if by a binocular lens. In one of very few examples of such framing in Machin's films, the spectator is guided to see through the white hunter's eyes and, therefore, from his perspective. This hunting film is also unusual for its lack of weapons: two monkeys are caught when they reach into a gourd filled with fruit and tied to a tree. The hunters display them to the camera, stretching out their ears and paws.[60] In a common racist trope equating Africans with children and animals, Pathé's catalog text for the film claims that the monkeys did not mind being caught as they "find in the native a devoted playmate" (CP, 612).

Machin targeted more formidable prey in *Grande chasse à l'hippopotame sur le Haut Nil* (Great hippopotamus hunt on the Upper Nile, 1910) and *Chasse à l'éléphant sur les bords du Nyanza* (Elephant hunt near Lake Nyanza, 1911). Pathé's catalog describes the filmed elephant hunt as a "grandiose and savage spectacle" made up of "gripping tableaux" (CP, 345, 364). Publicity for *Chasse à la girafe dans l'Ouganda (Afrique centrale)* (Giraffe hunt in Uganda [central Africa], 1910) noted that Roosevelt had also hunted in the region, "a veritable paradise for hunters" with "the greatest wild animals in existence" (CP, 349). The film, which has some hand coloring, has no intertitles at all.[61] A long first shot shows a river landscape through which a large hunting party becomes visible, crossing the frame from left to right and back again while walking toward a fixed camera. Africans are carrying equipment and supplies, and a European hunter, wearing the obligatory pith helmet, appears near the end of the long parade of men. The column stops in the next shot, and an African runs up to the white hunter and points into the distance. After the European shoots his rifle, the members of the hunting party encircle and touch a dead giraffe, which is displayed for a close-up like the leopard and monkeys of previous films, mouth held open. After skinning the animal, the African porters carry it back to camp; the film concludes with a panning long shot of them cooking and eating the meat.

In Machin's *Les chasseurs d'ivoire* (Ivory hunters, 1912), two Europeans wearing pith helmets and suit jackets and holding rifles track a herd of elephants, accompanied by twenty Africans with spears. The camera is fixed within each shot but moves to different locations as the film progresses. The hunters approach through tall grass, elephants pass, the white hunters shoot, and the entire group runs toward a scene described first by an intertitle: "Struck by a bullet in the head, the giant collapsed, only its huge ears still quivering." Surrounding the dead animal, the hunters touch various parts of its body, and the Africans among them push and pull, working to turn it over. We next see them dancing around the carcass, a few stopping to smile for the camera. A mustachioed European examines one of the elephant's tusks from all angles in a later shot; once imported, an intertitle tells us, the ivory will be "shaped by skilled workmen." Suddenly no longer in Africa, spectators see a room full of white men and women making everything from hairbrush and cutlery handles to religious sculptures, the finished products elegantly displayed in cases.[62] Pathé's catalog summary pronounced the film "stirring," adding that it was "one of the most picturesque spectacles to see the natives cut up and cook the enormous pachyderm" (CP, 592). But the final message is again the exploitation of African "raw material," as a last intertitle describes the ivory, which is to be transformed by European craftsmen into objects used by Europeans.

Also in color, Machin's *Comment une lettre nous parvient des grands lacs de l'Afrique centrale* (How a letter reaches us from the great lakes of central Africa, 1911) similarly situates its viewer firmly in Europe, waiting for a letter to arrive (CP, 438).[63] The letter's African travels were described by Pathé as "primitive and picturesque": by pirogue through swamps to the Nile, by felucca to the closest European post office, then by camel across the desert. Two larger boats, a train, and a postman bring the letter to a woman, who hands it to its "pretty little addressee," her daughter. Advertised as "a pleasing documentary view, whose goal went beyond simple description," the film gestures toward narrative via the fictional travels of a specific letter. Pathé did not invent an author for this letter or explain why he was in Africa; spectators would have seen enough travelogues and hunting films to make an educated guess.

Machin was the most prolific French hunter-cameraman in Africa, but he was by no means the only one. In Pathé's *Une chasse aux buffles dans l'Afrique centrale* (Buffalo hunt in central Africa, 1909), African hunters track, kill, and butcher a "powerful and fierce" buffalo: "The head and skin are taken back to camp, and the natives, thinking ahead, dry the flesh for difficult days ahead and make special shoes with the sturdy leather" (CP, 230). Gaumont's comparable releases included *Chasses aux panthères et aux buffles* (Panther and buffalo hunts, 1911) and Éclair's *Chasse au léopard* (Leopard hunt, 1913). Even during wartime, Pathé offered *Chasse à l'hippopotame en Haute-Gambie* (Hippopotamus hunt in Upper Gambia, 1917) and *Chasse au buffle en Haute-Gambie* (Buffalo hunt in Upper Gambia, 1918), both in Pathé-color. *Le courrier cinématographique* (Film news) reviewer Edmond Floury noted the "defiant character" of the hippopotamus as well as the decline in number of animals caused by increased hunting as "civilization penetrates" into central Africa.[64] Congratulating the cameraman for the "evident dose of energy" the capture of his uncommon images must have required, Floury informed readers that the film "details perfectly how this pachyderm is of service to us." And whereas *Chasseurs d'ivoire* reminded spectators of how they benefit from ivory extracted from African elephants, Floury explained that the ivory of hippopotamus teeth is "more beautiful and even finer than that of the elephant."

Catalogs and film magazines glorified those who filmed the hunting of wild animals, whether or not they were mentioned by name. Pathé proclaimed the bravery and skill of European cameramen who "accomplished veritable photographic feats, shooting from short distances" (CP, 146), in 1911 releasing *Le cinéma en Afrique* (Cinema in Africa), a film that took as its subject matter both filmer and filmed: "The cinema, penetrating into the least explored regions, finds the formidable inhabitants of central Africa where they live. . . . Hidden in the high grasses like a hunter in a blind, the cameraman lies in wait for the inevitable game. Captured *sur le vif*, a leopard leaping onto a graceful gazelle, young lion cubs at the edge of their den, a tribe of monkeys, a herd of elephants passing by, a family of vultures having a meal around a carcass" (CP, 407, 406). The most expert hunters, it seems, were holding cameras instead of guns, and Pathé described Machin as a man in whom "the qualities of an adept and intrepid hunter and a perfect cinematographer were combined" (CP, 703). Machin, like Mesguich before him and innumerable others after, called himself and his colleagues *chasseurs d'images*, image hunters, an inherited trope that would go on to structure French filmmaking in sub-Saharan Africa throughout the colonial era. In Jules Renard's 1896 *Histoires naturelles* (Natural histories), a collection of short observations of wild animals, the *chasseur d'images* heads out into nature without tools or weapons, his only nets his eyes, "where images imprison themselves."[65] A decade later, Machin's *chasseur* hunted images while hunting, capturing, and killing animals, the images not just remembered by the hunter but fixed on film.

In addition to traveling, hunting, and filming his travels and hunts, Machin wrote about traveling, hunting, and filming in a series of articles for *Ciné-Journal*. The metaphor of cinema as hunt took on a more military vocabulary in "The

Cinematograph and the Conquest of the World," published soon after Machin's first trip to sub-Saharan Africa. Repeating promises made by film companies to reveal to spectators the sensational truth of a continent, Machin wrote that, thanks to the cinema, "one can learn to know the entire world, be initiated into all of its curiosities and wonders."[66] Following up a week later, he observed that "more and more often . . . the cinematograph endeavors to violate the secrets of the most remote corners of our globe," detailing how cameramen prepare to film "in any savage region, far from civilization." Itineraries must be planned, transportation arranged, enough food, drink, medicine, and weapons supplied to last for many months, Machin explained, all so that "our good people, in cities and in the countryside, can travel around the world, without leaving home, remaining comfortably in their seats . . . without the slightest danger."[67]

European and North American hunters in Africa had long brought back trophies in the form of animals and animal parts but also in photographs, and historian Paul Landau notes that the 1860s saw parallel developments in the technologies of guns and cameras.[68] Concluding the third article of his series, Machin compared the camera to a weapon, praising "the valiant pioneers who march to conquer the world, armed with cameras, for the great glory of Cinematography."[69] In this argument, he and his fellow *chasseurs d'images* took risks and even violent action so that European spectators could receive accurate and complete instruction in the form of exciting entertainment delivered to their neighborhood theaters. Returning to the theme of cinematographic conquest two years later, Machin drew an even more explicit analogy between gun and camera in an essay titled "Shooting Guns and Films Across Central Africa." Directly addressing "you who, relaxing in your seat, watch as images of faraway lands pass before your eyes," he accused viewers of not grasping the risks taken for their edification and amusement. Just as Babin retraced Machin's first voyage in *L'illustration*, Machin himself retraced his second, with similarly ample photographic documentation, in a lengthy advertisement for his films and for Pathé as his sponsor and distributor. And for the first time, while asserting his effort and bravery, Machin wrote about Africans instead of just filming them. Calling his crew members "our natives," he incorporated them with the noisy cargo loaded in Khartoum: "mules, donkeys, goats, pigeons, chickens, hens, Negroes, all screeching."[70]

Chasseurs d'images like Machin hunted hunts, then, capturing what they saw and presenting their targets—landscapes, fauna, and people—as strange, exciting, and dangerous. After praising the educational possibilities of hunting films, Machin summarized quite dramatically the challenges and dangers faced by European cameraman in Africa: "You have to capture *sur le vif* the most thrilling, the most dramatic scenes, the agony of the lion and the death throes of the panther . . . and it is not always the wild animals that one hunts and kills, that one immolates on the altar of the Cinema god, like a sacrifice pleasing to the screen, that are to be feared the most; there are always the savage tribes, warlike and fierce, who lie in wait for the cameraman-explorer as he passes through."[71] Again equating Africans with wild animals, Machin described their capture on film not just as a daring exploit but as a bloody, burning gift to cinema itself. This figure of sacrifice would moreover allow for films that hunted only human beings. Machin's *Moeurs et coutumes des Chillouks* (Habits and customs of the Shilluk, 1910) and *Les Chillouks, tribu d'Afrique centrale* (The Shilluk, a central African tribe, 1910) were both made up of footage shot in Fashoda after traveling down the Nile from Khartoum. Categorized by Pathé as plein-air scenes, neither focuses on outdoor landscapes or wild animals (CP, 315, 341). *Moeurs et coutumes* shows "war dances, terrifying hairstyles," and "simulated combat," while *Les Chillouks* provides "a glimpse of the life of . . . a Central African tribe, whose members are tall and of a marked Negroid type and woolly hair." Spectators witnessed the construction of a house with a conical roof, a family leaving one of these typical dwellings, men and boys herding cattle, and women preparing food.

Machin's character of the brave cameraman shooting in Africa was built on existing mythology, aligning the *chasseurs d'images* with "explorers" Caillié and Brazza as well as military icons Jean-Baptiste Marchand, Commander and Minister of War Joseph Galliéni, and General, Minister of War, and Marshal Louis-Hubert Lyautey.[72] Film scholar Marc Henri Piault has linked this passion for discovery and conquest to the simultaneous births of cinema and ethnography, both of which depend on "going 'into the field.'" Arguing that the two grew out of an expansion of industry for which colonization was critical, Piault dubs them "the twin children of a common enterprise of discovery, of identification, of appropriation."[73] But if scholars have understood travelogues shot in colonized spaces in terms of ethnography, there is little critical agreement about what ethnography means with respect to early cinema.

Fatimah Tobing Rony's groundbreaking book on racialized representation in early nonfiction film begins with Regnault's chronophotographies of the 1895 exhibition in Paris. Regnault considered the colonized subjects he shot to be "raw data," Tobing Rony contends, and left this "positivist legacy" to both cinema and visual anthropology.[74] Skipping from Regnault to Flaherty to examine this legacy in films from the 1920s and '30s, she compares Regnault's "inscription" model of ethnography to the "taxidermic" model epitomized by Robert Flaherty's *Nanook of the North* (1922) and the "monstrosity" model of

Merian Cooper's and Ernest Schoedsack's *King Kong* (1933).[75] Griffiths builds on Tobing Rony's work to rethink pre-1915 travelogues as ethnographic films. Although both scholars ground early ethnographic cinema in precinematic arts and culture, Griffiths's working definition of ethnographic film is based not on any ideological or anthropological project but instead on "the looking relations between the initiator of the gaze and the recipient."[76] Not a cinematic genre or mode, it is a manifestation of race-based stereotypes. Katherine Groo similarly omits colonialism from her definition of early ethnographic cinema, understanding it simply as "a tactic of representation defined by departures both physical and conceptual" and extending its potential corpus to include unedited, unidentified, amateur footage.[77] With a potentially endless amount of film to choose from, Groo creates thematic groupings, unanchored in space or time, on which to reflect.

Their claims to nonfiction notwithstanding, the ethnographic detail of the films discussed here does not guarantee an accurate depiction of African lives and cultures. Yet anthropologist and specialist in visual ethnography Paul Henley includes Machin in an important overview of what he calls *reportage* films, invoking the language of investigative journalism. Acknowledging a colonialist "framing discourse," Henley argues that such works can nonetheless be read as "testimony to traditional forms of African social and cultural life in the early twentieth century, many of which have since been entirely abandoned."[78] Even should a spectator manage to read against the grain, however, this approach validates that of colonial cameramen, who asserted more and more often as decades passed that their films were especially valuable since what they recorded was doomed to disappear, this salvage anthropology argument at best ironic given their own role in the process. And unlike ethnographic documentaries of later decades, *Moeurs et coutumes des Chillouks* does not provide any information about the "habits and customs" displayed by Machin. The ethnographic attractions of travel and hunting films served colonial propaganda more than anthropological analysis.

Foregrounding colonial assets in Africa—understood to include landscapes, animals, and human beings—early nonfiction films also highlight French military and administrative power. Fashoda, the shooting location for Machin's films about the Shilluk people, was famous for the 1898 battle between the armies of Marchand and Sir Herbert Kitchener for control of the Upper Nile Valley, a conflict that resulted in France's cession of the region to Britain. Machin recounted that he was warmly welcomed by a local leader, who said a single word: the name *Marchand*. From this, Machin concluded that the man was remembering the day a white, French officer "treated [the Shilluk] with kindness and protected them."[79] The four-minute *En Afrique centrale—Fachoda* (In central Africa—Fashoda, 1910) is divided into six parts, with a first intertitle announcing a "General View," a slow pan left that starts on a cannon and stops at a brick building guarded by French soldiers (CP, 311). "The Native Village," in contrast, shows lines of large houses with pointed, thatched roofs, with women and children sitting outside. In "Native Troops," dozens of Black African soldiers line up in uniform with rifles and bayonets, perform training exercises, and march away from the village to the orders of a white commander. Finally, "Young Sudanese at School," "The Cafeteria," and "Recreation" show children sitting in front of a bearded, pith-helmeted white teacher, eating together from a large bowl, and playing the drums.[80] Whereas Pathé focused on the army and schools as colonial institutions, Gaumont's *Vues de Saint-Louis-Sénégal* (Views of Saint-Louis-Sénégal, 1912) and *Vues de Soudan Français-Tombouctou* (Views of French Sudan-Timbuktu, 1913) feature administrative and military leaders—Governor General of AOF William Ponty reviewing the troops and Military Governor Colonel Roulet with a Tuareg leader.[81]

A strong sense of French colonial cinema began to emerge, then, before World War I, combining the pleasures of tourism, ethnographic curiosity, and patriotic imperialism to accomplish the *mise en valeur* of places and peoples. Pathé's *Métiers, types, et coutumes* (Trades, types, and customs, 1913) opens with images of a tailor working on his sewing machine; women cooking a meal; artisans making pottery; fishermen bringing in their pirogues, nets, and catch; and children dancing. Shots of women in traditional dress and hairstyles are intercut with images of a large crowd of Africans lining a parade route decorated with French flags, assuring spectators that their patriotism was shared by those they had colonized.[82] Journalists often declared the power of such films even more explicitly than did the films themselves. Readers of *Le cinéma* in 1912 were told, for example, that "an indisputable use of the geographical film is that it helps link the colonies to the mother country" and "shows us all the outlets offered to French enterprise by our vast overseas possessions."[83] A year later, editor of *Ciné-Journal* Georges Dureau hoped that cinema would have a prominent place at the upcoming 1916 Colonial Exhibition. Colonial cinema, he wrote, provides "a living illustration of all of the corners of the world where the French flag flies." Dureau argued that the propaganda value of colonial films—more specifically, their capacity to recruit future colonizers—was intrinsically linked to their concrete and nonfictional nature. Cinema offered spectators "the exact representation of the nature and the people we cannot all go see," filling their eyes "with men, animals, plants whose life happens over there and that seem to have come to us to reveal themselves physically."[84]

Some travelogues were destined to promote the colonies to noncommercial audiences. Gaumont released a series of short films shot in French West Africa in the geography section of its educational cinematheque. An intertitle in *De Kouroussa à Bamako* (From Kouroussa to Bamako, 1913) identifies it with the Ministry of National Education and as part of the collection of the Pedagogical Museum in Paris, with "free loans" available. The film opens with a panoramic view of Kouroussa and concludes with the sun setting over the Niger River. In between, we see African women working and talking in a courtyard, a group of men identified as "the native tribunal," and Bamako residents packing into the open cars of a small train on the nearly ten-year-old railway line.[85] *De Kayes à Saint-Louis du Sénégal* (From Kayes to Saint-Louis in Senegal, 1913) combines city panoramas with scenes of African life—children bathing in a river and fishermen pushing their pirogues out to sea through crashing waves. The film concludes with Europeans in pith helmets, standing on large rocks to enjoy the view of the rapids. As the camera pans left, spectators see the landscape as if through their eyes.[86]

This focus on documentary as colonial propaganda intensified during the war. Readers of *Ciné-Journal* learned that "colonizing cinema" had a salutary influence on audience members, "to whom it reveals all of the marvels of our colonial domain," allowing spectators "to traverse very quickly and without fatigue the prestigious regions that, without it, they could never know."[87] In 1914, on the first page of the first issue of *Le film*, former editor of *Kinéma* journal Pierre Letorey maintained that he had long been calling for a cinema that would "make known, to all of the French, the sites, the output, and the diverse resources of our so rich and so interesting colonies." This was a crucial undertaking in the context of the war, he argued, since Germany was attacking the colonies it had cost France so much to acquire. Letorey believed that the indifference of most citizens to France's colonial possessions could be countered by films focused not just on the wealth to be gained from them but also on the "habits and customs" of their peoples. He therefore urged the French government to subsidize the production of such films and distribute inexpensive copies to exhibitors.[88] The same year, Pathé released *La ville de Saint-Louis du Sénégal* (The city of Saint-Louis in Senegal, 1914), which contrasts traditional straw dwellings and trades with the "modern" Faidherbe Bridge and colonial government complex, and *Kouroussa, Afrique Occidentale* (Kouroussa, West Africa, 1914), which highlights dried mud dwellings and native baobab, palm, and date trees, as well as "various native trades" of Malinké men (CP, 740, 767). Gaumont followed suit with *Vues d'Afrique Occidentale—Les textiles* (Views of West Africa—Textiles, 1914), among many others.

The French army created the SCA in 1915 in recognition of the importance of film to war propaganda, and Alfred Machin returned from working in Belgium to represent Pathé as one of four founding cameramen, each from a different company.[89] In Europe, the war brought a reminder of the elasticity of documentary with a return to the early cinema fashion of reenacted newsreels. Forbidden by army regulations from shooting during battles, cameramen would arrive at the front afterward and ask soldiers to perform previous combats. Wartime newsreels also mixed documentary and fictional scenes to provide narrative context, staging, for example, a soldier on leave for the birth of his child.[90] A few of the film unit's newsreels featured the *tirailleurs sénegalais*, African troops who, like the Africans in ethnographic exhibitions, were often brought to Europe by force. *Tirailleurs sénégalais en Alsace* (Senegalese sharpshooters in Alsace, 1917), for example, shows Black soldiers eating well, joking together, and engaging in playful swordplay.[91] Just as *La machine à écrire l'histoire* erased the reality of forced labor, this film erased that of forced conscription, brought to the screen only after independence in Senegalese director Ousmane Sembene's historical fiction *Emitai* (1971).

With official governmental initiatives put into place for the first time as the war began, films shot in France's overseas colonies resisted any narrative other than the valorization and exploitation of colonial resources. A note in *Ciné-Journal* in July 1914 informed readers that AOF Governor General Ponty, in collaboration with Commissioner Monsieur Guy, had hired a cameraman to "go on site to shoot the most difficult films."[92] The year 1916 saw the creation of Governor General of French Indochina Albert Sarraut's cinematographic mission, with the dual goal of shooting and screening films. The decree that established the mission described a need to produce "photographs and films relating to economic resources, population ethnographies, and general questions connected to a better understanding of the country and its resources."[93] These colonial propaganda films, like the earlier plein-air, travel, and hunting films, were conceived of as nonfiction.

In 1917, French deputies André Maginot and Pierre Perreau-Pradier, acting separately, each called for the creation of a committee for colonial propaganda.[94] And as the end of the war approached, the SCA began to produce not just newsreels but also longer films, including one designed to garner support for the colonial enterprise via the colonies' contributions to the war effort. *L'aide des colonies à la France* (The colonies' aid to France, 1918), distributed by Compagnie Universelle Cinématographique, was screened both in theaters and as a traveling show. The film is divided into two parts, the first shot mostly in French colonies and the second primarily in Europe.[95] At the

L'aide des colonies à la France, 1918.

start, two maps introduced by intertitles illustrate the expansion of French colonial possessions between 1870 and 1912, crediting the appropriation of one third of the African continent to the "brilliant vision" of a "great Frenchman": Jules Ferry, French prime minister in the 1880s. After an announcement of the economic importance to France of grain from Morocco and ammunition from Indochina, the film's emphasis shifts to military aid. Soldiers from Indochina and French colonies in North and sub-Saharan Africa "come to the rescue of a France under attack."

The second part of *L'aide des colonies à la France* traces the history of the *tirailleurs sénégalais* from the force's creation by French Governor of Senegal Louis Faidherbe in 1857. Intertitles quote various generals, including colonizer of Madagascar Joseph Galliéni, praising the loyalty, endurance, and bravery of the sixty thousand Black Africans who fought for France during the Great War. Along with scenes of *tirailleurs* training and fighting, the film, in the fashion of earlier travelogues, showcases their "games and dances," including traditional West African wrestling. Spectators are also shown part of a letter ostensibly sent by a mother in Segou to her son, a Mr. Diarra at war in France. Writing quite implausibly in French, Madame Diarra encourages her child to obey his superiors and show the French that he loves them and wishes to give his life for their cause. The film closes with an oval portrait image of war hero Mamadou Diarra, to whom an intertitle attributes "incomparable bravery and fierce energy." This element of fiction was designed to heighten the emotional connection of French spectators to colonial subjects imagined to be eternally subservient.[96] In the words of Roland Barthes, in his analysis of the myth of the *tirailleur* as represented on the cover of popular magazine *Paris-Match*, "there is no better response to the detractors of a supposed colonialism than the zeal of this Black man to serve his supposed oppressors."[97] Almost thirty years after independence and sixteen after *Emitai*, Sembene worked against this colonial myth in *Camp de Thiaroye* (Camp of Thiaroye, 1987), creating a counterhero to Diarra with a resonant name. After a group of World War II *tirailleurs* returns to their home continent, Sergeant Diatta loudly and clearly challenges the inequity of French treatment of African soldiers.

Calls for colonial propaganda continued in film and colonial publications as the war ended, grounded in hopes that the *mise en valeur* of the colonies could assure France's place in the postwar world. Maurice Landay, in a three-part series for *La dépêche coloniale* (Colonial dispatch) in 1918, repeated Dureau's claim that cinema could be "a marvelous propaganda instrument." "Let's take advantage of it, let's use it, let's abuse it!" he exulted, offering the support of his journal and colonial association to the task. The masses, stuck in France, could be encouraged to become "great and powerful colonizers" if films showed them "the still virgin riches" of the colonies, colonies Landay felt France was insufficiently exploiting.[98] The cinema, entertaining while it educated, could convince children and adults to build a "greater France," Landay argued, and he called on none other than the minister of colonies to demand the production of colonial films. Criticizing the first decade of French films shot in sub-Saharan Africa for inadequate messaging, he insisted that future colonial films should not be "kilometers of views of virgin forests more or less populated by marmosets or rattlesnakes, of Negro villages, or fishing trips on the Upper or Lower Niger" but instead show "the colonial mother-city, the roads and transportation, the organized ports."[99]

The earliest French films shot in sub-Saharan Africa, as we have seen, claimed to be documentaries. They used neither trick photography nor sets and actors, at least not in the conventional sense. Although views were selected and framed and actions performed for the camera, images were neither shot for nor edited into a fictional narrative, or much of a narrative at all. Yet these films were not faithful reflections of Africa and Africans; superficial and patronizing, they are imbued with and in turn bolstered colonial racism and avarice. Like earlier genres of French colonial visual art, they demonstrate the preconceptions and biases of those who filmed, produced, and distributed them as well as those who watched them. Describing the mechanism of colonial photographs and films, Piault notes that they rely on "the transportation of the Other from a place of absolute strangeness . . . to one within the reach of the measure of the white gaze."[100] The nonfictionality of these moving images of Africa was evaluated only in Europe, by white spectators for whom the images were attractive precisely because they were foreign and mysterious, because they represented a reality about which spectators were ignorant, their only knowledge gained from previous stereotypic representations.

Alfred Machin never returned to Africa for a third expedition, abandoning documentary claims to shoot fiction films that staged African hunting scenes. These films featured animals shipped from Africa, most famously a leopard named Mimir, and included episodes of two established series, one dramatic and one comic. The hero of *Babylas explorateur* (Babylas the explorer, 1911) is haunted by wild animals he killed on a previous hunting trip, during which he served as a guide for Roosevelt. In *Little Moritz chasse les grands fauves* (Little Moritz hunts great wild animals, 1911), Mimir shares top billing with comic actor Maurice Schwartz (CP, 431, 476). After leaving France to direct Pathé's subsidiary in Belgium, Machin made *Le diamant noir* (The black diamond, 1913), whose protagonist takes a job as assistant on a hunting expedition in Congo. Like *Comment une lettre nous parvient des grands lacs de l'Afrique centrale*, this film focuses on communication between African colonies and their metropoles, here telegraphs sent between Stanleyville and Brussels. Its "African" footage, however, including the heroic rescue of the main character's employer from a dangerous leopard, was shot in the Sonian Forest just southeast of Brussels.[101] After his wartime service with the SCA, Machin returned to filming imported African animals. When he died in 1929, not in the wilds of Africa but on the French Riviera, it was widely reported that one had attacked him during the shooting of *De la jungle à l'écran* (From the jungle to the screen). *Cinéa*'s obituary cited a massive heart attack—more likely if less poetic.[102]

Just prior to Machin's death, *Pour vous* magazine glossed over his early travel and hunting films in a single sentence to stress that he was the only director in France making movies "acted exclusively by animals."[103] Even into the twenty-first century, film historians and critics have preferred to remember Machin for these animal actors.[104] As much as we might now see the continuity between the films he shot in Africa and on the Côte d'Azur, however, Machin himself praised, in addition to his own bravery, his accomplishments as what we might call a visual ethnographer. When the Shilluk celebrated his arrival, he wrote, their "war dances, habits and customs were preciously recorded by the cinema."[105] In 1913, *Le courrier cinématographique* linked the entertainment value of travelogue films specifically to their ostensibly scientific representations of colonized peoples, which, like "the views of barbaric African and Australian tribes brought back by the Ethnological Society of London," made them "documents of primary importance."[106] And Armand Verhylle a year later illustrated his article asserting the authenticity of plein-air films with two still images of Africa. The first, a locomotive captioned "Africa Filmed on the Railway Line from the Cape to Cairo," was likely taken from Raleigh et Robert's 1907 *Du Cap au Caire*. In the second, two cameramen wearing pith helmets kneel in tall grass. The caption describes them as "pioneers of film . . . deep in the bush." They are, in fact, Alfred Machin and Julien Doux.[107]

Just as the nonfictional status of French films shot in sub-Saharan Africa from 1906 through World War I was central to the founding of a colonial cinema corpus, these colonial films proved fundamental to the emerging category of documentary cinema. Almost four decades after its release, André Debrie singled out *Du Cap au Caire* as a film "of the greatest interest" in his review of the history of French documentary for the First Conference on Documentary Film, cosponsored by the Organizational Committee of the Cinematographic Industry (COIC) and the Ministry of National Education. Debrie in the same speech drew attention to Machin's films for Pathé.[108] Machin's mythology of *chasseurs d'images* in Africa would structure French filmmaking in sub-Saharan Africa throughout the colonial period, as expeditions and films grew more frequent, lengthy, and elaborate, continuing to reflect the deeply unequal relationships between Europeans and Africans, filmers and filmed.

Notes

1. R. C., "Le cinema à l'Exposition coloniale," *La critique cinématographique*, no. 226 (1931): 45–46.

2. See Odile Goerg, *Tropical Dream Palaces: Cinema in Colonial West Africa*, trans. Melissa Thackway (Hurst, 2020), 13–15.

3. "Lettre du colonel Marchand," *Le film*, March 7, 1914, reproduced in Marcel L'Herbier, *Intelligence du cinématographe* (Corrêa, 1946), 93. Abel cites this letter as an early expression of the desire for cinematic propaganda but, attributing it to "a Colonel Marchand," does not recognize Marchand's military record of leading colonial armies in both West and North Africa. Richard Abel, *French Film Theory and Criticism, 1907–1939* (Princeton University Press, 1988), 29n58.

4. Elizabeth Grottle Strebel, "Imperialist Iconography of Anglo-Boer War Film Footage," in *Film Before Griffith*, ed. John Fell (University of California Press, 1983), 264–71.

5. See Convents, *À la recherche*, 69, 93, 94, 99; Jean-Jacques Meusy, *Paris-Palaces, ou le temps des cinémas (1894–1918)* (C.N.R.S., 1995), 183. For more on early documentaries produced by British and Belgian colonial organizations and businesses, see Guido Convents, "Documentaries and Propaganda Before 1914: A View on Early Cinema and Colonial History," *Framework*, no. 35 (1988): 109–11.

6. Guido Convents, "Africa: French Colonies," in *Encyclopedia of Early Cinema*, ed. Richard Abel (Routledge, 2005), 18.

7. Georges Sadoul, *Histoire du cinéma mondial, des origines à nos jours*, 7th ed. (Flammarion, 1963), 499; Georges Sadoul, *Le cinéma français* (Flammarion, 1962).

8. Richard Abel, *The Ciné Goes to Town: French Cinema, 1896–1914* (University of California Press, 1994), 91.

9. Stephen Bottomore, "Rediscovering Early Non-fiction Film," *Film History* 13, no. 2 (2001): 161, 164.

10. Alan Williams, *Republic of Images: A History of French Filmmaking* (Harvard University Press, 1992), 57–58.

11. Jacques Kermabon, ed., *Pathé, premier empire du cinéma* (Éditions du Centre Pompidou, 1994), 440.

12. Philippe d'Hugues and Dominique Muller, eds., *Gaumont, 90 ans de cinéma* (La Cinémathèque Française, 1986), 138–45, 190.

13. Daan Hertogs and Nico de Klerk, eds., *Nonfiction from the Teens* (Stichting Nederlands Filmmuseum, 1994); Daan Hertogs and Nico de Klerk, eds., *Uncharted Territory: Essays on Early Nonfiction* (Stichting Nederlands Filmmuseum, 1997); *1895, revue d'histoire du cinéma*, no. 18 (1995).

14. "Ce que l'on dit, ce que l'on sait," *Cinémagazine*, no. 32, August 26, 1921, 26.

15. Tom Gunning, "Before Documentary: Early Nonfiction Films and the 'View' Aesthetic," in Hertogs and de Klerk, *Uncharted Territory*, 23.

16. Tom Gunning, "The Cinema of Attractions: Early Film, Its Spectator and the Avant-Garde," in *Early Cinema: Space, France, Narrative*, ed. Thomas Elsaesser and Adam Barker (BFI, 1990), 57, 58.

17. Gunning, "Before Documentary," 11, 15.

18. Cited in Guy Gauthier, *Un siècle de documentaires français: Des tourneurs de manivelle aux voltigeurs du multimédia* (Armand Colin, 2004), 40. Alison Murray Levine, citing the *Trésor de la langue française*, traces *le documentaire* to 1915. See Murray Levine, *Framing the Nation*, 17; Roland Cosandey, "Some Thoughts on 'Early Documentary,'" in Hertogs and de Klerk, *Uncharted Territory*, 38, 47.

19. These titles and original accompanying catalog copy appear in Henri Bousquet's four-volume *Catalogue Pathé: Des années 1896 à 1914* (Henri Bousquet, 1996), 329, 448, 531, 565, 549, 594, 601, 538, 820, 575, 769. References to Bousquet's heroic compilation are parenthetical, indicated by *CP* and the relevant page number. When not referenced to Bousquet, Pathé catalog descriptions are from the archives of the Département des Arts du spectacle (Arsenal site) of the Bibliothèque

nationale de France or the former Bibliothèque du film in Paris, now incorporated into the Bibliothèque du film of the Cinémathèque Française. Portions are
available online at gparchives.com and, thanks to the Fondation Jérôme Seydoux-
Pathé, at https://www.fondation-jeromeseydoux-pathe.com.

20. For more on "the strange fashion of reenacted actualities," see Marcel Huret,
Ciné actualités: Histoire de la presse filmée 1895–1980 (Henri Veyrier, 1984), 24–27.

21. Abel, *Ciné Goes to Town*, 92.

22. *Pathé-Journal*, no. 37, October 6, 1913, cited in Meusy, *Paris-Palaces*, 259–60.

23. A. Verhylle, "Les coulisses du cinématographe: La confection d'un film," *La
science et la vie*, February 1914, 187.

24. J. Killian, "De la vérité," *Le film*, March 6, 1914, 1.

25. G.-Michel Coissac, *Histoire du cinématographe: De ses origines jusqu'à nos
jours* (Éditions du Cinéopse, 1925), 462.

26. Frédéric Delmeulle, "Le rêve encyclopédiste: Le cinéma documentaire
chez Gaumont, 1908–1928," in *Cinéma des premiers temps: Nouvelles contributions
françaises*, ed. T. Lefebvre and L. Mannoni (Presses de la Sorbonne nouvelle, 1996),
98, 101.

27. Frédéric Delmeulle, "Le monde selon l'Encyclopédie Gaumont," *1895, revue
d'histoire du cinéma*, no. 20 (1996): 24.

28. P. S., "Le 'Temps' et le cinéma," *Hebdo-Film*, no. 30, September 23, 1916, 13.

29. See Conklin, *A Mission to Civilize*, 5–8.

30. G.-Michel Coissac, "Le cinéma au service de la civilisation et de la propagande," *Tout-cinéma*, 1931, 70.

31. Charles Musser, "The Travel Genre in 1903–1904: Moving Towards Fictional
Narrative," in Elsaesser and Barker, *Early Cinema*, 123.

32. See Paula Amad, *Counter-Archive: Film, the Everyday, and Albert Kahn's
Archives de la Planète* (Columbia University Press, 2010). On Kahn's archives as
ethnographic project, see Paul Henley, *Beyond Observation: A History of Authorship
in Ethnographic Film* (Manchester University Press, 2020), 40–42.

33. Alison Griffiths, *Wondrous Difference: Cinema, Anthropology, and
Turn-of-the-Century Visual Culture* (Columbia University Press, 2002), xxvii, xxix,
53. See also Alison Griffiths, "'To the World the World We Show': Early Travelogues as Filmed Ethnography," *Film History* 11, no. 3 (1999): 282–307.

34. Jennifer Lynn Peterson, *Education in the School of Dreams: Travelogues and
Early Nonfiction Film* (Duke University Press, 2013), 89.

35. Neil Parsons, *Black and White Bioscope: Making Movies in Africa 1899–1925*
(Intellect, 2018), vii.

36. Panivong Norindr has opened new avenues of research by singling out Lumière films shot in French Indochina. Norindr, "Enlisting Early Cinema," 109–17.

37. Léon Cayla, "L'Afrique Occidentale Française à l'Exposition de Marseille,"
La dépêche coloniale illustrée, no. 17, September 15, 1906, 220.

38. *Exposition coloniale de Marseilles 1906, palmarès officiel* (Édition du Journal des Colonies, 1907), 206. Convents, "Africa," 18.

39. Peterson, *Education in the School of Dreams*, 150.

40. "Les grands films documentaires: L'Expedition Vandenbergh dans le 'Centre africain,'" *Cinémagazine*, no. 19, May 11, 1923, 243.

41. Another former Lumière employee with Jewish North African origins, Albert Samama Chikli would also go on to film around the world (though never in sub-Saharan Africa) for major French companies. In the early twenties, he would direct several feature fictions, both shot and screened in his native Tunisia.

42. *La dépêche*, November 7, 1907, 5; "Spectacles divers," *Le petit parisien*, December 1, 1906, 5.

43. *Photo-Ciné-Gazette*, 1907, 18, 115, cited in Convents, *À la recherche*, 116, 117.

44. Verhylle, "Les coulisses du cinématographe," 195–7; *Ciné-Journal*, no. 168, November 11, 1911, n.p.

45. The copy of this film held in the collections of the Library of Congress has been digitized and is available online. Library of Congress, 2006641955. See Griffiths, *Wondrous Difference*, 81–83.

46. Gaumont Pathé (GP) archives, 0000GR10201BIS and 2000GS 04771. When dates provided by the Gaumont Pathé archives catalog conflict with those in *Ciné-Journal* by Guido Convents, I use the latter. Convents, *À la recherche*, 132–33.

47. On late nineteenth-century and turn-of-the-century anthropology's use of photography to document the physiognomy of racial difference, see Elizabeth Edwards, "Photographic 'Types': The Pursuit of Method," *Visual Anthropology* 3, nos. 2–3 (1990): 235–58, and Coombes, *Reinventing Africa*, 136–41. I disagree here with Peterson, who sees in such moments a potential "look back" from filmed subjects, one that, if angry enough, can undermine the power of the colonizing camera and rescue early travelogues from being solely "bad objects." Peterson, *Education in the School of Dreams*, 169, 33. See also Paula Amad, "Visual Riposte," *Cinema Journal* 52, no. 3 (2013): 49–74.

48. Sadoul went so far as to omit Machin's hunting films shot in Africa from his filmography. Sadoul, *Le cinéma français*, 203. See also Abel, *Ciné Goes to Town*, 49, 204, 338.

49. Francis Lacassin, *Alfred Machin, 1877–1929* (Anthologie du Cinéma, 1968), 436.

50. Georges-Michel Coissac, "Les opérateurs de prises de vues," *Cinéopse*, no. 92, April 1, 1927, 338.

51. Francis Lacassin, *Alfred Machin: De la jungle à l'écran* (Dreamland Éditeur, 2001), 17–20.

52. Babin, "Les grandes chasses africaines," 254.

53. Lacassin, *Alfred Machin: De la jungle à l'écran*, 25.

54. Machin and his contemporaries used the term *panther* to designate what would now be identified as a leopard, a member of the panther family. *La chasse à la*

panthère has been restored from a stenciled color print in a collaboration between the Royal Cinematheque of Belgium (CINEMATEK) and Belgium's Royal Museum of Central Africa and Catholic University of Louvain.

55. A. M., "Notes d'un globe-trotter cinématographiste," *Ciné-Journal*, no. 43, June 11, 1909, 5.

56. See Gregory Waller, "Nonfiction Film in and out of the Moving Picture Theater: *Roosevelt in Africa* (1910)," in *A Companion to Documentary Film History*, ed. Joshua Malitsky (Wiley-Blackwell, 2021), 401–20.

57. Meusy, *Paris-Palaces*, 251. For more on Rainey's African safari films, see Griffiths, *Wondrous Difference*, 270–76.

58. Lacassin, *Alfred Machin: De la jungle à l'écran*, 26–27.

59. "Spectacles de Toulouse," *La dépêche*, November 4, 1913, 4.

60. GP Archives, 1912CNCPDOC 00119.

61. GP Archives, 1910CNCPDOC 00086.

62. GP Archives, 1912PDOC 00012. Machin's film appears to have been rereleased seventeen years later in the Pathé-Baby collection of educational films. See "La filmathèque Pathé-Baby: Nouveautés de mars 1929," *Le cinéma chez soi*, no. 29, March 1929, 8.

63. Additional information on Pathé films also held by the British Film Institute can be found on the invaluable "Colonial Film: Moving Images of the British Empire" site: http://colonialfilm.org.uk/home.

64. Edmond Floury, "Les films de la semaine," *Le courrier cinématographique*, no. 37, September 22, 1917, I.

65. Jules Renard, *Histoires naturelles* (Fayard, 1896), 2.

66. Alfred Machin, "Le cinématographe et la conquête du monde," *Ciné-Journal*, no. 36, 23–28, April 1909, 9.

67. Alfred Machin, "Le cinématographe dans le désert: Comment s'organise une expédition cinématographique," *Ciné-Journal*, no. 37, April 29–May 5, 1909, 6, 8.

68. Paul Landau, "Empire of the Visual: Photography and Colonial Administration in Africa," in Landau and Kaspin, *Images and Empires: Visuality in Colonial and Postcolonial Africa*, 147.

69. A. M., "Notes d'un globe-trotter cinématographiste," 5.

70. Alfred Machin, "À coups de fusil et d'objectif à travers l'Afrique centrale," in *Le livre d'or de la cinématographe* (Éditions de *Ciné-Journal*, 1911). Reprinted in Lacassin, *Alfred Machin: De la jungle à l'écran*, 190.

71. Machin, "Le cinématographe et la conquête du monde," 10.

72. On these explorers and military leaders as "imperial heroes," see Berny Sèbe, *Heroic Imperialists in Africa: The Promotion of British and French Colonial Heroes* (Manchester University Press, 2013), 31–36.

73. Marc Henri Piault, "L'exotisme et le cinéma ethnographique: La rupture de *La croisière noire*," *Journal of Film Preservation*, no. 63 (October 2001): 6.

74. Tobing Rony, *Third Eye*, 14.

75. Tobing Rony, *Third Eye*, 195.

76. Griffiths, *Wondrous Difference*, xxix. See Griffiths, "'To the World the World We Show,'" 282–307. Assenka Oksiloff reads German documentaries from the early cinema period through the 1920s as ethnographic. See chapters 2 and 3 of Oksiloff, *Picturing the Primitive: Visual Culture, Ethnography, and Early German Cinema* (Palgrave, 2001).

77. Groo, *Bad Film Histories*, 4. Groo's understanding of early ethnographic films leads her to conclude, contra my evidence here, that the majority "never reached an audience and never managed to intervene in popular culture" (256).

78. Paul Henley, "From *Vues* to Ethnofiction: French Ethnographic Filmmaking in Africa Before Jean Rouch," *Visual Anthropology* 33, no. 1 (2020): 34.

79. Machin, "À coups de fusil et d'objectif à travers l'Afrique centrale," 191–92.

80. GP Archives, 1910PDOC 00335.

81. Convents, *À la recherche*, 132.

82. GP Archives, 2000GS04355.

83. Burch, *Life to Those Shadows*, 53.

84. G. Dureau, "La cinématographie coloniale," *Ciné-Journal*, no. 257, 1913, 3.

85. GP Archives, 2000GS04371.

86. GP Archives, 2000GS04311.

87. H. C., "Le cinéma colonisateur," *Ciné-Journal*, no. 382, December 9, 1916, 7.

88. Pierre Letorey, "Le cinéma colonial," *Le film*, February 27, 1914, 7.

89. Huret, *Ciné actualités*, 43. This visual propaganda agency has endured within the French armed forces; as of 2001, it is known as ECPAD, the Communication and Audiovisual Production Establishments of the Ministry of Defense. Films produced by the SCA can be consulted at the Médiathèque de la Défense in Ivry.

90. Laurent Veray, "Fiction et 'non-fiction' dans les films sur la Grande Guerre de 1914 à 1928," *1895, revue d'histoire du cinéma*, no. 18 (1995): 238–39, 241.

91. Bloom, *French Colonial Documentary*, 49.

92. "Un hardi pionnier," *Ciné-Journal*, no. 308, July 18, 1914, 8.

93. André Touzet, *Une oeuvre de guerre et d'après-guerre: La mission ciné-matographique du gouvernement général d'Indochine* (Imprimerie d'Extrême Orient, 1919), 1.

94. Convents, *À la recherche*, 156–57.

95. ECPAD, 14.18B315. This film is included as a bonus track on the ECPAD's DVD release of *La force noire*, directed by Eric Deroo and Antoine Champeaux (2008).

96. In his analysis of the representation of the *tirailleur* in French colonial ideology of the late 1910s, Peter Bloom notes that a "projected colonial gaze" created the figure of an "infinitely obedient soldier," deployed in a range of contexts, from films like *L'aide des colonies* to the now-infamous advertisements for Banania chocolate breakfast drink powder. Bloom, *French Colonial Documentary*, 35, 43.

97. Roland Barthes, *Mythologies* (Seuil [Points], 1957), 201. In his short film *Vita Nuova* (2009), visual artist Vincent Meessen reveals what Barthes did not: Barthes's maternal grandfather was the late nineteenth century adventurer and colonial administrator Louis-Gustave Binger, conqueror and first governor of Côte-d'Ivoire. See T. J. Demos, *Return to the Postcolony: Specters of Colonialism in Contemporary Art* (Sternberg Press, 2013), 48–50.

98. Maurice Landay, "Propagande et cinéma," *La dépêche coloniale*, August 27, 1918, 13.

99. Maurice Landay, "Propagande et cinéma: Les leçons cinématographiques coloniales," *La dépêche coloniale*, September 3, 1918, 1–2; "Propagande et cinéma: Le film colonial," *La dépêche coloniale*, September 6, 1918, 1.

100. Piault, "L'exotisme et le cinéma ethnographique," 7.

101. Lacassin, *Alfred Machin, 1877–1929*, 456.

102. Pierre Leprohon, *L'exotisme et le cinéma: Les 'chasseurs d'images' à la conquête du monde* (Éditions J. Susse, 1945), 22; "Nécrologie," *Cinéa*, no. 136, July 1, 1929, 25–26.

103. Carlos Larronde, "Un ami des bêtes qu'on appelle sauvages," *Pour vous*, June 20, 1929, 2.

104. See Inga Pollman, "Environmental Aesthetics: Tracing a Latent Image from Early Safari Films to Contemporary Art Cinema," in *Cinema of Exploration: Essays on an Adventurous Film Practice*, ed. James Leo Cahill and Luca Caminati (Routledge, 2021), 107–24. The LUX Theater in Valence, France, in 2022 programmed a selection of Machin's films restored by the CNC under the title "Alfred Machin's Animals."

105. Machin, "À coups de fusil et d'objectif à travers l'Afrique centrale," 192.

106. "Les sujets de cinématographie," *Le courrier cinématographique*, no. 41, October 11, 1913, 52.

107. Verhylle, "Les coulisses du cinématographe," 196, 197. The same image appears in Coissac, "Les opérateurs de prises de vues," along with a short text by Machin.

108. "Congrès du film documentaire," *Le film*, April 17, 1943, 9.

2

ADVENTURE

Expeditions and the Grand Documentaire

The first scholarly discussions of French colonial cinema began with and remained limited to the interwar period, for some good reasons. Like the last third of the nineteenth century, it was an era of imperial fervor. In the wake of World War I, just as in 1870, concern about France's global importance heightened the desire for a greater France.[1] Efforts at colonial propaganda again accelerated, with newspapers, magazines, and journals publishing manifestos that called on cinema to contribute to the *mise en valeur* of the colonies. Beginning in 1906, as we have seen, French travel and hunting films shot in Africa built on and developed a racist, colonial discourse inherited from earlier visual media. In the 1920s and '30s, while still commercially produced and released, such films were also supported by new governmental institutions and networks. And spectators remained avid, with a reviewer for film magazine *Cinéa* claiming in 1924 that "Africa, despite all that literature and cinema have been able to reveal, remains the strangest and most troubling continent, the richest in marvels of all kinds."[2]

A year after the war ended, Alexandre Promio, who twenty years earlier had shot some of the first moving images of North Africa, became the director of the newly created photographic and cinematographic service of the Government General of Algeria, tasked with promoting the colony.[3] Also in 1919, Georges-Michel Coissac declared his interest in expanding on the propaganda work of earlier colonial films. An important figure in early French film criticism, Coissac published one of the first film projection manuals and founded *Le fascinateur*, a Catholic biweekly with an emphasis on photography and film.

His new monthly journal *Cinéopse* focused on cinema and education, and in the first issue, Coissac urged the use of film as propaganda in the French colonies to "develop a love of France on the part of the native . . . by showing him the varied marvels of our cities and countrysides . . . and, especially, teaching him new forms of industry and commerce."[4] He soon changed course, however, to argue for convincing the French of the value of their colonies by shooting propaganda films in Africa and screening them in France. Soon, Coissac wrote, thanks to an expedition by Auguste Jobez and Alfred Chaumel to French Equatorial Africa, Parisian spectators would have the pleasure of seeing "the diverse aspects of the regions . . . and their inhabitants with the customs that characterize them, the luxurious vegetation of the tropical forest with its rich and varied fauna," plus "grand and stirring elephant, hippopotamus, panther, gorilla, and antelope hunts." Coissac heartily approved of Jobez and Chaumel's plans to "push their propaganda into primary schools, high schools, middle schools, chambers of commerce, and entertainment venues."[5]

Coissac's language makes evident a thematic continuity through the decade, bridging pre- and postwar periods: sub-Saharan Africa was filmed for its exotic and huntable landscapes, animals, and people. His reference to public and private screening venues shows that, thinking systematically about colonial propaganda in filmic form, he saw no strict boundary between governmental and studio productions. In the late 1910s, Albert Sarraut proposed the creation in each of France's colonies of an economic agency charged with publicity in a variety of media, including film. Lacking production resources of their own, these agencies commissioned private studios to make films that were then collected and lent out for screenings.[6] Coissac noted in October 1920 that the Government General of French West Africa had just signed a contract with Pathé to send "one of its best cameramen" to film "scenes and views of all of the colonies of the group."[7] The next year, the AOF's economic agency, in a full-page advertisement on the back cover of *La dépêche coloniale illustrée* (The illustrated colonial dispatch), announced that its propaganda services included the distribution to conference organizers of "documents, photographs, and cinematographic films."[8] By the late 1940s, the economic agencies of AOF, AEF, Algeria, and Madagascar had created what journalist Marcel Lapierre called cinematheques: lending libraries of colonial documentaries intended "to draw attention to our overseas possessions, support commerce, and encourage colonial vocations."[9]

These practices continued throughout the interwar period amid debates about whether and how the French government should better propagandize via cinema. Sarraut, who by 1920 had returned to Paris as minister of colonies, declared to the Senate the "absolutely indispensable" need for "methodical, serious, constant propaganda, acting by word and by image, journal, conference, film, exhibition, in a word by all of the modern means of advertising."[10] Two years later, *Ciné-Journal* reported that a screen had been installed in the Senate chapel to project "the marvels and riches of our overseas possessions" in a series of "cinematographic matinées."[11] "Not only will our senators amuse themselves like big children," the piece concluded, but they will also support "our colonial expansion." At the end of the decade, the bulletin of the Agency General for the Colonies published a lengthy report on British colonial propaganda, asserting that British efforts had set an example for France to follow. The report noted the existence of government-funded "colonial cinemas" in London that featured titles such as *The Mysterious East, Life in Malaysia,* and *Cocoa in the Gold Coast.*[12] With concerns about attendance, however, the author went on to suggest that "it would be more profitable to show colonial propaganda films in ordinary movie theaters, inserted into programs in which a film star would attract audiences."[13] Once they saw "the unexpected riches over there and our unequaled methods of civilization," *Les annales coloniales* (Colonial chronicles) similarly proclaimed, "our children and grandchildren will decide to go collect the harvest of grains sown years ago."[14]

Interest in cinema as colonial propaganda escalated between the wars not just within the French government and its adjunct colonial lobby but also in the pages of major film publications, where columnists lamented that France did not measure up to its competitors in empire. After the Belgian minister of foreign affairs announced the production of documentary propaganda films to be shown around the world, *Ciné-Journal* asked, "What are we waiting for to organize similar propaganda tours in France?"[15] In the pages of the new illustrated film weekly *Cinémonde* (CineWorld), Jean Marguet with frustration answered no to the question "Does France, a colonial power, possess a colonial cinema?"[16] And Jean Andrieu deplored in *Cinéma* the ignorance of most French citizens about their colonial empire, which he described as "a jewel beyond compare, an object of envy for other peoples."[17] Only film, Andrieu argued—and more specifically, "a campaign of cinematic propaganda organized in a rational fashion across the metropole"—could encourage the exploration and exploitation of "so many unknown riches" and thus the accomplishment of the dream of greater France. Coissac in *Cinéopse* complained that he had long been asking that "a serious effort be made to intensify the production of documentaries that aim to make known all of the unrecognized treasures of France."[18] More than just recognition, the virtual travel provided by such films would encourage spectators to extract resources from the colonies. "Thanks to films," Coissac wrote, "we wander through any and all lands, not as tourists but as prospectors; they open themselves up to us in all of their features and with all of their resources and possibilities."[19]

Responding to these calls and to increased spectatorial enthusiasm for the colonies, French studios continued to produce travel and hunting films that displayed sensational African animals and people, explicitly framed as valuable possessions. The turn of the decade saw *Au Sénégal: Dakar* (In Senegal: Dakar, 1920) from Films de Stock; *St. Louis* (1920) from Pathé; and *Les nouvelles provinces africaines: Le Ruanda et l'Urundi* (New African provinces: Rwanda and Urundi, 1920) from Éclair. The 1922 Colonial Exhibition in Marseille by far eclipsed the 1906 edition both in size and attendance, and *Ciné-Journal* reported that the West Africa section featured "a very attractive movie theater . . . where only colonial films will be shown."[20] Up to three hundred audience members at a time were introduced, per *Le courrier cinématographique*, to "the many riches of our overseas possessions and their enchanting settings."[21] Gaumont was awarded the exhibition's grand prize for having organized and operated this theater, where its films were well represented. Arts daily *Comoedia* praised Gaumont, reminding its readers of the "usefulness of colonial cinema for the diffusion, in the metropole, of the precious resources of greater France."[22] And in the wake of the exhibition, *Le petit journal* organized its own "colonial cinema" program of ten films, eight of which were documentaries shot in sub-Saharan Africa: *Pêche au harpon sur le Niger* (Harpoon fishing on the Niger River), *Dans la falaise de Bandiagara* (In the Bandiagara Cliffs), *Chasse à l'hippopotame* (Hippopotamus hunt), *Divertissements à Kouroussa* (Entertainment in Kouroussa), *Port-Étienne*, *le palais des rois à Abomey* (The king's palace in Abomey), and *Passage de la barre en Côte d'Ivoire* (Crossing the sandbar in Ivory Coast). The ninth film was titled *L'utilisation de nos richesses coloniales* (The utilization of our colonial resources), and the tenth, enticement to attend or reward for sitting through the previous nine, was a Buster Keaton short.[23]

The interwar period saw, then, the crystallization of a particular nexus of colonial ideology and film, more specifically documentary—a very different tradition from feature fictions shot in Algeria, Morocco, and Tunisia. Yet scholars have followed Pierre Boulanger to designate these *colonial cinema*, identifying Jacques Feyder's *L'Atlantide* (1921) as the first of a string of popular melodramas and films noirs culminating with Julien Duvivier's *Pépé le Moko* (1936), all now classics of French cinema.[24] Very few such films were shot south of the Sahara, however, a difference that film critic Pierre Haffner later attributed to the difficulty of organizing a large shoot.[25] If this difficulty was indeed a contributing factor, it is also the case that the French colonial vision of sub-Saharan Africa and Black Africans differed greatly during this period from the romanticized, orientalist fantasy of the Maghreb. North Africa had a much larger settler population and, notes Peter Bloom, served as a popular French tourist destination in the early decades of the twentieth century.[26] There was no parallel distinction within British production, which in the 1930s saw a wave of fiction films set in sub-Saharan Africa, including *King Solomon's Mines* (1927), *Trader Horn* (1931), and the Tarzan movies.[27]

In the 1920s, the term *documentary* began to appear more frequently in Pathé catalogs. In the first year of the decade, Charles-Félix Tavano, filmmaker and future artistic director of Établissements Aubert, reinforced the link between travel films and other nonfiction genres in an essay for *Le film* titled "Voyages and Documentaries." Taking as one example a plein-air film made up of views of Saint-Louis, Senegal, he assured readers that the French public loved to travel, even and especially via the screen, and urged the production of "a wide variety of documentary and scientific films."[28] Ten years later, director J.-K. Raymond-Millet similarly assured readers of *Comoedia* that, among documentaries, "travel and tourism films are those that most keep the attention of spectators." "Excellent agents of propaganda," he stressed, such films "very usefully awake the adventurer that sleeps within us."[29]

Gaumont advertisements began to include a subheading for documentaries, listed after dramatic and comic films, in a sign of their newly distinct popularity. Frédéric Delmeulle observes that nonfiction film style changed so little through the 1920s that prewar films did not seem dated.[30] Gaumont's *Au travers de l'Afrique Equatoriale Française* (Across French Equatorial Africa, 1920), for example, consists of views as attractions, its images familiar from the travel, hunting, and early propaganda films of the prior decade: Africans as *tirailleurs*, on horseback, playing drums, and building a road and a bridge. Spectatorial desire for exotic fauna is fulfilled by shots of French men enjoying a game of tennis while lion cubs, a baby elephant, and ostriches wander around them. A flock of egrets takes off, and hippos swim in a river. Three concluding images convey in quick succession a message of possession: an outline of France, Africa with France's colonies identified by shading, and the French flag flying. Ten years later, and with almost exactly the same title, Gaumont's *À travers l'Afrique Equatoriale Française* (1930) includes a similar array of familiar images. Ducks and hippopotamuses swim in a river until bullets hit the water, then a group of African men drags out a dead hippo. Europeans in pith helmets can be glimpsed in the background as residents of a village go about daily activities—stacking logs, drying mud bricks, herding cattle—occasionally stopping to look at the camera.

These travel and hunting films can be difficult to identify, distinguish, and date. Responses to a 1930 survey sent by the French Ministry of Agriculture to over two hundred rural film programmers reported *Une chasse à l'hippopotame* (Hippopotamus hunt) as among its most popular offerings.[31] This may have been Ciné-Location-Éclipse's 1921 film, which had played at Paris's Maine-Palace and Delta-Palace theaters, or perhaps another with the same title. Pathé-Baby, a small camera and projector designed for home use, included a *Chasse à l'hippopotame* in its 1923 catalog, likely made up of Alfred Machin's footage from over a decade earlier. Pathé's *Chasse à l'hippopotame sur le Haut Zambèze* (Hippopotamus hunt on the Upper Zambezi River) was released in two virtually identical versions ten years apart (1921 and 1931) that match exactly the format of *Chasse à la panthère* and *Chasseurs d'ivoire*. A large group of Africans depart from a riverbank for a hippopotamus hunt, led by a European in a pith helmet; once an animal has been shot, they pull and push the carcass onto the bank, butcher it, and cook the head.

From 1906 through the early 1930s, growing interest in colonial propaganda through film was fed by an expanded production of travelogues and hunting films shot in Africa, which continued to feature not just African landscapes and fauna but also Africans. Éclair advertised *La vie des noirs dans un village du Congo* (The life of Blacks in a Congolese village, 1921), and Les Films Erka in June 1922 announced the opening of its new "department of documentary films," with a list of titles including *Chez les nègres de l'intérieur de l'Afrique* (With the Negroes of the African interior). Only after World War I, however, was the term *ethnography* used to refer to the representation of "curious" or "picturesque" customs on screen. In late 1920, Coissac's *Le fascinateur* summarized *Chez les Pygmées du Congo* (With the Pygmies in Congo) under the heading "Cinema in the Service of Ethnography."[32] Just over a year later, Pathé's Larousse encyclopedia series included a subsection of films categorized as "Ethnography." If new to the vocabulary of cinema, the nineteenth-century concept was familiar to visitors of Paris's Trocadero Palace, where France's ministry of education had established the Museum of Ethnography on the occasion of the 1878 Universal Exhibition.

Cinematic ethnography during the interwar period was a touristic and colonial enterprise rather than an academic one. Many productions were funded by France's colonial governments, as evidenced by the career of administrator and filmmaker René Bugniet. For *Dans l'extrême nord* (In the extreme north, 1919), sponsored by the High Commissariat of the French Republic, Bugniet traveled along the Logone River to Lake Chad, "contemplating villages, discovering the artisanal, musical, or sports activities of Cameroonians, and admiring the braided hairstyles of Cameroonian women, as well as their jewelry." *En pays foulbé* (In Fulbé country, 1927) presents the traditional clothing and daily chores of the inhabitants of seven villages. And the contemporaneous *Cameroun: Danses régionales* (Cameroon: Regional dances), supported by both the Ministry of Colonies and the Economic Agency of Cameroon and Autonomous Colonies, shows, often in extreme close-up, dancers from four regions of southern Cameroon. In a series completed in the 1930s for the Economic Agency of African Territories Under Mandate, Bugniet portrayed the pirogues, dwellings, dances, and foods of the Bamum and Bamileke ethnic groups, with several titles highlighting French colonial accomplishments in logging and the transportation of goods in the region. The same agency sponsored two films shot by André Lecurieux in 1929. *Le Togo: Le coton* (Togo: Cotton) demonstrates France's mechanization of the cultivation of cotton, a product to be exported to Europe, and contrasts living conditions in the European and African neighborhoods of capital city Lomé with those in the north.[33] Like forests and cotton, African traditions and cultures were exploitable resources.

More surprising, perhaps, is the degree to which commercial studio productions foregrounded France's colonial administrative and military presence in Africa. Éclair's *Le Congo belge* (Belgian Congo, 1919) begins with the arrival in Boma of Governor of French Congo Gabriel Angoulvant on a steamship named *Europe*. Angoulvant disappears from the film after a review of colonial troops, at which point spectators are given a tour of Boma's major avenues, governor's palace, and local markets, the military base in Banane, and a sanatorium where, an intertitle explains, "'colonials' . . . can take rest cures and convalesce." An introductory intertitle in Éclair's *La croisière de M. Maginot en Afrique Occidentale Française* (M. Maginot's cruise in French West Africa, 1929) reports that the Maginot mission, led by former war hero and current minister of colonies André Maginot, is en route to Dakar. Crowds of Europeans and Africans welcome the members of the group, which includes Senegalese deputy Blaise Diagne, as French flags flutter around them. Tours of Bamako and Gao are followed by a pilgrimage to the monastery of colonial officer turned cleric Charles de Foucauld across the desert in Beni Abbes.

Studio productions also continued to praise the European extraction of African resources. In Gaumont's *Les bois du Gabon* (Wood from Gabon, 1925), a familiar colonial narrative is enlivened by a fictional character, a genteel young woman first seen in Europe speaking with friends or investors. The scene almost immediately shifts to Port-Gentil, Gabon, where she is filmed by the ocean, then in a forest, smiling with two white colleagues as they watch a large group of African men clear brush and cut down an enormous tree. When the tree falls, our nameless heroine, in riding boots, scarf, and pith helmet, clenches her hands in excitement. The African workers saw the trunk into pieces, which are pulled by boat along the Ogooué River to Port-Gentil, then loaded onto a cargo ship. The woman reappears after the lumber has been unloaded in France, wearing a fur coat and surrounded by stacks of plywood in a warehouse; she and four men stand on a plank to demonstrate the strength of her product. An iris-out concludes the film, an eccentric mélange of genres designed to advertise the wealth available to adventurous (and stylish) colonialists.

If *Les bois du Gabon* stands alone as colonial documentary melodrama, conventional colonial travel and hunting films of the 1920s coexisted with a new strand of colonial-era documentary, differently conceived and better remembered. French adventurers had for centuries published accounts of their African expeditions, which, when sanctioned and supported by government agencies, gained the title of *mission*. Museums also began to sponsor such trips in exchange for the acquisition of objects for their collections. Filmmakers at first joined larger expeditions, sparing themselves the organizational work and costs of traveling on their own. Starting in the 1920s, however, expeditions to Africa were organized specifically for the films that would result. Only cinema, argued *Ciné-Miroir*, allowed spectators "to see explorers in action, near us . . . to become their companions." "The landscapes, the customs that unfold before their eyes," continued the journalist reviewing an American film shot in AEF with funding from both Famous Players-Lasky Corporation and the New York Museum of Natural History, "we in turn see them as if our own gazes had discovered them," all while remaining "comfortably seated" and "safe from tsetse flies and venomous serpents."[34]

In his 1920 essay on cinema as colonial propaganda, Coissac noted that Pathé's cameraman was asked to shoot films that would "please audiences, not only for their documentary interest, but especially for their artistic interest."[35] In a second divergence from the prewar period, those undertaking such efforts were now considered not just *chasseurs d'images* but also authors of creative works. If they followed often quite literally in the footsteps of Machin, he was never mentioned as an influence. When watching a Pathé newsreel, Lionel Landry announced in *Cinémagazine*, "we are in the presence of documentary, without a doubt," but documentaries could also be works of art, "as beautiful as a very simple drama."[36] By the end of the decade, *Cinémonde*'s Claude Jeantet was dismissive of pre-1920 documentaries that consisted of "a few views of cities or regions one after the other," contrasting these to the new category of the *grand documentaire*, made up of exploration films that "conserved the positive character of reproduced facts while giving their presentation an artistic character." "True documentary," Jean Marguet proclaimed in the same publication, was no longer the "moving postcards" of earlier decades, and film weekly *Pour vous* similarly privileged "shaped" or "fictionalized [*romancé*]" over "raw" documentary.[37]

In this second era of French colonial film shot in Africa, we find another origin story for the use of the noun *documentaire* to designate nonfiction film. Analyzing interwar exoticism, scholar Dudley Andrew traces the term to film historian and critic Léon Moussinac's *The Birth of the Cinema*, published in 1925, a year before John Grierson's review of Robert Flaherty's *Moana*.[38] Following a discussion of the distinction between educational films and documentaries, the penultimate section and page of Moussinac's book is simply titled "Documentaries" and consists of a list of twenty titles. The first seven, beginning with *The Germination of Plants*, are undated scientific films, while many of the rest are expedition films released in France in the early 1920s, including Flaherty's *Nanook of the North* (1922) and two shot in sub-Saharan Africa: Americans Martin and Osa Johnson's *Chez les Anthropophages* (*Among the Cannibal Isles of the South Pacific*, 1918/1921) and Swede Oscar Olsson's *Au coeur de l'Afrique sauvage* (*Bland vildar och vilda djur* [In the heart of wild Africa], 1921/1922).[39] Writing for *Ciné-Comoedia*, George Fronval like Jeantet and Marguet dismissed the popular travel and hunting films of the late 1900s and early to mid-1910s, insisting that only after Flaherty would a theater program a documentary as the main feature.[40] In France as elsewhere, *Nanook of the North* became a turning point and touchstone as what Landry deemed "a drama made almost entirely of scenes of real life, shot *sur le vif*."[41]

At the same time as he cited Flaherty's films as the first *grands documentaires*, Fronval contended that "Africa was the first to reveal its mysteries" in films by the Johnsons and Olsson.[42] The Johnsons' films were as popular in France as they had been in the United States, and *Ciné-Journal* described *Chez les anthropophages* as an "educational" and "sensational documentary."[43] Years before Fronval and Jeantet took up the expression, Coissac had described *Au coeur de l'Afrique sauvage* as a *grand documentaire*, claiming that it "calls documentary films into question and shows how captivating they are, even awe-inspiring, as long as they are real."[44] Olsson's expedition covered five thousand miles over the course of three years, from Nairobi to Kivu to Khartoum, his objective "to film wild animals in their native haunts and to obtain a pictorial record of life in general in the more remote parts of Central Africa."[45] A milestone in the history of films shot in sub-Saharan Africa, his documentary was a huge commercial success in France and became a point of reference for French filmmakers and critics for decades to come. *Au coeur de l'Afrique sauvage* opened at Paris's

Au coeur de l'Afrique sauvage at the Gaumont-Palace, 1922.

Gaumont-Palace, one of numerous cinema palaces to open in the early 1910s. The renovated hippodrome, originally designed by Gustave Eiffel for the 1900 Universal Exhibition, could accommodate fifty-five hundred seated and standing spectators; Gaumont declared it the largest movie theater in the world.[46]

Gaumont's publicity promised "a sensational documentary film" that exposed "the mysteries of the African bush and its unknown peoples."[47] A full-page advertisement in *Cinémagazine* began with "The must-see film!!!" and then announced "the greatest cinegraphic expedition ever undertaken, to reveal the customs of the Black peoples and the habits of the wild animals living as masters in the immense African jungle."[48] Another ad, placed in *Ciné-Journal*, targeted theater owners, affirming that "nothing is more interesting than studying the habits and customs of savage tribes on-site" and assuring that all of the film's "most curious scenes," taken *"sur le vif,"* would "enthrall" audiences. These enticements received official, governmental endorsement; *Cinéopse* published letters of congratulation sent to Gaumont by a representative of France's director of secondary education, the rector of the University of Paris, and the secretary general of the Society for Geography.[49] French schoolchildren and scholars were invited to a screening sponsored by the minister of public instruction and the minister of colonies; spectators young and old were reportedly overwhelmed by the "majestic attraction of the unknown continent that the cinema revealed to them in its complete splendor."[50]

Building on advertising in industry publications and movie magazines, Hachette published a literary adaptation of *Au coeur de l'Afrique sauvage* authored by Guy de Teramond, a former classmate of Olsson's who had accompanied the expedition.[51] And reviews of the film echoed its publicity, emphasizing that it was both exciting attraction and "the most exact and most abundant documentation of life in the African bush."[52] *Le courrier cinématographique* put the film on its cover, following Gaumont's lead to call it "the film that everyone wants to see" and "the most astounding document ever to have been screened."[53] *Cinémagazine* was perhaps the most concise in this dual claim, describing Olsson's film as, "in its documentary aspect, the most sensational recorded for screens." "Never has a cameraman managed to penetrate so deeply into these lands," the journalist continued, adding the trope of the courageous *chasseur d'images*, "to film so faithfully—at the cost of a thousand dangers—the habits and customs of the peoples and the fauna of central Africa."[54] A second review a week later noted that spectators would feel "amazement" and "admire equally the sangfroid of the cameraman and of the intrepid hunters" as the film allowed them to "live the exact life of the Blacks of this region."[55]

Publicizing its release of Svenska Film's follow-up a year later, also screened at the Gaumont-Palace, Gaumont took out a full-page ad asking theater owners, "Do you remember your box-office receipts from the sensational film *Au coeur de l'Afrique sauvage*? The Second Series of Great African Hunts, *En Afrique Équatoriale* [In Equatorial Africa] is now available."[56] The enthusiastic reception of Olsson's films by critics and spectators set the stage for a string of equally popular French expedition films shot in sub-Saharan Africa in subsequent years. Even the French army produced a *grand documentaire* with a successful

Vers le Tchad, 1922.

run in movie theaters. *Vers le Tchad* (Toward Chad, 1922), sponsored by the Under-Secretariat of State for Aeronautics and associated with a military research expedition to central Africa, was distributed by French Paramount and premiered at the Mogador Cinema in Paris. A grab bag of images and styles, the film begins with a shot of cameraman Maxime Dely with his camera, recalling the image hunter persona successfully exploited by Machin and Pathé. A map shows the route of a group of voyagers who will fly from Paris to Oran on airplanes named for French World War I aviators Jean Casale and Roland Garros, then travel by boat, car, and train from Oran to Gao, along the Niger River to Gaya, and on to Savé, Cotonou, and Dakar.

As they travel, these European adventurers take in exotic scenery and hunt buffalo while Africans work for them. Intertitles introduce and comment on landscapes, animals, and people, with "small trades," for example, followed by scenes of Africans spinning thread, weaving, and dying cloth; a traditional boxing match; and dancing and drumming. Moments of humor are achieved through patronizing, racist mockery, an "amused condescension," in the words of Jean-Michel Frodon, that was common in travelogues representing so-called exotic peoples.[57] The French travelers' truck appears to go out of its way to drive toward Africans who run away, terrified, and an intertitle jokes that "the crowd does not seem familiar with cars, nor with the rules of the road." *Le courrier des cinémas* called *Vers le Tchad* both a "first-rate 'document'" and an "adventure novel"—"unprecedented, exact, and, most importantly, evocative."[58] Paramount advertised the film in a two-page spread that featured praise from military officers, cinema professionals, and movie magazines, describing it as both "propaganda" and "intense poetry," both "patriotic work" and "work of art."[59]

In the private sector, manufacturers Citroën, Renault, and Peugeot sponsored documentaries starring vehicles that, Bloom maintains, "served as a mobile platform of geographic mastery."[60] The first of these, Paul Castelnau's *La traversée du Sahara en autochenilles* (Crossing the Sahara in half-tracks, 1923), was filmed during a Citroën-funded expedition from Touggourt to Timbuktu led by Georges-Marie Haardt and Louis Audouin-Dubreuil. Haardt worked for Citroën, Audouin-Dubreuil had already led an expedition, and Castelnau, who had previously worked for Albert Kahn, was hired to accompany the mission as geographer and cameraman. In opening intertitles, the film evokes a modern colonial undertaking: "From the dawn of antiquity, communication across the desert could only be assured by camel-driven caravans.... The vast French colonial domain in Africa requires more rapid communication ... made possible by courageous men, with the help of half-tracks."[61] Celebrating a new generation of brave French colonial adventurers in powerful automobiles, Castelnau incorporated familiar pleasures in his documentary, such as hippopotamus and crocodile hunts shot in Niger. *Ciné-Miroir* called the film a *grand documentaire*, and Gaumont released it simultaneously in thirty-two Paris theaters.[62]

Castelnau used excess footage from his expedition with Citroën to create *Le continent mystérieux* (The mysterious continent, 1924), a film in twelve parts that Établissements Aubert made available to theaters as either "one voyage" of seventeen hundred meters or "four stages" of four hundred meters each.[63] In terms we now recognize, Aubert advertised "a documentary that has the value of a great film" and a film displaying "the truth about the Black continent, habits, customs, existence"; reviewers for both *Cinéa* and *Ciné-Journal* hailed it as a *grand documentaire*.[64] Contrasting this second film with the earlier, official record of the expedition, Castelnau wrote that it revealed not just Africa but also Africans, providing "a synthesis of Saharan customs and landscapes, seeking out the most typical geographical features and penetrating into the natives' milieux."[65] After six chapters set in North Africa, the mission crosses the Sahara from Salah, in southern Algeria, to Timbuktu, where spectators are shown the houses of Scottish adventurer Alexander Gordon Laing, the first European to enter the city, and French hero René Caillié, the first to enter and return. After this homage, intertitles provide information about mosques, houses, city streets, and wells. "Many races meet in Timbuktu," an intertitle informs us further, and images of the hairstyles of Songhai women, a Tuareg musical instrument, and a French doctor and school follow. In Bamako, capital of French Sudan, Castelnau juxtaposes the European-style Hôtel des Postes and Koulouba governor's palace with the straw-roofed dwellings and livestock-filled roads of the "native city."

The third section of *Le continent mystérieux*, tracing the expedition's trip up the Niger River, includes an abbreviated version of Castelnau's *En chaland sur le moyen Niger* (Barge travel on the Middle Niger, 1925), a film distributed separately by Compagnie Universelle Cinématographique. Characterized as "travel notes," this shorter version opens with images of the river and its banks shot from a covered barge, which African men are working to move using poles and paddles. An intertitle nevertheless attributes to the boat trip "an inexpressibly relaxing calm," aligning spectators with unseen European passengers who soon emerge to hunt from the deck, wearing pith helmets. When the water drops rapidly in a channel, expedition members "requisition the populations of several villages," who pull the boat with ropes and dig the channel until the boat can pass through. Once again belying the pain of African labor, the film concludes with a peaceful sunset.

Renault and Peugeot joined Citroën to sponsor vehicle treks through Africa, which were publicized in films that similarly traded on the appeal of distant and unfamiliar landscapes and people. Gaumont's two-part *Mission Gradis au Sahara* (Gradis mission to the Sahara, 1924) records Renault's expedition from Algeria to French Sudan in three ten-horsepower vehicles. *Images d'Afrique* (Images of Africa, 1926), shot during a Peugeot expedition from Algiers to Dakar, was distributed in several different versions over the course of a decade. The year 1926 also saw the release of three feature-length French documentary productions shot in sub-Saharan Africa. The first two continued the trend of half-track vehicle travel, and all were expedition based. Coissac mentioned them when, a few years later, he announced that the era of documentary had finally arrived: "Henceforth the documentary film has the right to be programmed. . . . It has conquered the honor of exclusive first releases and plays as the principal attraction in enormous letters."[66] Several decades later, Georges Sadoul would list all three in support of his assertion that "most of the French *grands documentaires* were colonial."[67]

Aubert distributed footage of Renault's Gradis Delinguette mission from Oran to Cape Town as *Les mystères du continent noir* (Mysteries of the Black continent, 1926), its three parts titled *Au pays du soleil* (In the land of the sun),

Chez les primitifs du Centre-Afrique (With the primitives of central Africa), and *La maladie du sommeil et la mouche Tsé Tsé* (Sleeping sickness and the tsetse fly). An exclusive premiere at the Electric-Palace-Aubert Theater proved to *Cinéa* that "the intelligently conceived and artistically directed documentary finds favor with the general public."[68] *Cinéa* described the film as a "true ethnographic study" with "a scientific spirit," and *Cinéopse* found its ethnographic prowess emotionally thrilling. "The habits and customs of the peoples who live there were perfectly filmed," wrote Coissac; "There is an intense joy in being brought close to them."[69] Physicians at the French Academy of Medicine held a discussion of the Sara women with lip plates featured in *Les mystères du continent noir*, something that never would have happened, *Ciné-Journal* maintained, "if cinema cameramen hadn't made them news."[70] Sara women appeared regularly in colonial documentaries shot in AEF, as did African victims of sleeping sickness, with whom the film concludes. The doctors treating them were proof, according to *Ciné-Miroir*, that "wherever France appears, she brings civilization."[71]

Léon Poirier's feature-length *La croisière noire* (1925), shot during the second Haardt-Audouin-Dubreuil expedition for Citroën, was the biggest success among the African expedition films of the mid-1920s and the only one to achieve enduring stature within French film history. In a sixteen-member team, Poirier directed the film section, Georges Specht served as cameraman, and Alexandre Iacovleff produced visual art and ethnographic studies. They took eight months to cross the African continent, heading south, then east, shooting six thousand photographs and just under thirty thousand meters of film.[72] Even more so than previous such films, which had received significant governmental support, *La croisière noire* was a coproduction between Citroën and France. The French president himself went over the route map with Haardt and André Citroën prior to the departure of an expedition he described as being "in complete agreement with the convictions of the French government."[73] Before leaving Colomb-Béchar, Haardt and Audouin-Dubreuil sent a telegram to Minister of Colonies Edouard Daladier. "Our mission," they assured him, "will do everything possible to fulfill the expectations placed in it by you and those colonial figures who represent for us the spirit of initiative and progress."[74] Daladier in turn responded that the expedition would "brilliantly consecrate the work of pacification tirelessly pursued by France in the Sahara and forever bring together French West Africa and North Africa." *Le petit parisien* reminded readers that the mission's goals were documentary and colonial—"to study the regions traveled through, which constitute a reservoir of untapped and even incompletely inventoried wealth."[75]

Poirier's film was so well funded and received that it can be difficult to resist the claims of its status as a masterpiece. But *La croisière noire* is best understood as part of a tradition, if a technically accomplished and lengthy landmark. Like Machin, Poirier had worked for the French army's film unit during World War I, after which he replaced legend Louis Feuillade as Gaumont's artistic director. In the 1920s, he led Moussinac's French Cinema Club while his directing career progressed from literary adaptations *Jocelyn* (1922) and *La brière* (1924) to the immensely successful historical feature *Verdun, visions d'histoire* (Verdun, visions of history, 1928).[76] Unlike Machin, though, Poirier is remembered as the auteur not just of his fiction films but also of his documentary. If a few earlier films had been seen by critics as French answers to *Nanook*, it was Poirier who became the French Flaherty.

Recalling in his memoirs the excitement of traveling south of the Sahara, Poirier wrote that "central Africa . . . changes everything." He compared himself to Christopher Columbus, like Machin underscoring the importance of filming "the last primitive men" and of having recorded "while there is still time their customs and gestures that in ten years will be transformed by the Western invasion."[77] Poirier's mystic attraction to Africa and desire to preserve its purportedly doomed traditions was accompanied by condescension and contempt for Africans, along with support for European colonialism. If the Sara were "surprising specimens of this primitive life," he wrote, the Babinga people were "miserable and fearful beings who barely know how to make fire." The colonial capital of Stanleyville, Poirier continued, "situated in the very center of the most savage regions," was "a civilizing core around which the natives have already begun to evolve."[78] Once the expedition had concluded, Poirier glorified himself as had Machin, arguing that other filmmakers should follow his example. "We have marvelous colonies and a host of young, ardent cinegraphists," he wrote in *Ciné-Miroir*, thus "the exotic cinema will bear the mark of French genius."[79]

La croisière noire opened in exclusivity at the illustrious Marivaux Theater in Paris for three months, instead of the typical several weeks, and a series of postcards bearing images taken during the expedition was released simultaneously. One can still find the originals on eBay, where those of Sara women with lip plates fetch the highest prices. Critics emphasized the film's triple foundation—its exactitude, aesthetic achievement, and patriotism. In a discussion of cinematic exoticism, Pierre Leprohon raised *La croisière noire* from *grand* to *beau*, designating it "the first beautiful French documentary." René Jeanne, noting the increasing popularity of documentary films, considered it "the most personal work of the year, the most 'artistic' work."[80] Reviewers also stressed the film's successful support for the idea of greater France. *Ciné-Miroir*

Publicity postcard for Léon Poirier, *La croisière noire*, 1925.

maintained that Poirier's "magnificent documentary" better than any essay or novel refuted a characterization of France as "bad colonizer."[81] And *Cinéopse* located a sense of national accomplishment in the film's documentary nature. "A very captivating study in images of the flora and fauna, hunting scenes, native habits and customs," wrote Jehan de Vimbelle, all of which "make us yet again proud of our country."[82] The president of France attended a special gala screening of *La croisière noire* at the Paris Opera, an event announced as "national, documentary, and artistic": "National, because it is the visual narrative of a magnificent effort of French expansion in Africa. Documentary, because it provides the most curious revelations about mysterious lands and the unknown races of the black continent. Artistic, because it is the work of cinegraphist Léon Poirier." A brave and creative image hunter, *Comoedia* raved, Poirier "brings to life with a passionate intensity the adventures and the impressions of the most marvelous of voyages."[83]

Released a few months after *La croisière noire* but with less publicity and to slightly less acclaim, Marc Allégret's documentary feature *Voyage au Congo* (Voyage to Congo, 1926) is now widely available thanks to a new restoration with international distribution.[84] Although the two extended African travelogues were understood by contemporaries to be partner works, scholars have more recently opposed them to argue that Allégret's film escapes, at least partly, the colonial documentary tradition. Paul Henley describes *Voyage au Congo* as "a masterwork of French ethnographic cinema" and "very different from all other French expedition films of the interwar period," while Alison James argues it has been "unjustly identified" with films like *La croisière noire*.[85] Allégret was the fourth of six children of Élie Allégret, a Protestant pastor who traveled to Gabon and Cameroon as a missionary in the last decade of the nineteenth century and again after World War I. Better remembered for cinematic comedies from the 1930s and early '40s starring Raimu, Marcel Pagnol, and Josephine Baker, a young Allégret in 1925 and 1926 traveled through Belgian Congo and French Equatorial Africa with his much older lover, renowned French writer André Gide. Their eleven-month expedition followed a route very similar to Poirier's a year earlier. In addition to Allégret's film, which like much of his later work was produced by Pierre Braunberger, Gide recounted the trip in a series of articles and two lengthy travel diaries: *Voyage au Congo* (1927) and *Le retour du Tchad* (Returning from Chad, 1928).[86]

Allégret's *Voyage au Congo*, which bears the subtitle "Scenes of Native Life in Equatorial Africa," is itself a kind of travel diary; like the Citroën, Renault, and Peugeot films, it has no narrative arc other than geographical movement forward. After opening images of unidentified Europeans on a boat that stops in the Canary Islands before continuing south, each subsequent segment of African travel is preceded by a map and intertitles, which help the spectator-tourist navigate from one location to another. The camera remains stationary; occasional dissolves and iris-in or out shots were added during editing to enliven the filmed attractions—both wonders of the African landscape, including M'Bali Falls, and ethnographic wonders, such as the dancing that follows the excision ceremony of Nzakara girls. Viewers are introduced to "the spectacle" of Dakpa dances, the costumes and dancing masks of the Mundang, and the clay houses of the Massa. Bloom writes that *La traversée du Sahara* and *La croisière noire* display Africans as if in "a colonial geographic theme park of cultural and historical attractions," and the same is true for *Voyage au Congo*.[87] The film repeatedly erases the particular cultures of African ethnic groups by making global comparisons; one intertitle deems Mundang attire "strangely similar to Tibetan dress," and another notes that Massa houses are constructed "like Agrippa's Pantheon," which is to say from the top and without the aid of scaffolding. Recounting in his diary that he and Allégret had watched a performance of the same Dakpa dances that appear in *La croisière noire*, Gide mocked Poirier's presentation of them as a "mysterious or very rare" ceremony. He assumed that the members of the Citroën mission had paid the dancers to perform, just like Allégret and other traveling, "curious" Europeans.[88]

Crossing from Belgian to French territory, Allégret's film arrives in Fort-Archambault, Chad, where a French flag flies in a Sara village and African residents participate in a New Year's Day festival that involves horseback riding, javelin throwing, and wrestling. The tone shifts to comedy as a group of boys attempts to climb a greased pole, and this humor becomes even more condescending when we are shown a line of women wearing beads that an intertitle calls "their best pearl necklaces." The camera centers their bare breasts, then pans down their bodies, shown first from the front and then from behind. After this sexually exploitative moment, the scene concludes with African adults playing a game an intertitle calls "push ball," fulfilling the French stereotype of them as childlike. The French who supplied the giant rubber ball and would have been watching, however, are not visible in Allégret's images. These colonizers, like Allégret and Gide themselves, remain hidden so that viewers watch with them instead of watching them, catching only fleeting glimpses of a white man in a pith helmet who walks through the frame, looks at a dead hippopotamus hunted by the Kotoko, and views a parade of Fulbe notables on horseback.

After these New Year's games, the style of Allégret's film changes dramatically in a sequence that lasts twenty-eight minutes—a quarter of the length of the film. An intertitle asserting that the Sara are "particularly welcoming" and "willingly invite us into their private lives" introduces an illustratation of Sara marriage rituals in footage constructing the story of a young man and woman, Djimta and Kadde. The two meet at the river, where Djimta has come to water his horse. While swimming, Kadde hurts her foot, a "trick," suggests another intertitle, designed to attract Djimta's attention. An iris shot frames them, and Djimta soon brings a friend to negotiate with Kadde's father; the men drink millet beer to celebrate. In an intimate moment, the young couple talk and touch while turning repeatedly toward the camera. In contrast to the extractive flapper featured in *Bois du Gabon* a year earlier, Allégret's characters in this bare-bones fictional narrative are African and acting out their own "habits and customs." Thinking ahead to the work of Jean Rouch, Henley praises the originality of an "ethnofiction *avant la lettre*."[89] There is no sign here, however, of what Rouch later called *shared anthropology*, the participation in filmic framing or narration by those represented. The Djimta and Kadde story is rather an example of what Bill Nichols calls *documentary typification*, reenactments in which characters perform not prior events but "characteristic ones," representative "patterns, rituals, and routines."[90] A strategy that hearkens back to the European postcards of African "types" that similarly promised authentic illustration and representation, Flaherty had made ample use of it in *Nanook of the North*, his first *grand documentaire*.

Djimta and Kadde in Marc Allégret, *Voyage au Congo*, 1926.

Allégret's expedition, a much smaller undertaking than Poirier's for Citroën, was nonetheless also funded by the Ministry of Colonies. The voyagers received support from numerous colonial officials, including old friend and recently appointed Governor of Chad Marcel de Coppet and Governor of Oubangi-Chari Auguste Lamblin, assistance that is evident in Gide's books but concealed in Allégret's film. Gide in his writings criticized the use of forced labor by concessionary companies in central Africa, but he never questioned the colonial enterprise itself, instead calling for colonial administrators to rescue African laborers from exploitative private industry.[91] And Gide's limited criticism is completely absent from Allégret's *Voyage au Congo*. At the rubber production center in Bambari, Belgian Congo, which Congolese were obliged to supply once a month, Allégret shows groups of men, women, and children waiting for their contributions to be weighed. Shooting midway through the colonization of Congo, seventeen years after King Leopold II had ceded the region to Belgium following revelations of mass casualties during his decades-long rule, Allégret provides no sense of

Belgium's prior or current role in the rubber trade nor the terror that enforced it. Allégret's film praises Lamblin for French Congo's network of roads, thanks to which convoys of automobiles had, per an intertitle, "liberated the population from the harsh labor of portage." Deeply dishonest in at least two ways, this statement ignores the forced labor of Africans who built the roads as well as those impressed as porters to carry not just Allégret's and Gide's supplies but also Allégret and Gide themselves in sedan chairs called *tipoyes*.

Fine arts critic Émile Vuillermoz appreciated Gide and Allégret's "attractive [*beau*] geographical and ethnological film" for its style as well as slow tempo and length that allowed the spectator to "observe in detail the particularities" of "indigenous types." The movie camera, he argued, was now "an indispensable professional accessory for any explorer . . . colonial equipment just like the white cloth jacket and pith helmet."[92] The strength of the colonial documentary tradition seems to have warded off the rare 1920s French criticism of colonial cruelty, notably that of Gide and journalist Albert Londres in his likewise anti–forced labor if generally procolonial *Terre d'ébène* (Land of ebony, 1927). Detailing the unbearable suffering and mass death of Africans compelled by the Batignolles Company to build the Congo-Ocean Railroad, Londres parenthetically informed the minister of colonies that he had taken photographs, images "you will not find in propaganda films."[93] Londres was correct; advocating in 1928 no longer just for travel documentaries but for cinema as colonial propaganda, Charles-Félix Tavano maintained that when spectators saw "dazzling landscapes, luxuriant vegetation, leaping wild animals, mysterious and mystic tribes," they would "be proud to think that . . . we, the French, have not failed at our civilizing mission."[94] The governmental Committee of Colonial Propaganda by Film, led by Vice-President of the Chamber of Deputies Henry Paté, was formed the same year and based on the same belief, with the specific goal of producing a collection of films shot in the French colonies for the upcoming Colonial Exhibition, "a visitor's book in moving images that will evoke the glorious past, show the laborious present, and announce the fertile future."[95]

Continuing private and public colonial cooperation, the committee's first venture was *La marche vers le soleil* (March toward the sun, 1930), to be directed by René Le Somptier from a script cowritten with Léon Mirabel, director of the Economic Agency of AEF; filmed by Georges Specht, who had worked with Poirier on *La croisière noire*; and distributed by Établissements Aubert. Prior to the mission's departure, Henry Paté spoke at a lunch at the Hôtel Crillon attended by the governor general of AEF, Coissac of *Cinéopse*, and representatives of the *Petit parisien* newspaper, which had contracted to publish regular updates from Le Somptier and his crew. The committee had been created, Paté said, to "make our colonies known to all French citizens," especially young ones, so that they might volunteer "to go exploit our colonial domain." The films produced would be documentaries, he continued, "but with a script, since . . . we know from experience that one learns much better when entertained."[96]

Like Poirier, Le Somptier was already a well-known director. Following his exotic melodrama *Le sultane de l'amour* (Sultan of love, 1920), filmed in Nice, he had traveled to Morocco to shoot *Les fils du soleil* (Children of the sun, 1924), which starred his wife, actress Marquisette Bosky. For this next project, Le Somptier and Bosky traveled through AEF from Libreville to Brazzaville, then toward Chad via the Congo and Ubangi Rivers. The resulting film included reenactments of experiences of colonial adventurers, conquerors, and missionaries; a paean to French doctors treating patients with sleeping sickness; and a love story featuring Bosky. *Ciné-Comoedia* critic Jean-Paul Coutisson, however, found Bosky's scripted role "so vague that there is no need even to talk about it" and thus summarily declared *La marche vers le soleil* to be "a vast documentary . . . all to the glory of French colonization in Africa."[97] In late January 1930, it was screened during the French Colonial Union's gala at the Théâtre des Champs-Elysées, with President Gaston Doumergue in attendance.[98] Trained by tradition, the professional spectators of *Cinéa* and *La critique cinématographique*, like Coutisson for *Ciné-Comoedia*, eagerly subsumed fiction into documentary to call the film "the best colonial propaganda" and "a work of useful propaganda, since it shows the unquestionable benefits of colonialization."[99]

J. K. Raymond-Millet, who was traveling and filming in AEF at the same time as Le Somptier, began his career as a film critic, then published several colonial-themed books, including the memorably titled *Afrique si passionnément française* (Africa so passionately French, 1925). Raymond-Millet led so many expeditions in the 1930s—in central Africa, Madagascar, Martinique, and Guadeloupe—that he received more total funding from the French government to make colonial films than any other director or producer.[100] He publicized his work in numerous articles for the popular film press, affecting a light, ironic tone while crafting the persona of an intrepid image hunter. Raymond-Millet maintained that in his *Alger-Dakar et retour* (Alger-Dakar and back, 1930), he had "surprised" Black Africa in order to discover the secrets of its drums and dances.[101] And for the title of a travel diary in *Ciné-Miroir*, he appropriated a term popularized by renowned film critic Louis Delluc to ask, "Are Negroes photogenic?" The answer, perhaps unsurprisingly, was an "indisputable" yes to the *photogénie* of a young man displayed half naked in a large photograph, an aesthetic claim Raymond-Millet immediately tied to colonial propaganda by praising French doctors fighting sleeping sickness in Brazzaville as "the true face of France."[102]

J. K. Raymond-Millet, *France-Congo sur un cargo*, 1925.

The opening credits to Raymond-Millet's *France-Congo sur un cargo* (France-Congo on a cargo ship, 1930) categorize the film as "cinegraphic reportage." Conventional travel footage of the ports of Dakar and Grand Bassam shot by cameraman Charles Lemaire juxtaposes European and African neighborhoods and markets, then shows Africans working to prepare products for export—peanuts in Senegal and cocoa in Côte d'Ivoire. In Gabon, Raymond-Millet's approach is differently exploitative. Portrait shots of bare-breasted women are followed by a close-up of a man who seems to be mentally ill swiveling his hips and waving his hands; he is announced by a derisive intertitle as "the winner of the Charleston contest." In Congo, Raymond-Millet filmed Africans at church in support of France's Christianizing mission and the work of the Pasteur Institute in support of France's humanitarian mission. But the film's final images attest in detail to the profits to be made by logging the equatorial forest. Africans cut down trees and cut up massive trunks, which they load into a rail car to be transported to the river, then down the river to a ship waiting to take the "precious merchandise" to France. Writing about his documentary for *Cinéma*, Raymond-Millet described it as "national, touristic, and industrial propaganda."[103]

Made up of footage shot by Lemaire during the same expedition, Raymond-Millet's *Promenade en Afrique Equatoriale Française* (Excursion in French Equatorial Africa, 1931) even more explicitly endorses French colonialism. The film's opening credits recognize as producer the Intercolonial Service of Information and Documentation of the Ministry of Colonies and acknowledge footage supplied by the Economic Agency of AEF. After a reminder to the spectator that this colony was five times larger than France, several lengthy scenes track progress on the Congo-Ocean Railroad, never acknowledging that its construction caused the death of twenty thousand forced laborers. Whereas it once took days to cross the Mayombe mountain range, an intertitle informs us, the train will soon be able to cover the distance in a few hours. We witness African workers building platforms and bridges and preparing to blast rock to dig tunnels, making train travel in Africa possible for Europeans and enabling French companies to bring resources easily and quickly to ships in port. Raymond-Millet also shows African porters carrying their colonizers and even their colonizers' pets; a white man in a *tipoye* holds a monkey in his lap, just as Gide was inseparable from a potto adopted early in his travels.

Sound came to French cinema in 1929 and to documentaries shot abroad a bit later, in the form of voice-over commentaries accompanying silent footage. Marcel Huret insisted that this narration allowed newsreels to "attain a complete realism," but West African filmmaker and critic Paulin Soumanou Vieyra would later contrast French colonial silent and sound films quite differently: "During the silent era . . . the absence of sound and thus of voice-over commentary limited the noxiousness of these productions, even if the images . . . were often so vile that they did not require voice-overs. With sound, it was madness. It is truly through these films that we can comprehend the essence of colonization and the power of the cinema."[104] Voice-over commentary now narrated images moment by moment, and these images conversely illustrated the commentary. Edited to give the impression of objectivity, such films belong to what Bill Nichols named the expository mode of documentary.[105] The noxious madness noted by Vieyra is evident in Columbia Pictures's *Africa Speaks* (1930), which claimed to be the first sound film shot in sub-Saharan Africa. When distributed in France by Marcel Vandal and Charles Delac as *L'Afrique vous parle*, it was a remarkable success—advertised, like its predecessors, as "the most astonishing adventure shot in the African Bush." Despite the film's title, not a single African speaks, as would remain the case for virtually all colonial sound films, whether fiction or documentary. *Cinéopse* and *Ciné-Comoedia* nonetheless claimed that *L'Afrique vous parle* constitutes "the faithful expression of nature . . . without a false note" and "the naked truth, entirely without artifice."[106]

Colonial administrator turned filmmaker Alfred Chaumel directed one of the biggest documentary hits of 1930 and 1931: *Le réveil d'une race* (The awakening of a race, 1930), produced by his company, Les Films Exotiques, and released by Comptoir Français de Distribution de Film, or Franfilmdis. Chaumel's "cinematographic mission" through AEF in the early 1920s had traveled from Bordeaux, France, to Abéché, Chad, in sixty-eight days, covering 17,000 kilometers and shooting 11,500 meters of film. Publishing his itinerary, illustrated with photographs and details about "bizarre and savage landscapes," Chaumel stated that his goal was "to collect, on film, an entirely new archive to make our vast domain in central Africa better known."[107] Five years later, he left on another African expedition, commissioned by the Economic Agency of African Territories Under Mandate to travel to Cameroon with his wife, Geneviève, the daughter of adventurer and colonial administrator Émile Gentil. Early in their expedition, the Chaumels enjoyed a boat trip on the Djoué River with Marc Allégret and André Gide.[108]

Chaumel described *Le réveil d'une race* as a work in three parts: the first, an economic study of Cameroon under French mandate; the second, a study of sleeping sickness; and the third, a personal, atmospheric representation of Cameroon.[109] Originally silent, the film was rereleased with sound a year later by Gaumont-Franco-Film-Aubert, with an exclusive run on the Grands Boulevards at the Caméo Theater and a gala screening at the Théâtre des Champs-Elysées presided by the French president, the minister of colonies, and the minister of finance. In the pages of *Ciné-Miroir*, Pierre Bonardi maintained that *Le réveil d'une race* was the best kind of colonial film—both good propaganda and a commercial success.[110]

Part 1 of the 1930 original appears not to have been included in the 1931 version, which opens with footage of Chaumel sitting at a table and addressing the camera. Synchronized sound was rare for documentaries of the period, and Chaumel speaks directly to spectators, promising to show that "France's primary concern is to protect the native." His introduction is followed by maps of regions most affected by sleeping sickness and shots of the tsetse fly and the swampy landscape it infests. As the film progresses, voice-over narration accompanies images of sick African adults and children, illustrating various forms of the illness. Victims of sleeping sickness wait to be evaluated at Dr. Eugène Jamot's Ayos Hospital, and Chaumel follows in detail the diagnostic work and treatment protocols. When a white doctor arrives in a rural area, he and his assistants "proceed to the classification of the natives" by sex, age, and home village, then paint the dosage of medicine to be administered directly onto their patients' bodies. Statistics demonstrating a lowered mortality rate in the region are matched with shots of Africans who have been cured to attest to the effectiveness of the process. Coissac judged Chaumel's presentation of Jamot's work to constitute "the best and most intelligent of works of propaganda in favor of French colonization." Inspired to quote Chaumel himself, *Ciné-Miroir* pronounced that Jamot and his collaborators were leading Africans "to that stage of civilization where justice and peace reign, along with fraternity and liberty."[111]

The last section of *Le réveil d'une race* turns to expedition ethnography, with an orchestral soundtrack and voices added to silent footage of Bamileke landscapes, villages, and people. Intertitles sometimes identify and explain rites being performed, for example a "war dance" led by a chief wearing the jawbones of enemies he has killed. Spectatorial tourism continues along Cameroon's rivers from Foumban into Fulbe territory, where we see a village and market, women pounding millet, musicians, hairdressers and the hairstyles they create, blacksmiths, women potters, cattle herders, and fishermen. *Le courrier des cinémas* praised the film in phrases that had become routine, stating that Chaumel "shot *sur le vif* the curious customs and picturesque dances that make this region one of the most extraordinary in central Africa" and gathered "the richest harvest of documents about Cameroon ever to be seen."[112] But it was the most desperate of Chaumel's images that were used to sell tickets. A full-page ad in *Cinéopse* accompanied a still of sick Africans with dramatic shorthand: "The tom-tom of death, the spear dance, the sultan with 700 wives, Dantean visions, all of the horror of the curse that is ravaging central Africa, sleeping sickness."[113]

The commercial and critical success of these African expedition films proves that the French passion for colonial documentary was reaching a peak with the approach of the 1931 Colonial Exhibition in Paris. Coissac at the time described the exhibition as "the summary of the world" but also, and more specifically, "the affirmation of the oeuvre accomplished by France."[114] It surpassed by all measures the exhibitions held in Marseille in 1906 and 1922, and Raoul Girardet described it as "the apotheosis of 'greater France.'"[115] Coissac's and Girardet's judgments depended on the creation of enough colonial films to fill the cinematheques of multiple colonial offices with documentaries that, in Coissac's words, would "represent the very curious customs of tribes that have barely been touched by civilization" and "make known the unexpected wealth of our colonial domain." Only documentaries, director Raymond-Millet declared in a review of the exhibition, could be true *"films coloniaux."*[116]

Raymond-Millet considered the *grands documentaires* released by private film companies to be the best propaganda for the colonial cause, since they made the Colonial Exhibition an important showcase for cinema. The French army's film section had also prepared for the exhibition, however, by making *L'expansion coloniale de la France* (The colonial expansion of France, 1930), a survey of what one of its intertitles calls "the magnificent endeavor" of "colonial unity." From North to sub-Saharan Africa to Madagascar, Syria, and Turkey, the film details each step of France's colonial expansion as maps are progressively filled in to demonstrate successful "efforts at penetration" and, in a forceful use of the second-person plural, "our domination." Nineteenth-century colonial heroes Jules Ferry and Pierre Savorgnan de Brazza, shown in oval portrait photographs, are contrasted with African resistance leaders King Behanzin and Almamy Samory Touré, described as "tyrannical chiefs" defeated and deported by France. A concluding banner—"100 million French people . . . a France as big as Europe"—reinforces a greater France, as do the final intertitles: "The borders of France are not the edges of the small hexagon. . . . France is wherever a Frenchman, even if alone, accomplishes the ideal of his race!"

This passion for colonial documentary stoked more general popular and critical interest in nonfiction film. The very month of the exhibition's opening, Georges Dureau stated in *Ciné-Journal* that "documentary has henceforth won the place it deserves," his evidence the fact that prestigious theaters were programming documentaries as first-run features, "and these features bring in audiences!" Among Dureau's examples was *Le réveil d'une race*, and he concluded by looking forward to Chaumel's newest expedition film for Gaumont-Franco-Film-Aubert.[117] A few months later, *Pour vous* announced the first screening sponsored by Cinédocument, an association created to support documentary cinema and led by Louis Lumière himself, Georges Lecomte of the Académie Française, and former deputy and senator André Honnorat.[118] As enthusiasm for documentary film, French colonialism, and sub-Saharan Africa converged, a reviewer for *La critique cinématographique* described the trend in very French terms: "Another documentary about Africa . . . Yes, as there will always be new poems about love, new plays about adultery." *Pour vous* deemed Africa "very fashionable in the cinema," and *Cinémonde* similarly declared that "the Colonies are filmically in fashion. . . . Colonial film has conquered our screens." An informational bulletin printed during the exhibition asked, in the headline of an article highlighting the hairstyles of young Mangbetu women seen in *La croisière noire*, "Will 1931 Fashion be Colonial?"[119]

Léon Poirier was named artistic director for screenings at the exhibition's City of Information, where over three hundred films were shown—a million meters of footage, according to the guide published by the Ministry of Colonies.[120] The main theater, also used for conferences and social events, accommodated fifteen hundred spectators, while the theater in the newly constructed Museum of the Colonies could seat twelve hundred. Both silent and sound films were shown in the pavilions of each section of the exhibition, moreover, with programs noting that a screening room in the AOF section would play documentary footage continuously.[121] In one of many signs of public-private collaboration where colonial documentary was concerned, projection equipment and speakers across the exhibition were provided and installed by Poirier's studio, Gaumont-Franco-Film-Aubert, while those in the City of Information were equipped by Gaumont-Radio-Cinéma. A gala soirée in late September featured *La croisière noire*, and companies also supplied the Johnsons' *Simba* (released in France as *Cimbo*), *Images d'Afrique*, *La marche vers le soleil*, and *Le réveil d'une race*, among many others.[122] The governments general of the colonies provided over eighty thousand meters of footage for screening, and Pierre Ichac, a self-proclaimed *chasseur d'images* who had filmed in Egypt and the Sahara, held that "Pathé and its cameramen have for over a year been dredging French Africa and Madagascar."[123] One result of this dredging, Étienne Lallier's *Histoire de la plus grande France* (History of greater France, 1931) was coproduced by the Colonial Exhibition and Atlantic Film. Like the SCA's *Expansion coloniale de la France*, Lallier's sound film provided an overview of French colonial history, tracing and praising France's "civilizing mission" across the centuries. *La critique cinématographique* considered it "excellent propaganda" and noted that it was shown "every night to large, interested audiences."[124]

When the exhibition was over, Coissac published his own overview, not of French colonialism but of a tradition of colonial cinema "in the service of civilization and propaganda."[125] Beginning his history with those he called pioneers—Lumière, Promio, and Mesguich—Coissac included many of the filmmakers and works I have mentioned thus far. Machin appears as "an audacious young man of twenty-five" who teamed up with Charles Pathé to film wild animals in Africa so that spectators could watch an elephant hunt "without having to leave their seats."[126] The highlights of the 1920s followed: *Au coeur de l'Afrique sauvage*, *La croisière noire*, *La marche vers le soleil*, and *Le réveil d'une race*. At the apex point of the Colonial Exhibition, therefore, it is important to interrupt the building narrative of my film historical overview. This story of the popularity in France of films shot by French men in Africa has yet to account for a crucial element of interwar intellectual life in France, Paris's African diasporic community. The strength and consistency of the corpus of colonial documentaries conceals the vital reality that, at the same time as these films were being screened to popular and critical acclaim, a small but growing group of Black students and activists from the Caribbean, the United States, and sub-Saharan Africa were debating colonialism and its denigration of their home cultures, not only in person but also in print.

In the preface to his 1921 Goncourt Prize–winning *Batouala: Véritable roman nègre* (*Batouala*), Martinican-born colonial administrator and author René Maran condemned France's use of forced labor to construct the Congo-Ocean Railroad, writing with bitter sarcasm that "after all, if they die of hunger by the thousands, like flies, it's because their homeland is being valorized [*mis en valeur*]." *Batouala* portrays the same *ganza* ceremony shown in Léon Poirier's *La croisière noire*, but recounted from the perspective of Banda participants rather than traveling spectators.[127] Former *tirailleur* Lamine Senghor arrived in France from Senegal the year Maran's novel was published. A tireless anti-colonial activist, he founded the Committee, then League for the Defense of the Negro Race (LDRN), which published the newspapers *La voix des nègres* (Negro voice) and *La race nègre* (The Negro race), also authoring a didactic short novel titled *La violation d'un pays* (The violation of a land).[128] In 1924, Dahomeyan writer and lawyer Kojo Tovalou Houénou founded and coedited with Maran the short-lived pan-Africanist journal *Continents*. Maurice Satineau, originally from Guadeloupe, created *La dépêche africaine* (The African dispatch) in 1928, and three years later, Martinican Paulette Nardal cofounded the literary journal *La revue du monde noir* (The review of the Black world).[129]

Amid the outpouring of praise for documentaries shot in Africa in French film publications, a hint of skepticism appeared in a review of Chaumel's *Le réveil d'une race* for *La revue du cinéma* (Cinema review). Having expressed her appreciation of the film's entertainment value and depiction of Jamot's noble fight against sleeping sickness, journalist and Communist activist Germaine Ducaris suggested that France's primary concern might not be the protection of Africans.[130] French Communists were joined in their lack of zeal for the colonial project only by the surrealists, whose manifesto "Don't Visit the Colonial Exhibition" called the idea of greater France "intolerable" and "fraudulent."[131] While the Colonial Exhibition attracted over thirty million visitors, barely four thousand visited the surrealists' counterexhibition, "The Truth About the Colonies," which denounced, among other colonial crimes, the construction of the Congo-Ocean Railroad. The counterexhibition was cosponsored by the Communist Party and the LDRN, and French Sudan–born Tiémoko Kouyaté's *Le cri des nègres* (The cry of the Negro) published a series of articles condemning the Colonial Exhibition.[132] If Paris's interwar Black press quite understandably ignored French expedition documentaries, a rare and humorous African critique can be found in West African novelist Ousmane Socé's

1937 *Mirages de Paris* (Parisian mirages). Central character Fara, in town from Dakar for the 1931 exhibition, goes to a movie theater to hear a seminar given by a "cinema reporter" claiming to have completed "the first Paris-Zuluville voyage in an airplane." In the recounting of the seminar, we recognize "Zinder and its sultan with 150 wives" and "Negresses with lip plates" from films made by Poirier and his many colleagues. Of the imagined Zuluville, Socé's documentarist informs his audience that there "the Blacks do not roast Whites, but rather boil them."[133]

Another flurry of big-budget documentaries shot in Africa appeared after the exhibition, coasting on its success. *Ciné-Journal* advertised Baron de Gourgaud's *Le vrai visage de l'Afrique* (The true face of Africa, 1931), in fact, as "what you didn't see at the Colonial Exhibition."[134] Gourgaud, whose full name was Marie-Amédée-Henri-Napoléon Gourgaud, was the great-grandson of another Baron Gourgaud, a close ally of Napoléon Bonaparte. He and cameraman Joseph Barth traveled from the Cape of Good Hope through central and eastern Africa, making a final, memorial stop at Saint Helena. They shot silent footage of landscapes and hunting scenes as well as ethnographic images of the Zulu, Mangbetu, and Masai, from whose occasional practice of drinking cattle's blood they took their film's titillating subtitle: "In the Land of the Blood-Drinkers." When E. L. Massoulard Films released *Le vrai visage de l'Afrique* with a soundtrack added during postproduction, *Pour vous* judged it a "very beautiful and gripping documentary." Adopting the role of *chasseur d'images*, Gourgaud during interviews happily listed his dangerous encounters with elephants, lions, mosquitos, and tsetse flies while in pursuit of "all the truth, nothing but the truth" about Africa.[135] The director of the National Museum of Natural History in Paris agreed that Gourgaud had taken "precious filmed documents" during his "voyage of ethnographic and archeological research" and announced plans to screen the film in the museum's historic amphitheater.[136]

Cinematographic expeditions to Africa continued through the end of the decade, some organized by businesses and businessmen, some by film studios, and most associated with a *chasseur d'images*. Gourgaud was soon joined by another aristocrat with a long family history linked to France's imperial ambitions—Jean d'Esme, born Viscount Jean Marie Henri d'Esmenard. D'Esme studied at the École Coloniale, then published exotic novels set in Indochina, North and sub-Saharan Africa, and Madagascar. Organizing the Jean d'Esme Expedition across AEF, through Cameroon, Gabon, and Congo, he also created his own production company to distribute footage taken by cameraman René Moreau, former photographer and erstwhile friend of Alfred Machin. Moreau, identified by *Ciné-Journal* as a "globe-trotter" as early as 1912, shot numerous travelogues in North America, Europe, and North Africa throughout the 1910s and '20s.[137] He and d'Esme together produced *À travers le Cameroun, le Gabon, et le Congo* (Across Cameroon, Gabon, and Congo), *Les richesses de l'Afrique Equatoriale Française* (The riches of French Equatorial Africa), and *Les ressources agricoles et minières de l'Afrique Equatoriale Française* (The agricultural and mining resources of French Equatorial Africa), all released in 1928.

The biggest commercial success resulting from d'Esme and Moreau's expedition, however, was *Peaux noires* (Black skins, 1931 and 1932), distributed by Osso Films. Released just prior to the Colonial Exhibition in a silent version, like *Le réveil d'une race* it was rereleased a year later with an added voice-over commentary. *Courrier des cinémas* recommended *Peaux noires* highly "despite the recent abundance of films of the same genre," and *Hebdo-Film* gleefully followed suit: "After all the African documentaries that we have seen for quite some time, we thought that there was no more interest in this type of film. Well! We were wrong!"[138] Not only was *Peaux noires* a great success at the Marigny Theater, but the president of France requested it be included in a screening at the Sorbonne during the 1933 annual meeting of the Academy of Colonial Science, with an audience that included the minister of colonies, the governor general of AEF, and Marshal Lyautey. Just a few months earlier, the newly formed Society for Colonial Propaganda through Cinema had cosponsored with the Cinémathèque of the City of Paris and the Institut Colonial Français a screening of *Le réveil d'une race* at the Gaumont-Palace, introduced by Chaumel and attended by the president, the ministers of education and colonies, the undersecretary of state for the colonies, and schoolchildren from across the city.[139] D'Esme himself appended to his goal of helping audiences "get to know these so curious tribes of Equatorial Africa" that of "showing the importance of the work accomplished over there by France."[140]

D'Esme soon returned to Africa to shoot *La grande caravane* (The great caravan, 1935), which records the collection of salt in the Ténéré desert. The film was released by Franfilmdis, as was *Les sentinelles de l'empire* (Sentinels of the empire, 1938), which appeared as World War II approached. The Ministry for National Defense, the Ministry of Colonies, and the Government General of AOF financed the foregrounding of African soldiers in French uniform in the Nomad Group Number One of Meharist soldiers in Mauritania. Introductory text on screen announces that such troops patrol France's colonial empire and promises to provide information about the soldiers' lives "with scrupulous exactitude."[141] Over low-angle shots of the Meharists riding camels, the film's near constant voice-over asserts that they had been warlike until French occupation brought peace and provides ethnographic details about ceremonies, dances, and drumming. Employing the second-personal plural, the narrator notes that "we" took Mauritania at the cost of many deaths during 450 battles spread over thirty-five years, making *Les sentinelles de l'empire* one of few colonial-era films to acknowledge the violence of French conquest.

The primary argument of d'Esme's film, however, is that these African soldiers, led by European noncommissioned officers with automatic weapons and a small cannon, assure "French peace and civilization." Told that the Meharists serve France with "an obscure and formidable devotion," we watch them care for their camels, patrol the territory, and salute the French flag. To prove this caricatural loyalty, an acted fiction is abruptly introduced two-thirds of the way through the film, echoing the structure of Allégret's *Voyage au Congo*. The sentinels beat back a rebel group's attack, giving chase in a pursuit that, filmed from multiple angles, evidently required either multiple cameras or multiple takes. They track the rebels for days, over sand and rocks, then engage in a battle shot from overhead and with periodic close-ups; when the enemy flees across the border, they return to camp, their job well done. A fluttering tricolor flag concludes the film, overlaid on a low-angle shot not of the African soldiers but of a pith-helmeted French officer.

After the Colonial Exhibition, the French army focused its energies on the recruitment of such officers. The SCA's *Au service de la plus grande France* (In the service of greater France, 1935) attempted to do so by setting a fictional character against documentary footage of Africa. Alone in his attic room on a dark winter day, a French everyman opens a book of photographs. An inset image of an African landscape fills the screen and begins to move; villagers stand outside of their homes, then dance. Similarly hackneyed shots from Indochina give way to a poster bearing the message, "Young people . . . Go to the colonies," superimposed over African men in pirogues, fishing with spears. Closing the book, the man heads straight to the recruitment office, packs his bags, and "the beautiful journey begins." The film ends with brief scenes of the life of a soldier, seen marching through the countryside with his assigned group of *tirailleurs*.

Most of the films that have filled the pages of this chapter now seem minor and even embarrassing, which may in part explain their absence from discussions of interwar French cinema. When scholarship does address documentary, it is in the context of debates around *photogénie*, avant-garde experimentation, and the interpretation of social realities in works by Georges Lacombe, Jean Vigo, Luis Buñuel, and Joris Ivens. Yet the documentaries I have examined were not only popular with audiences and film journalists; they were also acclaimed by filmmakers, film critics, and film historians whom we still take very seriously. Writer and Montmartre bohemian Pierre Mac Orlan described *La croisière noire* as "one of the most powerful documentaries" he had ever seen, filled with diverse landscapes and "picturesque" people, noting that the spectator could also admire "the goals magnificently accomplished by Belgians in their great colony."[142] A version of *Images d'Afrique* was reedited by iconic avant-garde director and film theorist Jean Epstein and declared by *Cinéma* to be "an artistic film." Legend Abel Gance proposed to Minister of Colonies François Piétri a trip to French territories around the world to film footage for a "sincere colonial synthesis" to be screened at the Colonial Exhibition. And prominent critic Nino Frank, who would go on to coin the term *film noir*, presented Chaumel's *Le réveil d'une race* together with Flaherty's *Moana* and the Johnsons' *Simba* as the culmination of a documentary trajectory that began with simplistic, less sophisticated travel films.[143] In a review of *Le vrai visage de l'Afrique*, Frank praised Gourgaud's "sober and interesting" voice-over commentary, the film's "excellent" editing, and Barth's authentic images. Highlighting the wildness of animals and landscapes, he dehumanized Africans. "Elephants, hippopotamuses, monkeys and giraffes," Frank wrote, "the animals which are, with the Pygmies, Hottentots, and Zulus the actors of the film, do not prevent the landscapes . . . from impressing us with their violent beauty."[144]

Even when filmmakers and critics claimed to be deploying their analytical faculties, they were blinded by an exoticized vision of Africa and enthusiasm for the colonial project. Marcel Carné, future director of the masterpieces of French poetic realism *Le quai des brumes* (*Port of Shadows*, 1938) and *Le jour se lève* (*Daybreak*, 1939) as well as the classic melodrama *Les enfants du paradis* (*Children of Paradise*, 1945), praised colonial documentaries in a 1930 article titled "The Cinema out to Conquer the World." Giving as examples *Au coeur de l'Afrique sauvage*, *La croisière noire*, *Voyage au Congo*, and *Vers le Tchad*, Carné argued that in the wake of Flaherty's *Nanook of the North*, "the first *living* documentary," others had gone on to film *grands documentaires* that allow the spectator "to penetrate the least explored regions of the globe, across the burning sands of Africa or the arid steppes of Asia, the heavenly islands of the Pacific or the virgin forests of the New World."[145] Carné returned to the topic in a lengthy, amply illustrated essay inspired by the 1931 Colonial Exhibition. To those praising the exhibition for exposing the French to "faraway lands and native peoples," he retorted that cinema had been doing so for at least a decade and provided a history of what he called *exoticist cinema*, a category comprised exclusively of nonfiction films he deemed "pure documentaries."[146] Even more surprisingly, perhaps, high cultural theorist André Bazin also admired expedition films of the interwar period, including *La croisière noire* and the Johnsons' *Simba* and *Congorilla* (1932), praising their "poetic authenticity" and criticizing only the "decline" of the genre in the next decade.[147]

One constant of colonial exoticism from the earliest films advertised by Pathé is the coexistence of stereotypical images of Africa and claims to absolute novelty. After a 1930 expedition to Greenland, adventurer-director René Ginet, tired of educational and scientific films, declared "the death of documentary" and vowed to devote himself to "a production with great appeal." Instead of a *chasseur d'images*, Ginet decided, he would be a *cinéaste-reporter*. In this role—documentary's death apparently greatly exaggerated—he would provide "an exact image of the world."[148] In *Angola Pullman* (1933), produced by Compagnie Universelle Cinématographique and distributed by Lutèce Films, Ginet and cameraman Jean Goreaud recorded an expedition across Africa not on half-track vehicles but on the luxury Angola Pullman train, from the Atlantic to the Indian Ocean through Angola, Belgian Congo, Rhodesia, and Mozambique. Even more so than the amply funded *La croisière noire* and *Voyage au Congo*, *Angola Pullman* in many ways resembles a big-budget feature. A Dixieland jazz soundtrack accompanies a low-angle close-up of the train's wheels departing the first station, giving way to a shot of the train from the front, then a side view of European passengers leaning out of windows to wave. Ginet stated that his documentary film showed "the progress of 'civilization,'" and *Hebdo-Film* without scare quotes agreed that "this is a new face of Africa that we see; it is the Africa of industry . . . the Africa of commerce . . . civilized Africa."[149]

Despite the comfortable train, however, the film's voice-over commentary reverts to form, proclaiming "the battle between civilization and misery" and "the suffering of savage Africa" over panning shots of a crowd in a region of northern Angola where sleeping sickness is endemic. At first, the narrator recounts, Africans fled from the colonial hospital's white doctors, who ultimately managed to "tame them" and gain their trust. The European nations that "occupy the Black Continent and drag it out of its natural barbarism," he continues, have transformed health care in Africa. The mocking, demeaning humor of *Vers le Tchad* returns during a visit to village dignitaries, one of whom wears a bicorn hat; the voice-over names an elderly man in a loincloth standing next to him "the minister of finance." Africans who climb trees to pick coconuts are compared to monkeys as we are shown how adeptly they cut coconuts in half to dry. After informing viewers that the TransAfrican Railroad assists the exploitation of lands belonging to many colonial nations, from the copper mines of Katanga to tea plantations in Nyasaland, the film concludes as it began, with an invocation of "the continual progress of civilization." This progress is further represented by African soldiers wearing European uniforms, their tight formation contrasted with traditional "frenetic dances" shot from a low angle as performers look menacingly down at the camera.

Pierre Leprohon, who reviewed Ginet's *Angola Pullman* in the early 1930s, published a study of global travel films titled *Exoticism and the Cinema* a dozen years later. He used the same vocabulary as Machin and Carné to subtitle his book "The *'Chasseurs d'Images'* out to Conquer the World." Identifying 1920 as the year the "exploration documentary" came into being, surpassing travelogues that "scarcely went beyond the framework of the actuality," Leprohon cited Léon Poirier to assert an intimate and self-evident connection between exotic cinema and the truth.[150] Five years later, André Liotard and Samivel similarly drew attention to the advent in the '20s of a "cinema of exploration." Prior explorers, Europeans traveling in areas of the world they regarded as premodern or uncivilized, had produced drawings and photography Liotard and Samivel deemed "rare and episodic documents." Film by its very nature provided "impartial testimony" in support of colonialism, they contended, like their colleagues before them considering the movie camera a weapon: "Thus began a new era of the conquest of the Earth, that of the camera."[151]

This combined high emotion and critical praise of expedition documentaries relied on continuing admiration for men called *explorers*, whom I instead term *adventurers*. The double meaning in both French and English of the latter appellation, which also designates financial speculators, perfectly encapsulates the situation of colonial-era *chasseurs d'images*. Their position was also adopted by their spectators, noted Claude Vermorel in an article published during the Colonial Exhibition titled "The Explorer, in a Seat." Vermorel asserted that "the pleasure of exploration is one of the most complete the cinema gives to us."[152] "A bold document," he continued, "never seen before, without trick photography, that's what the public wants." The public also wanted to learn, and films made by French adventurers were said to convey the whole truth about Africa. "After all of the documentaries about African populations," wrote one reviewer of *Peaux noires*, "it seemed that nothing was unknown to us about their customs."[153] Yet it would be near impossible and extremely unpleasant to quote every racist stereotype included in the intertitles, voice-over commentaries, and press reviews of the films discussed here; they are innumerable. René Moreau crystallized the sense of domination felt by filmer toward filmed in an interview with *Ciné-Miroir*, stating that "the Negro is very docile . . . and for him, the white man, whether administrator, missionary, or cameraman, is a superior being to be feared and obeyed."[154]

Whether we call them exotic or exploration or expedition films, documentaries shot by image hunters force us to ask what it means to travel and shoot around the world. From Félix Mesguich to René Ginet, who could make documentary films about sub-Saharan Africa? The inaccessibility of training and equipment kept cameras out of the hands of Black Africans from 1906 through independence. The 1934 Laval Decree, moreover, announced for both AOF and AEF in the pages of *Ciné-Comoedia,* imposed explicit censorship on which films could be shown in France's African colonies while also legislating who was allowed to film there and how.[155] French cinemas programmed documentaries shot in Africa, but cinemas in colonized Africa programmed European and North American fiction films distributed by European distribution monopoly COMACICO, the Industrial and Commercial African Cinematographic Company. In Dakar, even colonial administrators could not see *Peaux noires,* but they could watch Greta Garbo in *Mata Hari,* which the governor of the district barred from being shown "in front of the native audience."[156] Throughout AOF, potential screenplays had to be examined and approved in advance by a commission, with shooting monitored by civil servants. In AEF, cameras had to be declared at customs, and licenses to film, which could be revoked at any moment for any reason, granted by the governor general. Applications for these licenses required two identity photos, a description of the project, and a detailed itinerary.

Writing in the early 1960s about essentially the same group of films as Leprohon, Liotard, and Samivel, René Jeanne and Charles Ford also identified a change in 1920, adopting the vocabulary of J.K. Raymond-Millet and René Ginet to describe a shift "from actualities to *grands reportages*" shot in Africa.[157] Reflecting the perspective of expedition filmmakers, this distinction also parallels our general understanding of the history of documentary. "The French who first used the term only meant travelogue," Grierson wrote a few years after reviewing *Moana,* arguing that documentary cinema had since advanced from "descriptions of natural material to arrangements, rearrangements, and creative shapings of it," progress he also understood in terms of the dramatic. In similar terms and at about the same time, Michel Vaucaire labeled Poirier's *La croisière noire* a *documentaire romancé* and as such the descendant of Flaherty's milestone *Nanook of the North.*[158]

Returning to Tom Gunning's work on early cinema, Anna Grimshaw reexamines *Nanook of the North* as an ethnographic cinema of attractions.[159] This shift of focus pulls a film so often cited as the first documentary, or more precisely the first *grand documentaire,* toward its roots in less narrative nonfiction, allowing us to grasp its transitional nature without undermining its accomplishments. We can understand the shared interests, goals, approaches, and tropes of the travel, hunting, and expedition documentaries I have discussed thus far in a comparable fashion. From 1906 through the mid-1930s, image hunters returned to Europe with simplistic and condescending representations of Africa and Africans that they asserted to be the whole truth. Without debating *petits* versus *grands documentaires*, an appreciation of the continuity of a colonial documentary tradition prepares us to understand its evolution in the last decades of the French Empire.

Notes

1. See Gary Wilder, "Framing Greater France Between the Wars," *Journal of Historical Sociology* 14, no. 2 (2001): 198–225.

2. "Le continent mystérieux, notes de voyage, en marge du raid Citroën," *Cinéa*, no. 10, April 1, 1924, 30.

3. Jean-Claude Seguin, "Aux origines du cinéma en Algérie: Alexandre Promio," in *Le Documentaire en Algérie coloniale*, ed. François Chevaldonné and André Raymond (IREMAM, 1997), 28–29.

4. G.-Michel Coissac, "Une ère nouvelle," *Cinéopse*, no. 1, September 1919, 7–8.

5. G.-Michel Coissac, "Le cinématographe utilisé comme propagande aux colonies," *Cinéopse*, no. 14, October 1920, 414.

6. See Bloom, *French Colonial Documentary*, 127–29, and Murray Levine, *Framing the Nation*, 121–25. On Sarraut and "greater France" more generally, see Wilder, "Framing Greater France Between the Wars," 203–12. Alison Murray, "Documentary Fiction: Images of Sub-Saharan Africa in Colonial Film Between the Wars," in *Proceedings of the Western Society for French History: Selected Papers of the Annual Meeting*, ed. Barry Rothaus (University Press of Colorado, 1998), 188.

7. Coissac, "Le cinématographe utilisé comme propagande aux colonies," 414.

8. *La dépêche coloniale illustrée*, December 1921, n.p.

9. Marcel Lapierre, *Les cent visages du cinéma* (Bernard Grasset, 1948), 301.

10. "Au Sénat, l'interpellation sur les colonies," *La dépêche coloniale et maritime*, no. 6685, April 3, 1920, 2.

11. "Au Sénat," *Ciné-Journal*, no. 667, May 27, 1922, 25.

12. Gabriel Fabre, "Une enquête sur la propagande coloniale anglaise," *Bulletin de l'Agence générale des colonies*, no. 240 (January 1929): 31, 9–35.

13. Fabre, "Une enquête," 32.

14. "Films coloniaux," *Les annales coloniales*, no. 30, February 22, 1924, 1.

15. "Propagande belge," *Ciné-Journal*, no. 644, December 17, 1921, 30.

16. Jean Marguet, "La France, puissance coloniale, possède-t-elle un cinéma colonial?," *Cinémonde*, no. 95, August 14, 1930, 519.

17. Jean Andrieu, "Pour la plus grande France," *Cinéma*, no. 31, April 1930, n.p.

18. Coissac, *Histoire du cinématographe*, 549.

19. Georges-Michel Coissac, "Vacances et exposition coloniale," *Cinéopse*, no. 145, September 1931, 387.

20. "À l'Exposition coloniale de Marseille," *Ciné-Journal*, no. 665, May 13, 1922, 28.

21. Georges Vial, "Le 'Courrier' à Marseille," *Le courrier cinématographique*, no. 23, June 10, 1922, 20.

22. "Une récompense méritée," *Comoedia*, November 9, 1922, 4.

23. "Cinéma colonial du 'Petit journal,'" *Le petit journal*, April 11, 1924, 4.

24. Pierre Boulanger, *Le cinéma colonial, de "L'Atlantide" à "Lawrence d'Arabie"* (Seghers, 1975). See, in chronological order, Richard Abel, *French Cinema, The First Wave, 1915–1929* (Princeton University Press, 1984), 151–60; Abdelkader Benali, *Le cinéma colonial au Maghreb: L'imaginaire en trompe-l'oeil* (Éditions du Cerf, 1998); and David Slavin, *Colonial Cinema and Imperial France, 1919–1939* (Johns Hopkins University Press, 2001). Benali does identify documentary-style moments in such films, the majority of which are adaptations of earlier literary works (52–66), and Slavin briefly discusses Léon Poirier's *La croisière noire* (61–63).

25. Pierre Haffner, *Palabres sur le cinématographe: Initiation au cinéma* (Les Presses Africaines, 1978), 151. Jacques de Baroncelli's colonial melodrama *L'homme du Niger* (The man of Niger, 1939) is a notable exception to this rule.

26. Bloom, *French Colonial Documentary*, 66.

27. See Kevin Dunn, "Lights . . . Camera . . . Africa: Images of Africa and Africans in Western Popular Films of the 1930s," *African Studies Review* 39, no. 1 (1996): 149–75. In an essay originally published in 1995, scholar of African film Femi Okiremuete Shaka limits his scope to British films, distinguishing between social documentaries and colonialist films to conclude that "most colonialist African films can be categorized as melodramas." Femi Okiremuete Shaka, "Politics of Cultural Conversion in Colonialist African Cinema," *Black Camera* 12, no. 2 (2021): 75.

28. C.-F.-T. Tavano, "Les voyages et les documentaires," *Le film*, April 1921, n.p.

29. J.-K. Raymond-Millet, "Le film de voyage documentaire ou reportage cinématographique a une valeur . . . ," *Comoedia*, June 22, 1930, 1.

30. Delmeulle, "Le rêve encyclopédiste," 107, 111n7.

31. This survey was part of a ministry initiative to collect and circulate educational documentaries. Alison Murray Levine, "Projections of Rural Life: The Agricultural Film Initiative in France, 1919–39," *Cinema Journal* 43, no. 4 (2004): 86, 89.

32. "Chronique cinématographique," *Le fascinateur*, no. 151, December 1920, 188.

33. Summaries of Bugniet's and Lecurieux's films are available via the Centre National du Cinéma et de l'image animée (CNC) Patrimoine site, http://www.cnc-aff.fr/home.aspx. For a more detailed analysis of Bugniet's work, contextualized within French colonial funding structures, see Murray Levine, *Framing the Nation*, 124–44. And on Bugniet's later *Sso* (1935), see Henley, *Beyond Observation*, 45.

34. "Le cinéma dans le centre africain: L'expédition Vandenbergh," *Ciné-Miroir*, no. 19, February 1, 1923, 42.

35. Coissac, "Le cinématographe utilisé comme propagande aux colonies," 414.

36. Lionel Landry, "Documentaires," *Cinémagazine*, no. 4, January 26, 1923, 154.

37. Claude Jeantet, "Opinion sur les documentaires," *Cinémonde*, no. 77, April 10, 1930, 227; J. M., "Le film documentaire," *Cinémonde*, no. 16, February 7, 1929, 296. R.-E. Bré, "Si vous aimez le documentaire, dites-nous . . . ," *Pour vous*, no. 132, May 28, 1931, 3.

38. Dudley Andrew, "Praying Mantis: Enchantment and Violence in French Cinema of the Exotic," in *Visions of the East: Orientalism in Film*, ed. Matthew Bernstein and Gaylyn Studlar (Rutgers University Press, 1997), 242.

39. Léon Moussinac, *Naissance du cinéma* (J. Povolozky et Cie, 1925), 165, 166, 177.

40. George Fronval, "Films documentaires," *Ciné-Comoedia*, August 30, 1928, 1.

41. Landry, "Documentaires," 154.

42. Fronval, "Films documentaires," 1.

43. "Echos," "Présentations de la semaine," *Ciné-Journal*, no. 619, June 25, 1921, 20, 41.

44. G.-Michel Coissac, "Un très beau film d'enseignement," *Cinéopse*, no. 34, 1922, 516. For the Swedish reception of Olsson's films, see Tommy Gustafsson, "The Visual Re-creation of Black People in a 'White' Country: Oscar Micheaux and Swedish Film Culture in the 1920s," *Cinema Journal* 47, no. 4 (2008): 37–40.

45. Oscar Olsson and Reginald Pound, "Five Thousand Miles on Foot in Central Africa," *Wide World Magazine*, no. 49 (1922): 514.

46. Meusy, *Paris-Palaces*, 285–88.

47. *Comoedia*, April 21, 1922, 5.

48. *Cinémagazine*, no. 14, April 7, 1922, 1.

49. Coissac, "Un très beau film d'enseignement," 517.

50. "Une présentation sensationnelle," *Ciné-Journal*, no. 662, April 22, 1922, 32.

51. Guy de Téramond, *Au coeur de l'Afrique sauvage* (Librairie Hachette, 1923).

52. *Ciné-Journal*, no. 665, May 13, 1922.

53. *Le courrier cinématographique*, no. 22, June 3, 1922.

54. *Cinémagazine*, no. 14, April 7, 1922, 23.

55. "Au coeur de l'Afrique sauvage," *Cinémagazine*, no. 15, April 14, 1922, 15, 41–42.

56. *Ciné-Journal*, no. 714, April 28, 1923.

57. Jean-Michel Frodon, *Le cinéma à l'épreuve du divers* (CNRS Éditions, 2021), 26. Tobing Rony notes this strategy of mocking "natives" to amuse spectators in US safari films. Tobing Rony, *Third Eye*, 86–87.

58. "Vers le Tchad," *Le courrier des cinémas*, March 5, 1926, 7.

59. *Cinémagazine*, no. 50, December 11, 1925, n.p.

60. Bloom, *French Colonial Documentary*, 65. Chapter 3 of Bloom's book is devoted to these films as "trans-Saharan" narratives, 65–93.

61. Bloom, *French Colonial Documentary*, 75.

62. "La traversée du Sahara en autochenilles, par la mission Haardt-Audouin-Dubreuil," *Ciné-Miroir*, no. 28, June 15, 1923, 183, 188.

63. *Cinéopse*, no. 59, July 1924. I would like to thank Peter Bloom for sharing this film with me.

64. "Le continent mystérieux, notes de voyage, en marge du raid Citroën," *Cinéa*, no. 10, April 1, 1924, 30; "Les grands documentaires," *Ciné-Journal*, no. 802, January 9, 1925, 27.

65. Paul Castelnau, "Le continent mystérieux, édité par Aubert," *Ciné-Miroir*, no. 49, May 1, 1924, 136.

66. G.-Michel Coissac, "Sous le signe du documentaire," *Cinéopse*, no. 133, September 1930, 3.

67. Georges Sadoul, *Histoire d'un art: Le cinéma, des origines à nos jours* (Flammarion, 1949), 283.

68. "Les mystères du continent noir," *Cinéa*, no. 66, July 31, 1926, 22.

69. *Cinéopse*, no. 83, July 1926, 588.

70. "Echos," *Ciné-Journal*, no. 900, November 26, 1926, 6.

71. "Les mystères du continent noir, film documentaire edité par Aubert," *Ciné-Miroir*, no. 103, August 1, 1926, 235.

72. Georges-Marie Haardt and Louis Audouin-Dubreuil, *La croisière noire: Expedition Citroën Centre-Afrique* (Librairie Plon, 1927), vi.

73. "L'expédition Citroën Centre-Afrique se dirige vers l'océan Indien," *Le petit journal*, May 6, 1925, 2.

74. "La liaison automobile intersaharienne," *Le matin*, October 30, 1924, 2.

75. "La deuxième mission Citroën a atteint le lac Tchad," *Le petit parisien*, December 19, 1924, 2.

76. Abel, *French Cinema, The First Wave*, 253.

77. Léon Poirier, *24 images à la seconde* (Maison Mame, 1953), 64.

78. Léon Poirier, *La croisière noire: Journal cinégraphique de l'expédition Citroën-Centre-Afrique* (Imprimerie Draeger, 1926), 13–14.

79. Léon Poirier, "Le cinéma exotique," *Ciné-Miroir*, no. 101, July 1, 1926, 195.

80. Pierre Leprohon, "L'exotisme au cinéma," *Cinémonde*, no. 45, August 29, 1929, 792; René Jeanne, "L'année cinématographique française," *Cinéopse*, no. 89, January 1927, 48.

81. Jean Vignaud, "Notre opinion," *Ciné-Miroir*, no. 98, May 15, 1926, 147.

82. Jehan de Vimbelle, "Chronique du cinéma éducateur," *Cinéopse*, no. 80, April 1926, 330.

83. *Comoedia*, February 24, 1926.

84. *Voyage au Congo* was restored for Bologna's Cinema Ritrovato Festival in 2018, then released on DVD by Les Films du Jeudi in France. A US release by Icarus Films followed a year later as *Travels in the Congo*, a title that unfortunately omits the sense of going to Congo from somewhere else. The *au* in the French title signifies both *to* and *in*.

85. Henley, "From *Vues* to Ethnofiction," 55, 54. James notes "striking moments" when Allégret's subjects look directly into the camera and, like Peterson, understands these to be moments of resistance through disruption. As we have seen, such moments had been prevalent in colonial documentary for almost two decades. Alison James, *The Documentary Imagination in Twentieth-Century French Literature* (Oxford University Press, 2020), 66, 72.

86. André Gide, *Voyage au Congo, suivi de Le retour du Tchad* (Gallimard Folio, 2002). On *Voyage au Congo* from book to film, see Damien Mottier, "*Voyage au Congo*: Cinéma, littérature et ethnographie," in Caroline Damiens' important edited collection *Ciné-Expéditions, Une zone de contact cinématographique* (AFRHC, 2022), 187–209. Mottier draws on the work of Gide scholar Daniel Durosay, notably his introduction and editor's notes to Allégret's *Carnets du Congo: Voyage avec André Gide* (CNRS, 1987).

87. Peter Bloom, "Trans-Saharan Automotive Cinema," in *Virtual Voyages: Cinema and Travel*, ed. Jeffrey Ruoff (Duke University Press, 2006), 149.

88. Gide, *Voyage au Congo, suivi de Le retour du Tchad*, 82n1.

89. Henley, "From *Vues* to Ethnofiction," 56.

90. Bill Nichols, *Speaking Truths with Film: Evidence, Ethics, Politics in Documentary* (University of California Press, 2016), 45.

91. In an interview with *Comoedia* after the film's release, Gide repeated hackneyed claims of a French civilizing mission, stating that "since the French occupation, these tribes have stopped making war on each other and have become peaceful, such that we thought for an instant about giving our film the title *Equatorial Arcadias*." Pierre Lagarde, "André Gide chez les anthropophages," *Comoedia*, February 25, 1927, 1. For a detailed reading of Gide and Allégret's expedition that focuses on the illustrated edition of Gide's *Voyage au Congo*, see Simon Dell, *The Portrait and the Colonial Imaginary: Photography Between France and Africa* (Leuven University Press, 2020), 55–115.

92. Emile Vuillermoz, "'Voyage au Congo,'" *Le temps*, June 18, 1927, 4. Within anthropology, *ethnology* is used to refer to comparative studies of cultures, whereas *ethnography* implies a deeper focus on a single culture. The terms appear to have been used interchangeably by nonspecialists such as Vuillermoz in the 1920s, '30s, and '40s.

93. Albert Londres, *Terre d'ébène* (Le Serpent à Plumes, 1998 [1929]), 246. For a recent historical recounting, see J. P. Daughton, *In the Forest of No Joy: The Congo-Océan Railroad and the Tragedy of French Colonialism* (W. W. Norton, 2021).

94. G.-Michel Coissac, "Le cinéma et la propagande coloniale," *Cinéopse*, no. 103, March 1, 1928, 259.

95. "La propagande coloniale par le film," *Cinéducateur*, no. 3, January 1928, 23. For more on the Comité de propagande coloniale par le film and colonial educational cinema, see Bloom, *French Colonial Documentary*, chapter 5.

96. Coissac, "Le cinéma et la propagande coloniale," 258.

97. Jean-Paul Coutisson, "Un grand documentaire, La marche vers le soleil," *Ciné-Comoedia*, no. 857, June 3, 1930, 1.

98. "Le president de la republique assiste a la presentation de la 'Marche vers le soleil,'" *Ciné-Journal*, no. 1066, January 31, 1930, 12.

99. Edmond Epardaud, "Le jubilé d'une grand maison française, Les Etablissements L. Aubert," *Cinéa*, no. 128, March 1, 1929, 28; "La marche vers le soleil," *La critique cinématographique*, no. 240, October 4, 1931, 49.

100. Le Roy, "Le fonds cinématographique colonial aux Archives du film," 59.

101. J. K. Raymond-Millet, "Alger-Dakar et retour," *Pour vous*, no. 85, July 3, 1930, 4.

102. J. K. Raymond-Millet, "Les nègres sont-ils photogéniques?," *Ciné-Miroir*, no. 227, August 9, 1929, 503.

103. J. K. Raymond-Millet, "France-Congo sur un cargo," *Cinéma*, no. 24, July–August 1929, n.p.

104. Huret, *Ciné actualités*, 58; Vieyra, *Réflexions d'un cineaste africain*, 61.

105. Nichols, *Representing Reality*, 34–35.

106. J. de Vimbelle, "L'Afrique vous parle," *Cinéopse*, no. 143, July 1931, 343; J.-P. Coutisson, "Un magnifique documentaire, 'L'Afrique vous parle,'" *Ciné-Comoedia*, April 11, 1931, 1.

107. Alfred Chaumel, "Mission cinématographique de l'A.E.F.," *Le monde colonial illustré*, no. 20, May 1925, 100.

108. Gide, *Voyage au Congo, suivi de Le retour du Tchad*, 26.

109. Nino Frank, "Un excellent documentaire: Notre oeuvre au 'Cameroun,'" *Pour vous*, no. 80, May 29, 1930, 8–9.

110. "Travaux de sonorisation," *Le courrier des cinémas*, no. 251–52, January 2 and 9, 1931, 20; Coissac, "Le cinéma au service de la civilisation et de la propagande," 71; Pierre Bonardi, "Pour le meilleur film colonial," *Ciné-Miroir*, no. 462, February 16, 1934, 102.

111. Coissac, "Le cinéma au service de la civilisation et de la propagande," 72; "Le réveil d'une race (au Cameroun)," *Ciné-Miroir*, no. 302, January 14, 1931, 52.

112. M. E. Tarquis, "Le réveil d'une race," *Le courrier des cinémas*, no. 258, February 20, 1931, 2.

113. *Cinéopse*, no. 139, March 1931, n.p.

114. G.-Michel Coissac, "Au service de la colonisation III," *Cinéopse*, no. 141, May 1, 1931, 217.

115. Girardet, *L'idée coloniale en France de 1871 à 1962*, 175–76. Too much good work has been published about the 1931 Colonial Exhibition for me to include a

comprehensive list here, although the place of cinema has been largely neglected. On architectural representations of colonial spaces, for example, see Patricia Morton, *Hybrid Modernities: Architecture and Representation at the 1931 Colonial Exhibition, Paris* (MIT Press, 2000); Panivong Norindr, *Phantasmatic Indochina: French Colonial Ideology in Architecture, Film, and Literature* (Duke University Press, 2006).

116. G.-Michel Coissac, "Au service de la colonisation II," *Cinéopse*, no. 140, April 1, 1931, 175; J. K. Raymond-Millet, "Le cinéma à l'Exposition coloniale," *Le courrier cinématographique*, no. 25, 1931, 6.

117. "Le cinéma documentaire," *Ciné-Journal*, no. 1131, May 1, 1931, 29.

118. Chamine, "Nudisme comparé: De Moana à Physiopolis," *Pour vous*, October 29, 1931, 2. For more on the connections between this organization (founded in late 1929), the associated journal that began publication two years later, and Chaumel's films, see Béatrice de Pastre, "Cinéma éducateur et propagande coloniale à Paris au début des années 1930," *Revue d'histoire moderne et contemporaine* 51, no. 4 (2004): 135–51.

119. "Peaux noires," *La critique cinématographique*, no. 259, February 21, 1932, 8; "Studios et plein air," *Pour vous*, March 26, 1931, 14; J. D., "Le réveil d'un race," *Cinémonde*, no. 117, January 15, 1931, 36; "La mode 1931 sera-t-elle coloniale?," in *Exposition coloniale internationale, Bulletin d'informations* (Commissariat Général, 1931), 13.

120. Bloom, *French Colonial Documentary*, 130.

121. *Paris et l'exposition coloniale*, 1931, 8, 9–10, 52.

122. "Informations – Communiqués," *Ciné-Journal*, no. 1131, May 1, 1931, 12; *Le petit parisien*, September 27, 1931, 5; "L'actualité," *La critique cinématographique*, no. 240, October 4, 1931, 11; F. Hertin, "L'Exposition coloniale et le cinéma," *L'echo d'Alger*, no. 7961, July 27, 1931, 2.

123. André Demaison, *À Paris en 1931, Exposition coloniale internationale, guide officiel* (1931), 15; Pierre Ichac, "Notes d'un chasseur d'images: Cinéma et colonies," *Cinéma*, no. 35, January 1931, n.p.

124. *La critique cinématographique*, no. 240, October 4, 1931, 48.

125. Coissac, "Le cinéma au service de la civilisation et de la propagande," 53–58.

126. Coissac, "Le cinéma au service de la civilisation et de la propagande," 59.

127. René Maran, *Batouala: Véritable roman nègre* (Albin Michel, 1938), 11, 101–12.

128. See David Murphy's introduction to Lamine Senghor, *La violation d'un pays et autres écrits anticolonialistes* (L'Harmattan, 2012).

129. See Brent Hayes Edwards's indispensable *The Practice of Diaspora: Literature, Translation, and the Rise of Black Internationalism* (Harvard University Press, 2003).

130. Germaine Decaris, "Le réveil d'un race, par Alfred Chaumel," *La revue du cinéma*, no. 24, July 1, 1931, 56.

131. "Ne visitez pas l'Exposition coloniale," in *Tracts surréalistes et déclarations collectives, 1922–1939* (Le terrain vague, 1980), 195.

132. Pap Ndiaye, "Présence africaine avant 'Présence africaine': La subjectivation politique noire en France dans l'entre-deux-guerres," *Gradhiva*, no. 10 (2009): 76; Edwards, *Practice of Diaspora*, 261.

133. Ousmane Socé, *Mirages de Paris* (Nouvelles éditions Latines, 1964), 65–67.

134. *Ciné-Journal*, October 23, 1931, n.p.

135. R. Thoumazeau, "Souvenirs de voyage du baron Gourgaud," *Pour vous*, November 26, 1931, 5; "Le vrai visage d'Afrique," *Ciné-Miroir*, no. 351, December 25, 1931, 842; Reine Hurel, "Au pays des grands fauves: Un hardi chasseur," *Cinémagazine*, no. 1, January 1932, 44–45.

136. Coissac, "Au service de la colonisation II," 177; "Le cinéma au Muséum d'histoire naturelle," *Cinéopse*, no. 152, April 1932, 175.

137. "Un globe trotter du cinéma," *Ciné-Journal*, no. 211, September 7, 1912, 7.

138. "Cette fois, c'est l'Afrique . . .," *Le courrier des cinémas*, nos. 300–1, March 1932, 2; "Les présentations," *Hebdo-Film*, February 20, 1932, 12–13.

139. "Le cinéma à la Sorbonne," *Cinéopse*, no. 164, April 1933, 137; "Chronique du cinéma éducateur," *Cinéopse*, no. 163, March 1933, 118; "La propagande coloniale par le cinématographe," *Ciné-Journal*, no. 1195, February 10, 1933, 21.

140. Roger Régent, "'Peaux noires,' film africain," *Pour vous*, no. 121, March 12, 1931, 4.

141. The copy held by Gaumont Pathé Archives dates from after the war and includes a patriotic, handwritten intertitle: "This film, entirely shot in the sands of Mauritania and Chad, was forbidden, seized, and burned by the Germans. It is dedicated to those who, from Chad and from Egypt, victoriously crossed 500 km of desert to return liberty and greatness to their fatherland."

142. Pierre Mac-Orlan, "Un grand film: *La croisière noire*," *L'intransigeant*, March 4, 1926, 1.

143. "Images d'Afrique," *Cinéma*, no. 31, April 1930, n.p.; Marguet, "La France, puissance coloniale," 519; Frank, "Un excellent documentaire," 8.

144. Nino Frank, "Le vrai visage de l'Afrique," *Pour vous*, December 3, 1931, 7.

145. Marcel Carné, "Le cinéma à la conquête du monde," *Cinémagazine*, no. 9, October 1930, 9–10.

146. Marcel Carné, "L'exotisme au cinéma, en marge de l'Exposition coloniale," *Cinémagazine*, no. 7, July 1931, 15, 16, 20. For his anthology of French film theory and criticism from the 1930s, Richard Abel instead chose Carné's "Cinema and the World" and "When Will the Cinema Go down into the Street," also published in *Cinémagazine*, both of which similarly advocate for films shot outside of the studio but without invoking colonial locales and ideology. Richard Abel, *French Film*

Theory and Criticism, vol. 2, *1929–1939* (Princeton University Press, 1988), 102–5, 127–29.

147. Bazin used the film's French title, *Cimbo*. André Bazin, "Le cinéma et l'exploration," in *Qu'est-ce que le cinéma?* (Éditions du Cerf, 1999 [1958]), 25.

148. René Ginet, "La mort du documentaire," *La critique cinématographique*, no. 236, September 6, 1931, 21–22; Pierre Leprohon, "Retour d'Afrique, René Ginet veut nous réveler une Afrique nouvelle," *Cinémonde*, no. 231, March 23, 1933, 240.

149. René Ginet, "Un nouveau film documentaire, Angola-Pullman," *Ciné-Miroir*, no. 429, June 23, 1933, 398; "Angola-Pullman," *Hebdo-Film*, no. 47, December 23, 1933, 14.

150. Leprohon, *L'exotisme et le cinéma*, 39, 57, 286, 296.

151. André Liotard, Samivel, and Jean Thévenot, *Cinéma d'exploration, cinéma au long cours* (Chavane, 1950), 7–8.

152. Claude Vermorel, "L'explorateur, dans un fauteil: L'écran nous a révélé les mystères du monde," *Pour vous*, August 13, 1931, 5.

153. "Peaux noires," *Ciné-Journal*, no. 1172, February 19, 1932, 11.

154. "Peaux noires: Film réalisé par M. Moreau, au course de l'expédition Jean d'Esme dans le centre africain," *Ciné-Miroir*, no. 381, July 22, 1932, 481.

155. "Désormais le cinéma aura en Afrique Occidentale Française un statut exemplaire," *Ciné-Comoedia*, March 13, 1934, 1; "Le nouveau contrôle des films en Afrique Equatoriale Française," *Ciné-Comoedia*, August 22, 1934, 1. For more on censorship and the Laval Decree, see Goerg, *Tropical Dream Palaces*, 60–62. And on France's postwar plans to use radio and cinema, particularly documentary films, as propaganda, see James Genova, "Cinema and the Struggle to (De)colonize the Mind in French/Francophone West Africa (1950s–1960s)," *Journal of the Midwest Modern Language Association* 39, no. 1 (2006): 52.

156. "Echos et informations," *Courrier cinématographique de l'Ouest Africain Français*, November 16, 1934, 1.

157. René Jeanne and Charles Ford, *Le cinéma et la presse, 1895–1960* (Armand Colin, 1961), 216.

158. John Grierson, "First Principles of Documentary," in *Nonfiction Film: Theory and Criticism*, ed. Richard Barsam (E. P. Dutton, 1976), 19, 20; Michel Vaucaire, "Un genre nouveau: Le documentaire romancé," *Pour vous*, no. 20, April 4, 1929, 11.

159. Anna Grimshaw, "Who Has the Last Laugh? *Nanook of the North* and Some New Thoughts on an Old Classic," *Visual Anthropology*, no. 27 (2014): 421–35.

3

RESEARCH

Ethnographic Filmmaking

In 1946, fifteen years after its release, Pierre Laubriet described *Peaux noires* in the journal of the Maritime and Colonial League as "a remarkable ethnographic document," regretting only that René Moreau's fifteen thousand meters of footage had been cut to a two-thousand-meter film.[1] Just a year earlier, Pierre Leprohon had affirmed that narrative works like *Au coeur de l'Afrique sauvage* and *Peaux noires*, unlike earlier travel films, were "of incontestable ethnographic value."[2] These post–World War II assessments of the ethnographic importance of interwar documentaries stand in stark contrast with the widespread praise of the films' "sensational," "astounding," and "curious" images upon their original release. Further complicating matters, in a brief 1948 investigation of what he called "the ethnological film," archeologist and anthropologist André Leroi-Gourhan repudiated the genre of the "exoticist documentary" that Marcel Carné and Leprohon so admired, dismissing it memorably as "the misshapen offspring of the notepad."[3] How are we to understand this simultaneous enthusiasm for ethnography on the part of colonial lobbyists and film critics and rejection of the films they considered ethnographic by a social scientist?

As is by now evident, French documentary from its first years manifested an ethnographic impulse inherited from earlier colonial literature and visual arts. French popular audiences were drawn to theaters by a keen interest in the lives of colonized peoples, especially those in Africa. Over time, as travelogues evolved into expedition films, ethnographic details came to occupy a larger portion of longer works. And over the course of the single decade of the 1930s, in the wake of the Colonial Exhibition, there was a qualitative change in both practitioners' and spectators' understanding of what Karl Heider and Paul Henley after him have called the "eth-nographicness" of documentary.[4] If the 1920s had seen the professionalization of the expedition documentary, in the final decades of the colonial era it was ethnographic filmmaking that became a vocation, an enterprise understood as scholarly and even scientific. By the mid-1940s, virtually all French nonfiction films shot in sub-Saharan Africa would claim ethnography as their primary project—a postwar return, André Bazin argued, to "documentary authenticity."[5]

This transformation occurred alongside a remaking of French anthropology and anthropological museums that had begun in the late nineteenth century. In his now classic essay "On Ethnographic Surrealism," James Clifford situates the surrealist movement's opposition to the Colonial Exhibition within Paul Rivet's decade-long transformation of the Trocadero Museum of Ethnography into the Musée de l'Homme (Museum of Mankind), housed in the new Chaillot Palace.[6] Building on Clifford's work, historian Alice Conklin details the evolution from biological-leaning anthropology to more culturally focused ethnography via the trajectories of both the Museum of Ethnography and the National Museum of Natural History, which, almost a century older, was founded in 1793 on the site of Louis XIII's Royal Garden of Medicinal Plants.[7] The Museum of Mankind combined the ethnographic collections of the earlier museums and housed the Institute of Ethnology, originally established at the Sorbonne in 1925. It also expanded on their range of media, opening in the late 1930s with its own movie theater and adding a department of cinematography after the war.[8]

In the oft-quoted opening lines of his celebrated *Tristes Tropiques*, anthropologist Claude Lévi-Strauss declared his hatred of "voyages and explorers," distinguishing himself from professional adventurers who drew large audiences to slide or moving picture shows accompanied by what he deemed "platitudes and banalities."[9] Just over twenty years earlier, however, Deputy Director of the Museum of Ethnography Georges-Henri Rivière had felt no need to draw such a distinction. A month before the opening of the 1931 Colonial Exhibition, Rivière wrote a rave review of *L'Afrique vous parle* for movie magazine *Pour vous*.[10] Praising the film as "the prototype of the talking *grand documentaire*" and "a rich contribution to ethnological scholarship," he argued for its conservation in the collections of the Smithsonian Institution. His own museum shared the film's goal that "primitive civilizations be better understood and loved," Rivière concluded, as did the upcoming Dakar–Djibouti mission to Africa led by his "dear friend" Marcel Griaule.

A key figure in the history of what are in French called the *human sciences*, Griaule joined the French air force in his late teens, in the last year of World

War I. After the war, he abandoned mathematics to learn Amharic and Ge'ez at the National School of Living Oriental Languages in Paris, then studied with Marcel Mauss at the École Pratique des Hautes Études (School for advanced studies). Griaule became the first scholar to obtain a *doctorat d'état* (second-level doctorate) in anthropology and at the end of his career composed an authoritative *Méthode de l'ethnographie* (Ethnographic methodology, 1957), yet he was never just an academic. When Griaule won the Gringoire Prize for the book about his first field expedition to Abyssinia, newspaper *Le petit journal* described him as "a civil servant who doubles as a scholar and an explorer."[11] He led five expeditions to sub-Saharan Africa, with film footage shot during three: Dakar–Djibouti in the early 1930s, Sahara–Sudan in the middle of the decade, and Sahara–Cameroon at decade's end.[12]

Clifford describes Griaule as "self-confident and theatrical," noting that in 1946, lecturing as the first chair in ethnology at the Sorbonne, he wore his World War I air force uniform.[13] Griaule participated fully in the construction of his persona as adventurer and, like the expeditions led by Poirier, Allégret, d'Esme, and Ginet, his were sanctioned as missions by the French government. Preparation for Dakar–Djibouti took place during the lead-up to the Colonial Exhibition and with corresponding zeal. In the months prior to their departure, team members attended one of the first screenings of *L'Afrique vous parle*, and Griaule met with President Gaston Doumergue to review the expedition route.[14] In just under two years, Griaule and his colleagues would cross the African continent from west to east: from Dakar to Djibouti through French West Africa, Cameroon, French Equatorial Africa, and Belgian Congo. Funding for the trip came from the Ministry of Colonies, the National Museum of Natural History, and the Institute of Ethnology, among other French governmental sources. The Ministry for Public Instruction and Fine Arts by itself promised 700,000 francs toward the study of indigenous "institutions, languages, and techniques," noting that the expedition would share its methodology with colonial administrations and thus "encourage their research and establish durable relationships."[15]

Griaule also received private support for the Dakar–Djibouti expedition—from the New York–based Rockefeller Foundation as well as from members of his Parisian literary and artistic circles who shared an enthusiasm for sub-Saharan Africa. Eccentric and influential writer Raymond Roussel donated 10,000 francs, and in mid-April, poet and avant-garde icon Jean Cocteau organized a gala boxing fundraiser featuring Panamanian world champion Al Brown; American superstar Josephine Baker was in attendance. In *Comoedia*, Georges Mouly assured readers that, despite considerable financial support,

Griaule would not profit from his voyage, which was motivated by "pure science, altruistic science."[16] This science was anchored in a circular logic that recalls the earliest *chasseurs d'images* in Africa and the written travel narratives that preceded them. In Mouly's summary, which repeated the reasoning of the law authorizing governmental funding for the expedition, the "European penetration" that brought "the benefits of progress to the natives" was also transforming their customs, a fact that lent urgency to Griaule's desire to observe and record "unknown civilizations."

The Trocadero Museum of Ethnography also contributed to Griaule's expedition, which pledged to add to its holdings. Before leaving Paris, expedition members collaborated on a slim handbook for ethnographer-collectors addressed specifically to members of the colonial administration. Basing their instructions on courses taught at the Institute of Ethnology, they, like Mouly, started from the premise that indigenous traditions were on the verge of disappearing as a result of European contact. It was therefore crucial to collect objects that would "fill the gaps that mar our Museum."[17] Indeed, soon after Griaule's arrival in Dakar, *Le journal* (The news) announced that the Trocadero museum was "getting richer" in African objects, including a large pirogue that had already been sent to Europe.[18] An exhibit drawn from the thirty-five hundred objects acquired and fifty-five hundred photographs taken by Griaule and his colleagues was officially opened by Minister of Colonies Albert Sarraut in June 1933.[19] A year later, Griaule and Rivière announced that objects from the Dakar–Djibouti expedition gallery would soon be on display alongside a diorama of animals from Equatorial Africa in the African Museum on the Île d'Aix, newly established by Baron Gourgaud and his wealthy American wife to house hunting trophies from their own African expeditions.[20]

Griaule's Sahara–Sudan expedition was much shorter than Dakar–Djibouti, covering three thousand kilometers in Renault vehicles over the course of three months: from Algiers to Hoggar to Tamanrasset, then across the Sahara to Gao, south to Hombou, and to the cliffs of Bandiagara. Funding came from many of the same sources, with the notable additions of the Air Force Ministry and Princess Marie Bonaparte. New Minister of Colonies Louis Rollin awarded Griaule 10,000 francs and his expedition the title of *scientific mission;* the proposed study of the Bandiagara cliffs received the approval of the governor general of AOF. In addition to conducting research in the domains of anthropology, ethnobotany, ethnozoology, and topography, Griaule was again charged with collecting objects, taking photographs, and shooting film footage, with two military planes provided in order so he could map the region in aerial photographs.[21] After the subsequent Sahara–Cameroon mission, to which a third minister of colonies, Marius Moutet, awarded 25,000 francs, Griaule participated in the 1935 Colonial Week organized throughout France and its territories, displaying "exotic" musical instruments at the Museum of Ethnography.[22]

If the events and publications surrounding the Dakar–Djibouti expedition had been the talk of the town thanks to famous athletes, artists, and performers, Griaule publicized Sahara–Sudan largely on his own. He narrated the voyage in a series of five articles in *Le journal* titled "The Sahara for All." Advertised in advance on the newspaper's front page—"Marcel Griaule's gripping reportage begins tomorrow"—these tales were told in a chatty, humorous tone and included no ethnographic information.[23] Griaule began by recounting the heat and difficult landscapes with poetic imagery and humor, this at the expense of a few African characters, whose words Griaule quoted in a pidgin French known at the time as *petit nègre*.[24] Subsequent pieces lightheartedly bemoaned the traffic jam of European tourists crossing the desert and told the dramatic story of a heroic French officer who committed suicide after being stranded at his post without food.[25] The very last mocked an African man Griaule encountered in Gao who was trying to avoid paying taxes to a colonial police commissioner.[26] Griaule returned to the pages of *Le journal* three months later with four articles about his time with the Dogon. Arguing the importance of extending "the work of exploration" to Bandiagara, he patronizingly described the region's people as "honest Black peasants, not too thick-lipped, whose skin is not that dark."[27] Inhabiting the role of intrepid explorer, Griaule remembered walking on a cliff's edge, then crawling through skull-filled caves until, at the end of a long, low passage, he "discovered" the longest mask in the world, which he took and sent to the Museum of Ethnography. To justify this appropriation of an African sacred object, Griaule contended that "the religions and skills of non-evolved peoples belong to their heritage, and also to our heritage, that of those who dominate them."[28] Despite his passionate interest in Dogon religion, Griaule did not respect it. Told by a priest that it was forbidden to enter an area wearing woven clothing, he stripped to his underwear, falsely asserting that it was made of rubber.[29]

Griaule's Sahara–Cameroon expedition was of great popular interest in France, since by the mid-1930s it was expected that Hitler would attempt to reclaim Germany's former colony. Beginning a series of articles in *Paris-Soir* with the French military plane that flew his crew across the desert, Griaule once again linked his roles as scholar and civil servant: "We were going to Cameroon ... to set up a scientific mission and also to see, at the same time, the work that France is accomplishing there."[30] Relating his astonishment at how quickly and enthusiastically Sara porters covered ground while carrying twenty kilograms of his supplies each, Griaule claimed, in a bit of colonial rivalry, that this was because the French treated them better than had the Germans. France governed the people of Cameroon, he concluded, with "liberalism and bonhomie." A week later, Griaule expressed the ugly underside of his comparison, deploring that "the Germans never did anything to tame these men."[31]

I preface Griaule's films with his academic and media profiles for two reasons. First, doing so is chronologically accurate; Griaule's films appeared years after his expeditions and the press narratives that recounted them. Second, Griaule's popular persona was quite different from the academic one for which he is now more often remembered. Although his discourse about Africa and Africans was not uncommon in France at the time, it stands in stark contrast to that of another member of the Dakar–Djibouti expedition, writer Michel Leiris, whom Griaule had asked to serve as secretary-archivist. After his return, Leiris published the almost seven-hundred-page *L'Afrique fantôme* (Phantom Africa, 1934), a work that outdid André Gide's *Voyage au Congo* both in length and skepticism of colonial mastery.[32] Despite his association with Leiris and the surrealist journal *Minotaure*, which published a special issue on Dakar–Djibouti, Griaule never actively protested the Colonial Exhibition nor colonialism itself. He and Leiris fell out after the publication of the latter's expedition notes, which revealed the forced purchase and outright theft of sacred objects as exploitative practices rather than humorous anecdotes.[33]

During the preparations for Dakar–Djibouti, Griaule and Rivière contacted French Paramount to request that a film crew accompany their mission. Paramount declined, perhaps because Griaule insisted that any rights be held by the Institute of Ethnology.[34] Most of Griaule's own footage proved unusable, so for Sahara–Sudan, he hired a professional, Roger Mourlan, who shot ten thousand meters of film. Sirius Films distributed *Au pays des Dogons* (In Dogon country, 1940) and *Sous les masques noirs* (Under the black masks, 1940) with Griaule's voice-over commentary added to Mourlan's images. Less widely reviewed than the *grands documentaires* of the late 1920s and early '30s, Griaule's documentaries were shown in both movie theaters and museums, often part of an event, conference, or gala sponsored by colonial organizations like the Maritime and Colonial League. If his on-site ethnographic practice was by many accounts innovative, his cinema, like his expedition planning and publicity, is utterly familiar, shaped by an implication in colonial funding circuits as well as the hunter-adventurer model of African travel and resource acquisition. When his films had not been completed in time to be screened at a 1939 exhibit, the Museum of Mankind simply substituted *La croisière noire*.[35]

Au pays des Dogons opens with orchestral music accompanied by credits that authenticate what audiences are about to see: a film shot during "an official mission led by Marcel Griaule." Rolling text on screen introduces "the Niger, great French river of the black continent" and "the immense Sudanese plain, enriched by the colonizing genius and the will of France, guided first by a long line of pioneers" and now by Georges Mandel, minister of colonies. Situating West Africa as greater France and the Bandiagara cliffs as "French Africa," this text and Griaule's voice-over describe "the curious tribe of the Dogon" as "a hardworking population that trusts us, and that we have the noble objective of lifting up to our level." Panning shots across and up and down the landscape of cliffs and cliff dwellings precede the film's first images of Dogon people: children at play, drumming and dancing. Griaule's hitherto condescending commentary becomes mocking, echoing *Vers le Tchad* and *Angola Pullman*.[36] The problem of drought, he quips, "is unfortunately not solved by dancing." After showing and describing how Dogon women and children prepare the onions they grow, Griaule pokes fun at women carrying baskets of onion balls to market, winding their way up the cliff. Addressing an imagined spectator whom he asks to compare French and African infrastructures, Griaule exclaims, "Do you see? Dogon highways are difficult for pedestrians!" A propagandistic tone returns over images of wide stairs cut up the cliffside. "Don't think that this staircase . . . was the initiative of the natives," Griaule warns, claiming it as an accomplishment of the colonial administration. Noting that at the local market, a cowry shell is equivalent to one hundred francs, Griaule ignores the cruelty of a French colonial system of taxation reliant on forced labor to joke that, when it is time to pay taxes, "the administration does not accept shells!"

The credits for *Sous les masques noirs* resemble those of *Au pays des Dogons*, with the cinema service of the Ministry of Colonies listed as producer. Another rolling text on screen introduces "the immense Sudanese plain, fertilized by the colonizing genius of France." Here, we are told, "tribes . . . respect ancient customs" maintained thanks to the French colonial administration, which is also credited with "the miracle of the creation of wealth through work under French patronage." The text takes care to identify the film as a "documentary" that will show spectators "one of the most mysterious peoples of black Africa." If thus far we could be watching the army's 1918 *L'aide des colonies à la France*, *Sous les masques noirs* changes course when Griaule appears on screen for the first time, sitting with a notebook in front of two elderly men. Although they have been recruited "to explain all of the techniques, all of the mystique, of the masks," we neither see them speak nor hear their words; it is Griaule who explains their mask-making rituals. His commentary narrates every stage of the process as two younger men walk into the countryside, pour sacred water on a carefully selected tree, cut it down, and carve a mask from its trunk. The film concludes with a funeral ceremony also narrated by Griaule, enlivened for spectators by a montage of low-angle shots of a drummer and clips of dancing feet, which gives way to a series of staged fights with bows, arrows, and guns.

Griaule completed two additional *grands reportages* in 1942. Both reuse footage—*Le Soudan mystérieux* (Mysterious Sudan) from *Sous les masques noirs* and *Technique chez les noirs* (Skills of Black Africans) from *Au pays du Dogon*—with sequences of differing lengths in different order. The sustained voice-over commentary of *Le Soudan mystérieux*, written but no longer read by Griaule, promises to reveal what the region is trying to keep secret, "its customs and its soul, which it guards jealously and only reveals parsimoniously to patient observers." Dances of the Dogon masks are performed one by one for the camera, accompanied by narration that insists on the religious nature of the "sacred choreography" without discussing the religion in question. *Technique chez les noirs* does provide ethnographic information; we learn, for example, that the village blacksmith is esteemed and feared and that legends recount his descent to earth with bellows filled with air from the sky. But the conclusion of the film evokes *Au Congo* and *Promenade au Soudan*, travelogues shot thirty years before, as the voice-over describes a "swarming crowd" at a regional market.

Of all the narrative products of the Dakar–Djibouti expedition, Griaule's films are perhaps the least interesting. Unlike Leiris's incisive and fragmented *L'Afrique fantôme*, they are thoroughly conventional, both omniscient and coherent. Despite his academic training and ambitions, Griaule's representation of Africa and Africans, like his understanding of documentary form and realism, falls neatly in line with prior travel, hunting, and expedition films. When describing his filmmaking process to George Fronval of *Cinémonde*, Griaule claimed that "the shooting was all done *sur le vif* like real newsreels [*actualités*]. You cannot ask the natives to do a reenactment or even a rehearsal. For them, everything is spontaneous and if you trouble them with details, they are lost." To film funeral rituals, he waited for a village resident to die, he continued, and therefore "the documents recorded by our camera are therefore precise and faithful accounts and unquestionably authentic."[37] These assertions, like the stereotypes on which they were based, are manifestly untrue, with Leiris's diary entries providing evidence of many staged ceremonies. No such acknowledgment made it into any of Griaule's films, however, which would have been greatly enriched by the inclusion of an episode he witnessed and described to Fronval—Dogon men acting out a parody of the ethnographers studying them.[38]

Unlike Leiris and Lévi-Strauss, Griaule never dissociated himself from the tradition of the colonial expedition. In 1945, in fact, he published a book titled *Les grands explorateurs* (Great explorers), which began with Alexander the Great and continued through Christopher Columbus to René Caillié and Stanley and Livingstone. Most of these men were motivated by a desire for land and goods, Griaule acknowledged, and for this reason he believed that "the explorers of today and tomorrow should be ethnographers," driven by scientific interest rather than greed.[39] Yet the distinction between acquisitive and ethnographic adventurers was not as clear as Griaule led readers to believe. A decade earlier, discussing his upcoming Sahara–Sudan expedition with journalist Jean Pédron, Griaule announced its purpose as the "prospecting" of Dogon land. Not interested in coffee or cotton or tropical wood, he was instead in search of valuable information and cultural objects, with the goal of producing an "extremely complete" study of ceremonies, sacred spaces, myths, social organization, fauna, flora, and topography.[40]

Griaule's ethnographic method relied on gathering information through extended, detailed fieldwork. Working toward comprehensive and definitive descriptions, he stationed expedition members at different locations to record multiple observations of Dogon ceremonies in a variety of media. Suspecting that Africans were trying to withhold information from his team, Griaule also insisted on series of interviews that resembled interrogations, with repeated questions and cross-checking to eliminate inconsistencies. Information was matched by objects; Griaule collected a hundred Dogon masks, which, he promised, would constitute "the best collection in Europe, and about each one we have the totality of explanations."[41] Griaule's approach to documentary filmmaking was similarly characterized by a sense of mastery. Cinema, he told Fronval, was an ethnographer's "indispensable collaborator." "Thanks to the lens, from now on not a single detail will escape us," Griaule declared, and "henceforth, every explorer who leaves on a scholarly mission must take a cameraman with him."[42] In his search for knowledge about Africa, Griaule exemplified Mudimbe's observation that eighteenth- and nineteenth-century "travelers" and twentieth-century "anthropologists and colonizers" shared the same perspective and as a result took the same actions.[43]

After Griaule's return from Cameroon and with another war approaching, a return to unequivocal propaganda interrupted the ascent of ethnographic filmmaking. Distribution Parisienne des Films concluded the decade by releasing an unusual feature-length production, *La France est un empire* (France is an empire, 1939). Based on an idea and screenplay credited to Jean d'Agraives, the film received financial support from the Ministry of Colonies, the Ministries of Air, the Navy, and Foreign Affairs, and the governors general of the colonies filmed, with five directors assigned each to a region of the French empire.[44] Screened so widely that it was reviewed in fashion magazine *Marie-Claire*, the documentary presents France as the savior of its colonies. After the standard set of maps, it offers spectators a step-by-step history of French colonization, starting with the conquest of Algiers in 1830 and continuing to Faidherbe in Senegal, Brazza in central Africa, and the 1918 acquisition of Cameroon and Togo.[45]

La France est un empire is organized thematically, with footage from multiple colonies in each section. With respect to health, voice-over commentary announces that traditional medicine and slavery have contributed to the suffering of native inhabitants. We are then shown the Mandel Sanatorium in Dakar, a French flag flying on its roof. Returning to the popular topic of sleeping sickness, like *Le réveil d'une race*, the film displays African patients whose treatment doses have been painted on their skin. Addressing education, the narrator claims that Black and white children, shown sharing a classroom, are treated equally. And for religion he implausibly contends that "souls are conquered without violence" such that Africans tell their beloved missionaries, "You are both my father and my mother."

Continuing the colonial documentary tradition of a *mise en valeur* of France's colonies, *La France est un empire* foregrounds the removal of riches. Refusing to acknowledge forced labor, the film maintains that the French administration "endeavored to give the natives a taste for work, by facilitating it." Spectators watch African workers collect and pack coffee, peanuts, oil, soap, bananas, and oranges for shipment to France. Logging is also performed by "natives," who, the voice-over narrator sneers, "in times past, would only venture into the forest trembling." The colonial forestry administration regulates the industry, and the commentary notes that each tree is now worth a small fortune. Like Guinean gold, this fortune is said to be "extracted from the soil of our empire" by African workers, who are also shown building the empire's roads. Seeking to debunk "rumors" of any resistance to colonization, the film includes images of Africans marching in a parade, carrying banners that read "France Is Our Mother" and "France Is Our Fatherland." This footage was shot without synchronous sound, but cheering was added to the soundtrack during editing. The last seven minutes of *La France est un empire* address the coming war, announcing that *tirailleurs* drawn from the 110 million inhabitants of the French empire are coming to the aid of the metropole. Concluding with the paradoxical assertion that these colonized soldiers wish to "live free or die," the film in a last image depicts a child writing the words "France Is Our Fatherland," linking enforced liberty to literacy in French.

La France est un empire, 1939.

Among the many French newsreels and longer documentaries made during World War II were titles such as *Réalisations coloniales françaises en Afrique* (French colonial accomplishments in Africa, 1942) and *Réalisations coloniales en Afrique Occidentale Française* (Colonial accomplishments in French West Africa, 1942). The collaborationist Vichy government created a division within its General Secretariat for Information and Propaganda specifically devoted to supporting colonialism.[46] France-Actualités Pathé-Gaumont distributed *Français, vous avez un empire* (French citizens, you have an empire, 1941), a montage of previously shot images from Africa and Indochina edited together by Georges Manue and screened in every movie theater in France as part of Vichy's Week of Overseas France.[47] Accompanied by a pamphlet of the same title, the film encouraged spectators in the metropole to develop an emotional and practical investment in the colonial enterprise. In a historical overview that like *La France est un empire* begins with the conquest of Algeria in 1830, the voice-over narration recounts the slow but sure building of the empire by explorers, soldiers, missionaries, businessmen, and colonists. France is once again presented as Africa's savior by virtue of medical treatment, education, and the construction of roads and railroads; Africans are again shown laboring while surveilled by a European man in a pith helmet. And on-screen text presents the differences in area and population between metropolitan France and the French empire—550,000 square kilometers as opposed to 5,500,000 and 40 million inhabitants as opposed to 110 million—as well as the increase over time in French imports of goods extracted from the colonies: 3,000,000 tons in 1913 versus 7,700,000 in 1936. Reinforcing the value of empire to metropolitan France, graphs of increases in hectares farmed and production of cotton, tea, coffee, bananas, sugar, rubber, and lumber overlay images of African and Indochinese men and women at work. A unity of metropole and colonies, the commentary concludes over a long close-up of Vichy head of state Marshal Philippe Pétain, will restore France's "pride and greatness."

Maurice Noël made three documentaries for the French army's film unit in the early years of the war, all of which rehearse these same themes while emphasizing the need to recruit both officers for the colonies and colonial troops for the armed forces. *Aux confins de l'empire, les solitaires de la grande forêt* (At the edges of the empire, the solitary troops of the great forest, 1941) asserts that French officers have brought "French law" and hygiene to Côte d'Ivoire, while showing Africans farming coffee and collecting sap from rubber trees. *Aux confins de l'empire, les grands nomades de l'armée* (The great nomads of the army, 1941) praises the young French officers leading colonial troops in Agadez, its voice-over narrator exclaiming, "What a marvelous life for a French man who is twenty to twenty-five years old!" And *La garde de l'empire, de l'Atlantique au Tchad* (Guarding the empire, from the Atlantic to Chad, 1941) calls spectators to promote the "greatness of France" by serving in West Africa, to protect and administer the territory.

Films produced by Charles de Gaulle's Free France government in exile were similar. Released by the French Office for Cinematographic News (OFIC), *Efforts français en Afrique* (French efforts in Africa, 1944) belies its title by featuring only the work of Africans, who log trees, sift for gold, and build roads. A spear fight was added as an ethnographic attraction. Like Griaule's Dakar–Djibouti expedition, such projects attracted the interest of prominent avant-garde artists, as evidenced by two collaborations between director François Villiers and photographer Germaine Krull, who spent the second half of the war in De Gaulle's headquarters in French Equatorial Africa. *Autour de Brazzaville* (Around Brazzaville, 1944) opens with a quote on screen: "The crime of the armistice was to have capitulated as if France did not have an empire." De Gaulle spoke these words on BBC radio in late August 1940, celebrating the commitment of first colonial Chad, then Cameroon, and ultimately all of AEF to an alliance with his forces, whereas the metropole had surrendered early and easily to Nazi Germany. Brazzaville became, in the words of the voice-over commentary, "a French capital," the only independent French soil on which De Gaulle could tread. Free and independent, of course, in this case meant free from German but not French occupation, independent for Europeans but not Africans.

A conventionally colonial filmic portrayal of AEF, *Autour de Brazzaville* puts forth a patriotic vision similar to that of *L'aide des colonies à la France* during World War I, one reliant on both African *tirailleurs* and African workers. Despite several admiring low-angle close-ups of soldiers, the bulk of the film is devoted to the benefits to France of African labor.[48] After introducing modern routes in sub-Saharan Africa—the roads, waterways, railways, and airways that are crucial to the war effort—the voice-over narration deems these to be both "the constant concern of administrators and colonists" and "a place of exertion and joy for the native." Footage of Africans building roads and bridges and loading goods onto boats gives way to images of Europeans eating in the restaurant car of a comfortable train on the Congo-Ocean Railroad; only a spectator identifying with the latter group could imagine any joy in the exertion of the former. Villiers's presentation of AEF as a wartime resource continues along familiar lines, cataloging materials to be extracted and exported. In Cameroon and Gabon, African workers harvest sap to produce rubber. In Gabon, enormous logs of mahogany are sawed into pieces, loaded onto trucks, and tied together to be floated downriver to factories in Port-Gentil, where they are processed into plywood. Chadian laborers pick cotton and pick and dry coffee beans. "One can live without coffee," acknowledges the commentary, "but coffee counts among the privations that the French have felt the most cruelly." In Congo, a group of forty men cuts paths through the jungle, carrying supplies as well as a French engineer who will spend months looking for gold for the Brazzaville Mining Service. And like countless travelogues and expedition films, *Autour de Brazzaville* also highlights spectacular waterfalls and French medical efforts in AEF, specifically Jamot's Ayos hospital and mobile sleeping sickness treatment units. Unlike earlier films, however, this one states explicitly that colonial medical aid assures healthy African laborers for French work sites.

Film historian Jean-Pierre Bertin-Maghit includes *Autour de Brazzaville* in his list of French wartime propaganda documentaries but leaves out a second film by Villiers and Krull, *L'amitié noire* (Black friendship, 1945).[49] Published release dates vary, but both films were screened in October 1945 at the month-long France Overseas Exhibition at the Grand Palais in Paris, an event that also featured tastings of coffee, tea, cocoa, and rum from the colonies.[50] Although the works are in many ways quite similar, *L'amitié noire* is notable for a voice-over commentary written and read by Jean Cocteau, a decade and a half after he raised money for Dakar–Djibouti. Cocteau opens the film by introducing the short-wave radio transmitter in De Gaulle's Brazzaville headquarters that connects the capital of "fighting France" to Paris and the rest of the world.[51] A wipe transition leads to a labeled map of AEF and a second to footage of African boys carrying a colonial administrator seated in a *tipoye* to his rural post. As the man is rowed down the river in a pirogue, Cocteau proclaims his ignorance of Gabon's landscape and fauna: "I don't know the name of this bird, but don't be surprised, since you are going to see and hear some of the least-known signs in the world." The African forest is not just mysterious, however. "At first glance," says Cocteau, "it resembles our innocent undergrowth," but "this is one of its tricks." "Made like a trap," he continues, "it remains immobile, attentive, ferocious."

Contrary to Griaule, then, Cocteau claimed no expertise about Africa and Africans. Content with stereotype and poetic speculation, he describes a man's gait as "primitive," then muses about "the depths of time," finding it difficult to believe that a market scene belongs to the present and not the past, "that these solemn women exist, that they live now in 1945." Cocteau describes artisans working iron and making pottery as "types," and a series of familiar scenes follows: Sara women with lip plates, a village of mud dwellings, men fishing from pirogues, women pounding grain and dying cloth. Speaking about several women in particular, his commentary spins tales that seem equal parts colonial condescension and surrealist fancy. The first, a weaver, "embodies the nobility of these profound races." In a section of narration that was excised from the CNC's restored version of the film, Cocteau calls a second, bare-breasted woman "the bronze Venus, who marries her victim, then kills him." A third woman is shown with a man who reaches to touch one of her breasts, then the other. Cocteau claims an unlikely ethnographic signification: "This simple caress means that the young girl accepts a husband."

In his voice-over, Cocteau repeatedly compares Africans to animals, plants, and characters from European mythology and art. Dancing women who shake their heads side to side are said to be like Scheherazade, Russian ballet dancers, and the furies of the Oresteia. As we watch another group of women dance, Cocteau gives himself over to mocking wordplay: "Do their sentimental asses come out of these straw skirts? [*Leurs cuculs de culs ont-ils leur origine dans ces tutus de faille?*]" To conclude the film, Cocteau tells spectators, whom he presumes to be non-African, that it is time to "tear ourselves away from these somber dreams and return to the land of men." Over abruptly introduced footage of men on horseback, the documentary's last words—also cut from the restored version—are suddenly propagandistic and not at all poetic: "For centuries, these great races massacred each other. Muslims and animists hated each other, destroyed each other. Since the arrival of the French, they have stopped hating each other. At the signal of General de Gaulle, they came together to undertake a long voyage and to defend France." It is startling, then, that film scholar Richard Barsam in the 1970s described *Amitié noire* as "a sensitive ethnographic film about Negroes."[52] More recently, expert on Germaine Krull's photographic work Kim Sichel has acknowledged the film's colonialist rhetoric but blamed it entirely on Cocteau, giving Krull credit for "beautiful imagery" that "honored native culture and industries."[53] For the most part, though, those interested in French and avant-garde cinema of the period have preferred simply to ignore *Amitié noire*, which Georges Sadoul left out of Cocteau's filmography just as he omitted Alfred Machin's hunting films.[54]

Before *Amitié noire* was strategically forgotten, it was screened in September 1952 at the Friends of Cinema ciné-club in Paris, programmed with Eli Lotar's celebrated *Aubervilliers* (1945) as a "social and scientific short film."[55] Lotar himself in the same year shot a documentary in central Africa, *Bois d'Afrique* (Wood from Africa, 1952), a film referenced even less frequently than *Amitié noire*. Lotar apprenticed with Germaine Krull in the 1920s, before working on Luis Buñuel's landmark documentary *Las Hurdes* (*Land Without Bread*, 1932).[56] The scrolling text that opens *Aubervilliers* announces that the film's goal is to "draw attention to the living conditions and hard labor of the inhabitants of 'insalubrious blocks' of big cities." But *Bois d'Afrique*, shot far from urban Europe, has no such concerns. "African peasants and workers," the film's voice-over commentary asserts, "assist the efforts of whites to improve their well-being and the economic development of their continent, . . . without having lost their primitive joy and their insouciance." Yet again, spectators see Black Africans building roads and bridges, then logging a forest. Footage of a laboratory in France where tropical wood is studied in order to increase profit margins is followed by images of a factory in Côte d'Ivoire. "The destiny of the forest has been mastered," concludes the narration, adding a final sentence as colonialist as it is poetic: "Fall, fall O trees of Africa; you have not completed your service."

Alfred Chaumel and Franfilmdis returned to screens during the war with *Sortilège exotique* (Exotic enchantment, 1942), a film that like *La France est un empire* is composed in five parts, one per region colonized by France. The last of these, titled *Continent noir* (Black continent), is made up of footage characterized as "documents" collected by Chaumel and his wife, Geneviève, and several desert scenes contributed by Jean d'Esme. Director, critic, and editor of *Cinéa* Jean Tedesco authored the commentary, which begins with the familiar cliché of "penetrating into the heart of Africa."[57] The film is less geographically specific than the expedition films of the 1920s and '30s; shots of herds of cattle and of Fulbé women pounding grain give way to images of the Logone River accompanied by contemplative orchestral music. "Life in the region is limited to fishing from pirogues," spectators are told, "on these vast expanses defined by a sad horizon in the total calm of faraway, infinite spaces." The voice-over narration contrasts this calm with footage of a spear combat in the court of a sultan with one hundred wives, after which *Continent noir* continues south beyond unidentified waterfalls to "a primitive region" where "the tom-tom of animist tribes proclaims the glory of fetishist gods." As the rhythm of the editing quickens, the narrator provides little concrete information about the images on screen. Despite the many political and cinematic differences that separated Chaumel from Villiers, it seems that the fundamental similarity of *Sortilège exotique* and *Amitié noire* was recognized in a joint screening of the films in a 1947 program titled "Songs and Dances of the Union Française."[58]

As Jean Rouch would aptly note fifteen years later, Chaumel's postwar effort was "outdated before it reached the screen."[59] Yet Henri Reynaud, organizing biweekly screenings at the Museum of Mankind after its reopening in October 1945, nonetheless hoped to show films by Poirier and Chaumel as well as those produced by the French army.[60] The SCA continued shooting in Africa after the war, and films such as *De Trêves à Abidjan* (From Trêves to Abidjan, 1946) combined military propaganda with ethnography. Amid scenes of military training maneuvers in West Africa, French pilots visit the market in Bamako. "In this picturesque region," voice-over narration announces, "everything is a pretext for dancing and singing." We then join the pilots to watch the Dogon masks. If equally outdated, hunting films were still popular after the war, as evidenced by, among many others, Albert Mahuzier's *Grandes chasses en A.O.F.* (Great hunts in AOF, 1947), *Regards sur l'Afrique noire* (Visions of Black Africa, 1947), and *À la poursuite des gorilles* (In pursuit of gorilles, 1952), the last of these shot during a thirty-five-thousand-kilometer expedition undertaken with his wife and nine children. Also past their time were Léon Poirier's hagiographic biopic *Brazza, ou l'épopée du Congo* (Brazza, or the Congo epic, 1939) and the very few feature fictions shot in AOF and AEF just before and soon after the war. In Jacques de Baroncelli's *L'homme du Niger* (The man of Niger, 1939), two military officers compete for a woman's love against the background of the construction of a dam on the Niger River. And Georges Régnier's *Paysans noirs* (Black peasants, 1948) tells the story of a heroic young French colonial administrator who frees

Senufo farmers from the Dyula who have been oppressing them—frees them, that is, to cultivate peanuts to sell to a French company that has just built an oil factory.

The vast majority of French films shot in sub-Saharan Africa between the war and independence were still documentaries, but the colonial documentary tradition now built on Griaule's blend of expedition and ethnographic filmmaking. In 1937, Louis Audouin-Dubreuil, codirector of the Citroën expedition that had produced *La croisière noire*, became president of the newly created French Explorers and Travelers Club. An early list of members is a who's who of French ethnography, including Marcel Griaule, Louis Liotard, Germaine Dieterlen, André Leroi-Gourhan, and, after World War II, Jean Rouch. The group, still in existence today (as a society instead of club), held its events at the illustrious Salle Pleyel, a three-thousand-seat concert hall named for the famous French piano manufacturing company. In addition to musical performances and film screenings, Parisians flocked to hear "fantastic narratives of astonishing explorers," as when, in the club's first year, "Paul-Émile Victor recounted the history of Eskimo seal hunting, . . . Bertrand Flornoy placed on the table, as a preamble to his presentation on the Amazon rainforest, a real miniature head, . . . [and] Commander Guyot and Marcel Griaule presented their Dakar-Djibouti mission."[61] The Liotard Group, made up of some of the club's younger explorers and travelers, was formed in 1945 under the leadership of Noël Ballif, who was studying at the Institute of Ethnology with Griaule, Leiris, and Leroi-Gourhan. A few years later, the French government created a Grand Prize for Exploration also named in honor of Liotard, who had been killed in Tibet in 1940.[62]

In the late 1940s, the Liotard Group sponsored two major expeditions: Ogooué–Congo in 1946–1947 and Hoggar–Congo–Niger in 1949. As head filmmaker, Ballif hired Jacques Dupont, the first director with academic training to appear in this history of French documentary in Africa. Allied as an adolescent with the extreme right-wing Action Française movement, Dupont spent much of the war in prison and then joined the first graduating class of the French Institute for Advanced Cinematographic Studies (IDHEC). In July 1946, he set off for AEF with Ballif, cameramen Edmond Sechan and Pierre Gaisseau, physical anthropologist Raoul Hartweg, a couple of archeologists, and a geologist. A team led by André Didier and accompanied by musicologist Gilbert Rouget developed new techniques for on-site recording of sound on disc. The French air force provided four planes to transport the personnel and equipment, and the Company for Cinematographic Applications (SDAC) contributed cameras, film, and blank discs, also promising to pay future laboratory costs.[63] After traveling 6,000 kilometers from Brazzaville, Congo, to Ouesso and through Gabon, the group returned with 650 records, 4,000 photographs, and 2,300 objects for the Museum of Mankind.[64] Dupont made two sets of films, adding voice-over commentary to footage that he shot with Sechan and Gaisseau and sound recorded by Didier and Rouget.

Following Griaule's example, Ballif publicized his expedition in seven articles for newspaper *Ce soir* (This evening) in February and March 1947, a series titled "Two Months with the Pygmies." In the introductory teaser, he stressed the youth of his team members and the range of their areas of specialization, explaining that their primary goal was to meet "those mysterious small men that very few white people have been able to approach."[65] After a piece about vehicle trouble and another detailing the expedition route, Ballif described his group's first contacts with the Babenzélé group of the Babinga, claiming to have told them, "When we will be in France, we will recount how the Babenzélé live."[66] The fourth of his articles is the only one to do so, however, with a focus on how the group uses nets to hunt.[67] The fifth began by relating how expedition members bought objects from the Babenzélé for the Museum of Mankind, then noted the forty measurements per individual Hartweg recorded on "anthropometric forms," adding photographs taken both from the front and in profile.[68] To this retrograde attention to physical type, Ballif in his last articles added familiar tales of buffalo and elephant hunts.[69] Less than a decade later, he rewrote and expanded the articles into a more scholarly book, *Les danseurs de Dieu* (Dancers of God).[70]

The illustrated weekly *Images du monde* (Images of the world) put the adventurers of the Ogooué–Congo mission on its cover with the teaser "a sensational reportage," and Dupont joined Ballif to promote the expedition in the popular press.[71] Doing so, Dupont constructed his persona as audacious *chasseur d'images* by minimizing the extensive assistance provided by various colonial administrators on site, information detailed in Ballif's subsequent book.[72] In an article for the journal of the French Federation of Ciné-clubs titled "L'Afrique vous parle," Dupont invoked the earlier Columbia Pictures hit while relaying the difficulty of convincing producers and distributors that a film shot in Africa could be a technical and commercial success. Explicitly situating his films in the documentary lineage traced here, Dupont later deemed Léon Poirier his "double, or rather . . . closest mentor," a precursor whose career path he had not just followed but imitated.[73] Like Poirier, he described Africa as an exciting haven for the European creative artist, a place to "live the African adventure to its fullest." The role of adventurer-director was a lifelong calling, Dupont affirmed, a desire always to "go further . . . work with fiercer and more attractive races, unknown faces and regions, unexplored continents." His ultimate goal, reminiscent of the reviews of early travelogues and interwar expedition films, was to transform spectators into colonizers by making them forget that they were seated in a theater. "They will gallop in the savanna," Dupont exulted; "They will have the souls of conquerors, of discoverers of new lands!"[74]

The best-known of Dupont's documentaries from the Ogouée–Congo mission, *Danses congolaises* (Congolese dances), *Au pays des Pygmées* (In the land of the Pygmies), and *Pirogues sur l'Ogooué* (Pirogues on the Ogooué) were all released in 1947, distributed by Ciné Sélection and Atlantic Film. Credits acknowledge support from a wide range of governmental agencies in France and in the colonies, including the Ministry of France Overseas, the French air force, the Civil and Military Authorities of AEF, the Museum of Mankind, and the National Conservatory of Arts and Trades. The shortest of the three films, *Danses congolaises* brings together the different regions traversed by the expedition; dancers are shot in close-up and from a variety of angles, some wearing masks, some headdresses. Moving seamlessly from one ethnic group to another, the voice-over narrator explains that "in all of Black Africa," where "dance rhythms and copies the great activities of men," dancing is both entertainment and sacred ceremony grounded in local myths and symbolism. When providing ethnographic information, the commentary relies on colonial stereotypes of warlike Africans, claiming for example that the Bateke, who in the past had been powerful fighters, now dance for hours, pounding the ground with their feet "to calm their rage."

Yet two of Dupont's films diverge in circumscribed but important ways from the exoticist and paternalistic model tracked in these pages. *Au pays des Pygmées* begins with a conventional commentary that introduces the "Babinga Negroes" as "the last representatives of a very ancient race, which has for the most part disappeared," then describes their physical attributes and social practices. As the film begins its ethnographic portrait, however, the first voice-over narrator is replaced by a second, who speaks from an African perspective in accented French. Over footage of village inhabitants conducting both daily and less frequent activities, the second narrator explains how hunting nets are woven and used, how meat and caterpillars are prepared and eaten, and how, when there is not enough food, the Babinga trade with ethnic groups that live outside of the forest. He introduces and translates a few Baka words and provides the names of some of the Babinga on screen: Mangazou, Njaoubé, and Mouniéka.

This second speaker was not Babinga; absent from the credits, he is elsewhere identified as Habib Benglia.[75] Benglia, born in Algeria to West African parents, is considered the first Black actor in France for his over two-decade long career on Parisian stages. The narration he performed for Dupont's film neither accepts nor completely rejects European superiority, commenting that "the Black man and the white man, it's like the father and the child. . . . The child doesn't know anything, but the father doesn't know everything." Watching footage of a hunt, we are told that "the white man laughed" when he heard the Babinga singing, wrongly believing that it would scare away the forest animals. And the voice-over explains why a Babinga elder refused the French commandant's order to cultivate grain; God told them to hunt, and they have done so for generations. At times, Benglia's commentary seems to be translating recordings of men speaking Baka, and the singing that accompanies a filmed hunt is authentic if not synchronous. Yet *Au pays des Pygmées* ultimately retreats to attractions and mastery. After a sensationally quick-cut night scene of singing, drumming, and dancing, the first narrator returns to conclude that "this has been the primitive life of the Pygmies, in the equatorial forest in the heart of Africa."

The introductory voice-over of *Pirogues sur l'Ogooué* commemorates Pierre Savorgnan de Brazza's first travels in the region. Spectators are told and shown on a map that France at the time held only a few posts on the coast; in 1876, Brazza left Lambaréné to travel up the Ogooué River as far as the Congo Basin, then "penetrate into the heart of the African continent." Forced to abandon his mission at the Boubara Waterfalls after the death of his companion François Rigail de Lastours, Brazza founded Franceville before turning back. Dupont and his colleagues start from Franceville and retrace Brazza's voyage in reverse, going down the river to Lambaréné in six pirogues rowed by 110 African oarsmen. Sechan and Dupont's footage was shot from the boat; the commentary narrates the sights and provides information about the food, music, and rivalries of ethnic groups that live along the river.

Like *Au pays des Pygmées*, *Pirogues sur l'Ogooué* experiments with voice and perspective. When the African crew changes at Boué, new head boatman Pierre Moignon introduces himself on the soundtrack. The voice-over narrator returns to present the rest of the boatmen, but their recorded voices are later heard discussing how best to cut up an elephant they have killed, a sequence that hints at Rouch's postsynchronized films of over a decade later. Stylized camera work accentuates the hard labor of the Africans who transport the crew that is studying, recording, and filming them. Dupont also for the first time drew back the documentary curtain to reveal what was happening behind the scenes. In a village where the expedition stops for the night, he filmed not only a performance of African songs and dances but also the French team member doing the sound recording, wearing headphones and adjusting knobs on his equipment.

As had Leiris but not Griaule, Dupont and Ballif subsequently made clear that their ethnographic documentaries were stage managed and sometimes outright staged. In pursuit of "local color," Dupont told the boatmen of *Pirogues sur l'Ogooué* to change out of their shorts and shirts and put on raffia loincloths. They reluctantly agreed to wear such outdated clothing, he admitted, only when he asked a colonial officer to insist on his behalf.[76] In a more elaborate instance, Dupont told Ballif that he needed to film "sensational evidence [*documents*] . . . an elephant or a gorilla." With no elephants in the area, an administrator in Brazzaville hired a Makéta gorilla hunter; expedition members gave him a gun, planning to join him once the weather improved. He returned first, however, with a dead gorilla. Dupont improvised, filming the carcass from every angle, then asked a Babinga man to hold the dead animal's hand. As recounted in his memoirs, he later "edited the footage together with unrelated images of a hunter shooting a gun."[77] The voice-over narration of *Au pays des Pygmées* fills in the gaps, telling a dramatic story about how the hunter lured the gorilla by imitating the cries of its young.

Dupont's first set of films gained recognition in colonial, ethnographic, and cinematographic contexts, both noncommercial and commercial. *Au pays des Pygmées* and *Pirogues sur l'Ogooué* premiered at a gala fundraiser for the French Red Cross held at the Salle Pleyel. *Au pays des Pygmées* won the Grand Prize at the 1947 International Congress on Ethnographic and Human Geography Films organized by André Leroi-Gourhan at the Museum of Mankind, and *Pirogues sur l'Ogooué* was judged the best documentary at the 1948 Cannes Film Festival. The journal of the Maritime and Colonial League reported that, in addition to a selection of SCA films, its cinema service had available to lend "the three famous documentaries shot by the Liotard group."[78] And when *Au pays des Pygmées* was included in the Festival of Documentary Film sponsored by *Science et vie* (Science and life) in 1950, the magazine reported that tickets sold out a week in advance, with audiences applauding after each screening. Footage from the films was recut into a US release titled *Congolaise* and later renamed *Wild Rapture*.[79]

In the wake of this success, Dupont returned to sub-Saharan Africa to work as assistant director on Régnier's *Paysans noirs*. He then undertook a second documentary voyage, the Liotard group's Hoggar–Congo–Niger expedition, modeled on those of Citroën, Renault, and Peugeot in the 1920s. In a jeep and two British ambulances brought from Paris to Algiers via Marseille, the team drove across the Sahara, through Nigeria and Chad, and into Cameroon. Dupont used the footage he shot to make five films, which range from five to twenty-five minutes long. Released in 1951, all five were produced by the SDAC, with several receiving additional funding from the territorial government of French Cameroon. Yves Baudrier's orchestral music compensates for a

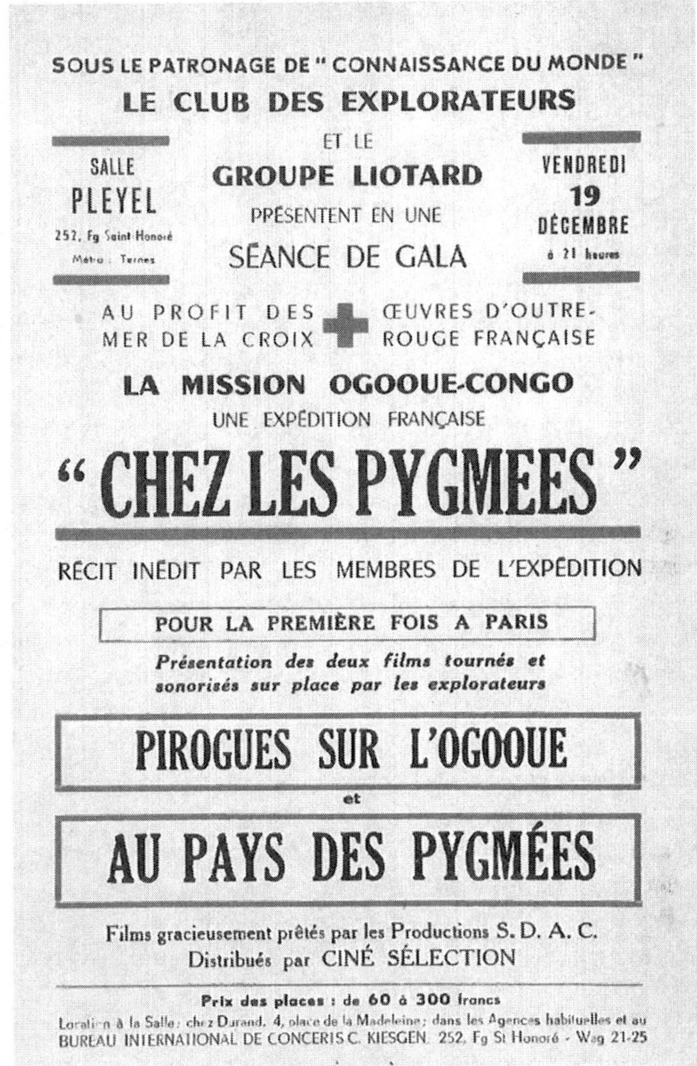

Jacques Dupont's films at the Salle Pleyel, 1947.

markedly diminished selection of recorded sound, setting a different tone from
the films in Dupont's earlier series.

La grande case (The great house), which announces as its subject "the ancient
political institutions of Cameroon," is the only of the films with pretensions to
ethnography. After a panning shot that comes to rest on the eponymous house
with a conical roof, voice-over narrator Louis Arbessier explains that each

Bamileke district has a chiefdom, "a large village in the center of which the great house is constructed." Although only village leaders and those who wear traditional masks are allowed to enter this sacred dwelling, Dupont's spectators are able to witness the assembly held inside. The commentary addresses totems, sculptures, ritual dancing, and the role of the village council, claiming to provide a comprehensive overview of Bamileke religion and society. After this relatively bland beginning, however, *La grande case* shifts course. A long scene of a palaver under a sacred tree centers on a discussion in Bamileke about who will become the next leader of the chiefdom. The narrator translates the words of men who stand to speak, filmed in low-angle shots, inflecting his voice to indicate the alternation of roles. The newly chosen leader is carried into the village for a celebration, and the voice-over characterizes this and other Bamileke traditions as unchanging across the centuries despite "the invasions, wars, exoduses, which have made Cameroon a mosaic of races." The film concludes with a sudden flashback to the distant past, reenacting the arrival of Muslim Fulani horsemen in central Cameroon and their war against local farmers who resisted them.

The rest of the films in Dupont's second set of documentaries are quite standard colonial propaganda. *Palmes* (Palm trees) and *Okoumé* purport to show how modernization brought by France has improved traditional African agriculture and forestry. *Palmes* begins with the lengthy process of manually extracting oil from the pulp and pit of coconuts, set in contrast to the "intensive and rational exploitation of African palm groves" being formulated by scientists in a French governmental research institute. African palm trees must be protected from Africans, the voice-over narrator contends; new European factories will produce a purer oil to the benefit of all consumers. *Okoumé* makes a similar argument about the exploitation of Gabonese forests, praising the modern factories built by the French to process tree trunks into lumber and plywood. Dupont reused images from *Au pays des Pygmées* to accompany the commentary's assertion that France's water and forest service had "civilized" both African workers and the African forest, "no longer the hell of fear and shadows described by the first explorers."

L'éveil d'un monde (The awakening of a world) and *Voilà nous!* (Here we are!) similarly take as their subject the French modernization of sub-Saharan Africa. Like so many earlier films, *L'éveil d'un monde* retraces the history of European colonization by filling in maps with the names of conquered regions and the faces of "explorers." The world to be awoken is an Africa described by voice-over commentary as inaccessible and "frozen in the past," its deserts, forests, and waterfalls inhospitable to "the pioneers who attempted its discovery and

conquest." Also like its antecedents, Dupont's film focuses on French colonizers who taught new trades and established schools as well as medical staff who
used "European science" to treat sleeping sickness, malaria, and leprosy. Ballif
later revealed that these last scenes were acted out by local residents and expedition members, with anthropologist Hartweg playing the role of a visiting
doctor.[80]

Commissioned by the Investment Fund for Economic and Social Development (FIDES), *L'éveil d'un monde* pays equal tribute to transportation
networks—airplanes, trucks, and bulldozers—that "liberate" the African
countryside. Echoing *Voyage au Congo*, the film's narrator maintains that
French roads have freed Africans from the work of forced porterage. Admit-
ting that "it was necessary to use forced labor to open and maintain these
roads," the voice-over never acknowledges that this paradox might vitiate
any argument for the beneficence of colonialism. Themes of successful exploitation and *mise en valeur* reappear from *Palmes* and *Okoumé*, along with
some of the same footage, as spectators are shown a sawmill in Cameroon,
a paper mill in Cote d'Ivoire, a peanut oil factory in Senegal, and palm oil
factories along the Atlantic coast. The commentary concludes, over images of
gas stations, apartment blocks, multistory buildings, and an African driving
a tractor, that the continent "has woken from its millennial slumber and . . .
is ready to master its destiny." The pith helmet on the tractor operator's head
accentuates the message that the destiny Africans are now ready to master
was fashioned by France.

Reprising the conclusion of *La France est un empire*, the last of the films begins with a close-up of an African boy at his school desk, writing with chalk on
a slate; a cut to the slate reveals the title, *Voilà nous!* As in *Au pays des Pygmées*,
the commentary consists of two alternating narrators, one French (Arbessier is
named in the credits) and one unidentified but seemingly African. Both speak
in the first-person plural; rather than converse or debate, they together build a
unified narrative of French-led African advancement. The African voice begins
the film by stating that Cameroon "has made rapid progress under French
mandate," expressing pride in "the evolution of our beautiful land." The French
voice provides details about this evolution, manifested by the appearance of
a class of Africans that has adopted not just European clothing but also "our
culture and customs." A Europeanized African family poses for a photographic
portrait, set against close-ups of African sculptures said to represent "primitive
life in hostile nature, populated by cruel gods." When the African narrator returns to tell a so-called legend in which the white man brought "the treasures
of paradise" to happy Africans, the French narrator promptly takes credit for

civilization and machines. A large outdoor Catholic mass led by a white priest is then accompanied by the claim that Africans trained by Europeans will build the future of Cameroon and indeed all of Africa. The last images of the film, shot in France, show the advanced stages of such training; African deputies visit Versailles, and African students walk through Saint-Germain-des-Prés.

Dupont's expedition documentaries are more skillfully shot and edited than their predecessors, and, despite their chauvinism, they are sometimes more innovative in their approach to ethnography and less objectionable in their portrayal of Africans. Dupont went on to direct feature fictions, his career coming to a high point with *Les distractions* (The distractions, 1960), starring Jean-Paul Belmondo. He then joined the extreme right-wing and terrorist Secret Armed Organization (OAS) to fight against Algerian independence and was arrested and sentenced in the Paris Plot of 1961. When Dupont was released from prison, nobody would hire him, and he has since been an uncomfortable figure in the history of French cinema, his nonfiction films never restored and rarely mentioned. Yet some light can be shed on Dupont's early work by contemporaneous director Jacques Becker's film *Rendez-vous de juillet* (July rendezvous), a commercial and critical success that won the Louis Delluc Prize for Best French Film of 1949. Becker staged the lives of a group of young, bohemian, postwar Parisians—an avid jazz trumpet player with a diploma from the IDHEC and several actors. Whether working, middle, or upper-middle class, all have parents who do not understand them. The film's central character, Lucien Bonnard, is studying at the Museum of Mankind and dreams of leading an ethnographic expedition to photograph and film Pygmies in Congo. Becker based Bonnard on Noël Ballif and asked him to play the role.[81]

Rendez-vous de juillet reflects France's postwar colonial enthusiasm for Africa in multiple ways. It is hard to imagine any other nation generating a film that combines youth culture and rebellion with ethnography. And it is simultaneously astonishing and completely predictable that in a film that tells the story of a passion for the "Black continent," a single Black person appears on screen, for just a few minutes, and never speaks—Duke Ellington Orchestra cornetist Rex Stewart in a cameo role as a visiting jazz musician from the United States. This absence of Black Africans is particularly glaring for a time when Black artists, musicians, and writers were making increasing contributions to Parisian intellectual life. In the 1930s, poet, philosopher, and future president of Senegal Léopold Sédar Senghor, together with poet, playwright, essayist, and future mayor of Fort-de-France Aimé Césaire and poet, essayist, and future Guyanese deputy Léon-Gontran Damas, laid the foundations of what is known as the Negritude movement. Alioune Diop's transformative journal

Présence Africaine was founded in 1947, a year before the release of *Rendez-vous de juillet*, yet it had seemingly little impact on the conception and reception of French films shot in Africa.

The 1947 Congress on Ethnological Film at which *Au pays des Pygmées* won the Grand Prize marked a new stage of professionalization for French ethnographic documentary. In the title of the essay with which I began this chapter, André Leroi-Gourhan posed a fundamental question: "Does the ethnological film exist?" His answer, after a review of three categories of film with ethnological aspects, was essentially "not yet."[82] Commercial travel and expedition films had for four decades presented scenes of African life, and film footage had been shot for research purposes for at least as long, but for Leroi-Gourhan, the true ethnological film would be equal parts research and crafted aesthetic product. The film director most often credited and celebrated for joining serious ethnographic study and *grand documentaire* is not Dupont but Jean Rouch, whose first film appeared the same year as both Dupont's first film series and Leroi-Gourhon's conference. Like Dupont, Rouch situated himself within the documentary genealogy I have outlined, claiming at various times that a Dogon leader called him "the son of Griaule" and that *Rendez-vous de juillet* was about him and not Ballif.[83]

Jean Rouch constitutes a hinge figure within this history of nonfiction films shot in sub-Saharan Africa. More than simply occupying a point of juncture, he overshadows our view of colonial-era French documentaries while haunting postcolonial African documentarists, as is evident in the second half of this book. By far the most prolific French ethnographic filmmaker, Rouch completed over one hundred films, which have been the subject of innumerable reviews and analyses. Many were released commercially and are now available for viewing both in theaters and at home in carefully restored and digitized versions. Éditions Montparnasse even distributes *Il était une fois Jean Rouch* (Once upon a time, Jean Rouch), a box set of documentary films *about* Rouch and his films. Equally revered in the domains of cultural anthropology and cinema studies, Rouch was a favorite of *Cahiers du cinéma* in the late 1950s and '60s and became one of the best-known French directors of the twentieth century. After his death in 2004, anthropologist Faye Ginsburg judged that Rouch had created "an entirely new kind of ethnographic and documentary film practice." In the same collection of tributes, film scholar Sam Di Iorio emphasized Rouch's influence on celebrated filmmakers of the French New Wave, noting that Jean-Luc Godard credited him with having saved French cinema like Joan of Arc had saved France.[84] There is too much excellent scholarship on Rouch to list here, and my purpose is not to contribute to that literature.[85]

Whereas others have focused on Rouch's ethnographic and cinematographic innovations—on how he was different and unprecedented—I wish instead to locate his work within a tradition.[86]

Rouch himself established in many essays and interviews a prehistory and history of ethnographic filmmaking, culminating with his work and that of his colleagues at the Museum of Mankind. He considered Félix Regnault's chronophotographs to mark the field's birth, just as Regnault had envisioned a museum of films that would constitute the birth of ethnology.[87] Regnault and the Lumière brothers just prior to the turn of the twentieth century were Rouch's "prophets," while in the 1920s Dziga Vertov, a pioneer of sociological cinema, and Flaherty, an ethnographer without professional training, were "precursors." Griaule was a "pioneer" in the early '30s for having shot "the first French ethnographic films," an accolade Rouch almost immediately retracted, deeming these works mere "laboratory experiments."[88] And although Rouch sometimes identified Dupont's *Au pays des Pygmées* as "Africa's first ethnographic film" thanks to the Ogooué–Congo expedition's on-site sound recordings, he never failed to note that his own simultaneous recording of image and magnetic sound in the 1950s constituted a significant improvement.[89]

Reacting to Ousmane Sembene's charge that Rouch had filmed Africans as if they were insects, American critic and journalist James Hoberman maintains that "Rouch, hardly so scientific, was more of an explorer."[90] Competent defense or not, the accuracy of Hoberman's assertion is evident in the start of Rouch's career in the early 1940s, just after the release of Griaule's documentaries and before Dupont enrolled at the IDHEC. A cinephile who frequented Henri Langlois's Cinémathèque Française, Rouch attended Marcel Griaule's seminars at the Museum of Mankind.[91] After completing a degree in civil engineering, he traveled to sub-Saharan Africa for the first time in 1942, sent by the French government to work in Niger. When Rouch arrived in Niamey, he later recounted, he could see only images from a film he had viewed as a child, not the African reality before his eyes. This was not just any film—"it was those views from *La croisière noire* that . . . welcomed me on this plateau of dusty laterite above the valley of the Niger River."[92] Rouch oversaw teams of African forced laborers that constructed and repaired roads, railways, and bridges, an experience that alienated him from other members of the colonial community.[93]

Inspired by what he had seen, Rouch began a correspondence with Griaule, who would later advise his doctoral thesis in anthropology. With Griaule's backing, Rouch was able to undertake an expedition to Niger in 1946 and 1947, accompanied by his friends and engineering colleagues Jean Sauvy and Pierre

Ponty. The trio was also supported by Ballif and Dupont, with whom they hitched a ride to Gao on an airplane provided for the Ogooué–Congo expedition. Rouch knew both men from the Caveau des Lorientais, the jazz club fictionalized in Jacques Becker's *Rendez-vous de juillet*; he often told the story of how Ballif had encouraged him to buy his first Bell and Howell camera at a Paris flea market and how Edmond Sechan, Dupont's cinematographer, had shown him how to use it during an unplanned stopover in Aguelhok on the way to Gao. Over the course of seven months, Rouch, Sauvy, and Ponty, along with their guides, porters, and a cook, followed the four thousand kilometers of the Niger River to its source, an accomplishment for which Rouch received the Liotard Prize for Exploration from the French Explorers and Travelers Club.

Unlike Dupont, Rouch had no training in filmmaking, and most of his footage from the trip was unusable. Yet he and his colleagues had made a stop in Ayorou, a village where he had been posted during the war, and received authorization from colonial officials to return to film a group of fishermen performing a hippopotamus hunt with harpoons.[94] Back in Paris, Rouch screened this footage for an august group of spectators that included Griaule, Michel Leiris, and Claude Lévi-Strauss. Working with Ponty and Sauvy, he completed *Chasse à l'hippopotame* (Hippopotamus hunt, 1947), which was shown at the Museum of Mankind.[95] Rouch's earliest extant film, it joined a long list of French documentary films about hippopotamus hunts in Africa. Later the same year, Actualités Françaises edited some of the footage into the shorter *Au pays des mages noirs* (In the land of the black sorcerers, 1947). This title, which Rouch later called "abominable," advertised ethnography as even more of an attraction than the hunting of exotic animals.[96] Opening text on screen attributes the poor quality of Rouch's images to his bravery, asserting that "the *chasseur d'images* who managed to film the public and secret lives of a village in Niger, in the center of Black Africa, had to take the most extreme precautions to record gripping scenes of the dance of possession." In between opening and closing clichés about a land "frozen in the original purity of a kind of prehistory," the film's incessant voice-over commentary narrates everyday life in the village—artisans working, women pounding millet, men going out to fish—as well as the hunt and the dance. Blown up from 16 mm to 35mm, *Au pays des mages noirs* was programmed widely in theaters, paired with Italian neorealist Roberto Rossellini's *Stromboli*.

Jean Rouch's first two documentaries were also screened at the Salle Pleyel in 1948 in the context of a seminar on the Upper Niger River. *Ciné-Miroir* reported on the event, the journalist noting that cineaste Becker, very interested in the hippopotamus hunt, was seated two rows ahead of him.[97] Like Griaule and Dupont, Rouch was eager to gain attention in the media and traveled to present the narrative and films of his "sensational expedition" in Rennes, Le Mans, and Nantes. The journal of the Maritime and Colonial League described his lecture as "brilliant" and stressed Rouch's heritage as an adventurer, introducing him as the son of Commandant Jules Rouch, a naval officer who had assisted Jean-Baptiste Charcot during his 1904–1907 expedition to the Antarctic.[98] Rouch spent several years of his childhood in Morocco thanks to his father's career, and he grew into his pedigree, sharing themes, passions, production companies, and screening venues with Poirier, Griaule, and Dupont. This sense of lineage is reinforced by his claim that the first film he ever saw, at the age of five, was Flaherty's *Nanook of the North*.[99] As late as 1961, Rouch considered *La croisière noire* to be "an exemplary film about Black Africa" that shows "the most representative aspects of the populations encountered during this voyage."[100]

Thanks to the success of *Au pays des mages noirs*, Rouch embarked on another expedition, shooting in color for the first time. In Niger, he traveled with Damouré Zika, a wartime acquaintance, and Ibrahim Dia, known as Lam—both became longtime collaborators. The short *La circoncision* (Circumcision, 1949) follows a group of Hombori boys undergoing circumcision rituals, while the longer *Les magiciens de Wanzerbé* (Magicians of Wanzerbé, 1949) and *Initiation à la danse des possédés* (Initiation into possession dance, 1949) feature the dances of spirit possession that fascinated Rouch throughout his career. The text rolling over a map of Africa that begins *Les magiciens de Wanzerbé* asserts the film's documentary nature, comparing Rouch's camera to a note-taking pencil: "The observer was content to film scenes of everyday life in a village of black sorcerers without instigating any of these scenes and without even attempting the slightest special effect." Rouch's voice-over then introduces the flora, fauna, and geography of the region. If the scenes of habits and customs and smiling portrait shots that follow recall much earlier travelogues, their level of ethnographic detail goes far beyond that of even Griaule's and Dupont's films, particularly with respect to the work of the sorcerers who initiate boys, prepare magic charms, read cowry shells, and dance themselves into a state of ecstasy.

In 1950, Rouch went back to Niger, this time in the company of linguist Roger Rosfelder and with funding from the National Center for Scientific Research (CNRS) and CNC, as well as additional support from the French Institute of Black Africa (IFAN) in Dakar. In *Cimetières dans la falaise* (Cemeteries on the cliff, 1951), his first sound film, Rouch narrates over the singing and music of funeral ceremonies, revealing the significance of the habits and customs shown on screen. *Yenendi, les hommes qui font la pluie* (Yenendi, the rainmakers, 1952) similarly begins with Rouch's voice-over commentary, which announces a drought that will be resolved by possession dances. Spectators hear African voices on the soundtrack, but it is Rouch who transmits meaning and eventually brings closure to the film, declaring after images of approaching storms that "the sky gods" have kept their promise. Shot during the same expedition, *Bataille sur le grand fleuve* (Battle on the great river, 1952) returns to hippopotamus hunts and dances of spirit possession. In his authoritative commentary, Rouch again explains, step by step, the details of both. When a woman is shown to be possessed by the spirit of the water, he narrates the spirit's words, and in a subsequent possession scene, Rouch translates from the "secret language" of the Hauka to speak for other spirits.

Rouch had returned to Ayorou, the site of his first hippopotamus hunt with Sorko fishermen, to make *Bataille sur le grand fleuve*. He described the film almost three decades later as a kind of remake not of the original, ethnographically focused *Chasse à l'hippopotame* shown at the Museum of Mankind but of the Actualités Françaises version screened in commercial theaters.[101] Rouch's assertion is less surprising when we consider his early writings, in which he used the persona of the image hunter in Africa to appeal to a wide audience. Agence France-Presse paid Rouch, Sauvy, and Ponty to report their journey in dramatic fashion; they published articles under the portmanteau name Jean Pierjant, and additional pieces authored by Rouch alone appeared in newspaper *Le franc-tireur* (The maverick) in 1951.[102] He began the first of these with an invocation of Scottish adventurer Mungo Park's 1796 arrival at the Niger River, noting that exactly 150 years later, he had embarked on the same voyage. Journalist Catherine Valogne introduced Rouch to readers of *Ce soir* as a more scholarly version of the *chasseur d'images*—"a boy of about thirty-five years old, tanned, with dreamy blue eyes and a bounce in his step"—in a piece tellingly titled "A Cinema Without Special Effects and Without Artifice: Films About Lived Travel and Adventures." Valogne explained that, after three expeditions to West Africa, Rouch hoped for more screenings of his films at theaters for the general public. Travel films shot without camera tricks, he told her, are "of interest to everyone when the voice-over commentary explains the why and the how of what is happening on screen."[103]

Despite Rouch's university training and support from research institutions, his films from the start did appeal to nonacademic audiences, if not always the masses. Experimental filmmaker Dimitri Kirsanoff provided editing advice for *Chasse à l'hippopotame*, and *Initiation à la danse des possédés* reconnected Rouch to the world of the artistic avant-garde. Selected for Jean Cocteau's Festival of

Cursed Films in Biarritz before Rouch had even completed the soundtrack, it won the Prize for Best 16mm Film after Rouch performed a live voice-over commentary. Cocteau was joined on the jury by luminaries Henri Langlois, Jacques Doniol-Valcroze, and André Bazin, and François Truffaut, Jean-Luc Godard, and Jacques Rivette attended the screening—a decade before becoming the faces of the New Wave.[104] It was at this festival, moreover, that Pierre Braunberger, who two decades prior had produced Allégret's *Voyage au Congo*, approached Rouch and offered to produce his future films.

If Griaule was a Paris-trained ethnographer who learned filmmaking in Africa and Dupont a Paris-trained filmmaker who learned ethnography in Africa, Rouch learned ethnography, filmmaking, and Africa at the same time. Although he pursued recognition in Parisian film circles, he never abandoned academic ethnography, and in 1952, he and Leroi-Gourhan cofounded the Committee for Ethnographic Film (CFE) at the Museum of Mankind. Both professional association and home base where prospective ethnographic filmmakers could seek sponsorship for expeditions, the CFE offered editing equipment and a film catalog while sponsoring screenings that, at the height of the ciné-club era, attracted specialist and nonspecialist audiences. Its list of founding members includes Griaule, in memoriam; Lévi-Strauss; Rivière, who had moved to the Museum of Popular Arts and Traditions; Langlois from the Cinémathèque Française; Jacques Chausserie-Laprée from the CNC; and directors Marc Allégret and Alain Resnais.[105]

Most films shot in sub-Saharan Africa by CFE-sponsored directors were never destined for commercial theaters, yet in content and style, the work of Serge Ricci, Guy Le Moal, Georges Bourdelon, Igor de Garine, Marc Piault, and others differs little from the expedition films of prior decades.[106] Ricci's 1953 *Noces d'eau* (Water wedding), for example, opens with a map of Africa, then cuts to a more detailed map of central Mali and western Upper Volta. Voice-over commentary describes the life of the Bobo people over images of men weaving nets and fishing and women gathering and smoking fish to sell at market. The customs, songs, and dances of Africans on screen are described and interpreted by a self-assured, authoritative filmmaker-ethnographer. "I had not come to this land to live like Black people," Rouch wrote in *Le franc-tireur*, "but to be the impartial witness to their lives."[107]

Such films continued to be produced during the decade preceding the independence of France's sub-Saharan African colonies, while the Laval Decree prevented Africans from shooting their own films in these spaces. A few important exceptions nonetheless trouble the travelogue to expedition to ethnography tradition I have elaborated thus far, each diverging in its own way.

Never prevalent or similar enough to cohere into a countertradition, as a group they illuminate the rules they were breaking. We know almost nothing about the first, a unique short titled *Rythme noir* (Black rhythm, 1938) that provides the slightest of hints of a road not taken.[108] A single, introductory intertitle identifies the location of shooting and the people filmed: "Sound cinema has recorded for the first time the songs and dances of the Ndézé tribes in the heart of central Africa." There is no voice-over commentary to provide explanatory information or speak for the Africans on screen. Instead, background music and crowd sounds accompany shots of a large outdoor market, men holding spears, and women clapping. Men stand in a circle, singing and drumming, and the musical soundtrack matches their moving lips and hands.

The first avowedly anticolonial French documentary film shot in Africa appeared only after World War II. At the age of twenty-one, just a year after receiving his diploma from the IDHEC, René Vautier was commissioned by the nonprofit Ligue de l'Enseignement (Educational League) to shoot a film for schoolchildren showing the lives of West African villagers. Vautier was to accompany an expedition team that included an ethnographer, a doctor, a teacher, a photographer, and two university students, he recalled, and "bring back images of African reality."[109] Traveling through the region in 1949 and 1950 in a truck provided by the governor of French Sudan, Vautier was appalled by what he saw and decided to subvert the project. He worked with leaders of the African Democratic Assembly (RDA) party to shoot in secret, without the required authorization and surveillance. As a result, his negatives were confiscated, and he was sentenced to a year in prison. Vautier recounted in his memoirs that, informed of these consequences, Rouch protested with surprise that he himself had never had any trouble filming in Africa. "Perhaps the representatives of French authority in Africa think your films go along with the colonialism they are charged with maintaining," Vautier caustically replied.[110]

Vautier succeeded in smuggling a third of his footage out of West Africa, and these reels became *Afrique 50* (1950), a film banned by the French government for almost fifty years. The documentary's strong voice-over commentary is radically different from those of Griaule, Dupont, and Rouch, all of whom ignored colonial exploitation to focus on the illustration and explication of traditional practices. Vautier's narration points directly to such abuse; he speaks with emotion, using the second person singular and informal *tu* to interpolate the spectator. Introducing a group of children on screen, Vautier suggests that we follow them. "You will see some very picturesque things, without a doubt," he notes, "but little by little you will realize that this picturesqueness cannot hide extreme poverty." These instructions inflect viewers' understanding of sights familiar from previous films: men making bricks, women braiding hair and washing clothes, fishermen repairing their nets and boats, and children playing and swimming in the Niger River. Vautier was judged and condemned, Paulin Soumanou Vieyra wrote just over a decade later, "for having seen something other than elephants and crocodiles in Africa."[111] But it was less what he saw than how he showed it on screen that made the difference.

Rejecting his original commission, Vautier made the revolutionary decision to turn both filmically and politically away from ethnography. The music on the soundtrack of *Afrique 50* was recorded not by academic researchers but by West African musician Fodéba Keita. And Vautier's commentary contradicts decades of colonial-era vaunting of French accomplishments in education and health care for Africans. Noting that his spectator will not see schools and doctors, Vautier declares that "in Africa, schools are opened when the big colonial companies need accountants. A doctor is sent when the big colonial companies are at risk of not having enough workers." Over footage of a village in northern Côte d'Ivoire that was destroyed by French troops for not having paid its taxes in full, his voice rises in anger, recounting the men, women, and children killed, "assassinated in our name, people of France." "Colonization," he concludes, "here as everywhere, is the reign of the vultures." Vautier was the first French documentarist, indeed the first French filmmaker, to deem the back-breaking work of colonized Africans not just profitable but unjust. Watching Africans build a road, spectators learn that their labor is cheaper than the steamrollers used in Europe, and watching Africans push a boat stuck in sand, that their labor is cheaper than fuel for a tugboat. Although forced labor had been illegal since 1946, Vautier explains, Africans worked for colonial companies for only fifty francs a day in order to pay the taxes imposed on them by the French colonial government.

The same year that Vautier completed his illicit, activist documentary, young filmmakers Chris Marker and Alain Resnais were commissioned by *Présence Africaine* to make a film about Negro art, an invitation issued by editorial board member and ethnographer George Balandier.[112] *Les statues meurent aussi* (Statues also die, 1953), which like *Afrique 50* would be banned in France, was filmed not in Africa but in anthropological museums in England, Belgium, and France, including Paris's Museum of Mankind. Highlighting artifacts to challenge their placement, Marker and Resnais questioned why African art objects were in the Museum of Mankind instead of the Louvre—and why they were trapped in European museums at all, deprived of the use value that would give them life.

Les statues meurent aussi is made up of two types of footage, some shot for the documentary and the rest reused from previously released films. None of this recycled footage is identified in the credits, but it is just as important as the images of statues. While no official justification was provided for the French government's decision to ban Marker's and Resnais's film, approval was granted several years later for distribution of a shortened version. Removed were images of colonial administrators and French politicians traveling in sub-Saharan Africa, including a young François Mitterand, and footage from Actualités Françaises newsreels *Le Président Auriol au Niger et en Guinée* (President Auriol in Niger and Guinea, 1947) and *Village moderne à Dakar* (Modern village in Dakar, 1950).[113] Censors were untroubled by clips taken from Castelnau's *En Chaland sur le moyen Niger*, Chaumel's *Sortilège exotique*, Villiers's *L'amitié noire* and *Autour de Brazzaville*, and Dupont's *Au pays des Pygmées* and *Pirogues sur l'Ogooué*—these last likely obtained by Dupont's cameraman Edmond Sechan, who collaborated with Marker and Resnais on the film. *Les statues meurent aussi* never questions the perspective of this borrowed footage, and Resnais described it afterwards as merely illustrative, "a bit of African reality, real documents taken either from newsreels or from short films shot in Africa."[114]

Marker's and Resnais's documentary quickly achieved iconic status in French film circles. After the minister of the interior requested it not be accepted at the Cannes Film Festival, it was screened in secret and awarded the 1954 Jean Vigo Prize. In the same year, *Cahiers du cinéma* described *Les statues meurent aussi* as an ethnographic film.[115] Senegalese director Sembene later remarked that it was not typical of French ethnographic filmmaking of the time, also noting that Resnais and Marker "only dealt with statues and masks."[116] Not only did the filmmakers not travel to Africa, but no Africans appear in their film. Resnais acknowledged a decade and a half after the film's completion that he and Marker had known nothing about the African art their film was commissioned to address. And with the government ban having only just been lifted, he reminded potential African audiences that the film had been made in 1953 and not 1969; "the simplifications," he pointed out, "for '69, would be too coarse."[117] An African had finally spoken on French screens in Marker's postindependence *Joli mai* (The lovely month of May, 1963), which features an extended interview with a Dahomeyan student in Paris.

By the late 1950s, a decade after the founding of *Présence Africaine*, the fight for African political and cultural independence was fully engaged. Marker, Resnais, and Rouch had become fellow travelers, if in a sometimes ambiguous and always less direct fashion than Vautier. Rouch recounted that African students at the IDHEC in 1955 asked Griaule, a regular contributor to Alioune Diop's journal, to request that the Ministry of France Overseas repeal the Laval

Image from François Villiers, *Amitié noire*, 1945, as used in Alain Resnais and Chris Marker, *Les statues meurent aussi*, 1953.

Image from Jacques Dupont, *Pirogues sur l'Ogooué*, 1947, as used in Alain Resnais and Chris Marker, *Les statues meurent aussi*, 1953.

Decree.[118] Rouch's story is uncorroborated, and there is no evidence that Griaule, almost certainly the "metaphysical and Dogonish ethnographer" enemy targeted by Aimé Césaire in *Discourse on Colonialism* the same year, ever did.[119] The 1956 International Congress of Black Writers and Artists in Paris, sponsored by *Présence Africaine* and attended by Césaire, Léopold Sédar Senghor, Frantz Fanon, James Baldwin, and Richard Wright, among many others, is unmistakable evidence of the demand for such action.

Most scholarly accounts of Rouch's work, like the major multi-DVD editions of his films that have been released in Europe and North America, begin with the last years of the colonial era.[120] *Les maîtres fous* (*The Mad Masters*, 1956), a turning point in his career, grew out of his second hippopotamus hunt film. Hauka priests who saw *Bataille sur le grand fleuve* in Accra, Rouch remembered, asked him to film one of their possession ceremonies in Kumasi, Gold Coast (now Ghana).[121] The resulting documentary was a critical success, winning a prize for ethnographic filmmaking at the Venice Biennale, and at the same time extraordinarily controversial, particularly for a scene in which the Hauka kill and eat a dog. André Bazin described it as "a document of rare quality" filmed with "an extraordinary realism," finding Rouch's voice-over to be "vibrantly objective, simple, useful."[122] Yet Rouch reported that both his mentor Marcel Griaule and young West African filmmaker Paulin Soumanou Vieyra were furious after a screening at the Museum of Mankind. "For once," Vieyra said to Rouch, "I agree with Professor Griaule; this film is a scandal."[123]

Beyond the question of the documentary truth of *Les maîtres fous*, and beyond the debate about whether this truth should be put on screen, by whom, and how, the film marked Rouch's first effort to establish a dialogue with his African subjects, bringing them into his filmmaking process. The next attempt again arose from *Bataille sur le grand fleuve*; in early 1954, Rouch returned to Ayorou and screened the finished film for its participants.[124] One spectator recommended that Rouch make another hunting film, and *Chasse au lion à l'arc* (*The Lion Hunters*) appeared in 1965, winning the Golden Lion for Best Film in Venice. Such screenings were a vital aspect of a practice Rouch came to call "shared anthropology," the acquisition of knowledge via "an endless quest where ethnographers and those whom they study meet."[125] Unlike the directors of earlier travel, expedition, and ethnographic films—even his own—Rouch began to include the names of African participants in the credits of his films. Damouré and Lam went from serving as guides and porters to starring as actors who also contributed, in their own French, to the films' voice-overs.

Rouch's shift toward an experimental cinematic practice diverged from what is still the conventional understanding of ethnographic film, in which, per Karl

Heider, "film is the tool and ethnography the goal."[126] And although Rouch never stopped making conventional ethnographic documentaries, those of his films he called "ciné-fictions" weakened the definitional claims of colonial documentary, leading scholars and critics to identify them as the point of transition from colonial French to postcolonial African cinema.[127] Rouch is often credited not just with reinventing documentary but with founding African filmmaking. He tended to accept this credit, and he thanked his touchstone documentarist Flaherty for having modeled the success of "dramatized documentary [*la mise en scène du documentaire*]."[128] Changing his anthropological focus from hunting and possession rites to migration, Rouch spent extended periods of time in Gold Coast, Ivory Coast, Togo, and Upper Volta (now Burkina Faso). *Jaguar*, filmed at the same time as *Les maîtres fous*, was his first feature-length work as well as his first film to use fiction to convey a fuller picture of reality. Rouch staged a crossing from Niger to Gold Coast, for example, after asking the permission of border guards. When not being filmed walking, his subjects, now characters, rode in a Land Rover with Rouch and his wife, Jane. This footage was shot silent, and the narration improvised later, while watching it.[129] Aside from a very few moments in Dupont's films, these were the first African voices heard in a French documentary shot in Africa. But decades later, Rouch noticed a difference of opinion about *Jaguar* between his French and African spectators, just as with *Les maîtres fous*. He did not understand why *Jaguar*, his favorite among his films, "annoys my African friends so much, but enchanted Sadoul, Langlois, or Rossellini."[130]

Rouch went on to train many of his African collaborators to be filmmakers themselves and established the first film production facilities in sub-Saharan Africa. He continued to narrate his films, but his voice became more speculative, with African voices joining in to tell at least part of the story. This was not always the case, however; anthropologist Mick Eaton notes that as late as *Les funérailles à Bongo: le vieil Anai* (Funerary rites for Old Anai, 1972/1979), filmed with colleague Germaine Dieterlen, Rouch in his voice-over commentary speaks the words of all of the participants in a Dogon funeral rite.[131] Practitioners and scholars of ethnographic filmmaking Jean-Paul Colleyn and Paul Henley observe that a truly shared anthropology, in the sense of collective, equal authorship, was not possible given inequalities that persisted after the end of French colonial rule.[132] The most paradoxical aspect of Rouch's shared anthropology and ciné-fiction may be that these strategies also served to provide him the status of auteur, detracting from the participation of his ethnographic subjects by acclaiming him for having enabled it.

Jean-Luc Godard reviewed Rouch's *Moi, un noir* (I, a Black man, 1958) just a year before his own breakthrough film *À bout de souffle* (Breathless, 1960) became a critical and commercial hit. Like *Jaguar, Moi, un noir* features an improvised voice-over narration recorded by the actors after editing was complete. Godard stressed the influence of *Moi, un noir* on the French New Wave, declaring that "all great fiction films tend toward documentary, just as all great documentaries tend toward fiction." For the title of his review, like Jacques Dupont he reached back to invoke *L'Afrique vous parle*, linking Rouch's accomplishments to the exploitative American adventure documentary that had sparked French interest with its sound.[133] Godard and theorist Gilles Deleuze after him quite astonishingly extolled Rouch's innovative filmmaking techniques for having transformed the director himself into the *I* of the film's title. Rouch, in their reading, is the true Black man, not the character of Edward G. Robinson played by Nigerien Oumarou Ganda.[134] Ganda, who disavowed his work with Rouch once he became a filmmaker himself, had a very different opinion. "Every time I make a film," he is said to have proclaimed during an appearance at the Algiers Cinematheque, "I kill Jean Rouch."[135] We find once again a disconnect between French praise and African criticism of Rouch's shared anthropology, one that French literary and film scholar Marie-Claire Ropars-Wuilleumier understood as a consequence of Rouch having chosen to documentarize fiction rather than fictionalize documentary. African critics discerned in *Moi, un noir* a misleading representation of reality, she argued, "that was all the more dangerous for having the appearance of authenticity."[136]

Less famous than Jean Rouch both then and now, French filmmaker Jean-Luc Magneron in the year before Mauritanian independence made a film that manifests both the desire to innovate and the limitations of French documentary shot in late colonial sub-Saharan Africa. Produced by renowned studio Le Film d'art, *Seigneurs de l'horizon* (Lords of the horizon, 1959) uses a divided voice-over to make room for an African viewpoint, while also putting its director on screen with his subjects. Magneron filmed and was filmed while living with a group of nomads in the Tagant Plateau region. His narration and that attributed to the leader of this group reflect on local customs as well as on the filmmaking habits of traveling Europeans. It becomes evident, however, that Magneron authored both strands of commentary, relying on ethnographic knowledge acquired during his stay and his own critique of filmmakers like himself. Magneron's remark that his counterpart has "a mug made for close-ups" brings the retort that "he comes to shoot images . . . that he will sell in his country." And his African interlocutor argues that Europeans misunderstand his people's actions, such as the enslavement of Black women and the use of a medical pomade to style hair. By the end of the film, Magneron is frustrated: "I'm trying to understand your customs. . . . I know that for you, I'm always the foreigner, the tourist." Still showing images of everyday life, he begins to issue warnings. Children should be sent to the colonial school, Magneron states, since "your country's future depends on it." Traditional Mauritania will soon disappear, he continues, bringing back the salvage anthropology argument of the early *chasseurs d'images*, and "you will have to renounce nomadism to stay put and build your country." The ambiguity of Magneron's position is reflected in his advice that Africans should adapt to a French version of modernity without losing their personality, abandoning certain traditions while keeping their generosity and sense of solidarity.

I began this chapter with Pierre Leprohon's 1946 praise for the "ethnographic value" of exoticist films from the 1920s and '30s. In 1960, the year of independence for many of France's sub-Saharan African colonies, Leprohon published a second book addressing colonial documentaries shot in Africa. For this book's title, he chose Alfred Machin's preferred term for his profession. "The *chasseur d'images* is a reporter, a curious man, an ethnographer, a sociologist, an explorer, an athlete, a dreamer, a philosopher, or a poet," Leprohon began, promising to introduce readers to models of each.[137] Although a paragraph was devoted to Lumière, Pathé, and Gaumont, and a few pages to Flaherty, Poirier, and Ginet, Leprohon was now more interested in Dupont and Rouch, the latter discussed at length in a chapter called "The Ethnographer with a Camera." In the 1940s and '50s, as we have seen, Dupont and Rouch introduced noteworthy innovations to a documentary tradition that began in 1906. These were praised at the time and have been widely recognized since. Given this sweeping acclaim in a range of venues, it is striking how well their work nonetheless perpetuates crucial aspects of the tradition, a continuity recognized by Vieyra, Sembene, and Ganda. With Vautier's *Afrique 50* the sole anticolonial French film shot in sub-Saharan Africa before independence, a sustained documentary rejection of colonial political and filmic domination would arrive only with the first independent African filmmakers.

Notes

1. Laubriet, "L'outre-mer vu par le cinéma," 13.

2. Leprohon, *L'exotisme et le cinéma*, 218.

3. André Leroi-Gourhan, "Cinéma et sciences humaines: Le film ethnologique existe-t-il?," *Revue de géographie humaine et d'ethnologie*, no. 3 (July–September 1948): 50.

4. Karl G. Heider, *Ethnographic Film*, rev. ed. (University of Texas Press, 2006 [1976]), 1–4, 50–109; Henley, *Beyond Observation*, 15–18.

5. Bazin, "Le cinéma et l'exploration," 27.

6. Originally published in 1981, a revised version is included in Clifford, *Predicament of Culture*, 117–51.

7. Alice Conklin, *In the Museum of Man: Race, Anthropology, and Empire in France, 1850–1950* (Cornell University Press, 2013), 1–35. On the roles of explorers, ethnography, and museums in the construction of a French "Africanism" from the 1870s through the 1920s, see Emmanuelle Sibeud, *Une science impériale pour l'Afrique?* (Éditions de l'EHESS, 2002). Recent archival work by Alice Gallois, Eric Jolly, and Damien Mottier allows an inside look at the development of a discipline of ethnographic filmmaking in France in the 1930s and '40s and challenges myths forged by early practitioners.

8. Alice Gallois, "Le cinéma au Musée de l'homme: La construction d'un patrimoine, l'invention d'une culture? Première partie: 1937–1960," *Journal des anthropologues*, nos. 134–35 (2013): 376, 380.

9. Claude Lévi-Strauss, *Tristes tropiques* (PLON Pocket, 1961 [1955]), 9–10. John Russell's 1961 translation into English turns *explorateurs* into "travelers," erasing important resonances.

10. Georges-Henri Rivière, "Toute la vie de la forêt évoquée par ses bruits et ses images: 'L'Afrique vous parle,'" *Pour vous*, no. 124, April 2, 1931, 8–9.

11. "Le Prix Gringoire récompense cette année un jeune explorateur: M. Marcel Griaule," *Le petit journal*, February 12, 1935, 5.

12. For a detailed overview of Griaule's film work, see Eric Jolly, "Les missions Griaule et le cinéma ethnographique," in *À la naissance de l'ethnologie française: Les missions ethnographique en Afrique subsaharienne (1928–1939)*, 2016, http:// naissanceethnologie.fr/files/pdf/43.pdf.

13. Clifford, *Predicament of Culture*, 55.

14. "A l'Elysée," *Le journal*, March 4, 1931, 2; Jolly, "Les missions Griaule et le cinéma ethnographique," 3–4.

15. P.-E. Flandin, Gaston Doumergue, and M. Roustan, "Mission ethnographique et linguistique Dakar-Djibouti," *Journal de la Société des Africanistes* 1, no. 2 (1931): 300–303.

16. Georges Mouly, "La mission Dakar-Djibouti sous la direction de son chef M. Marcel Griaule s'embarquera le 13 mai pour l'Afrique," *Comoedia*, April 30, 1931, 6.

17. Musée d'ethnographie et mission scientifique Dakar-Djibouti, *Instructions sommaires pour les collecteurs d'objets ethnographiques* (Musée de l'homme, 1931), 6–7.

18. Jean Pédron, "Le Musée du Trocadéro s'enrichit," *Le journal*, September 20, 1931, 1.

19. J. P., "L'exposition de la mission Dakar-Djibouti et de trois autres expositions sera inaugurée ce soir," *Le journal*, June 1, 1933, 4. Jean Jamin counts six thousand photographs taken during the expedition, of which three thousand became part of the photography collection of the Museum of Mankind. Michel Leiris, *Miroir de l'Afrique* (Gallimard, 1996), 26.

20. Georges-Henri Rivière and Marcel Griaule, "Le Musée de l'Ile d'Aix," *Beaux-Arts*, no. 73 (1934): 1. One of these trophies was a rhinoceros killed by Gourgaud near Lake Rodolphe, a hunt captured on film by Barth. Marie-Claude Aristégui, "Cet incroyable rhinocéros," *Sud Ouest*, July 28, 2011, https://www.sudouest.fr/2011/07/28/cet-incroyable-rhinoceros-462037-1391.php.

21. Louis Rollin, "Missions," *Journal officiel de la République française*, March 30, 1935, 3610.

22. Marius Moutet, "Rapport," *Journal officiel de la République française*, October 11, 1936, 10724; "Les fêtes et les expositions de la Semaine coloniale de 1935," *Le journal*, May 20, 1935, 2.

23. *Le journal*, May 13, 1935, 1–2.

24. Marcel Griaule, "Le Sahara pour tous: Sol noir, pierres calcinées," *Le journal*, May 14, 1935, 1–2.

25. Marcel Griaule, "Une route . . . presque un boulevard," *Le journal*, May 15, 1935, 1–2; Marcel Griaule, "Le suicidé de Tin Zouaten," *Le journal*, May 17, 1935, 8.

26. Marcel Griaule, "Gao, la grand'ville," *Le journal*, May 18, 1935, 4.

27. Marcel Griaule, "Des petits épargnants qui dévorent leurs semblables," *Le journal*, August 25, 1935, 6.

28. Marcel Griaule, "Avec la mère des masques dans les entrailles d'une nécropole," *Le journal*, August 27, 1935, 1–2; Marcel Griaule, "L'avion blanc sur la falaise noire," *Le journal*, August 29, 1935, 6.

29. Marcel Griaule, "Le lamantin dans la falaise et le margouillat protecteur," *Le journal*, August 28, 1935, 1–2.

30. Marcel Griaule, "La leçon du Cameroun," *Paris-Soir*, November 16, 1936, 1, 3.

31. Marcel Griaule, "Le Cameroun s'est imprégné de l'influence française," *Paris-Soir*, November 17, 1936, 3; Marcel Griaule, "Les Noirs du Cameroun ne sont pas des troupeaux à vendre ni des gages à échanger contre des promesses," *Paris-Soir*, November 24, 1936, 5.

32. Leiris's text is beyond my scope here. See James Clifford, "Interrupting the Whole," *Conjunctions*, no. 6 (1984): 282–95; Clifford, *Predicament of Culture*, 165–74.

33. Sébastien Côté, "Michel Leiris et la fuite impossible: Ethnographie, autobiographie et altérité féminine dans *L'Afrique fantôme*," *MLN*, no. 120 (2005): 856n10.

34. Conklin, *In the Museum of Man*, 206–7.

35. Eric Jolly, "Les missions Griaule et le cinéma ethnographique" and "Démasquer la société dogon: Sahara-Soudan, janvier–avril 1935," *Les carnets de Bérose*, no. 4 (2014): 96–100; Henley, "From *Vues* to Ethnofiction," 64.

36. Henley notes that the condescension of Griaule's voice-over is also found in his *Méthode de l'ethnographie*. Henley, *Beyond Observation*, 48.

37. George Fronval, "Haut les masques!," *Cinémonde*, March 17, 1938, 213. Griaule went on to contradict himself, stating that "the Dogon are excellent actors," who "played the roles intended for them in accordance with the planned layout."

38. Fronval, "Haut les masques!," 213.

39. Marcel Griaule, *Les grands explorateurs* (Presses universitaires de France [Que sais-je?], 1945), 119.

40. Jean Pédron, "Entretien avec M. Marcel Griaule chef de la mission ethnographique qui va explorer les étranges falaises de Bandiagara au Soudan," *Le journal*, January 3, 1935, 2.

41. J. P., "Deux missions scientifiques rentrent en France," *Le journal*, April 16, 1935, 4.

42. Fronval, "Haut les masques!," 213.

43. Mudimbe, *Invention of Africa*, 22.

44. For an analysis of the film's production, see Alison Murray Levine, "Film, Propaganda, and Politics: *La France est un empire*, 1939–1943," *Contemporary French Civilization* 40, no. 1 (2015): 71–90.

45. "Marie-Claire note les films," *Marie-Claire*, April 5, 1940, 9.

46. Jean-Pierre Bertin-Maghit, *Propaganda Documentaries in France, 1940–1944*, trans. Marcelline Block (Rowman and Littlefield, 2016), 84.

47. Murray Levine, "Film, Propaganda, and Politics," 82; GP Archives, PJM1941298; Pascal Blanchard and Ruth Ginio, "Imperial Revolution, Vichy's Colonial Myth (1940–1944)," in *Colonial Culture in France Since the Revolution*, ed. Pascal Blanchard, Sandrine Lemaire, et al. (Indiana University Press, 2014), 316.

48. Krull's commission specified "a film about the production of gold, rubber, and timber." Eric Jennings, *Free French Africa in World War II: The African Resistance* (Cambridge University Press, 2014), 179.

49. Bertin-Maghit, *Propaganda Documentaries in France*.

50. *Paris-presse, L'intransigeant*, October 30, 1945, 2.

51. Kim Sichel, "Germaine Krull and *L'Amitié noire*," in *Colonialist Photography: Imag(in)ing Race and Place*, ed. Eleanor Hight and Gary Sampson (Routledge, 2002), 258.

52. Richard Barsam, *Nonfiction Film: A Critical History* (Indiana University Press, 1992 [1973]), 213.

53. Sichel, "Germaine Krull and *L'Amitié noire*," 258.

54. Sadoul, *Le cinéma français*, 173.

55. *L'aurore*, September 24, 1952, n.p.

56. On Lotar's career and best-known work, see Steven Ungar, "'Toute la misère du monde': Eli Lotar's *Aubervilliers* and a Sense of Place," *Romanic Review* 105, nos. 1–2 (2014): 37–51.

57. Chaumel recycled much of this footage in *Le char des dieux* (The chariot of the gods, 1946) four years later.

58. "La vie des lettres," *Les lettres françaises*, February 7, 1947, 4.

59. Jean Rouch, "The Situation and Tendencies of the Cinema in Africa," in *Ciné-Ethnography*, trans. and ed. Steven Feld (University of Minnesota Press, 2003), 55.

60. Gallois, "Le cinéma au Musée de l'homme," 382–83.

61. A history of the Société des Explorateurs Français and list of early members is available at https://www.societe-explorateurs.org/la-societe/histoire/.

62. Liotard's father, Victor, who had been trained as a pharmacist, became an "explorer" and then colonial administrator, serving first in AEF and then as governor in Dahomey, New Caledonia, and Guinea.

63. Noël Ballif, *Les pygmées de la grande forêt* (L'Harmattan, 1992), 22–23.

64. Noël Ballif, "Deux mois chez les pygmées avec la mission Ogooué-Congo," *Ce soir*, February 2–3, 1947, 1.

65. Ballif, "Deux mois chez les pygmées avec la mission Ogooué-Congo," 1.

66. Noël Ballif, "La route de paille prend feu," *Ce soir*, February 4, 1947, 1–2; Noël Ballif, "'La guerre est-elle finie?' m'a demandé Motozélé . . . ," *Ce soir*, February 6, 1947, 1–2.

67. Noël Ballif, "Mougounzi et ses hommes nous ont invité à chasser," *Ce soir*, February 8, 1947, 2.

68. Noël Ballif, "Les Babenzélé se sont laissé filmer avec complaisance et ont reconnu leurs chants," *Ce soir*, February 9, 1947, 2.

69. Noël Ballif, "Nous avons descendu l'Ogooué en pirogues," *Ce soir*, February 13, 1947, 2; Noël Ballif, "De Lastoursville à Lambaréné," *Ce soir*, March 21, 1947, 2.

70. Noël Ballif, *Les danseurs de Dieu* (Hachette, 1954). Almost three decades after publishing his expedition narrative, Ballif would defend a two-volume third-cycle doctoral thesis titled *Analyse critique et synthèse des connaissances sur les Pygmées africains* (1981).

71. *Images du monde*, no. 110, February 11, 1947; Marie Alter, "Douze explorateurs français vivent la vie des populations nomades de l'Afrique noire," *L'aube*, no. 3422 (1948): 1.

72. See, for example, Ballif, *Les danseurs de Dieu*, 24, 34–35, 45, 58, 203, and 241–42.

73. Jacques Dupont, "L'Afrique vous parle," *Ciné-Club* no. 7, 1948, 2; Jacques Dupont, *Profession: Cinéaste, politiquement incorrect!* (Italiques, 2013), 240.

74. Dupont, "L'Afrique vous parle," 2.

75. UNESCO, *Premier catalogue sélectif international de films ethnographiques sur l'Afrique noire*, 83.

76. Dupont, *Profession*, 55.

77. Ballif, *Les danseurs de Dieu*, 147–97; Dupont, *Profession*, 52.

78. "Service cinématographique," *Mer outre-mer*, no. 1 (1948): 14.

79. "Plein succès du Festival du film documentaire," *La science et la vie*, March 1, 1950, 193. The English-language version erases Dupont's measured innovations and reverts to the earlier norm of expedition films like *Africa Speaks*, adding maps, intertitles, and a completely new voice-over, which begins by invoking "Africa, the dark continent."

80. Ballif, *Les danseurs de Dieu*, 45.

81. For this and more information about Becker's film and its links to Dupont and Rouch, see Damien Mottier, "Jean Rouch au rendez-vous de juillet: Métamorphose d'un ethnologue cinéaste," *Journal des Africanistes* 87, no. 1–2 (2017): 66–71.

82. Leroi-Gourhan, "Cinéma et sciences humaines," 42.

83. Paul Stoller, *The Cinematic Griot: The Ethnography of Jean Rouch* (University of Chicago Press, 1992), 18.

84. Faye Ginsburg, "*Dans le bain avec Rouch*: A Reminiscence," *American Anthropologist* 107, no. 1 (2005): 111; Sam DiIorio, "Notes on Jean Rouch and French Cinema," *American Anthropologist* 107, no. 1 (2005): 121.

85. The major monographs on Rouch include Paul Henley, *The Adventure of the Real: Jean Rouch and the Craft of Ethnographic Cinema* (University of Chicago Press, 2009), revised and translated into French as *L'aventure du réel* (Presses universitaires de Rennes, 2020), as well as, among edited collections, Mick Eaton, ed., *Anthropology-Reality-Cinema: The Films of Jean Rouch* (BFI, 1979); Joram ten Brink, ed., *Building Bridges: The Cinema of Jean Rouch* (Wallflower Press, 2007). Collections of Rouch's interviews and essays exist in French and in English translation. See Jean-Paul Colleyn, ed., *Jean Rouch: Cinéma et anthropologie* (Cahiers du cinéma/INA, 2009); Rouch, *Ciné-Ethnography*. Henley and Feld provide comprehensive filmographies.

86. See also Peter Bloom, "Unraveling the Ethnographic Encounter," *French Forum* 35, nos. 2–3 (2010): 87–89.

87. Jean Rouch, "Le film ethnographique," in *Ethnologie générale*, ed. Jean Poirier (Gallimard, 1968), 436; Tobing Rony, *The Third Eye*, 14, 23, 48; Félix Regnault, "Un musée de films," *Bulletins et mémoires de la Société d'anthropologie de Paris* 6, no. 3 (1912): 95–96.

88. Rouch, "Le film ethnographique," 437, 440, 447, 456.

89. Rouch, "Situation and Tendencies," 72; Rouch, "Le film ethnographique," 458–59.

90. J. Hoberman, "The Film Is the Search," *Artforum* 54, no. 3 (2015): 281.

91. Jean Rouch, "L'ethnographe et le cineaste: Un 'véloportrait' des origines," *Afrique contemporaine*, no. 196 (2000): 6.

92. Jean Rouch, *Connaissance de l'Afrique noire* (Le Livre de Paris, 1957), 32.

93. Rouch, *Ciné-Ethnography*, 105.

94. Stoller, *Cinematic Griot*, 37; Claire Devarrieux and Marie-Christine de Navacelle, *Cinéma du réel* (Éditions Autrement, 1988), 15.

95. Rouch, "L'ethnographe et le cinéaste," 10.

96. Jean Rouch with Lucien Taylor, "A Life on the Edge of Film and Anthropology," in Rouch, *Ciné-Ethnography*, 136. Philippe Lourdou, who compares the production contexts of *Au pays des Dogons*, *Sous les masques noirs*, and *Au pays des mages noirs*, distances both Griaule and Rouch from the films. Philippe Lourdou, "The Dawning Commentary in Ethnographic Film: Marcel Griaule's Cinematographic Work," *Visual Anthropology*, no. 6 (1993): 65–84.

97. "La chronique de Goupi-Cancans," *Ciné-Miroir*, March 30, 1948, 9.

98. "4.200 kilomètres en pirogue sur le Niger," *Mer outre-mer*, no. 9 (1948): 15.

99. Devarrieux and de Navacelle, *Cinéma du réel*, 10; Rouch, *Ciné-Ethnography*, 161.

100. Rouch, "Le cinéma africain," 1. This assertion also appears in Rouch, "Situation and Tendencies," 49. Feld's translation unfortunately turns *exemplaire* into *noteworthy*, eliminating the sense of a model to follow.

101. Rouch, *Ciné-Ethnography*, 162.

102. These have been collected as Jean Rouch, *Alors le Noir et le Blanc seront amis* (Mille et une nuits, 2008).

103. Catherine Valogne, "Un cinéma sans truquage et sans artifice: Les films de voyage et d'aventures vécues," *Ce soir*, June 27, 1952, 2.

104. Henley, *Adventure of the Real*, 48.

105. Alice Gallois, "Le cinéma ethnographique en France: Le Comité du Film Ethnographique, instrument de son institutionnalisation? (1950–1970)," *1895, revue d'histoire du cinéma*, no. 58 (2009): 89. See also Carolyn Eades, "Le Comité du film ethnographique: De la création au bilan," *Décadrages*, no. 40–42 (2019): 9–30.

106. Piault would not have agreed. He contrasted the ethnographic efforts of Poirier, Griaule, Villiers, and Dupont with his generation's "ethnocinéma" in *Anthropologie & Cinéma: Passage à l'image, passage par l'image*, 2nd ed. (Téraèdre, 2016 [2000]), 118–24, 137–40, 195–232.

107. Rouch, *Alors le Noir et le Blanc seront amis*, 113.

108. The Gaumont Pathé Archives follows the CNC to list a release date of 1930 for *Rythme noir*, but this is extremely unlikely given that sound was recorded on site. The film appears in *Paris-Soir* and *Paris-Midi* as screened at the Splendid Theater on February 13, 1938, and I was unable to locate any earlier reference to it.

109. René Vautier, *Caméra citoyenne: Mémoires* (Éditions Apogée, 1998), 29–30.

110. Vautier, *Caméra citoyenne*, 29. For a sustained analysis of Vautier's film in French cinema history, see Steven Ungar, "Making Waves: René Vautier's *Afrique 50* and the Emergence of Anti-colonial Cinema," *L'esprit créateur* 51, no. 3 (2011): 34–46. As is clear in the previous chapter of this book, I disagree with Ungar with respect to Poirier's *La croisière noire* and Allégret's *Voyage au Congo*.

111. Vieyra, *Le cinéma et l'Afrique*, 101–2.

112. For more details, see Sam Di Iorio, "Les vivants et les morts: Marker, Resnais et *Les statues meurent aussi*," *Trafic*, no. 105 (2018): 53.

113. For an overview and discussion of Marker's and Resnais's use of montage in *Les statues meurent aussi* and Resnais's in *Nuit et brouillard* (*Night and Fog*, 1956), see Ivan Čerečina, "Historical Assemblages: Montage in the Films of Nicole Vedrès, Alain Resnais and Chris Marker 1947–1957" (PhD diss., University of Sydney, 2019), 165–210.

114. Reprint of a 1972 interview with Resnais conducted by René Vautier and Nicole Le Garrec, *Ode au grand art africain: Les statues meurent aussi* (Monnaie de Paris, 2010), 36.

115. Max Favalelli, "Au Festival de Cannes," *Paris-presse, L'intransigeant*, April 26, 1953, 1; Jean-José Richer, "Le cinéma de demain," *Cahiers du cinéma* 7, no. 41 (1954): 32–33.

116. Paulin Soumanou Vieyra, *Sembène Ousmane, cineaste* (Présence africaine, 1972), 170.

117. "Alain Resnais à propos de l'interdiction du film '*Les statues meurent aussi*,'" April 1, 1969, https://www.ina.fr/audio/P12123747/alain-resnais-a-propos-de-l -interdiction-du-film-les-statues-meurent-aussi-audio.html.

118. Jean Rouch, "Préface," in UNESCO, *Premier catalogue sélectif international de films ethnographiques sur l'Afrique noire*, 21. On Vautier's *Afrique 50*, Marker's and Resnais's *Les statues meurent aussi*, and Rouch's *Moi, un noir* within the history of French social documentary, see Steven Ungar, *Critical Mass: Social Documentary in France from the Silent Era to the New Wave* (University of Minnesota Press, 2018), 136–66.

119. Aimé Césaire, *Discours sur le colonialisme* (Présence Africaine, 2011 [1955]), 38.

120. In France, Éditions Montparnasse's *Jean Rouch, Le geste cinématographique* (2005), and in the United States, Icarus Film's *Eight Films by Jean Rouch* (2017). On reflexive ethnography in *Moi, un noir* and the later work of Rouch, Marker, and Resnais, for example, see Laure Astourian, *The Ethnographic Optic* (Indiana University Press, 2024).

121. Rouch, *Ciné-Ethnography*, 189. For a lengthy reflection on ethnographic films about possession rituals with a particular focus on Rouch and *Les maîtres fous*, see Catherine Russell, *Experimental Ethnography: The Work of Film in the Age of Video* (Duke University Press, 1999), 193–327.

122. André Bazin, "Les maîtres fous," *France-Observateur*, no. 24 (October 1957): 1.

123. Colleyn, *Jean Rouch*, 40–41.

124. Henley, *Adventure of the Real*, 64.

125. Rouch, *Ciné-Ethnography*, 101.

126. Heider, *Ethnographic Film*, 3.

127. Most of these films were produced by Braunberger. See Catherine Papanicolaou, "Des *Fils de l'eau* à *Jaguar*: Zoom sur la collaboration Jean Rouch-Pierre Braunberger," *1895, revue d'histoire du cinéma*, no. 63 (2011): 104–19.

128. Jean Rouch, "Le cinéma africain," *Les lettres françaises*, no. 893 (1961): 7.

129. Henley, *Adventure of the Real*, 73–74.

130. Jean Rouch, "Cartes postales," *L'Afrique littéraire*, no. 68–69 (1983): 11.

131. Eaton, *Anthropology-Reality-Cinema*, 49.

132. Henley, *Beyond Observation*, 253.

133. Jean-Luc Godard, "L'Afrique vous parle de la fin et des moyens," *Cahiers du cinéma*, no. 94 (1959): 21–22.

134. Gilles Deleuze, *Cinéma 2: L'image-temps* (Les Editions de Minuit, 1985), 199, 291.

135. Despite its evident appeal, this quote may be mythical. The sources I have discovered bear the same byline: Boudjemaâ Karèche, "Hommage à Jean Rouch,"

Le matin, 2004, http://www.algerie-dz.com/article10.html; Boudjemaâ Karèche, "Juste un mot: L'ami nigérien," *El Watan*, 2014, https://www.elwatan.com/archives/culture-archives/juste-un-mot-lami-nigerien-2-30-01-2014.

136. Marie-Claire Ropars-Wuilleumier, "Naissance d'un cinéma," reprinted in Vieyra, *Sembène Ousmane, cinéaste*, 195.

137. Pierre Leprohon, *Chasseurs d'images* (Éditions André Bonne, 1960).

PART 2

West and Central African Documentary, 1960–2023

Burkinabé filmmaker Idrissa Ouédraogo and over thirty colleagues from around the world used a restored, hand-cranked Lumière Brothers cinematograph to shoot films for the 1995 *Lumière et Compagnie* (*Lumière & Company*) project celebrating the centenary of cinema. Trained at the short-lived African Institute for Cinematographic Studies (INAFEC) in Burkina Faso and the ID-HEC in France, Ouédraogo became a giant of postindependence sub-Saharan African cinema. His career, cut tragically short by his untimely death in 2018, began in the early 1980s with short fictions and documentaries, then continued with feature fictions *Yam Daabo* (The choice, 1987), *Yaaba* (Grandmother, 1989), and *Tilaï* (The law, 1990). For his contribution to the *Lumière et Compagnie* collection, Ouédraogo opted for a direct response to the earliest documentary footage of Black Africans—the Lumière films shot at ethnographic exhibitions in France and the travelogues shot in sub-Saharan Africa. Asserting his role as African director, he mocked the archetype of the heroic European *chasseur d'images*.

Ouédraogo's two-minute, untitled short begins with a peaceful view of a wide West African river; two men in a pirogue cross the frame from right to left. After a few seconds, we are shown a very different view of the same river—one that includes the near bank, on which Ouédraogo himself stands, looking out at three pirogues on the water with his back to the camera. Whereas Lumière productions were silent, the soundtrack to Ouédraogo's film is designed to subvert a colonial documentary template. As the first pirogue glides down the river, a dissonant clanking of filmmaking equipment reminds viewers that they are not glimpsing Africa caught unawares. Ouédraogo then speaks to the boatmen in Mooré, with no French-language translation provided. Another cut reveals a dozen African men on the bank, surrounding a bearded European seated on a dolly behind a camera and tripod. As one of the Africans pushes the dolly along a short track, the others break into raucous laughter. Switching to French, Ouédraogo calls out criticisms and instructions, then enters the frame. "You're tiring out the white guy," he tells his assistant. When Ouédraogo wonders aloud why his crew members are always arguing, one offers a possible response—"we're stupid"—which is followed by more laughter. The film stages the creative control of a Black African director who patronizes a silent European cameraman to the hilarity of his Black African crew. They find the suggestion that they might be unintelligent equally amusing.

The next cut brings us to a fifty-second sequence shot with the Lumière camera on black-and-white film stock provided by the Museum of Cinema in Lyon. Within the narrative of Ouédraogo's film, this footage is shot from the dolly by the passive *chasseur d'images*. In images that evoke those of Africans canoeing and swimming in *Baignade de nègres*, we see men fishing from the pirogues, another man in the water, and a woman washing clothes from the bank. All run screaming from what turns out to be a man wearing a crocodile mask, and uproarious laughter once again fills the soundtrack. A man who fled returns with a wooden club to battle the crocodile in a vaudeville version of the Ashanti village saber dances. Extended by similitude and analogy to the Lumière films of a century prior, this humor points to their ludicrous representation of Africans. Undermining the energy and authority of the traveling image hunter, Ouédraogo proclaims an African second century of cinema.

Ouédraogo's brilliant encapsulation of the cinema's past in Africa and simultaneous link to its African future is the perfect prologue to the second half of this book, which delineates an African documentary tradition in counterpoint to the French tradition that preceded it in the same geographical space. Colonial-era French cinema inspired African filmmakers to "shoot back," as scholar Melissa Thackway has argued, no matter the genre they chose.[1] For *Présence Africaine*'s Alioune Diop, this meant to "Africanize" the cinema.[2] A resolution issued by the arts commission of the journal's Second International Congress of Black Writers and Artists in Rome in 1959, a year after Sekou Touré's Guinea said no to membership in Charles de Gaulle's proposed French Union, asserted that colonial cinema had "devitalized the autochthonous culture of Black Africa and was an instrument of propaganda and indoctrination that often worked against the self-esteem and national pride of African peoples." Independent African nations would therefore use cinema to the opposite end, if similarly as a "means of communication, education, and indoctrination."[3]

Idrissa Ouédraogo and crew in *Lumière et Compagnie*, 1995.

Acutely aware of the racism, condescension, and inaccuracy of the European documentary tradition, the first generation of African documentary filmmakers was forced to rethink the conventions of the craft—in the words of Paulin Soumanou Vieyra, to "use the same weapons to cure the illness."[4] Reacting against the colonial travel, hunting, expedition, and ethnographic films that came before, they engaged a revolution of documentary style as well as content to reinvent nonfiction film for Africa, opposing colonial filmic discourse and seeking self-definition in words and images.

At the 1958 Universal Exhibition in Brussels, *chasseur d'images* Pierre Ichac participated in a workshop on cinema and sub-Saharan Africa, with former propagandists Étienne Lallier and François Villiers, ethnographer Jean Rouch, and Vieyra also in attendance. At the same time as Ichac claimed to be pleased that Africans might begin making their own films, he worried that "many Africans seem to sometimes forget their own culture," such that "'Africanists' often show themselves to be more African than Africans themselves."[5] Ichac's strange assertion that he and other French documentarists who had filmed in Africa were more African than Africans is in fact a logical—if extreme—conclusion drawn from decades of French colonial filmmaking. Before 1960, directors and critics often applied the term *African films* to French films shot in Africa, and this deceptive shorthand continued even after independence. In 1962, *Le Monde* reported the cancellation of a "festival of African film" intended to foster "cultural exchange."[6] The program had included films by Poirier, Cocteau, Ichac, and Rouch, not an African among them. Reviewing the "Festival of African Film" held in 1963 at the Museum of Decorative Arts and UNESCO headquarters in Paris, Pierre Ajame noted that all the films to be shown were made by European and American directors.[7] And as late as 1968, French theater director Pierre Debauche organized the "Week of African Cinema" in Nanterre with a program that included three films by Rouch, Marker's and Resnais's *Les statues meurent aussi*, and a single film by an African director, Ousmane Sembene's *La Noire de . . .* (*Black Girl*, 1966).[8] Sembene, Blaise Senghor, and other African filmmakers who attended a 1966 conference on documentary film in Africa and Asia sponsored by the Vienna Institute for Development noted the neocolonial attitude evident in the programming of mostly European films. With characteristically perceptive forthrightness, Sembene stated, "I have the impression . . . that we were invited here to see what Europe wants to do in Africa and how it is trying to understand us."[9]

In addition to being one of the first Black African filmmakers, Vieyra was the first sub-Saharan African film critic and first scholar of sub-Saharan African cinema.[10] He also worked as a producer of African films, both feature and documentary, most notably in a longstanding partnership with Sembene. In his earliest writings, Vieyra addressed the confusion between Africanist and African directors, between a cinema filmed in Africa and one, still to come, that would be African. Observing in 1957 that "there are still domains in which Europe speaks and continues to speak exclusively in Africa's name, among others the cinematographic domain," Vieyra divided European directors still speaking for Africa into four categories: colonialists, ideologues, paternalists, and realists. In this last, smallest group were those he called "our true friends"—René Vautier, Alain Resnais, Chris Marker, and Jean Rouch—whom he considered predecessors of African cinema for having portrayed, in films he noted were documentaries, "essential truths about Africa."[11] Only after political independence was African cinema able to "reestablish the truth about Africa," Vieyra wrote, "once Africans themselves had taken charge of their cinema."[12] Sembene described this transformation at a personal level, affirming that "What is important is for us to have our own cinema: that is to say, to see ourselves anew, to take control of ourselves, to understand ourselves via the mirror of the screen."[13]

Vieyra believed from the start that documentary would be an essential and dynamic component of sub-Saharan African cinema. Writing just prior to independence about "the responsibilities of the cinema in the formation of an African national consciousness," he envisaged six categories of independent African film—feature-length fiction, feature-length documentary, short fiction, short documentary, educational, and newsreel—two-thirds of which were nonfictional.[14] The vast majority of the more than thirty films Vieyra directed during a career lasting over three decades were documentaries. Film scholars have largely ignored these films, however, along with the larger sub-Saharan African documentary tradition born with independence. The second edition of Erik Barnouw's *Documentary: A History of the Non-fiction Film* is one of few such books to mention even a single African film. As evidence of "documentary film eruptions in new places," however, Barnouw cites the oeuvre of Ousmane Sembene, illustrated by a still from *Tauw* (1970).[15] *Tauw* is a short fiction; of Sembene's more than a dozen movies, only the commissioned but never released *Empire Sonhraï* (Songhay empire, 1963) was to be nonfiction. Similarly, in a short essay about "documentary cinema in Africa," Dominique Jutras selects Cheikh Oumar Sissoko's ninety-minute fiction *Nyamanton* (The garbage boys, 1986) as a case study, because "the actors in the film are non-professionals, the budget approaches that of Western documentaries, [and] reality is presented without much mise en scène."[16] The desire for ethnography that infused French colonial documentary from its beginnings is still present; reading fictions as anthropological resources, European spectators and critics have understood all African films to be simple reflections of customs and traditions.

More perplexing than this ignorance of African documentary within documentary studies is its long absence from academic studies of sub-Saharan African cinema. The first English-language overviews of African filmmaking, Manthia Diawara's 1992 *African Cinema, Politics and Culture* and Frank Ukadike's 1994 *Black African Cinema*, did not systematically distinguish documentaries from feature films, instead characterizing all African films as realist fiction. Despite having addressed the importance in the 1960s of newsreels in Senegal and Côte d'Ivoire and educational films in Guinea, Diawara concluded by dividing later African cinema into three categories of fiction: social realist, colonial confrontation, and return to the source.[17] Ukadike, who also mentioned early newsreels and educational documentaries, focused on the cinematic transformation of African oral narrative into feature-length fiction.[18] He did identify a specifically documentary tradition in Angola and Mozambique, and a year later published a short, groundbreaking essay dating an "emerging trend" of sub-Saharan African documentary to the 1990s. In earlier decades,

Ukadike maintained, "the fictional and the documentary coexist to illuminate and expand the borders of reality."[19] Film scholar and critic Clément Tapsoba has likewise recognized documentary "tendencies" and not a "documentary school" in African film history, noting, for example, a "documentary temptation" in Sembene's first short, *Borom Sarret* (The cart driver, 1963).[20]

Due in part to this amalgamation of African feature fiction and documentary films in the fields of both documentary cinema studies and African cinema studies, scholars and audiences have been slow to recognize the importance, and even the existence of African documentary. Although the line of demarcation between fiction and nonfiction film has never been clear in any region of the world, it is impossible to establish a corpus of documentary films without this distinction. And without a corpus, it is impossible to establish the history of an African documentary tradition that could claim its place within global documentary cinema. Of the twenty-five films screened at the first Ouagadougou Pan-African Film Festival (FESPACO) in Upper Volta in 1969, sixteen were made by African directors and nine by Europeans. Considering the history of French colonial documentary traced in the first half of this book, it is not surprising that all nine European films were documentaries. Given the lack of critical attention to African nonfiction film, however, it is remarkable that seven of the sixteen African films—almost half—were documentaries.[21] When we ignore early African documentary, we fail to recognize the emergence of an important tradition, one that flourishes today.

Like the French colonial films of the three previous chapters, the documentaries I discuss in the three chapters that follow were made primarily for commercial distribution. It is a rich and varied group of films released over the course of six decades: shot on 16mm and 35mm film, video, and digital video; in black and white and in color; short, medium, and feature length; and shown at festivals, in movie theaters, on television, and streaming. Chapter 4 begins just a few years before 1960, the year many former French colonies in West and central Africa gained their independence, charting a striking range of experimentation in both content and form in the first dozen years of documentary film production in the region. Chapter 5 continues from the early 1970s through the late '80s as documentary production and distribution was outweighed by an acceleration of feature fiction films, with directors such as Ouédraogo, Sembene, and Souleymane Cissé coming to international attention. This period of transformation brought African women to documentary and launched the careers of several of Africa's most accomplished documentarists.

If chapters 4 and 5 occasionally manifest an impulse to catalog, it is because the wealth of the first three decades of documentary in the region has been so little recognized and these films are so difficult to find. Chapter 6 begins at the turn of the 1990s, a moment when a second generation of sub-Saharan African filmmakers turned to documentary. As technologies of shooting and screening have advanced and become more affordable and accessible, the production of nonfiction moving images has grown exponentially, with creators continuing to challenge outsider claims to unquestionable authenticity as they transform the language of objectivity on which colonial documentary relied. Like Uka-dike, many scholars locate the origins of African documentary during this period, with African documentary finally attracting sustained attention from international festival programmers and film critics.[22] This delayed but substantive recognition was marked on the African continent by the 2007 creation of a documentary section within FESPACO's official competition. Many Africa-based documentary festivals and seminars have been launched since, and African films are more and more often selected for global documentary festivals, including Visions of the Real in Switzerland, Cinema of the Real in France, Dok Leipzig in Germany, ZagrebDox in Croatia, Hot Docs in Canada, and AFI Docs in the United States. French directors have continued to shoot documentaries in sub-Saharan Africa, but the second half of this book alludes to such work only to draw contrasts. Following the development of a sub-Saharan African documentary tradition where Alfred Machin, Léon Poirier, Marc Allégret, Marcel Griaule, Jacques Dupont, and Jean Rouch hunted, adventured, and collected ethnographic data, we witness the gradual decentering of European ideological and generic models for film and media.

Notes

1. Melissa Thackway, *Africa Shoots Back: Alternative Perspectives in Sub-Saharan Francophone African Film* (Indiana University Press, 2003).

2. Iwiyè Kala-Lobe, "Alioune Diop et le cinéma africain," *Présence Africaine*, no. 125 (1983): 340, 349.

3. "Résolution de la commission des arts," *Présence Africaine*, no. 24/25 (1959): 415–16.

4. Vieyra, *Réflexions d'un cineaste africain*, 63.

5. *Rapport général du groupe ciné-photo: Section du Congo-belge et du Ruanda-Urundi* (Brussels, 1959), 16.

6. "Un festival du film africain est interdit," *Le Monde*, March 31, 1962.

7. Pierre Ajame, "En noir et blanc," *Les nouvelles littéraires*, no. 1865 (May 30, 1963).

8. P. C., "Deux festivals africains à Paris," *Jeune Afrique*, no. 380 (1968): 46.

9. Vienna Symposium, "The Documentary Film in Africa and Asia" (Vienna Institute for Development, 1966), 99.

10. Excerpts from Vieyra's critical writings have recently been translated into English for the first time. See Mélissa Gélinas, "In Translation: Paulin Soumanou Vieyra," *Journal of Cinema and Media Studies* 58, no. 3 (2019): 118–36.

11. Vieyra, "Quand le cinéma français parle au nom de l'Afrique noire," 143; Vieyra, *Le cinéma et l'Afrique*, 179.

12. Vieyra, *Réflexions d'un cineaste africain*, 132.

13. Vieyra, *Sembène Ousmane, cinéaste*, 166.

14. Paulin Soumanou Vieyra, "Responsabilités du cinéma dans la formation d'une conscience nationale africaine," *Présence Africaine*, no. 27/28 (1959): 309.

15. Erik Barnouw, *Documentary: A History of the Non-fiction Film*, 2nd ed. (Oxford University Press, 1993), 206.

16. Dominique Jutras, "Le cinéma documentaire en Afrique," *24 images*, no. 46 (1989): 34.

17. Manthia Diawara, *African Cinema: Politics and Culture* (Indiana University Press, 1992), 58–59, 65, 71, 141, 152, 159.

18. Frank Ukadike, *Black African Cinema* (University of California Press, 1994), 69.

19. Ukadike, *Black African Cinema*, 231–45. Frank Ukadike, "African Cinematic Reality: The Documentary Tradition as an Emerging Trend," *Research in African Literatures* 26, no. 3 (1995): 91.

20. Clément Tapsoba, "Filmer l'Afrique," *Ecrans d'Afrique*, no. 16 (1996): 51.

21. Hamidou Ouedraogo, *Naissance et évolution du FESPACO de 1969 à 1973* (Imprimerie Nationale du Burkina, 1995), 51–52.

22. See for example Thackway, *Africa Shoots Back*, 97, and Anjali Prabhu, *Contemporary Cinema of Africa and the Diaspora* (Wiley-Blackwell, 2014), 157–71.

4

INDEPENDENCE

Renewing Nonfiction

If Ousmane Sembene was the father of sub-Saharan African cinema, Paulin Soumanou Vieyra was the first sub-Saharan African documentarist, one of few African filmmakers of his generation to work consistently in documentary. Vieyra was born in Porto Novo, Dahomey, in 1925; his father, a civil servant in the French colonial administration, sent Vieyra to boarding school in France at the age of ten. He lived with a French family during school vacations and did not return home for twenty-five years, by which point he was no longer able to speak his mother tongue.[1] Soon after World War II, Vieyra developed tuberculosis, which forced him to take several convalescent breaks during his university studies first of biology and then of cinema. His first contact with filmmaking came in 1947, when he was recruited from an international student residence hall to play an African soldier in Claude Autant-Lara's *Le diable au corps* (Devil in the flesh). Intrigued by the world of cinema and sensing its "great usefulness" in and for Africa, Vieyra passed the elaborate and lengthy entrance exam for the IDHEC, becoming one of its first sub-Saharan African students and the first to earn a diploma.[2] He studied with Georges Sadoul, graduating less than a decade after Jacques Dupont; two decades later, Jean Rouch would serve as adviser for Vieyra's doctorat d'état thesis at the Université de Paris X, titled "In Search of African Cinema."

While Vieyra was preparing for the entrance exam and starting at the IDHEC, the first films made by Black Africans appeared in what was known as Belgian Congo. Albert Mongita, a journalist and member of the Ciné-Club Congolais of Léopoldville (now Kinshasa), shot *Leçon de cinéma* (Film class, 1951) with fellow club members. Emmanuel Lubalu, who acted in several educational films made by Catholic missionary Abbé Cornil, directed *Les pneus gonflés* (Inflated tires, 1953).[3] In Paris, Guinean Mamadou Touré filmed *Mouramani*, a short based on a West African tale, and Malian Amadou Cissé established Publi Afric Film to make African newsreels.[4] Nothing remains of these initiatives, leaving Vieyra's graduation project as the earliest extant work by a sub-Saharan African filmmaker. The opening credits to the somewhat autobiographical *C'était il y a quatre ans* (It was four years ago, 1954) immediately identify him as African: "Directed by Paulin Vieyra, originally from Dahomey (AOF)." As an unnamed African student reads Paul Hazard's *La crise de la conscience européenne* (*The Crisis of the European Mind*, 1935), the camera pans to a sheet of paper on which is written, "The crisis of westernized African consciousness??" Vieyra dramatized his fraught position as an African student in France through his character's self-interrogation, this questioning itself staged via a work of French intellectual history. The film develops this theme by contrasting the character's memories of African music and dancing with the classical music his French girlfriend plays on a record player. Twenty years later, Vieyra maintained that, of all his works, this was a favorite.[5]

After graduating, Vieyra formed the African Cinema Group with friends Jacques Mélo Kane and Mamadou Sarr, both from Senegal, and Robert Caristan, who was originally from French Guiana but had attended high school in Dakar. Prevented from filming in Africa by the Laval Decree, the group decided to shoot in France and in 1955 completed *Afrique sur Seine*, a twenty-minute short depicting the lives of African students in Paris. Vieyra described the film as "an overview of the varied existences of black people in Paris . . . with a flashback to a mythic Africa and a circumstantial vision of the West."[6] Refused permission to shoot on his native continent, Vieyra was paradoxically obliged to borrow images for the flashback from René Vautier, whom he knew from the IDHEC; Vautier had filmed them while in Côte d'Ivoire for the commissioned project that became *Afrique 50*. A voice-over commentary cowritten by Vieyra and Sarr begins in the second-person plural, seeming to describe the carefree, noisy children swimming and playing on screen: "We called out our independence to the sun and to our ancestors, possessive, insouciant, unaware of the world that surrounded us." Imagining the children's future while acknowledging the filmmakers' present reality, the narration sets the scene for the transition to Europe: "It was necessary to grow up, leave the country, for Paris, capital of the world, capital of Black Africa." After this cry of African independence and subsequent reminder of colonial power, the camera pans slowly past monuments and monumental spaces in the colonial capital—the Sorbonne, the

Paulin Soumanou Vieyra and the African Cinema Group, Paris, 1955.

Paulin Soumanou Vieyra, *Afrique sur Seine*, 1955.

Pantheon, Notre Dame, the Quartier Latin—in a long shot described by David Murphy as designed to "inscribe the African presence in the city."[7]

Painting a comprehensive if not detailed portrait, *Afrique sur Seine* is by turns optimistic and pessimistic about this presence. The film follows unnamed Black men and women as they appropriate the spaces of the colonial capital, and a varied commentary guides viewers' perception of their experiences. Narrating images of smiling mixed-race couples, for example, the voice-over speaks of unity and urges the overcoming of ingrained stereotypes: "The crowd in the Latin Quarter assembles and assimilates, trying to melt antique barriers of prejudice and of monuments to hate in the sun of love, in order to come closer, to understand itself despite the classifications that men have made out of the history of righteous peoples." A less optimistic vision of African Paris—"the Paris of days without bread, the Paris of days without hope"—is evident in shots of a mendicant, a street sweeper, and, in a cameo appearance by Vieyra, a blind man walking with a cane.[8] For filmmaker Sarah Maldoror, who was born in France to parents from Guadeloupe and spent a significant portion of her career in sub-Saharan Africa, *Afrique sur Seine* was a revelation in that "we were watching others, we were no longer 'the watched.'"[9] Filming their compatriots, Vieyra and his colleagues broke the spell under which colonial French documentarists had claimed full and accurate authorship of the lives of Black subjects.

Afrique sur Seine's voice-over commentary provides information—a function conventionally coded as documentary—and shares poetic reflections.

The film shows young Africans in Paris from an African perspective, but this human reality is illustrated neither in a montage of previously recorded footage nor by a purely observational camera. The students on screen are acting for the camera, a fact acknowledged in the double meaning of the film's title, both *Africa on the Seine* and *Africa on stage* (*scène*). There are no developed characters and no sustained storyline in the performed scenes, however, and the actors, including Marpessa Dawn from the United States and Philippe Mory from Gabon, are credited under the ambiguous heading "with the cooperation of." Maria Loftus calls Vieyra's film a docufiction, qualifying its narration as documentary and its images as fictional, but these components cannot be neatly opposed. The use of the term *docufiction* to designate a mixture of nonfiction and fiction leaves works in limbo, neither one nor the other.[10] The hybrid appellation is unnecessary, moreover, since documentary cinema has always relied on some part of plotting and performance—defining characteristics, as we have seen, of the colonial-era *grands documentaires*. This is not merely a question of terminology. Understanding *Afrique sur Seine* to be documentary allows us, in the words of film scholar Michael Renov, to "expand the received boundaries of the documentary form."[11] Whereas Renov is addressing generic boundaries, the boundaries under consideration here are also geographic. The African Cinema Group's first film inaugurates a tradition of African documentary.

Afrique sur Seine was made quite literally in the interstices of the Paris film industry. Vieyra wrote that it took several months to create a film from the footage: "It wasn't always possible to obtain an editing room and equipment. . . . We had to be devious, adding the soundtrack in secret, at night."[12] At the same time, the format and lack of resources allowed for a certain freedom. Vieyra was an active participant in the vibrant African and African diaspora intellectual circles of 1950s Paris, publishing frequently in Diop's *Présence Africaine*. Situating his work in an international context to argue that short-form documentary could combat prejudice and transform our vision of reality, he cited as examples films by Robert Flaherty, John Grierson, Joris Ivens, Sergei Eisenstein, and Jean Rouch.[13] Vieyra also referred to the 1953 manifesto of the Group of Thirty, composed of members of the French film industry who advocated for government funding for the documentary short subject in order to facilitate the creation of strongly political and formally inventive work.[14] In several essays, Vieyra acknowledged Vautier's *Afrique 50*, Marker's and Resnais's *Les statues meurent aussi*, and Rouch's *Jaguar* and *Moi, un noir* as exceptions to the rule of colonial nonfiction filmmaking.[15] And he was in contact with French documentary filmmakers who shared his interest in African cultures: Vautier, Resnais, and Rouch, whose Ethnographic Film Committee at the Museum of Mankind funded *Afrique sur Seine*.

Vieyra and his colleagues insisted on the importance of African cinema for showing "African realities," and Vieyra equally insisted that African cinema was "an extremely important contribution to universal art."[16] From its beginnings, African film was international and cosmopolitan out of both desire and necessity. With no film schools in sub-Saharan Africa in the decade before or the first decades after independence, aspiring filmmakers trained in France, Italy, the Soviet Union, Yugoslavia, and even the United States. They learned technique as well as European and North American film traditions, often living and working in a community of Africans from a variety of regions and ethnic and religious backgrounds. The prevalence of coproductions with European directors and production companies during this period also forces us to think of early African documentary in a global context. Doing so, however, it becomes clear that, as Vieyra maintained during the 1958 workshop in Brussels, "every time that Africans have made decisions about their destiny, they have done so in a very different manner than that anticipated by Europeans."[17]

Working in France during the last decade of French colonial rule in Africa, the African Cinema Group considered itself to be participating in the fight for independence. There was no doubt, Vieyra asserted, "that the cinematographic expression of an authentically African reality would come only with the national sovereignty of African countries."[18] Yet although African filmmakers and scholars have honored Vieyra as an influential pioneer, some have been ill at ease with the idea of an African cinema born in Europe. Senegalese director Cheikh Ngaïdo Bâ named Momar Thiam's *Sarzan* (1963) as the first sub-Saharan African film, dismissing *Afrique sur Seine* as made "in a school in Paris with students."[19] Biographer of Sembene Samba Gadjigo specifies that, although Vieyra did indeed make a film first, Sembene was "the first African to make a film about Africa in Africa and for Africans."[20] As a compromise, *Afrique sur Seine* is commonly credited as the first film directed by a Black African and Sembene's *Borom Sarret* (1963) as the first Black African film. Without entering into the debate over origins, an examination of Vieyra's career reminds us of the significance of documentary to the birth of sub-Saharan African cinema.

Both Bâ and Gadjigo neglect not only *Afrique sur Seine* but also the first African documentaries shot in West Africa. Paulin Vieyra and his colleagues left Paris for Dakar, Senegal, in 1957, soon after the French Parliament passed the *loi-cadre*, which gave a certain amount of autonomy to sub-Saharan African territories. In the three years that followed, Vieyra held three jobs, following a path that mirrored the quickly changing political and cinematic landscapes surrounding independence. In 1958, he became director of the cinema section of the High Commissariat of French West Africa (AOF) and made the short newsreel *Le Niger aujourd'hui* (Niger today). In 1959, Vieyra took over as head of the cinema service of the Mali Federation and shot *Présence Africaine à Rome* (*Présence Africaine* in Rome), a chronicle of the Second Congress of Black Writers and Artists. In 1960, after independence and the merging of the cinema services of the Mali Federation and Senegal, he joined the Actualités Sénégalaises, the newsreel section of the Senegalese Ministry of Information. Vieyra trained filmmakers, shot footage, and edited films, many of which documented President Léopold Sédar Senghor's trips abroad as head of state.

In his history of Senegalese cinema, Vieyra maintained that "any state that becomes independent wants to have primarily national news."[21] At independence, 80 percent of movie theaters in Senegal were owned by European conglomerates SECMA and COMACICO, which showed newsreels produced by French companies.[22] A year later, at the encouragement of the French Ministry of Cooperation, the four major French newsreel companies—Actualités Françaises, Éclair, Gaumont, and Pathé—banded together to form the International Audiovisual Consortium (CAI), which contracted to make newsreels for eight new African nations.[23] The Actualités Sénégalaises struggled to obtain distribution until the Senegalese government passed a law banning foreign newsreels; films produced weekly were shown first in Dakar and then in theaters around the country. This model was adopted in other former French colonies, including Chad, Côte d'Ivoire, Dahomey, Togo, and Cameroon. On the other hand, multiple attempts to create African distribution companies to compete with SECMA and COMACICO failed, even after Upper Volta in 1969 and Mali, Senegal, and Dahomey in the years that followed took control of their theaters by nationalizing them.

In 1963, the third year of what François Kodjo later called the neocolonial era of African filmmaking, the French Ministry of Cooperation created its Bureau of Cinema, which administered a program called Aid to African Cinema.[24] The office was led by Jean-René Debrix, who in the postwar years had served as deputy director of the IDHEC. At a time when many new African governments saw cinema as a propaganda tool or an unnecessary luxury, France offered financial and technical assistance for editing and printing films in exchange for noncommercial distribution rights. This structure meant not only that directors had to find other resources to shoot their films but also that topic and style could be taken into account when funding decisions were made, with requirements often placed on how films would be finalized during the editing process. This "cooperation," if highly controversial, nonetheless enabled the completion of a number of African films in the first decade after independence, including documentaries.[25] France was the primary but not the only European country to fund early West and central African cinema; filmmakers from countries aligned with the Soviet bloc had other partnership opportunities, which entailed other kinds of censorship.

In 1964, Ivorian director Timité Bassori bemoaned the European control of film distribution in Africa and the focus of African governments on newsreel production, which together left filmmakers with very limited options. A true African cinema, Bassori believed, must be creative: "Filmed images, even those with origins in reality, can only attain the 'cinematographic miracle' if this reality is aesthetically formed into a work of art."[26] Senegalese filmmaker Blaise Senghor noted the same problem. African directors trained in Europe, then returned to Africa with the desire to make African films. They found jobs at national newsreel services but soon realized that they had become civil servants, rarely able to pursue artistic visions.[27] When Africans were able to make films other than newsreels, with or without French funding, these were screened at European festivals or French cultural centers. The European distribution companies that controlled the few existing theaters in Africa refused to buy African productions, instead circulating what Sembene described as "freight cars worth of third-rate European films."[28] At the 1966 World Festival of Negro Arts in Dakar, filmmakers therefore adopted a series of resolutions to promote the development of African cinema. These included calls for the creation of an inter-African administrative body for production, distribution, and exhibition; the establishment of national cinematheques; and the reinvestment of box office proceeds into production.[29] The second half of the 1960s also saw the creation of two African film festivals: the Carthage Film Festival (JCC) in 1966 and FESPACO in 1969. The Pan-African Federation of Filmmakers (FEPACI) was formed in 1969 and inaugurated the following year in Carthage, with the goal of advocating for African national cinemas and African control of distribution and exhibition circuits.[30]

Cameroonian filmmaker Urbain Dia-Moukori agreed with Bassori and Senghor that the new African cinema had to be both grounded in reality and conceived of as art. Without a film tradition of their own, he argued, African directors "must act like all technical orphans: risk, produce, film, in a word, live, and even live dangerously."[31] Creating a tradition meant taking financial as well as aesthetic risks. Given the scarcity and complexity of funding structures, it was easier to make short films than feature-length ones, and easier to make documentaries, without sets to build and actors to rehearse, than fiction films. In addition to newsreels, the Actualités Sénégalaises occasionally funded documentary short subjects, which, Vieyra noted, "allowed independent filmmakers to take their first steps."[32] Vieyra reedited newsreel footage to make the satiric short *Écrit du Caire* (Written from Cairo, 1964), for example, using images shot during the Conference of African Heads of State in Egypt, which he had attended with President Senghor. His *Écrits de Dakar* (Writings from Dakar, 1971) depicts French president Georges Pompidou's visit to Senegal with a comic touch. Vieyra believed that nonfiction films could and should be not just works of art but also a "lifelong occupation," rather than merely a first step before directing feature fictions.[33] Yet his life-long documentary work has been overshadowed by *Afrique sur Seine*, the only of his post-IDHEC films to have received sustained critical attention, and, not coincidentally, the only to have been shot in Europe.

While at the Actualités Sénégalaises, Vieyra documented African in-dependence ceremonies in newsreels such as *L'indépendance du Cameroun*, *L'indépendance du Togo*, *L'indépendance du Congo*, and *L'indépendance de Madagascar*, all shot during his travels with Senghor. In 1961, he became the head of the cinema service of the Senegalese Ministry of Information, overseeing more than just newsreels. That year, to celebrate the first anniversary of inde-pendence, the ministry funded a different kind of independence film, Vieyra's *Une nation est née: La république du Sénégal* (A nation was born: The Republic of Senegal, 1961). Widely successful in Senegal and the winner of prizes at the Kar-lovy Vary Festival in Czechoslovakia and the Locarno Festival in Switzerland, it was "ostracized" by French authorities, Vieyra remarked, and particularly those at the French embassy in Dakar, for having told "the principal truths about the French colonization of Senegal."[34] In a mix of recorded footage and reenactments, Vieyra had conveyed a strong message of independence via the representation of an African history that had never been filmed. Reflecting on the role of the political documentary in African cinema, Vieyra later cited *Une nation est née* as an example of the fact that "the limit between the documentary short and the short fictional film is not always well drawn."[35]

Une nation est née provides an overview of Senegalese history from precolo-nial times to the present. The film's first few minutes are accompanied by music, as panning shots tour forests, traditional villages with farmers, and oceans and rivers with fishermen. The scene set, a voice-over commentary written by Vieyra and read by Bachir Touré begins: "A long, a very long time ago, in this corner of Africa . . . a hardworking and peaceful population lived by the rhythm of the seasons, in love with work well done." Vieyra presents an allegorical vision of West African life in precolonial times in a series of images of hunters, boat build-ers, and artisans, of dancing, drumming, and wrestling. He then introduces viewers to Senegal's four landscapes—the forest, the sea, the savanna, and the village—as a couple dances in each setting in turn. An extraordinary portrayal of colonial conquest follows, narrated by a quotation from Cheikh Hamidou

Kane's newly published *L'aventure ambiguë* (*Ambiguous Adventure*): "Strange dawn of the West! . . . It was a morning of birthing pains . . . a birth that took place in mud and in blood. . . . Those who were arriving were white and frenzied. Nothing like it had ever been seen before. . . . They fought among themselves to dominate the land."[36] The dancing couple, Abdoulaye Diop and Henriette Bathily of the famed Ballets Africains, again represent precolonial Africa. First reaching out with gestures of welcome, they hurl clumps of dirt at their attackers and fall to the ground when artillery fire is heard on the soundtrack. The victorious invading nations are symbolized on screen by their flags, such that no European characters appear on screen.

The anticolonial novel *L'aventure ambiguë*, which tells the story of Samba Diallo, a young man sent by his royal West African family to study in France, had autobiographical resonance for Vieyra. Diallo discovers upon his return home years later that, although he never felt comfortable in Europe, he has lost a fundamental connection to his native culture and religion. Having evoked colonial violence as well as what Kenyan author and activist Ngugi wa Thiong'o called the colonization of the mind, the narration for Vieyra's *Une nation est née* describes colonial forced labor and moves on to the period of anticolonial resistance that led to the birth of the Republic of Senegal. Only now, two-thirds of the way into the film, does Vieyra include archival footage. He refused to use any images shot by colonial-era travelers, opting to show recordings only of independence festivities and speeches. These are accompanied by a triumphant voice-over recitation of the words of the Senegalese national anthem, written by president and poet Senghor, concluding with "Arise brothers, and behold Africa, united." The most explicitly political of Vieyra's documentaries, the film ends with the announcement of a "new battle" for economic independence.

The other films celebrating West African independence in the early 1960s were made by French directors. The Ministry of Information of Upper Volta hired Serge Ricci to make the country's first film, *À minuit, l'indépendance* (At midnight, independence, 1961), for the anniversary of the independence of Upper Volta, Dahomey, Niger, and Côte d'Ivoire. Ricci had worked in AOF while based at Rouch's Committee for Ethnographic Film, and he would go on to produce the majority of films made in Upper Volta in the dozen years following independence, including educational titles like *L'utilisation du savon* (Using soap, 1967).[37] In the contrast between Ricci's *À minuit, l'indépendance* and *Une nation est née*, we can grasp the extent of Vieyra's innovation. Although released at the same time and for the same occasion as Vieyra's film, *À minuit, l'indépendance* is very different in form and message. Ricci wrote and read the third-person omniscient voice-over commentary and directed, shot, and edited the film, which is composed of footage of independence ceremonies interspersed with performances of traditional singing and dancing. Despite an ostensible focus on independence, the documentary relies on speeches by both African leaders and French delegates, accompanied by images of West African and French flags flying together. Ricci's narration similarly stresses unity with France rather than separation, asserting that African civil servants trained by the French "will be the first to create a synthesis of the values brought by Western culture and the ancient African wisdom inherited from their ancestors." In a clip taken from a newsreel shot in Niamey, Niger, Charles de Gaulle's representative Louis Jacquinot states that independence was declared "with feelings of solidarity, friendship, and fraternity with France." And footage from Upper Volta shows President Maurice Yaméogo thanking the French for having trained his country's civil servants, then crying out, "Long live independent Upper Volta! Long live France!" Jean Rouch's *Fêtes du Niger* (Celebrations of Niger, 1962) and Robert Donio's *Reunification* (1962) are likewise composed primarily of newsreel footage accompanied by conventional, third-person omniscient voice-over commentaries.

Claims for *Sarzan* and *Borom Sarret* as the first sub-Saharan African films also overlook Blaise Senghor's *Grand Magal à Touba* (Grand Magal in Touba, 1962), produced by Senghor's private, Dakar-based company, African Cinematographic Union (UCINA). Senghor, who was seven years younger than Vieyra, also studied filmmaking at the IDHEC before returning home to Senegal. He worked as a producer until his tragically early death at the age of forty-four, but *Grand Magal à Touba*, shot in 35mm color and winner of a Silver Bear at the Berlin Film Festival, was his first and only film as director. Senghor's goal, which he urged other African filmmakers to adopt as well, was "to make Africa better known to Africans."[38] The documentary begins with maps of Dakar and Touba, Senegal, accompanied by a French-language voice-over that introduces and explains the stages of the yearly Mouride pilgrimage to the Touba mosque. The narrator describes what viewers are shown as members of the brotherhood travel on trains and buses from the train station in Dakar past Thiaroye, Rufisque, and Thiès. When pilgrims arrive at the mosque, they are greeted by performances and other entertainment; the next day, they line up to be blessed by the caliph and visit the tomb of Cheikh Ahmadou Bamba. At the end of the film, the commentary informatively (if prosaically) announces that "the caliph's secretary, the president, and the caliph himself will speak to thank the crowd and recall the principles on which the brotherhood is based, the pledge of membership, and the economic role of these ardent workers in the country's development."

Black French critic D'dée opposed *Grand Magal à Touba*, an African film about Africa, to European films, identifying in Senghor's work "a dimension and a tone that we don't find in documentaries shot by Africanists."[39] Senghor's documentary is evidence that early African filmmakers were eager to record and interpret their own societies and cultures for audiences both at home and abroad. French Africanists, however, could not conceive of a filmic category in which they could do so. Jean Rouch insisted on defining ethnology as "the study of a culture which is not your own. That's it."[40] In the classic ethnographic paradigm, the society and culture represented on-screen are foreign to both filmmaker and audience; documentary scholar Bill Nichols describes the model as "we speak about them to us."[41] Perpetuating what Paulin Vieyra called a "cultivation of difference," colonial films, and particularly films by "foreign ethnologists," stressed "the strangeness of this unknown entity, the African continent."[42] This was not a difference among equals, and African filmmakers felt the condescension keenly. While a student in Paris, Blaise Senghor saw Rouch's *Maîtres fous* at the movie theater La Pagode, where Pierre Braunberger had arranged an unlikely pairing with Swedish art house auteur Ingmar Bergman's *Sawdust and Tinsel*. "When I left the theater," Senghor told Rouch years later, "all of the white spectators were looking at me, the only Black spectator." Humiliated, he guessed what they were thinking: "There's another one who is going to eat a dog."[43]

In *Grand Magal à Touba*, Senghor worked to appropriate the concept and form of ethnographic documentary, in which, as we have amply seen, Africans had been filmed objects rather than filming subjects. Well aware that French documentaries claiming to represent Africans and their traditions objectively and comprehensively were not as accurate as they claimed to be, Senghor would eventually condemn ethnographic filmmaking altogether. "The African is badly understood by the world," he affirmed, "victim in the past and present of a collection of prejudices that always consist of showing Africans as savages or people who dance naked around a wood fire."[44] Vieyra, also acutely aware of the colonial tradition that preceded him, considered the term *ethnography* inappropriate for films like Senghor's precisely to distinguish them from prior French efforts. He suggested that African documentaries about African societies and cultures instead be called "social anthropology films" or "sociological films."[45] In addition to *contact zone*, we might adopt the term *autoethnography* from the work of Mary Louise Pratt, who uses it to designate not "autochthonous or 'authentic' forms of representation" but rather texts "in which people undertake to describe themselves in ways that engage with representations others have made of them."[46]

The first independent African filmmakers, if born under French colonial rule, were no longer colonized subjects. The oldest of those discussed in this chapter, Vieyra was thirty-five years old at independence; the youngest, Pierre-Marie Dong and Djibril Diop Mambéty, were fifteen. Yet all were conscious of working within a neocolonial system while taking up a medium and mode that had been exploitative in European hands. Describing the Brussels workshop conducted on the eve of independence, Vieyra commented on "the paternalistic spirit of the formulations of certain proposals and the possessive adjectives abusively employed by some to speak about African populations." "It was necessary to acknowledge," he concluded, "that for African cinema to be truly African it would have to be the work of Africans themselves."[47] A few years after independence, Alioune Diop established a cinema commission within the African Society for Culture; members included Vieyra, Bassori, Senghor, Sembene, and Dia-Moukori. In a memorandum submitted to UNESCO, the commission announced the objective of shooting as many educational, social, cultural, ethnographic, and sociological films as possible. This document was circulated to African heads of state and used to prepare a conference in Genoa titled "Negro-African Culture and Its Cinematographic Expressions," which advocated for a Black African cinema with "its own identity," anchored in the representation of African cultures and traditions for African audiences.[48]

In the early years of African documentary cinema, this goal was elusive. Film is always a collective endeavor, so it can be difficult to disentangle the roles of "cooperating" French and African filmmakers—particularly since, as Pratt notes, autoethnographies are addressed to both members of one's own society and audiences in the metropole.[49] Jean-Paul N'Gassa, born in Bana-Bafang, Cameroon, studied first in Yaoundé and then at the IDHEC in Paris, where he codirected the documentary short *Aventure en France* (Adventure in France, 1963). N'Gassa returned to Cameroon in the mid-1960s to direct the cinema service of the Ministry of Information and the weekly Cameroun Actualités, and historians of African cinema identify him as the director of *La grande case Bamiléké* (The Bamileke great house, 1966). A coproduction of Cameroun Actualités and French Pathé, the documentary won a prize at the 1966 festival in Dakar and was selected for the Saint-Cast Festival of African and Malagasy Film in northwestern France. Yet French cameraman William Hamon, who also worked for Cameroun Actualités, appears in the film's credits as director, with N'Gassa listed as director of production.

La grande case Bamiléké was in fact an almost exclusively French creation, with voice-over commentary written by Marcel Huret, who had worked for several French newsreel companies, and read by Henri Champetier, previously the voice-over narrator of the French army's *Nos soldats en Afrique noire* (Our soldiers in Black Africa, 1952). In its content, form, and message of an unchanging Africa relegated to an eternal past, Hamon's and N'Gassa's film belongs to the tradition of French ethnographic documentary, within which multiple films were made about Bamileke dwellings in the 1950s. A series of scenes documents the construction of the great house, described as the future location of community meetings and traditional ceremonies. The voice-over commentary proclaims that the new house will be identical to the one it is replacing, stressing that the building techniques are the same as those used 130 years prior. And when sacred dances are performed to celebrate the house's completion, the narration concludes with the Griaule-like assertion that now "the eternal spirit of Africa can continue, intact, unchanging, in all of its purity." The film's comparison of the Bamileke great house to medieval European cathedrals and the Eiffel Tower, moreover, led Paulin Vieyra to suspect that N'Gassa did not have much of a role in its crafting.[50]

The documentary films of Pascal Abikanlou, like Senghor's *Grand Magal à Touba*, are more convincingly autoethnographic, anchored in explanatory commentary from an insider's perspective. Originally from Pobé, in Dahomey, Abikanlou trained as a draftsman before taking correspondence courses in photography and working as a reporter and assistant cameraman. In the early 1960s, when the Dahomeyan Cinema Company (SODACI) was created in cooperation with France's CAI, Abikanlou worked as cameraman on weekly national newsreels.[51] After an internship in France, he began to direct his own films, which were also funded by the SODACI. The voice-over narrator of *Premières offrandes* (First offerings, 1969) explains the ritual that begins the harvest season in a region where "Nago clans cultivate for the most part the yam, a voluminous tuber that is the base of their diet." The film cuts from one fixed shot to another, showing the community preparing for the ceremony "according to tradition." Abikanlou's *La fête de l'igname* (The yam festival, 1969), a more detailed presentation of the yam ceremony, was followed by *Escale au Dahomey* (Stopover in Dahomey, 1968), a panoramic presentation of the country and its culture.

Senegalese director Momar Thiam shared Abikanlou's approach in films depicting touchstones of West African culture. Thiam attended both Quranic and French schools in Dakar, worked briefly as an accountant, and then left for France to study photography. He returned to work at the Actualités Sénégalaises and began his directorial career with *Sarzan* (1962), an adaptation of a short story by Senegalese author Birago Diop.[52] For *Luttes casamançaises* (Casamance wrestling, 1968), Thiam worked with cameraman Abdou Fary

Faye to film a wrestling competition held in a Dakar neighborhood. Voice-over commentary informs spectators that children in Casamance begin to wrestle at the age of eight; spectators are shown several bouts and the triumphant celebration of the winner, who is carried by the crowd. Thiam followed up with *Simb: Jeu de faux lion* (Simb: Game of the false lion, 1969), which also begins with third-person narration: "Simb, or the game of the false lion, is a popular performance that was born in the river region. . . . Its history goes back more than a century. It is generally organized to accompany a big meeting or a popular performance." After listing the names of famous false lions, said to share the qualities of the lion for having been clawed by one, the narrator introduces the performer we will watch, Pierre N'Gom. The film's conclusion teaches the lesson that "Simb, for the Senegalese, belongs to the folkloric universe of our national artistic heritage."

Two years later, Abdou Fary Faye made *Ballet de la forêt sacrée de Casamance* (Ballet of the sacred forest of Casamance, 1970), and Thiam served as his assistant. Faye's autoethnography, however, has no voice-over commentary. Following an intertitle that reads, "The call of the tom-tom and the voice of Africa," additional intertitles introduce the two parts of the performance: "Ontine or the sacred river" and "Magic tom-tom." To portray the ballet of his title, Faye edited together fixed shots from different angles and distances, showing drummers and dancers in a mix of medium shots and close-ups of hands and feet. Several years earlier, Paulin Vieyra's *Avec l'ensemble national* (With the national company, 1964) had represented performances by the Senegalese National Ballet in a more conventional style. And journalist Thérèse Sita Bella recorded traditional dances performed by Cameroon's national troupe for *Tam tam à Paris* (Tom-tom in Paris, 1963), a coproduction of Cameroon's Ministry of National Education and the CAI. Featured at the first FESPACO at the end of the decade but now lost, Sita Bella's documentary was likely the first film made by a Black African woman.

West and central African cinema and television services commissioned films about African cultural festivals to link African traditions to contemporary, politically independent nations. Vieyra's *Le Sénégal et le Festival mondial des arts nègres* (Senegal and the World Festival of Negro Arts, 1966) begins with aerial views of Dakar, a city, voice-over narration informs us, that just over a hundred years ago was "a humble fishing village with straw huts, which have given way to genuine skyscrapers."[53] Guinean Sekou Amadou Yonfila filmed the First Pan-African Cultural Festival in Algiers in 1969 for *L'Afrique danse* (Africa dances, 1970). The commentary that introduces each set of performances declares that the parades of national delegations in traditional costume exemplify "the richness of the African imagination." The first film director from the Republic of the Congo, Sebastien Kamba, filmed the same festival for *Le premier festival culturel panafricain d'Alger* (The First Pan-African Cultural Festival of Algiers, 1969). Trained as a teacher, Kamba had completed an internship in France in order to work for Congolese television. Once back in Brazzaville, he joined the camera club of the French Cultural Center and shot a documentary about neighboring Democratic Republic of Congo's fight for independence from Belgium titled *Le peuple du Congo-Léo vaincra* (The people of Congo-Léo will triumph, 1965). After Algiers, Kamba made a second festival film—*Le festival culturel de Guinée* (The Guinean cultural festival, 1970)—and a series of shorts documenting political ceremonies.[54]

Not all commissioned documentaries were ethnographic during this period, and nationalism took different turns. Moustapha Alassane's *L'arachide de Santchira* (Santchira peanuts, 1966) was coproduced by Niger's Ministry of National Education in support of a local peanut company. Abikanlou's *Opération SO.NA.DER dans le Mono* (The SO.NA.DER Project in Mono, 1971) addresses the arrival of mechanization in the village of Houin, in the Mono region of Dahomey. Following instructions from the government, peasants form the SO.NA.DER agricultural cooperative to learn new farming methods. Ivorian Timité Bassori, best remembered for his short fiction *Sur la dune de la solitude* (On the dunes of solitude, 1964) and feature-length *La femme au couteau* (Woman with a knife, 1968), also made documentaries on commission. Bassori studied theater in Paris, where he performed with future filmmakers Ababacar Samb and Sarah Maldoror in the Griots' Dramatic Art Troupe. When he enrolled at the IDHEC in the late 1950s, he became a classmate of Blaise Senghor. Upon his return home, Bassori joined the Ivorian Cinema Company (SIC) and worked to launch Côte d'Ivoire's first national television station. In *Les forestiers* (Forest rangers, 1963), he addressed questions of conservation, and in *L'Abidjan-Niger* (The Abidjan-Niger line, 1963), West African train networks.[55] Bassori's *Feux de brousse* (Brush fires, 1968) was coproduced by the SIC and the CAI. Over opening shots of a courtroom, a voice-over commentary informs us that a man has just been charged with destroying a thousand hectares of land. The film's stated goal, to alert viewers to "the harmful effects of certain practices on vegetation and thus on the national economy," is accomplished via an expository introduction, direct advice to peasant farmers, and a lengthy series of shots of fires raging out of control, accompanied by a syncopated jazz score and the sound of a crying child. This creative touch was recognized by Paris-based magazine *Jeune Afrique*, which praised *Feux de brousse* for being both educational and of interest to a wide audience.[56]

In president and dictator Sekou Touré's socialist Guinea, commissioned documentaries mixed autoethnography with government propaganda. At independence, Touré nationalized all aspects of the Guinean film industry, creating the Syli-Cinema company to control production, distribution, and exhibition. Directors were instructed to produce educational and ethnographic documentaries that would inform Guineans about their history and culture.[57] Moussa Kemoko Diakité, who had studied in Frankfurt, West Germany, shot a number of films for Syli-Cinema, including *Riziculture dans le Bagata* (Rice cultivation in Bagata, 1969); *Le 14 mai 1970* (1970), about the birth of Touré's Democratic Party of Guinea (PDG); *Les funérailles de Kwame Nkrumah* (The funeral of Kwame Nkrumah, 1972); and *Fidel Castro, un voyage en Guinée* (Fidel Castro in Guinea, 1972). Diakité's feature-length *Hirde Dyama* (People's celebration, 1971) depicts the two-week-long First National Cultural Festival held in Conakry in 1970. The film was coproduced by the East German state-owned DEFA company; Diakité codirected with Gerhard Jentsch, who wrote and read the German voice-over commentary, and most of the members of the crew were East German.[58] In a sign of the prevalence of European funding during the first dozen years after independence, *Hirde Dyama* was awarded the newly created Special Prize for African Authenticity at the 1972 edition of FESPACO despite its German codirection and narrative perspective.[59]

Hirde Dyama begins with a long shot of a sunset over the ocean, followed by close-ups, one by one, of individual Guineans—children, women, and men. The film's German-language voice-over narration introduces the capital of Conakry, and thousands of performers arrive in an endless parade of theater, ballet, and instrumental troupes, choirs, and orchestras. Cultural and political propaganda come together as Sekou Touré is shown inside the People's Palace, announcing that the objective of the festival is to show the rich traditions of African culture and art as both entertainment and forces of social liberation. The festival begins, with songs of praise to Touré's PDG followed by excerpts of plays about resistance heroes Almamy Samory Touré and Alpha Yaya, modern African music based on traditional themes performed by Bembeya Jazz National, and dances with historical, anticolonial themes performed by the National Ballet of Guinea. *Hirde Dyama* adds praise of Guinea's accomplishments in the areas of education and industrial development to its celebration of independence and traditional culture. "The chains have fallen," the voice-over narrator announces as workers celebrate the opening of a new power plant, "and with these the shackles of economic backwardness have also been thrown off."

Struggling for filmic independence through the 1960s and into the early 70s, then, African filmmakers produced works about their countries and a range of African cultural traditions and events. Yet French fellow traveler of early African cinema Pierre Haffner expressed frustration that African directors did not make more ethnographic films. Haffner understood this choice as a sign of the "subjective, even narcissistic character of their approach, their individualism, the distance between them and the ordinary people from whom they are descended," going so far as to suggest in an interview with Paulin Vieyra that it might be easier for a white filmmaker to speak with elders in a village. Vieyra disagreed.[60] It seems that African filmmakers were not making what Haffner considered to be ethnographic films, which is to say not following the model epitomized by Marcel Griaule, Jacques Dupont, and Jean Rouch, whose *Chasse au lion à l'arc* Haffner considered exemplary. Given what we have learned from the beginnings of African documentary, perhaps the distinction between ethnographic and autoethnographic film is unnecessary, indeed counterproductive.

Even with regard to the decades after independence, scholarly and critical attention to innovations in ethnographic filmmaking in sub-Saharan Africa has been limited to the work of non-African filmmakers: Rouch, but also Chris Marker, Trinh Minh-ha, and Peter Kubelka, among others. Our nonfiction film history, already grounded in an inclusive definition of documentary, requires a definition of ethnographic cinema capacious enough to allow African directors to contribute to its canon. Early African documentarists, seeking to reflect African realities, reversed European ethnography's perspective on Africa while challenging its form, exploring a range of strategies to widen colonial cinema's circumscribed approach. If we set aside Rouch's insistence that the ethnographer be an outsider to the culture represented, we might better examine how, to take up once again Renov's phrasing, African documentary has expanded the received boundaries of ethnographic cinema *tout court*.[61]

When Paulin Vieyra arrived in Dakar from Paris in 1957, his first project was a film tentatively titled *Un homme, un idéal, une vie* (A man, an ideal, a life). The African Cinema Group lacked the funding to edit and add commentary and a soundtrack to the silent, color footage, and it took almost a decade to complete and release what became *Môl* (Fisherman, 1966). The film depicts life in a fishing village near Dakar through the story of a central character, Ousmane. After the opening credits, we watch a boy on the beach throw stones into the ocean, and the voice-over begins: "When Ousmane was a child, he dreamed of becoming a man of the sea, a great fisherman." Following a panning shot of the village of Cayar, the commentary becomes informational, identifying "one of the most important fishing centers in the region," then recounting Ousmane's day at work and his visits to friends afterward, characterizing both as typical of young men in Cayar. Spectators also see Ousmane's girlfriend, Aissata, doing chores and visiting her female friends. "Today," the narrator states, "Ousmane will confide in Aissata that he has decided to buy a motor for his pirogue." This decision is the result of a transformation in local fishing patterns: "The fish are going farther and farther from the coast. The work of a fisherman is getting more and more difficult and dangerous. And it would be absurd not to use what progress offers."

Môl constructs characters but does not account for the fullness of individual lives. Vieyra's project was rather to illustrate and analyze the life of a Senegalese fisherman working in a traditional occupation that faces contemporary pressures. Three decades after *Nanook of the North* and *Voyage au Congo*, Vieyra and his colleagues would similarly use representative reenactments, or typifications, in their ethnographies. Unlike Flaherty and Allégret, however, they did so from the perspectives of the dynamic societies they were filming. The elders of Cayar are concerned, relates *Môl*'s voice-over, that "Ousmane's project will interfere with customs. And how will the spirits answer?" After deliberating, the elders consult the ancestors, whose approval Vieyra conveys through quick, intercut shots of a baobab tree, masks, and drums, time-honored cultural symbols. When Ousmane leaves to buy the motor, the commentary describes his departure rituals, reassuring spectators that "all was done according to tradition." Ousmane's attempt to borrow money from an uncle in Saint-Louis is unsuccessful, so he continues to Dakar. At the industrial equipment office of the French West-African Company (CFAO), a colonial trading enterprise that began distributing American agricultural machinery in the 1950s, the narrator explains how the system of credit functions. Ousmane works at the port to earn money for his down payment, then returns to Cayar, where villagers are overjoyed to see him and "welcome progress" in the form of a shiny, red Johnson boat motor. Ousmane and Aissata can now marry; "the dreams of a little boy are fulfilled."

Like *Grand Magal à Touba*, *Môl* is didactic, in this case a combination of ethnography and educational film, a third subset of documentary with colonial European roots in sub-Saharan Africa. Having represented the daily life and traditional customs of Ousmane's village, Vieyra shows that Ousmane's dream has come true thanks to modern technology approved by the ancestors. And like *Une nation est née*, *Môl* is political as well as allegorical, bringing together different regions of Senegal—in this case Cayar, Saint-Louis, and the capital city of Dakar, where Ousmane is amazed by the skyscrapers, broad streets, and international port. The film's voice-over narration, bolstered by the story of Ousmane and Aissata, encourages viewers to join the new to time-honored tradition. Vieyra was ultimately critical, however, of the final version of his film's commentary, written by Renée Clarke and read by Mauritanian actor and future filmmaker Med Hondo. He found its sensibility European rather than African and its commentary "too realistic, repeating the image and explaining it, a common fault in French film commentaries."[62] *Môl* proved too conventionally ethnographic for its own director.

Paulin Vieyra similarly criticized the voice-over commentary of Blaise Senghor's *Grand Magal à Touba* for being "ponderous."[63] The entire film, in his opinion, too much resembled an outsider's view on the Mouride pilgrimage to Touba.[64] Moustapha Alassane on the contrary rebelled against colonial-era film style in his first work, *Aouré* (Marriage, 1962), which joins *Une nation est née* and *Grand Magal à Touba* among the very first sub-Saharan African films. Upon the film's release, D'dée praised Alassane in an article titled "Finally, True African Cinema," writing that *Aouré* evinced "a truly authentic African character."[65] Born in Dahomey in the early 1940s, Alassane moved with his family to Niger a decade later. He came to cinema through a talent for drawing and, while working as a clerk at the IFAN ethnographic museum in Niamey, experimented with drawing directly on film stock. It was at the IFAN that Alassane met Jean Rouch, who taught him about cinema and helped arrange an internship with Canadian animator Norman McLaren. Although known primarily for his animated shorts, adaptations of traditional tales, and a parody western, Alassane also made several short nonfiction films.[66] In an interview conducted at the first FESPACO, Alassane like Vieyra stressed the urgent need for African documentaries to counter the European documentaries filmed in Africa. He criticized European ethnographers for portraying a timeless and unchanging Africa instead of "contemporary African reality." "In this situation," Alassane argued, "it is important that we, as African filmmakers, prove to these European spectators . . . that the past is over, that today Africa is independent."[67] To this end, he would experiment with characterization, voice-over narration, and editing.

Alassane described *Aouré*, a coproduction of the IFAN and the French Ministry of Cooperation, as a "short film of an ethnographic type, that described a Djerma [Zarma] marriage." Like *Grand Magal à Touba*, the film was acclaimed in Europe, winning a silver medal at the Cannes Amateur Film Festival and the Prize for Ethnographic Film at Saint-Cast.[68] *Aouré*, like *Môl*, uses character development to draw in its spectators. And, like Allégret's *Voyage au Congo*, the documentary illustrates how courtship leads to marriage through the story of a young couple.[69] Early in Alassane's voice-over commentary, he pointedly informs viewers that "marriage is of great importance in our country." This *our* identifies him as an African and more specifically Nigerien documentarist, representing his people on screen.

Aouré's narration both summarizes actions on screen and speaks occasional lines of dialogue, recounting the love story of characters Mariam and Garba as traditional and typical. When the two decide to marry, the voice-over details the steps of the process, all of which require the participation of members of their community. After making a promise to Mariam, Garba speaks to his father, a fisherman, about their plans. His father agrees to the marriage, and village griots visit Mariam's family to ask for her hand in marriage on Garba's behalf. Garba's father then delivers the *sougi* or dowry, which Alassane notes is "often a sum of 25,000 or 30,000 francs." Mumbling the requisite prayers from the Quran, Alassane as narrator again places himself within the filmed community. "Marriage is quite a remarkable ceremony in Niger," he continues, but afterward, the young couple will return to their daily tasks. *Aouré* concludes with a short scene scripted to exemplify, with a bit of humor, the state of marriage. Mariam wants to buy a pillow cover from a traveling merchant, but Garba refuses. They argue, Mariam prevails, and work begins again.

Released a year after *Aouré* and in the same year as *Sarzan* and *Borom Sarret*, Paulin Vieyra's *Lamb* (Wrestling, 1963), shot in color, is devoted to traditional Senegalese wrestling. Although produced by the Senegalese Ministry of Information, it is in some ways Vieyra's most innovative short film and became, according to Vieyra, the first "entirely African film" to be screened in official competition at the Cannes Film Festival.[70] Whereas *Afrique sur Seine* and *Une nation est née* illustrate African history and contemporary reality from an African perspective without an ethnographic focus, and *Môl* incorporates ethnography into an educational film, *Lamb*'s ethnography consists both of performances in which wrestlers illustrate their sport and of recorded footage of wrestling matches, tied together by voice-over commentary. Vieyra consciously addressed a diverse audience, aiming to present Senegalese wrestling "at the same time to connoisseurs and to those who know nothing about it."[71] And he used humor to appeal to these viewers, explaining that the film was "a creation, that is to say the expression of a personal point of view on wrestling."[72]

Returning to the nationalist political message of *Une nation est née*, *Lamb* begins by asserting a Senegalese unity made up of diverse occupations and ethnic groups. Images of landscapes, cattle, and pirogues are supported by narration stating that farmers and fishermen, Wolof, Toucouleur, Serer, and Djolof, are all "children of Senegal." Traditional wrestling brings them together; "truly a national sport," we are told, it "goes beyond sport." Less formal than that of Vieyra's previous films, the commentary continues: "To appreciate it, you must

Moustapha Alassane, *Aouré*, 1962.

know it. And so here is a demonstration." *Lamb* shows and explains *lamb* to its viewers, from wrestlers training on the beach, smiling and swinging their arms as they jog, through the conclusion of several matches. The narrator names each move as two men wrestle on a beach, watched by a few fishermen, and as a single wrestler performs different positions for falling. After a cut to recorded footage of a match in a small stadium, wrestlers prepare, busloads of spectators arrive, and suddenly, in a transition via overhead shots of traffic, we see a much bigger stadium in a large city. The match footage is edited discontinuously throughout the remaining two-thirds of the film, alternating between close-ups and long shots, views of wrestlers and audience members from different angles, and wrestling matches in different stadiums.

Like its editing, *Lamb*'s commentary is heterogeneous and unconventional, by turns informational, literary, philosophical, joking, and enthusiastic as it weaves together multiple aspects and examples of wrestling. Introducing the match in the large stadium, the voice-over narrator explains that "this muscle festival is a festival of the people; from the head of state to the humblest citizen, they come to see, they come to listen, for here, the word makes the man, and it makes him a hero." Next, as if a participant in the event, the narrator cries out excitedly, "To your seats! The show is about to start!" As viewers see and hear a band, crowds, and wrestlers, he works in a reference to Senegalese literature. Citing Birago Diop's poem "Souffles" (Breaths, 1951), he urges us to "listen, as the poet said, listen more often to things than to beings, the voice of the ancestors will be heard," then calls out again, "To your seats!" Ousmane Sembene, at the time a rising young filmmaker, listens to a wrestling match on the radio in an on-screen cameo. Again interpolating as if we were at the stadium, the voice-over narrator interjects: "The show is about to start! Place your bets!" As *Lamb* comes to an end, Sembene and his friends celebrate a win by their favored wrestler, and spectators at the different matches leave the stadiums. The commentary concludes that *lamb* is "a sport, a spectacle, a game, life," and the film's last images are of two children play wrestling. Vieyra's documentary elaborates the present reality of an African tradition—one that these boys, like Alassane's Mariam and Garba, will carry into the future.

Like Blaise Senghor, Moustapha Alassane, and Paulin Vieyra, Cameroonian filmmaker Moïse Zé sought in his work to break from "traditional ethnographic cinema," which he characterized as "an abusive enterprise." In such films, Zé asserted, foreign directors arrive with a foreign crew to film local populations that neither contribute to the finished product nor profit from it. He called for the founding of an African "research cinema" informed by a deep knowledge of its topics.[73] Zé had attended secondary school in Yaoundé before undertaking university studies of economics and filmmaking in Paris. When he returned to Cameroon, Zé founded his own production company, MOZES'Films. Named for a traditional musical instrument and style of performance, his innovative *Le Mvet* (1965/1972) won the prize for Best Research Film for the Conservation and Diffusion of African Cultures at the Carthage Festival. Zé's collaborative first-person voice-over in dialogue with Jackie Maman accompanies the representation of a Cameroonian musical tradition, but he insisted that it does not merely narrate the film. It is "an evocation of the *mvet* narratives" with a threefold charge: to describe the film's images, allow those portrayed in the film to speak for themselves, and present the filmmaker's analysis of the topic.[74]

When introducing the ethnographic films of Pascal Abikanlou, I intentionally skipped over his first effort, which was more distinctive than his subsequent work. In *Ganvié mon village* (Ganvié my village, 1967), Abikanlou like Zé experimented with documentary narration, opting to provide not just an African frame of reference, constant throughout his career, but also a first-person voice. In autobiographical commentary written by Abikanlou and read by Richard Dogbeh, the unseen narrator of *Ganvié* returns to his lakeside village many years after having left for high school. "Here I am again," he

Paulin Soumanou Vieyra, *Lamb*, 1963.

announces, "completely changed." Traveling in a boat piloted by a man who has not "betrayed" the village by leaving, the narrator visits his family's house on stilts over the water and explains the work they have done for generations as fishermen, the house's construction, and the village's social organization and structure. Addressing the boatman as well as the entire village in the second-person singular, he says, "You have remained unchanged. . . . Ganvié my village, I love you." The film concludes with panning shots through the village from the boat, aerial shots from a plane, and more praise of Ganvié, "my village, not like the others." Abikanlou's intimate voice-over conveys ethnographic information while hinting at an individual story of colonial and neocolonial education in exile.

First- and second-person voices also narrate the ethnographic films of director Richard de Medeiros. Originally from Ouidah, Dahomey, de Medeiros studied classical and modern literature in France, then taught at the university level in Algiers and Cotonou. His first documentary was made for Algerian television. Historical and anticolonial, *Le roi est mort en exil* (The king died in exile, 1969) recounts the imprisonment and 1906 death of King Behanzin, the last ruler of the kingdom of Dahomey. Behanzin and his soldiers fought the invading French army in the last decade of the nineteenth century; after surrendering, he was deported first to Martinique and later to Blida. Three years later, in *Téké, hymne au Borgou* (Teke, hymn to Borgou, 1972), de Medeiros shifted to a cultural topic, the baton dance of the Bariba in northeastern Dahomey, a ritual performed for a period of seven days during the celebration of a king's ascension to the throne. The film begins with drumming and singing in a small village. Voice-over commentary, read by Jean Biaou, joins the singing and switches to French: "Bouye bouye bouye bou, hello, all of you here; we welcome you." The narrator lists the names of the descendants of great Bariba warriors and then addresses them: "Hear me. Hear your griot who comes to praise you this evening. . . . We came to start off the *teke* for you." He translates into French the history of the dynasty as told by an elder, detailing the professions and familial relationships of all those on screen.

Reciting proverbs and stories associated with the dance, the voice-over narrator again addresses the film's spectators, now pointedly assumed to be African: "Listen to the story of our fathers." Like Alassane's narrator, he also consistently and explicitly places himself within the culture he is engaging as he shares ethnographic information. Explaining that *teke* dancing imitates the movements of a small black insect that circles on the water's surface, for example, he says, "That's what we imitate when we dance." This positioning was crucial for de Medeiros who, critiquing the films of Jean Rouch, explained, "That's the problem with ethnology, just like it is the problem of history and the historian; depending on the place from which you see the battlefield, you don't see the same thing."[75] De Medeiros also took care to bring the ancestral tradition of *teke* into the present; viewers both learn about the past of the Borgou region and see its modern factories and schools. The film concludes with images shot by a twirling camera that mimics *teke* dancing, while the narrator takes his leave: "*Teke* dancers, I honor you. My friends everywhere, I honor you all."

Coining a phrase that could also apply to *Ganvié mon village* and *Téké, hymne au Borgou*, Paulin Vieyra described Senegalese director Tidiane Aw's *Réalité* (Reality, 1969) as a work of "theatrical ethnology."[76] Aw studied photography in Germany and radio journalism in France, then returned to Senegal in 1965 to work in television. He went on to head Senegal's cinema bureau and direct several popular full-length fiction films. In *Réalité*, which was partially funded by Debrix's Bureau of Cinema, Aw took an innovative approach to the representation of the *n'doep* ceremony, a ritual to cure victims of possession featured in a number of French ethnographic films made both before and after independence. In Michel Meignant's *N'doep* (1967), for example, spectators are introduced to the custom by a long interview with a European doctor who contrasts Western psychiatry with what he terms "savage psychiatry." Clips from a recorded *n'doep* ceremony are accompanied by an omniscient, explanatory voice-over.

Aw begins *Réalité* very differently, with an acted scene in which a certain Mr. Diop tries to awaken his wife from a nightmare. A voice-over narrator then explains that "this film, which takes place in Senegal, shows yet again that Africa remains very attached to its traditions." "The world of spirits and demons," he continues, "the supernatural world, is a reality for the African." Desperate to cure his wife, Diop seeks out a traditional healer, who diagnoses the illness and performs the necessary rite. Unlike the *n'doep* ceremony depicted by Meignant, Aw's is overtly performed for the camera, and the film concludes with Mrs. Diop dancing and rolling on the ground, imitating the lion *rabe*, or spirit, that has possessed her in order to liberate herself from it. The image blurs as we see incarnations of other spirits, and the commentary pronounces the last words of the film: "*N'doep* endures yesterday, today, and tomorrow." Aw shows *n'doep* to be a real cure for a culturally significant illness, with none of the patronizing distance of Meignant and his psychiatrist. The "reality" of the title refers both to the cure and the film itself, which uses acted scenes understood to provide more authentic information than had the ostensibly scientific recordings made by Europeans.

In an interesting counterpoint to the ethnographic *I* and *we* used by Alassane, Vieyra, and de Medeiros, several early African documentarists turned their cameras on the French. Guinean director Alpha Adama, a former architecture student, produced *L'imprévu* (Unforeseen, 1964), a film described by Paulin Vieyra as "an African vision of the life of young people in France, a bit in the style of the gaze of a Western ethnographer on Africa."[77] Cameroonian filmmaker Jean-Pierre Dikongue-Pipa, who worked as a journalist in Côte d'Ivoire before training in Paris, addressed the question of infidelity in European society in *Les cornes* (Horns, 1966). Rather than remake or reverse ethnography, another group of filmmakers opted to address cultural traditions in a poetic, reflective, and even formally reflexive mode. These films further trouble the standard narrative of the first decades of African filmmaking, which, as we have seen, obscures the role of documentary through a focus on realist fictions with nonprofessional actors. Even Guy Hennebelle, a French critic who like Haffner was extremely interested in Black African cinema from its beginnings, saw it as limited to a simple realism Europe had already outgrown. "African cinemas overall have drawn their inspiration from dated, if not outdated, aesthetics," he contended, and "the 'modernist' influence, when present, has only manifested itself as alienated mimicry."[78] This charge of alienation recalls the insistence of colonial-era cameramen and directors that authentic African culture was by definition locked in the past. By the time Hennebelle wrote these words in 1972, African filmmakers had already proven themselves skilled at taking modernist cinematic influences in new directions.

Some documentarists addressed African artistic and performance traditions by opting for an expressive, avant-garde style that dispensed with ethnographic explanation. Vieyra described Yves Diagne's *Delou Thyossane* (Return to traditions, 1966), a coproduction of the Actualités Françaises and CAI, as "an art film about art."[79] Diagne, who was born in Dakar, studied in Paris, graduating from the IDHEC in 1962. While in France, he codirected *L'Afrique noire en piste* (Black Africa on track, 1965), a documentary about African athletes training to represent their countries at the First All-Africa Games in Brazzaville. Back in Senegal, Diagne served as director of Senegal's Cinematographic Import and Distribution Company (SIDEC) and made a few films. *Delou Thyossane*'s first images are of African masks and traditional sculpture, which the camera approaches in zooms and traveling shots. In images reminiscent of Resnais's and Marker's *Les statues meurent aussi*, viewers see works of art isolated against a black background. Accompanied on the soundtrack by a jazz score, Diagne's voice-over narrator speaks in both the third and first person. "The virtue of Negro art is to be neither pure aesthetic pleasure nor a game, but to signify," the commentary affirms, without identifying any of the pieces shown on screen or their locations. Citing Léopold Sédar Senghor in a film styled to match the objects it features, Diagne concludes that African art, suggestive and rhythmic, restores the unity of man with his world, of flesh with spirit.[80]

Costadès Diagne's *Les hommes de la danse* (Men of dance, 1966) also echoes *Les statues meurent aussi*, particularly in its focus on the inappropriateness of the European museum setting for African art. Diagne, also known as Costa, was born in Guinea to a Guinean mother and a Greek father. After studying in France, he moved to the State Institute of Cinema (VGIK) in Soviet Moscow; *Les hommes de la danse*, his graduation film, won the Golden Antelope Award at the Festival of Negro Arts in Dakar. The short subject shows cameraman and fellow Guinean Himi Sylla touring an exhibit of African art in a Moscow museum, where he and Diagne encounter a mask from their home country.[81] The accompanying voice-over narration is not explanatory but instead quotes from writings by dancer, poet, and politician Fodéba Keita, founder of the Guinean national ballet. The film concludes with an excerpt from Senghor's poem "Prayer to the Masks," which replaces the exploitative colonial perception of Africans as "men of cotton of coffee or oil" with "men of dance." "Only an African could shoot this script," Diagne said of his film, maintaining that its topic was not African art. It was about his "emotions toward and impressions of" African art, Diagne argued, "which someone from another country or continent would not have been able to express."[82]

African art is similarly at the heart of *Sources d'inspiration* (Sources of inspiration, 1967), one of three student films made by world-renowned Malian director Souleymane Cissé. Cissé worked as a projectionist in Bamako before attending the VGIK several years after Diagne. *Sources d'inspiration* examines the work of painter Mamadou Somé Coulibaly, another Malian studying in the Soviet Union, in the context of contemporary international politics, using newsreel footage of protests and violence against Black Africans and Americans in South Africa, Rhodesia, Angola, and Alabama. Opening shots of a drawing of colonial soldiers overseeing the forced labor of Africans are followed by an intertitle that cites poet and theorist Aimé Césaire: "A civilization which uses its principles to deceive is a moribund civilization." Cissé then elaborates an anticolonial argument in sequential clips of Martin Luther King Jr. and Patrice Lumumba, accompanied by readings of poems by Césaire and Senghor and songs by South African and pan-African activist Miriam Makeba. Although he is best known for his later feature fiction films, Cissé said that it was a 1962 documentary about Lumumba's arrest that convinced him of the importance and power of cinema.[83] And when he returned to Mali from the Soviet Union, Cissé worked for the cinema service of the Ministry of Information, where in just two years he made thirty newsreels and five documentaries, some ethnographic.[84] *Degal à Dialloubé* (Degal in Dialloubé, 1970), shows cattle herders crossing the Niger river in an annual search for new pastures, and *Fête de Sanke* (Sanke Festival, 1971) highlights an annual celebration of fishermen in southeastern Mali.

Not all early African documentary filmmakers opted to focus on the recovery or valorization of precolonial cultural traditions. Urbain Dia-Moukori, in the same essay in which he called for a daring approach on the part of the African director, expressed his frustration with the stereotypical images and sounds of Africa in both European and African films. "Please, no nighttime tom-tom on the village square!" he pleaded somewhat provocatively; "I can affirm that I have never heard as many tom-toms as in the European theaters where films about Africa were shown."[85] The end of the decade of independence saw a return to the historical and political focus of Vieyra's *Une nation est née*, in renewed celebrations of African independence that critiqued persistent remnants of colonial power.

Documentary in Guinea was strongly influenced by the Soviet montage tradition, with filmmakers given more leeway for aesthetic than political experimentation. When Costa Diagne returned from the Soviet Union in 1967, he, like Moussa Diakité, was urged to make propaganda films. Diagne released

Huit et vingt (Eight and twenty, 1968), a lengthy presentation of the eighth convention of Sekou Touré's PDG that Paulin Vieyra deemed "a bad and deadly boring propaganda film which is also technically poor." Vieyra had high praise, however, for Diagne's *Hier, aujourd'hui, demain* (Yesterday, today, tomorrow, 1968) of the same year, a medium-length documentary that was presented at the Carthage Festival and won the Joris Ivens Prize at the Leipzig Film Festival in Germany. The film traces Guinean history from the colonial period to independence to the future of current development efforts, evidencing at the same time, in Vieyra's words, "aesthetic experimentation used to support artistic expression."[86] Touré, on the other hand, believed that Guineans would not understand *Hier, aujourd'hui, demain*.[87] Diagne was arrested in the 1971 purge of Guinean filmmakers, two years after the arrest and assassination of Fodéba Keita, and imprisoned for seven years at the notorious Camp Boiro.

A colleague of Diagne's, Guinean Sekoumar Barry trained in Belgrade, Yugoslavia, and made *Et vint la liberté* (Thus arrived liberty, 1968) in a studio in Warsaw, Poland. *Et vint la liberté* was featured at the Pan-African Cultural Festival in Algiers, and Touré liked it so much that he screened it frequently, perhaps the reason that Barry spent only a year in Camp Boiro.[88] Barry's work, like Diagne's, recounts both colonization and decolonization using archival documents: colonial-era drawings and photos from the Guinean National Institute of Research and Documentation and newsreel footage from Syli-Cinema. The film begins by evoking slavery, with sounds of cannons firing, drawings of enslaved people, and text on screen that reads "Africa torn apart, humiliated, and wounded!" Several more titles follow, apostrophizing a wounded continent: "Africa! They killed your kings and your sublime monarchs, denied your culture, your civilization, your history!" The camera follows the paths of the African diaspora on a world map, and the last title announces a mission: "Peoples of Africa, together we will reestablish the truth of history!"

After a voice-over overview of Guinean geography, music on the soundtrack becomes ominous, anticipating the arrival of French and Portuguese slave ships. The narration provides biographical information about late nineteenth-century resistance fighters Samory Touré, Alpha Yaya, and Dina Salifou, all of whom were captured and imprisoned by the French. Addressing the subsequent colonial period, *Et vint la liberté* compares forced labor to the slavery that preceded it. In an Africa divided among colonial powers, Barry's commentary asserts, "the African became a foreigner in his own country." The film then jumps to 1947 and Sekou Touré's founding of the PDG, followed by the 1957 formation of the first semiautonomous Guinean government. To highlight Touré's leading role in the process that brought Guinean independence, Barry includes newsreel footage of the president's declaration, in front of Charles de Gaulle, that "we prefer poverty and liberty to wealth and slavery." Over additional footage of Guineans voting for independence from France, the voice-over commentary returns to Samory's deportation in 1898, now avenged by the proclamation of the Republic of Guinea. Barry's Soviet training is evident in the montage technique used throughout the film; at the moment his narrative arrives at independence, shots of fallen, decayed European statues are linked to images of the new flag flying and a performance of the Guinean national anthem. Intercut footage of triumphant rallies and visiting dignitaries gives way to Touré visiting New York as global pan-African leader, featured on the cover of *Ebony* magazine. *Et vint la liberté* concludes at the moment of its own creation, with celebrations of the tenth anniversary of Guinean independence and aerial city shots of new buildings symbolizing a modern nation.

In the same watershed year, Senegalese filmmaker Djibril Diop Mambety released an equally experimental, reflexive, and anticolonial documentary with a very different narrative style and without Barry's archival images or propagandistic bent. Mambety, who was born in Dakar, took a few theater classes after dropping out of high school and then acted at the national Daniel Sorano Theater. *Contras' City* (1968), his second short subject, was shot on 16mm in six days and on a shoestring budget raised from private investors.[89] Mambety is now regarded as one of sub-Saharan Africa's best and most idiosyncratic filmmakers for his feature fictions *Touki Bouki* (1973) and *Hyènes* (Hyenas, 1992), both of which exhibit the "very personal filmic style" that Paulin Vieyra discerned in his earlier work.[90]

Vieyra described *Contras' City* as a "critical essay about life in Dakar starting from its colonial heritage."[91] The film begins with symphonic music and images of the city's colonial-era architecture; the camera changes angles, zooming in and out on wrought iron gates, then pans down from the sky to a building with a clock tower, the *hôtel de ville* or city hall. Mambety's voice-over narration, like that of Moïse Zé, is dialogic. To a woman's "O, my sweet France," a man responds, "Your sweet France doesn't seem to handle the sun very well. . . . her France . . . well, my dear, this is Dakar." His joking sarcasm recalls Vieyra's *Lamb* but with a sharper tone, one that scholar Sada Niang characterizes as "taunting."[92] The camera continues its downward movement to arrive at the Senegalese flag, at which point the sound of a record scratch interrupts the classical music on the soundtrack. From a greater distance but still in front of the formerly French and now Senegalese city hall, we see a man leading a horse-drawn cart, around and in which are a white cameraman and our African and European narrators, director Mambety and script girl Inge

Djibril Diop Mambéty, *Contras' City*, 1968.

Hirschnitz. In this reflexive reference to Ousmane Sembene's already iconic *Borom Sarret*, Mambety asserts his film's Africanness in the face of the ostentatiously nonnative building, situating his work within a young Senegalese and sub-Saharan African filmic tradition. Only now does the title appear, written on the side of a clapboard and followed by the opening credits.

Mambety shows viewers colonial buildings housing Total Oil and the chamber of commerce as well as the Sorano Theater, built in 1966 for the Festival of Negro Arts. In their dialogue, the earnest female and sarcastic male narrators comment on all three. Hennebelle attributed to *Contras' City* the distinction of being "the first comic African film," and art historian Steven Nelson has more recently called it "Africa's first mockumentary."[93] Mambety himself said that the film's humor comes from the "aesthetic contradictions" of its subject, the city of Dakar. "I found it funny," he explained, "that we have a Sudanese style cathedral and a chamber of commerce that looks like a theater, when the theater looks like public housing."[94] Foregrounding these contradictions, he also identifies others. In front of the presidential palace gate, for example, the camera retreats farther and farther from a close-up on a guard while Mambety's stilted and distorted voice reads from a speech given by President Senghor about his policies supporting women. Shots of Senegalese women looking at European women's magazines follow, with exaggerated groans on the soundtrack, the juxtaposition mocking Senghor's self-congratulation as well as stereotypical images of European and African women.

From colonial European buildings and culture, Mambety moves to other parts of Dakar, the neighborhoods where Africans live. On the opposite side of the same bridge featured in Sembene's *La Noire de...*, bearing the same Air Afrique advertisement, we see rows of shacks with tin roofs and hear music played on West African instruments. A series of close-ups shows inhabitants working and shopping in street markets, and the female narrator singles out a passing man with long dreadlocks to observe, "Oh, a hippie!" Her counterpart, suddenly serious, corrects her misunderstanding by explaining that this man is a Mouride and follower of spiritual leader Cheikh Ahmadou Bamba. When she asks her voice-over partner if he himself is Muslim, his joking tone returns; Mambety, whose father was an imam, quickly subverts the film's sole piece of ethnographic information with, "Oh, sort of." Leagues away from the didacticism of Blaise Senghor's *Grand Magal à Touba*, Mambety parodies the relationship of African religious leaders to France's neocolonial presence in West Africa. Her "father," France, his narrator continues, built a few distilleries, and many marabouts have since traded their Coran for cognac.[95] The theme of religion then takes spectators back to the colonial side of Dakar, where church bells and choir music accompany residents standing on the steps of the Cathedral of African Memory.

Again using music to travel through his city, Mambety leads viewers to a staircase atop a ruined building via the strains of "La Marseillaise," played by a brass band. The camera repeats a strategy, pulling back to reveal that this building, dated 1911, overshadows the shacks and dirt roads of the Colobane neighborhood. Humor returns as the continuing differentiation of European and African Dakar gives way to an extreme close-up of a Gauloise cigarette advertisement with the slogan "French Taste." Mambety again mocks Dakar's cultural confusion as the film approaches its conclusion. A shot of a transportation route from the hôtel de ville to Clichy elicits an eager cry from the female voice-over, "But, it's Paris!" A quick cut reveals that the map is in fact posted in a small bus in Dakar. Viewers are taken inside the bus to see the Moorish arch of the Kermel Market through its window, then back outside to watch the bus depart. The cart driver reappears in front of the Dakar train station, his cart bearing a clapboard that reads "The End." Mambety's juxtaposed images and ironic voice-over expose the colonial roots of contemporary Dakar, as *Contras' City*—its inflected English title a short escape from the suffocation of *francophonie*—simultaneously makes clear that Dakar and Paris, Senegal and France, Africa and Europe, are architecturally and culturally inseparable.

Combining Mambety's eccentric eye and Barry's montage technique, Simon Augé's *Il était une fois... Libreville* (Once upon a time... Libreville, 1972) incorporates a range of narrative strategies into an extraordinary compilation of documents, interviews, and acted scenes retracing Gabonese history from the fifteenth century to the present. Born in Port-Gentil, Augé had trained at the French Office of Radio and Television (ORTF) and, during a later stay in Paris, at the National Audiovisual Institute (INA). This was his first film, and his career would change course soon after the release of the medium-length documentary. An ethnographic short titled *Mbigou, poésie du Gabon* (Mbigou, Gabonese poetry, 1976) would be his last before becoming the director of Gabonese Radio and Television (RTG) and, in 1985, the head of Gabon's National Center for Cinema.

Augé understood *Il était une fois... Libreville* to be an African work of African history, "a return to the past... always aiming to make known what we really are."[96] He distinguished his own perspective from that of colonial histories and media products; these had created false stereotypes and preconceptions that needed to be debunked to "reestablish truth." The film was a production of the RTG, its voice-over commentary cowritten by Augé and Gaston Rapontchombo, director of the archives at the Gabonese National Library, and read by Gabonese actor and filmmaker Philippe Mory with Eugene Philippe Ndjenno. Augé begins his history in the prehistoric period, showing tools and providing information about the area's first inhabitants. The narration interprets photos and drawings that lead viewers through the arrival of the Portuguese in the fifteenth century, and a blank map is filled in with the names of regions, towns, and European nations who passed through, along with the materials and numbers of enslaved people they took with them. Focusing on the arrival of the French in the nineteenth century, Augé stresses the importance of an 1839 treaty signed by Antchuwè Kowè Rapontchombo, also known as King Denis, a concession of sovereignty that began the era of colonization.

As did Mambety with Dakar, Augé centers his analysis of the colonial and postcolonial periods around a capital city—Libreville—noting that its name refers to its 1846 founding to house people freed from a captured slave ship. Also like Mambety, Augé pays attention to architecture, detailing the growth of Libreville's European neighborhood over time and in contrast with other parts of the city. When the first images of contemporary Libreville appear just over halfway through the film, its style changes unexpectedly from expository nonfiction to fictional narrative. An African man in a European suit and elegant shoes, played by fellow Gabonese filmmaker Pierre-Marie Dong, steps out of a car that has gotten stuck in mud. He walks to a village, seeking out a woman, with whom he speaks in Fang. The man pays her, then replaces his European clothes and shoes with a white sheet tied around his waist. In the film's sole but central ethnographic moment, she performs a Bwiti initiation ritual, hitting him with leafy branches that he then uses to scrub himself before washing. From this allegorical shedding of neocolonial language and garb, Augé returns suddenly to archival documentary materials—first a photograph from August 27, 1960, the day of Gabonese independence, then newsreel footage of new president Léon Mba walking with a French general behind him. Voice-over narration recounts Mba's death in 1967 and the accession of Vice President Albert-Bernard Bongo to the presidency; footage of these ceremonies is followed by orchestrated scenes of Bongo holding a series of meetings.[97]

The third part of *Il était une fois . . . Libreville* is again different from the first two. Paulin Vieyra criticized it for catering to Bongo, who would remain president of Gabon until 2009.[98] Amid shots of Bongo at work, the commentary states that his presidency has marked an increase in modern construction in Libreville. In interviews, residents of the capital discuss the Westernization of Gabonese customs; a young man expresses a sense of distance from his people's traditions and laments their loss. Suggesting that modernization need not be accompanied by loss of ancestral heritage, Augé incorporates a second fictional scene into his film. A Gabonese family watches television in its living room, and we see, on the screen within our screen, a television news anchor announce that two men are about to walk on the moon. Answering a ringing telephone, the anchor says, "I think Houston is calling. Hello, Houston?" In a shot-countershot sequence, Augé cuts back and forth from newsreel images of the first moon landing to the family watching, mouths agape. This fiction is completely different from the first, performing not a return to precolonial tradition but instead Africa's central role in the world's scientific future.[99] *Il était une fois . . . Libreville* concludes with additional interviews of Libreville residents, who respond in the negative to a question about a "return to the sources," and images of modern apartment blocks, gas stations, schools, and government buildings. Augé's staged television sequence brings this modern Libreville to Houston, Houston to Libreville, and both to the moon.

Pierre-Marie Dong's role in *Il était une fois . . . Libreville* enacted a theme central to his own work. Born and raised in Libreville, Dong studied filmmaking at the IDHEC in Paris in the late 1960s. He returned home to work for the RTG, eventually becoming its general manager, and made several commissioned documentary shorts including *Gabon, pays de contrastes* (Gabon, country of

Simon Augé, *Il était une fois . . . Libreville*, 1972.

contrasts, 1969).[100] With *Sur le sentier du requiem* (On the path to requiem, 1971), shot on bits and pieces of black-and-white film left over from a Philippe Mory production, Dong found a new direction. The film shares aesthetic and thematic interests with those of Mambety and Augé yet abandons narrative altogether. In its first shot, the director appears holding a movie camera; the camera that is filming him pulls back, and he turns slightly to face it. Unidentified footage of Black and white men and women—cyclists on a busy street, ballerinas and boxers, toddlers playing near a palm tree—follows, intercut with scenes of war—bombs falling, tanks and airplanes, soldiers running—all without explanatory commentary. A calm, unidentified voice-over narrator intones, "Happy, those who have the souls of poor men," and the images shift: from a church to young people dancing to rock music; to mass demonstrations in Asia and Africa; back to the nightclub; and to police breaking up the demonstrations.

Having set the violent and creative global scene of the late 1960s and early '70s, Dong's film continues to juxtapose locations and music styles, eventually settling on a man in a white robe who walks across sand, again intercut with a nightclub scene. The man pours water from a bottle onto the sand and his head, then lights a patch of grass on fire in a mysterious rite. Dramatic cuts take viewers back and forth between an Air Afrique plane on an airport tarmac and two fashionable young women, one Black and one white, who pose on the beach wearing white minidresses. The camera retreats twice to reveal a man who walks, arms outstretched, toward each woman, one after the other. His very gendered choice between them is never made, but leads to the last shot of the film: a Black man's shackled foot stepping across a log in the equatorial forest. With only the opening image of Dong as mooring, we understand the explosive footage of the late '60s to be focalized through the filmmaker, who is as tied to the young *soixante-huitards* dancing to rock music as he is to the enslaved body of the work's conclusion.

Sur le sentier du requiem won second prize in the short film category at FESPACO in 1972 but, despite its innovative structure and resonance with global filmmaking of the period, has never been restored or distributed. Winner of the Prize for African Authenticity at FESPACO, Dong's first feature fiction, *Identité* (1972), became his best-received film. A less experimental representation of the alienated postcolonial African intellectual, it stages the return to the source of an autobiographical character. Returning from France, Pierre abandons bourgeois city life for his native village where, like the character in *Il était une fois . . . Libreville*, he is initiated into the practice of Bwiti. But Pierre ultimately returns to the city, as Dong suggests that contemporary Africa is inseparable from contemporary Europe. Like Mambety and Augé, Dong rejected a strict opposition of village tradition and urban modernity. In later years, he produced mainly propaganda pieces for Bongo, a fan of cinema who installed a four-hundred-seat screening room in his palace.[101] *Demain, un jour nouveau* (Tomorrow, a new day, 1978) was adapted from the dictator's autobiography; like Sekou Touré, Bongo was not a fan of avant-garde or reflective filmmaking.

Chadian director Edouard Sailly came to the same conclusion about nighttime drumming as Urbain Dia-Moukori at about the same time, and like Mambety, Augé, and Dong, his artistic vision led him to experimental documentary. Born in Abéché, Sailly completed only primary school before working as a mechanic, a veterinary nurse, and the projectionist for the Normandy Theater in Fort-Lamy (now N'Djamena). Just after independence, he received a scholarship to spend two years in Paris, where he held internships in a Kodak laboratory and at the Actualités Françaises. Sailly returned to Chad to serve as director of the cinema service of the Ministry of Information, where he was also responsible for newsreel production. Over the course of a decade, the ministry funded a series of his short films, all between five and thirty-five minutes long and for the most part ethnographic. In *Les pecheurs du Chari* (Chari fishermen, 1964), voice-over narration praises the beauty and power of the Chari River, describing the fishing customs and economy of the men, women, and children of the region. The commentary alternates between poetic and informational modes. Announcing that for three months of the year, "the gestures of fishing will set the rhythm of their days," it then states that the Chari River is one of the richest sources of fish in the world. "Chad is one of the biggest producers of fish in Africa," Sailly's first film concludes quite prosaically, exporting dried fish to the Republic of the Congo, the Central African Republic, and Nigeria. *Les pecheurs du Chari* was followed by *Le Lac Tchad* (Lake Chad), *Les abattoirs de Forcha* (The slaughterhouses of Forcha), and *Ballet Tchadien* (Chadian ballet).

In *Le troisième jour* (The third day, 1966), however, Sailly renounces ethnography. Screened at the First Tashkent Festival of African and Asian Cinema and winner of the grand prize for short subjects at Saint-Cast, the film's formal experimentation impressed Parisian critic D'dée, who described it as "a very personal use of cinema in search of a truly African cinematographic expression."[102] Recovered along with works by Alassane, Thiam, and Kamba for the International Film Festival Rotterdam's 2010 "Where Is Africa?" program, *Le troisième jour* is once again near impossible to view.[103] Shot in 35mm black and white two years before *Contras' City* and five before *Sur le sentier du requiem*, the film has no voice-over, no dialogue, no historical documents or footage, and no clear narrative arc. Several introductory sentences on screen hint at a story: "The loss of his mother is first a shock, a perhaps unhealable wound in the life of a boy. It is also often the beginning of a voyage toward the worse or the better. Memories remain, however, and it is a bit as if the absent one was still speaking." The only recurring character in the film, however, is not a boy but a man, and spectators learn nothing about his mother.

From the film's opening moments, which evoke an abstract voyage linked to memories of the dead, Sailly disorients viewers with a series of shots from varying angles and without countershots, linked by montage and rhythmic repetition. An image of two men fishing on the bank of a river gives way to a low-angle shot of a group of people carrying a coffin across a bridge, then to a high-angle shot of the river from the bridge. Another low-angle shot of the people on the bridge follows, seemingly from the opposite bank but without an establishing point of view. An unidentified man walks over an arid landscape and crosses the bridge alone. His journey continues in fragments, through a seemingly abandoned village, on a boat on the river, and through the market street of a larger town, where Sailly's camera for the first time shares images

Edouard Sailly, *Le troisième jour*, 1966.

of daily life. When the man is arrested and taken to a police station, a dissolve returns us to the opening shots of a bridge and funeral procession. Although these are now focalized as though they are his memories, he is included in the images. After leaving the station, the man recedes into the distance only to reappear in a low-angle shot from the front that breaks the 180-degree rule, his face obscured by the glare of the sun. *Le troisième jour* concludes with the river; a series of shots from multiple angles show fishermen throwing their nets, then two men cross in a boat in a final long shot that recalls the fishermen of Chari. Watching a film that epitomizes Bill Nichols's category of performative documentary, Sailly's spectator must make meaning out of discontinuous edited images that cohere neither as fictional story nor as informational narrative. This "highly suggestive, clearly fabricated, referential but not necessarily reflexive form of documentary filmmaking," argued Nichols, "presents a distinct disturbance to ethnographic film," interrupting and deferring documentary referentiality.[104] This is the most recent mode in Nichols's taxonomy, said to have developed in the 1980s, but we see signs of it at the origins of sub-Saharan African documentary, decades ahead of its time.

Looking back almost forty years after independence, Pierre Haffner argued that African cinema arose from African, essentially Franco-African, newsreels and was therefore, in contrast to Italian neorealism, "stuck in a sort of *realism complex*."[105] Yet we have seen that this was not the case—not even, or perhaps especially not, for documentary films. African nonfiction filmmaking was innovative and varied from its very beginnings, spurred by an energy to create a countertradition to the expedition and ethnography-based French colonial documentary that had come before. Too many nonfiction films from the first dozen years after independence have been lost or remain virtually inaccessible, however, leading scholars to continue to make generalizations like Haffner's. In an absorbing essay that considers Franco-Senegalese filmmaker Mati Diop's *Mille soleils* (A thousand suns, 2013) to be a transformative documentary, for example, James Williams relegates early West African documentary to a footnote, summarized as "formulaic exercises in ideological self-congratulation."[106] This process of forgetting is illustrated even within the trajectory of Haffner's own scholarship. Addressing the enduring influence of the earliest African films fifteen years before his critique above, he had described them as "for the most part documentaries" and praised the "astonishing modernity" of Paulin Vieyra's *Afrique sur Seine*.[107]

Notes

1. Françoise Pfaff, *Twenty-Five Black African Filmmakers* (Greenwood Press, 1988), 289.

2. Vieyra, *Le cinéma et l'Afrique*, 18.

3. Rik Otten, *Le cinéma au Zaïre, au Rwanda, et au Burundi* (OCIC, 1984), 22.

4. Paulin Soumanou Vieyra, *Le cinéma africain: Des origines à 1973* (Présence africaine, 1975), 15; Victor Bachy, *Le cinéma au Mali* (OCIC, 1983), 11.

5. Vieyra, *Le cinéma africain*, 155.

6. Paulin Soumanou Vieyra, *Le cinéma au Sénégal* (OCIC, 1983), 53.

7. David Murphy, "Francophone West African Cinema, 1955–1969: False Starts and New Beginnings," in *Africa's Lost Classics: New Histories of African Cinema*, ed. Lizelle Bisschoff and David Murphy (Legenda, 2014), 52.

8. See Brett Bowles, "Paulin Vieyra's *Afrique sur Seine* (1955): Black Ethno-fiction and French New Wave Prototype," *French Politics, Culture & Society* 41, no. 3 (2023): 11. Bowles reads this cameo as proof of "frustrated *auteurisme*" on Vieyra's part rather than the desire to place himself among those represented on screen.

9. Sarah Maldoror, "À toi Paulin . . .," *Présence Africaine*, no. 170 (2004): 23.

10. Maria Loftus, "The Appeal of Hybrid Documentary Forms in West Africa," *French Forum* 35, no. 2–3 (2010): 40. Whereas Loftus uses the term *docufiction* to

describe *Afrique sur Seine*, James Genova characterizes all West African fiction films from the 1960s and '70s as docufiction. James Genova, *Cinema and Development in West Africa* (Indiana University Press, 2013), 93, 113, 144. In his analyses of contemporary African films, James Williams uses such attestations to "the historical impurity of African documentary" to support his lack of distinction between feature fiction and documentary cinema. James S. Williams, *Ethics and Aesthetics in Contemporary African Cinema: The Politics of Beauty* (Bloomsbury, 2019), 123, 35.

11. Michael Renov, "Toward a Poetics of Documentary," in *Theorizing Documentary*, ed. Michael Renov (Routledge, 1993), 34.

12. Vieyra, *Le cinéma et l'Afrique*, 8.

13. Vieyra, *Le cinéma et l'Afrique*, 107–8.

14. Ungar, *Critical Mass*, 178.

15. Paulin Soumanou Vieyra, "Quand le cinéma français parle au nom de l'Afrique noire," *Présence Africaine*, no. 11 (1956): 142–45; Paulin Soumanou Vieyra, "Le cinéma et la révolution africaine," *Présence Africaine*, no. 34/35 (1960): 92–103.

16. Vieyra, *Le cinéma africain*, 246.

17. *Rapport général du groupe ciné-photo, section du Congo-belge et du Ruanda-Urundi*, 15.

18. Vieyra, *Le cinéma et l'Afrique*, 8.

19. Françoise Pfaff, *À l'écoute du cinéma sénégalais* (L'Harmattan, 2010), 52.

20. Pamela Cohn, "Samba Gadjigo and Jason Silverman," *Bomb Magazine*, 2015, https://bombmagazine.org/articles/2015/04/28/samba-gadjigo-and-jason -silverman/.

21. Vieyra, *Le cinéma au Sénégal*, 19. On early documentary in Ghana via the nationalization and transformation of Britain's Gold Coast Film Unit, see Rebecca Ohene-Asah, "Documenting Africa on Film and Nkrumah's Legacy in Pan-Africanist Africa," *Historical Journal of Film, Radio and Television* 41, no. 4 (2021): 808–18.

22. For more on the creation and development of national cinema services and inter-African cooperation in the former French colonies, see Diawara, *African Cinema*, 104–15.

23. See Guy Hennebelle, "Economique: Entretien avec Jean-René Debrix," *L'Afrique littéraire et artistique*, no. 49 (1978): 153–54.

24. François Kodjo, "Les cinéastes africains face à l'avenir du cinéma en Afrique," *Tiers-monde* 20, no. 79 (1979): 608.

25. Debrix claimed that the Bureau of Cinema funded 125 of the 185 films produced in the former French colonies of West and central Africa between 1963 and 1975. Hennebelle, "Economique," 153. For a detailed overview of the functioning of French aid to African cinema in the 1960s and 1970s, see Claire Andrade-Watkins, "France's Bureau of Cinema: Financial and Technical Assistance Between 1961 & 1977," *Visual Anthropology Review* 6, no. 2 (1990): 80–93. With respect to French support for documentary production in the early years of independence, see

Vincent Bouchard, "African Documentaries, Critical Interventions: The Non-fiction Film Production at the Origins of Francophone West African Film Production," *Critical Interventions* 11, no. 3 (2017): 214–27.

26. Timité Bassori, "Un cinéma mort-né?," *Présence Africaine*, no. 49 (1964): 112.

27. Vienna Symposium, "Documentary Film in Africa and Asia," 18–19.

28. Jean-Claude Morellet, "Quatre cinéastes africains: 'Nationalisons les salles!,'" *Jeune Afrique*, no. 335 (June 11, 1967): 45. In 1968, of the 180 theaters in France's former sub-Saharan African colonies that could project 35mm films, 150 were owned by COMACICO and SECMA. Jean-R. Debrix, "Le cinéma africain," *Afrique contemporaine*, no. 40 (1968): 2.

29. Debrix, "Le cinéma africain," 6.

30. Diawara, *African Cinema*, 40.

31. Dia-Moukori, "Intuition d'un langage cinématographique africain," 208.

32. Vieyra, *Le cinéma au Sénégal*, 20–21, 38.

33. Vieyra, *Réflexions d'un cineaste africain*, 127.

34. Paulin Soumanou Vieyra, "Le film africain d'expression française," *African Arts* 1, no. 3 (1968): 66.

35. Vieyra, *Réflexions d'un cineaste africain*, 128.

36. Cheikh Hamidou Kane, *L'aventure ambigüe* (10/18, 2003 [1961]).

37. Vieyra, *Le cinéma africain*, 115; Teresa Hoefert de Turégano, *African Cinema and Europe: Close-Up on Burkina Faso* (European Press Academic, 2004), 40. Ricci also trained Burkinabé technicians and advised the French government on audiovisual cooperation. Bouchard, "African Documentaries, Critical Interventions," 222.

38. Blaise Senghor, "Le point de vue d'un futur producteur africain," *La vie africaine*, no. 15 (1961): 39.

39. D'dée, "Jeune cinéma d'Afrique noire," *L'Afrique actuelle*, no. 15 (1967): 18.

40. Guy Hennebelle, "Jean Rouch et l'éthique du cinéma ethnographique," *L'Afrique littéraire*, nos. 61–62 (1981): 47.

41. Nichols, *Blurred Boundaries*, 86.

42. Vieyra, *Réflexions d'un cineaste africain*, 61. The French word *étrangeté* signifies both strangeness and foreignness.

43. Colleyn, *Jean Rouch*, 45.

44. Olympe Bhely-Quenum, "Interview exclusive de Blaise Senghor," *L'Afrique actuelle*, no. 19 (1967): 13.

45. Vieyra, *Réflexions d'un cineaste africain*, 128.

46. Mary Louise Pratt, "Transculturation and Autoethnography: Peru, 1615/1980," in *Colonial Discourse / Postcolonial Theory*, ed. Francis Barker, Peter Hulme, and Margaret Iversen (Manchester University Press, 1994), 28. Vincent Debaene identifies the parallel if earlier appearance of the African ethnographic novel in the 1930s with Paul Hazoumé's *Doguicimi*. Vincent Debaene, *Far Afield:*

French Anthropology Between Science and Literature (University of Chicago Press, 2014), 285.

47. Vieyra, *Le cinéma et l'Afrique*, 140.

48. Kala-Lobe, "Alioune Diop et le cinéma africain," 333–35.

49. Pratt, "Transculturation and Autoethnography," 29.

50. Vieyra, "Le film africain d'expression française," 67.

51. Vieyra, *Le cinéma africain*, 62.

52. Pfaff, *Twenty-Five Black African Filmmakers*, 267.

53. On the rediscovery and restoration of this film, see Marco Lena, "Paulin Soumanou Vieyra in the Documents of the Rediscovered Audiovisual Archive of the Senegalese Ministry of Culture," *Black Camera* 13, no. 2 (2022): 482–87.

54. Guy Hennebelle, *Les cinémas africains en 1972* (Société Africaine d'Edition, 1972), 244.

55. Pfaff, *Twenty-Five Black African Filmmakers*, 35.

56. "Où en est le cinéma ivoirien?," *Jeune Afrique*, no. 409 (November 4–10, 1968): 16.

57. Jeanne Cousin, *Histoire du cinéma en Guinée depuis 1958* (L'Harmattan, 2017), 31.

58. The film was made in German and French versions, of which only the German remains. Olivier Barlet, "De Sekou Touré à aujourd'hui," *Africultures*, 2011, https://africultures.com/de-sekou-toure-a-aujourdhui-10079/.

59. Patrick Ilboudo, *Le FESPACO, 1969–1989: Les cinéastes africains et leurs oeuvres* (Éditions La Mante, 1988), 240.

60. Pierre Haffner, "L'esthétique des films," *L'Afrique littéraire*, no. 68–69 (1983): 70; Pierre Haffner and Paulin Soumanou Vieyra, "Propos sur le cinéma africain," *Présence Africaine*, no. 170 (2004): 50.

61. Catherine Russell interrogates autoethnography in order to expand rather than abandon the concept, considering a range of experimental works filmed around the world as autoethnographic in the sense of representing a split self. Russell, *Experimental Ethnography*, 277.

62. Vieyra, "Le film africain d'expression française," 66.

63. Vieyra, "Le film africain d'expression française," 65.

64. Pierre Haffner, "Quatre entretiens avec Paulin Soumanou Vieyra (III): Deuxième partie," *Peuples noirs, peuples africains*, no. 40 (1984), https://mongobeti .arts.uwa.edu.au/issues/pnpa40/pnpa40_04.html#haut.

65. D'dée, "Enfin du vrai cinéma africain," *La vie africaine*, no. 29 (1962): 47.

66. On Alassane's work in animation, see chapter 5 of Sada Niang, *Nationalist African Cinema: Legacy and Transformations* (Lexington Books, 2014).

67. Ouedraogo, *Naissance et évolution du FESPACO de 1969 à 1973*, 67.

68. "Alassane Mustapha," *L'Afrique littéraire et artistique*, no. 49 (1978): 15. Amélie Garin-Davet, formerly of the cultural services of the French Embassy in New York,

organized in 2018 the first North American retrospective of Alassane's films, which included a restored version of *Aouré*.

69. David Murphy reads *Aouré*'s acted ethnography as marking the birth of African entertainment cinema, posing the intriguing question of how our understanding of African film history might differ were Alassane attributed the role of founding father. Murphy, "Francophone West African Cinema, 1955–1969," 54.

70. Vieyra, *Le cinéma au Sénégal*, 58.

71. Vieyra, "Le film africain d'expression française," 66.

72. Vieyra, *Le cinéma africain*, 157; Vieyra, *Le cinéma au Sénégal*, 58.

73. Julien Sormery, "'J'ai vu le Mvet': Introït pour un nouveau cinéma africain," *Cinéma pratique*, no. 129 (1974): 8.

74. Sormery, "'J'ai vu le Mvet,'" 6, 8.

75. Pierre Haffner, "Jean Rouch jugé par six cinéastes d'Afrique noire," *L'Afrique littéraire*, no. 61–62 (1981): 67.

76. Vieyra, *Le cinéma africain*, 188.

77. Vieyra, *Le cinéma africain*, 106.

78. Hennebelle, *Les cinémas africains en 1972*, 100.

79. Vieyra, *Le cinéma au Sénégal*, 71.

80. Léopold Sédar Senghor, *Négritude et humanisme* (Éditions du Seuil, 1964).

81. Cousin, *Histoire du cinéma en Guinée depuis 1958*, 64; Gabrielle Chomentowski, "Going Abroad to Study the Craft of Filmmaking in the USSR During the Period 1960–1970," in *Saving Bruce Lee: African and Arab Cinema in the Era of Soviet Cultural Diplomacy* (Haus der Kulturen der Welt, 2018), 29.

82. Documents from the Russian state archives regarding Diagne's film are reproduced in English translation in *Saving Bruce Lee*, 50, 51.

83. Bachy, *Le cinéma au Mali*, 39.

84. Bachy, *Le cinéma au Mali*, 40.

85. Dia-Moukori, "Intuition d'un langage cinématographique africain," 217.

86. Vieyra, *Le cinéma africain*, 107–8.

87. Cousin, *Histoire du cinéma en Guinée depuis 1958*, 42.

88. Cousin, *Histoire du cinéma en Guinée depuis 1958*, 39.

89. Pfaff, *Twenty-Five Black African Filmmakers*, 217.

90. Vieyra, *Le cinéma au Sénégal*, 74.

91. Vieyra, *Le cinéma africain*, 182. *Contras' City* is available in a restored 4K version on the Criterion Collection DVD release of Mambety's *Touki Bouki* (1973).

92. Sada Niang, *Djibril Diop Mambety: Un cinéaste à contre-courant* (L'Harmattan, 2002), 54. Niang's chapter on *Contras' City* situates the film in great detail in various neighborhoods of Dakar.

93. Hennebelle, *Les cinémas africains en 1972*, 330; Steven Nelson, "A Tale of Two Cities," *Artforum International* 47, no. 3 (2008): 307.

94. "Diop-Mambety Djibril," *L'Afrique littéraire et artistique*, no. 49 (1978): 43.

95. I have maintained the French spelling of *Quran* in the interest of Mambety's play on words with *cognac*.

96. Victor Bachy, *Le cinéma au Gabon* (OCIC, 1986), 86.

97. Bongo changed his first name to Omar after converting to Islam in 1973.

98. Vieyra, *Le cinéma africain*, 94. Vieyra elsewhere described the desire of men in power for documentary glorification, calling filmmakers who provided it "griots in the worst sense of the term." Vieyra, *Réflexions d'un cineaste africain*, 127.

99. Augé's film contains echoes of Edward Mukuka Nkoloso's short-lived and perhaps ironically conceived Zambian Space Program (1964–1965), born with independence and remembered in Frances Bodomo's short film *Afronauts* (2014). Closer to home, it recalls a film produced eight years earlier by the RTG, which was at the time under the direction of Jean-Luc Magneron. In *Chouchou cosmonaute*, the first Gabonese cosmonaut takes off in a rocket called the Ogooué. https://www.lepratiquedugabon.com/gros-plan-sur-le-gabon/.

100. Pfaff, *Twenty-Five Black African Filmmakers*, 79.

101. Bachy, *Le cinéma au Gabon*, 27.

102. D'dée, "Jeune cinéma d'Afrique noire," 17.

103. Lindiwe Dovey, *Curating Africa in the Age of Film Festivals* (Palgrave Macmillan, 2015), 70.

104. Nichols, *Blurred Boundaries*, 95, 96.

105. Pierre Haffner, "Nations nègres et cinéma," *Les cahiers de médiologie* 1, no. 3 (1997): 151.

106. James S. Williams, "A Thousand Suns: Traversing the Archive and Transforming Documentary in Mari Diop's *Mille Soleils*," *Film Quarterly* 70, no. 1 (2016): 95n11.

107. Pierre Haffner, "L'esthétique des films," 60.

5

EXPANSION

Ethnography Remade

If Paulin Vieyra had been publishing articles in *Présence Africaine* since the 1950s, it was at the turn of the '70s that his work began to appear in book form—a collection of his earlier essays as *Le cinéma et l'Afrique* (Cinema and Africa) in 1969, *Sembène Ousmane, cinéaste* (Ousmane Sembene, filmmaker) in 1972, *Le cinéma africain, des origines à 1973* (African cinema, from its origins to 1973) in 1975, and *Le cinéma au Sénégal* (Cinema in Senegal) in 1983. The development of African film history and criticism accompanied a crucial transitional period for sub-Saharan African cinema, one that Tunisian filmmaker, screenwriter, and critic Férid Boughedir described as "after the era of pioneers and amateurs."[1] Jean-René Debrix, who directed the Bureau of Cinema until his death in the late 1970s, asserted mid-decade that "Black African cinema has left its childhood years to enter into adulthood."[2] As proof of this maturation, Debrix noted an increase in not just the technical quality of films but the number and prominence of feature-length fictions as opposed to documentaries. Attesting to the same phenomenon with a contrary evaluation, Vieyra in 1974 bemoaned the fact that many African directors, associating the status of cineaste with feature fictions, had given up on documentary.[3] At the same time, though, a new group of dedicated documentarists was joining the field, including the first women filmmakers. Documentary almost as much as fiction would transform the look and sound of sub-Saharan African cinema.

The story of production and distribution funding during the second and third decades of independent sub-Saharan African cinema is one of many manifestos and many more acronyms, and scholars from Manthia Diawara to Teresa

Hoefert de Turégano have told it in more detail than I can here. Governmental organizations were created and dissolved both in Europe and in African nations as political winds changed direction, and historical and critical writing about African cinema has dealt as much or more with the transformations of agencies and policies than with the films these did or did not support. France's Ministry of Cooperation continued funding African films until the elimination of its cinema office by the government of President Valéry Giscard d'Estaing.[4] In the 1980s, under François Mitterand, the ministry began to distribute funding to groups like the African and Mauritian Communal Organization (OCAM) instead of to individual filmmakers.[5] Films were also funded by France's Agency for Cultural and Technical Cooperation (ACCT), established in 1970 with a list of member nations that included Canada, Luxembourg, and Belgium as well as former colonies in East Asia and Africa. After Debrix's death, his work was to some extent taken over by the Technical Association for Audiovisual Research and Information (ATRIA), a nonprofit founded by Paris-based film editor Andrée Davanture in 1980 and supported by France's Ministry of Cooperation and CNC.[6] In the same year, Jean Rouch returned to Paris from training future filmmakers in newly independent Mozambique and created the Ateliers Varan, a twelve-week workshop in ethnographic filmmaking still in existence today.

Boughedir marked the early 1970s as the start of a period of cinematic nationalization in Africa. From Senegal to Tanzania to Madagascar to Congo, the era brought increased governmental support for film production as well as some restrictions on European monopolies of distribution.[7] The year 1970 saw the creation of the Voltaic National Cinema Company (SONAVOCI) in what is now Burkina Faso, followed by a National Center for Cinema (CNC) in 1977.[8] In late 1972, the Senegalese Ministry of Culture formed a cinema bureau as well as the semipublic National Cinema Company (SNC), which funded films selected from submitted scripts.[9] And Cameroon in 1973 created the Development Fund for the Cinema Industry (FODIC), which, in addition to direct funding, adopted the French model of *avance sur recettes*.

By 1973, both Upper Volta and Senegal had at least in theory also nationalized film distribution via SONAVOCI and SIDEC. Gabon's branch of European monopoly COMACICO became the Gabonese Cinema Company (SOGACI). And at the end of the decade, after years of discussion, the Inter-African Consortium for Cinematographic Distribution (CIDC) was established, led by Nigerien filmmaker Inoussa Ousseini. The CIDC created a common market for distribution across the fourteen countries in formerly French West and central Africa—Senegal, Mali, Mauritania, Guinea, Côte d'Ivoire, Burkina Faso, Niger, Togo, Benin, Cameroon, Gabon, Congo, Chad, and the Central African Republic—but was operational for only four years, from 1981 to 1984.[10] Senegal's SNC lasted five years, and the African Institute for Cinematographic Education (INAFEC) where Idrissa Ouédraogo began his filmmaking training was open for ten; founded in 1976 at the University of Ouagadougou with support from UNESCO, it closed its doors in 1987. Governments never provided enough support to create fully functional national cinemas, much less to enable them to thrive. Historian and critic Mbye-Boubacar Cham described the West African film industry as "plagued by a chronic lack of capital, equipment, production facilities and effective exhibition channels."[11] Boughedir recognized with frustration that it was neocolonial French funding that kept West and central African cinema in existence.[12]

FEPACI, the advocacy group created at the first editions of pan-African film festivals in Carthage and Ouagadougou in the late 1960s, proved durable if also underfunded. National associations of directors could become members, and under the leadership of Senegalese filmmaker Ababacar Samb-Makharam the organization urged African governments to nationalize importation and distribution of films, refrain from taxing sales of tickets for African films, and use revenue from ticket sales and taxes on imported films to support African cinema. In 1972, Timité Bassori became president of the Association of Cinema Professionals of the Ivory Coast, a position he held for fifteen years while also heading the Abidjan office of the African Committee of Cineastes (CAC). And a series of international meetings of media professionals from formerly colonized regions we now refer to as the Global South generated further activism in the form of prescriptive manifestos, most notably the "Resolutions of the Third World Film-Makers Meeting" held in Algiers in 1973 and FEPACI's 1975 "Algiers Charter on African Cinema" and 1982 "Niamey Manifesto."[13]

Descendants of Paulin Vieyra's 1959 "Responsibilities of the Cinema in the Formation of an African National Consciousness," these manifestos called for films that would advance what the Third World Film-Makers Meeting called "the revalorization of national cultural heritage." Delegates on a subcommittee chaired by Ousmane Sembene repeated that "the role of cinema in the third world is to promote culture through films."[14] Two years later, FEPACI representatives proclaimed cinema's power to counter "cultural domination" via "education, information and consciousness raising."[15] This focus on the authenticity of cultural content was accompanied by appeals to make films in African languages. Echoing the conclusions of the manifesto released following the 1969 Pan-African Cultural Festival in Algiers, Vieyra gave the example of Wolof in Senegal to assert that films in local languages have "a certain authenticity" and reach audiences beyond the educated elite.[16] African languages "reflect cultures," he noted in an interview at FESPACO, and African actors are more at ease when speaking them.[17]

The desire to film in African languages was often in tension with the need for French government funding, which usually required that a film be in French. Autocratic rulers at home added other constraints, and with production funding and distribution so difficult to obtain and exhibition spaces close to non-existent, it is little wonder that many early African directors had short-lived careers in the cinema. Documentary was particularly impacted by these challenges, such that by the early 1970s, as we have seen, some documentarists had abandoned filmmaking to work for national media agencies, while others had switched to feature fiction. Yet there remained a strong sense of the importance of documentary—to African cinema, but also to sub-Saharan African societies and cultures more generally. Participants in the 1974 "Seminar on the Role of the African Filmmaker in Rousing an Awareness of Black Civilization" in Ouagadougou set the goals of independent African cinema against Africa's experience of colonial-era European films that supported and justified "domination and economic exploitation."[18] Their final report argued that, in order to show an "interior vision" of Africa, filmmakers had to become both historians and archivists. In addition to fiction films, one resolution insisted, "the production of documentaries is immediately recommended and encouraged, so as to describe every aspect of African life, its techniques and its traditional arts."[19]

Pushing back against the continued predominance of European ethnographic filmmakers, especially Rouch, Senegalese director Mahama Traoré a few years earlier had similarly insisted on a local perspective for ethnography.[20] As the decade progressed and manifestos multiplied, films fitting his prescription dominated a documentary corpus with a diminished range. Just over a decade after *Aouré*, Nigerien Moustapha Alassane presented a second interior vision of Africa in *Shaki* (1973). An ethnographic short sponsored by Rouch's CFE and Museum of Mankind as well as the CNRS, *Shaki* shares with Alassane's earlier documentary a narrative voice that is individual and informal. Over high-angle panning shots of a relatively large town in southeastern Nigeria, a French-language commentary introduces the history of the people of Shaki, shown going about everyday activities. Half of all residents go abroad to trade, planning to return and build multistory houses as signs of wealth, the voice-over explains, but also as "revenge against the colonial past." Another aspect of this continuing resistance to British colonial influence, the narrator continues, is a refusal to abandon ancestral beliefs and culture. "Prepare a religion and arrive in Shaki," he jokes, and you may gain followers, but you will never destroy the beliefs that preceded you.

Arriving at the central focus of his film, Alassane explains the rites associated with enthroning the new king of Shaki while also speaking the dialogue of the participants, translated into French. The authority overseeing the coronation, for example, calls out to those in attendance, "Are you sure you have found your new king? . . . Will you permit me to call him?" Once the ceremony is over, the royal court of Shaki can resume functioning; spectators watch new king Abimbola and his advisers settle conflicts brought before them. The last words of the film are attributed to Abimbola. "Shaki has never been conquered," the voice-over narrator proclaims, the town's refusal of illegitimate governance bringing a message of self-determination to the portrayal of African traditions that have persisted and thrived despite European colonization.

Alassane had taken classes in different aspects of filmmaking at the Franco-Nigerien Cultural Center in Niamey. These were taught by French *coopérants* Jean Rouch, Serge Ricci, and Serge Moati, with Oumarou Ganda, Inoussa Ousseini, Djingarey Maïga, and Moustapha Diop also in attendance.[21] All these future African filmmakers perceived the benefits and burdens of Rouch's tutelage, with Ganda most vocal about the burdens, saying later that he had served "under the dictatorship of Jean Rouch."[22] As a teenager, Ousseini founded a ciné-club at his Niamey high school and assisted on several of Moati's films. He finished high school in France, where he heard Rouch speak about shared anthropology on the radio. The young Ousseini sent Rouch a postcard announcing that he would soon film white people just as Rouch had filmed Africans.[23] Rouch agreed to act in Ousseini's *La sangsue* (The leech, 1974), an ethnographic short about French sexuality, Ousseini later claimed, but never showed up for the shoot. *La sangsue* was followed by *Paris c'est joli* (Paris is pretty, 1974), a fictional representation of life as an undocumented African. Returning to Niger, Ousseini became the director of the CIDC and Ciprofilms as well as of the audiovisual department of the National Center for Scientific Research (CNRS) Rouch had established in Niamey.

Ousseini believed he could replace Rouch in a changing of the ethnographic guard that would "make films with the same scenes, but such that we want to see them, and to lead people to accept this perspective on reality."[24] His *Luttes sahariennes* (Saharan wrestling, 1977) begins with a voice-over announcing in West African–accented French the popularity of traditional wrestling. Explanatory commentary describes and interprets action on screen, both the moves of wrestlers and the reactions of those attending seven recorded matches. "Spectators always reward the wrestlers," the narrator concludes, highlighting the audience's role for his own audience; "in Niger wrestling is above all a free performance in which the spectators are also actors." In *Fantasia* (1980),

Ousseini attests to the importance of traditional ceremonies of horsemanship in Niger, maintained long after horses ceased to be the best means of transportation between villages. Viewers again witness the details of local rituals while a voice-over narrator provides explanations. In the same year and vein, Ousseini released a series of short ethnographic documentaries titled "Popular Festivals and Traditions in Niger."

Ousseini's commitment to documentary, and more specifically to ethnographic films made by Africans to be appreciated by African audiences, was career long, culminating after four decades with the establishment of the annual African Forum on Documentary Film in Niamey. It was Djingarey Maïga, however, who had the longest career of the Nigerien pioneers of African cinema, one that lasted from the early 1970s into the 2010s. Maïga's interest in cinema was sparked shortly after independence, when he saw Alassane's *Aouré* at the Niamey IFAN. He acted for Alassane in the parody Western *Le retour de l'aventurier* (Return of an adventurer, 1968) and the social drama *FVVA: Femmes voitures villas argent* (Women, cars, villas, money, 1972). Maïga became Alassane's assistant director and, while also serving as Ousseini's cameraman, began to make his own films. Like the authors of the decade's African cinema manifestos, and like Alassane and Ousseini, Maïga's goal was the valorization of African culture through the description of techniques and traditional arts of African life. Codirected with French documentarist and producer Yves Billon, Maïga's first documentary, *Autour de l'hippopotame* (About the hippopotamus, 1979), portrays a Sorko hippopotamus hunt with harpoons and the butchering of an animal on the riverbank. Maïga provides voice-over commentary and also appears on screen remembering the hunts he witnessed as a child, during the period when Rouch was filming *Bataille sur le grand fleuve*. In *La danse des dieux* (Dance of the gods, 1982), filmed in a village near Niamey, narration read by Thérèse Keita explains the preparations for a ceremony in which each dance has a specific meaning and addresses an individual god. Among those performed are dances of the Moro Naba in western Niger and the Hauka in Gold Coast, ethnic groups featured in Rouch's early films.

Serving as director, cameraman, and editor, Maïga continued to make lowbudget ethnographic documentaries. Shot in Mali, *Paysans des sables* (Peasants of the sand, 1984) traces the history of the city of Gao to the fifteenth-century empire of Askia Muhammed Touré. While many scenes explain local traditions such as marriage dances, the film also shows the region's contemporary reality. The Niger River has receded amid a serious drought, leaving the earth dry and cracked. Interviews in French and Songhai with a Nigerien professor, a French medical aid worker, and the president of a Gao cooperative bring to light

Pascal Abikanlou, *Sous le signe du Vodun*, 1973.

additional struggles, including a cholera epidemic. And scenes filmed in a classroom reveal not children but adult farmers and Tuareg herders who, seeking to adapt to their new reality, are learning to read and write. In *Paysans du fleuve* (Peasants of the river, 1987), Maïga focuses on new techniques being developed by a farmers' cooperative to irrigate rice crops using water funneled from the river. Interviewing farmers, fishermen, and a government representative sent to advise them, Maïga shows peasants to be the prime movers of change.

Whereas Alassane in the 1970s shifted away from the reenactment strategy central to *Aouré*, with Ousseini and Maïga following suit, Dahomey's Pascal Abikanlou moved in the opposite direction, for the first time using illustrative characters in his ethnographic filmmaking. The hundred-minute *Sous le signe du Vodun* (In the light of Vodun, 1973) is narrated by the French-language voice-over of the character Codjo, played by actor Gratien Zossou, who recounts his initiation into the Vodun religion as spectators watch him perform the ritual. More complex than the representation of a single event or series of events in a single place, Abikanlou's film follows Codjo from his village to the capital of Cotonou and back, critiquing the imposition of a national agricultural campaign on rural inhabitants in the process. A fire destroys Codjo's familial house and fields, leading him to seek work in the city. Distanced from his home, earning a living by cleaning Air Afrique planes at the Cotonou airport, Codjo is haunted by dreams of the Vodun rituals he has abandoned. After his father's death, he returns to the village with Assiba, a student he met in Cotonou, and the young couple together return to Vodun traditions.

Directors Kollo Sanou and Moussa Yoro Bathily, from Burkina Faso and Senegal, respectively, also used fictional characters to ethnographic ends. Sanou studied in Abidjan, Côte d'Ivoire, then trained in Paris at both the Independent Conservatory of French Cinema and the INA. His *Les Dodos* (The monsters, 1980) is centered around a hunter who, crossing a forest, witnesses the supernatural apparition of a lion that transforms into a man. Trying to comprehend what he has seen, the hunter teaches his children about the Dodos, performance groups introduced to the Mossi people by the Hausa. Sanou's presentation is not just ethnographic but also historical and sociological, stressing the integration of the Dodos into national cultural associations in Upper Volta. Bathily similarly employs a framing story to represent the traditions surrounding the rite of circumcision in his feature-length *Tiyabu-biru* (Circumcision, 1978). Several boys are desperate to participate but not yet old enough. Through the boys' eyes, spectators watch initiates who are progressing through the stages of the ritual, at the same time witnessing scenes of daily life in a rural village. Via the experiences of these characters and other village residents, Bathily addresses conflicts between African and imported European customs, between traditional African and colonial European educations.

After attending university and the same Dakar ciné-club as fellow future filmmakers Djibril Diop Mambéty, Mahama Traoré, Ben Diogaye Beye, and Samba Félix Ndiaye, Moussa Bathily taught high school and worked as a journalist. Captivated by the nascent world of West African cinema, he began to write scripts and assisted on Sembene's *Xala* (1975) and *Ceddo* (1977). *Tiyabu-biru* was one of a few productions funded by the SNC in the second half of the decade and received additional support from France's ACCT and INA. The documentary's subject, like that of Maïga's *Autour de l'hippopotame*, had been treated in one of Jean Rouch's first films. But Bathily's perspective was internal, not just as a West African but as a former resident of Tiyabu, the rural village where *Tiyabu-biru* was shot. *Biru* means shelter or barn in Soninke, thus newly circumcised adolescents live in *tiyabu biru* while they recover. Bathily emphasized the film's autobiographical roots, stating that his goal had been to make it "as if I had never left my village."[25] Yet the voice-over commentary begins with the nostalgic pronouncement that "each year that passes takes me farther from my village, from my customs," and Bathily's narrator worries that he will lose these customs altogether. "So let me evoke one last time," he tells spectators, "a circumcision ceremony from my childhood."

Tiyabu-biru's French-language narration remains consistently in the first person, providing information but also addressing the film's spectators and even participants: "You have to decide, guys. Have some nerve!" Dialogues among the characters are virtually all in Soninke. When the boys encounter another young resident of the village on his way to school dressed in European clothes and carrying a book bag, they angrily accuse him of being an *élève*, or student, one of the few French words they know. They feel as much contempt for the *élève* as they feel admiration for the recently circumcised teenagers working in the fields. When a local herder threatens the successful completion of the circumcision ritual by refusing to sell cattle to the village, the boys plot to prevent the purchase of the cattle at a higher price by a wealthy buyer, who appears in European clothes and wearing a watch. Tradition is preserved thanks to their actions, but the herder files a police complaint against Tiyabu. First a police officer and then the prefect, whom the voice-over narrator calls a "white Negro," come from the neighboring town of Bakel to adjudicate the case, eventually reaching an agreement and payment plan with the village elders. Realizing that their autonomy is waning, the elders continue their discussion after the prefect's departure and decide to send the circumcised initiates "to find money in the land of the White men." "Our world is dying," they declare, and the last shots of the film show the boys waiting in line at the French school while their older idols trudge away, each carrying a few possessions in a cloth bag.

A critical and even commercial success, *Tiyabu-biru* was presented at the Cannes Film Festival in 1978 and FESPACO in 1979 and screened in theaters in Senegal, Mali, Mauritania, and Benin. Complaining that European critics and festival organizers had considered it ethnography, however, Bathily insisted that, despite its ethnographic content, it was "not an ethnographic film." The jury of a festival of ethnographic film had called it fiction, proof for Bathily that his film, created both to bear witness to a ritual that was disappearing and to entertain a Senegalese audience, "challenges classifications."[26] Nichols notes that the observational mode of documentary, grounded in "the nonintervention of the filmmaker," is associated with the North American Direct Cinema movement of the 1950s and '60s as well as with North American and European ethnographic filmmaking and visual anthropology.[27] Bathily's challenge to the conventions of this model, like Tidiane Aw's "theatrical ethnology" of the *n'doep* ceremony in *Réalité*, echoed the Ouagadougou seminar's rejection of the observational "ethnographic gaze" several years earlier. Boughedir, who deemed this gaze "scientific," set it in contrast to the "warmth and sympathy" of someone from the culture represented.[28] The Third World Film-Makers Meeting had similarly denounced ethnology as a "pseudo-scientific process" that was "for the most part in the service of the colonizer."[29]

Discussing ethnography, Bathily noted the difficulties involved in producing a "faithful" description of the circumcision ceremony. Not least of these was the fact that the ceremony at the heart of his film had not taken place in Tiyabu for twenty years and therefore had to be reenacted for *Tiyabu-biru*. For a different reason than his young characters, Bathily himself had also been excluded from ritual circumcision; he underwent the procedure in a medical clinic. In the wake of the film's release, Bathily claimed that he had now "exorcised" this childhood deprivation and could leave documentary for "pure fiction."[30] Malian director Souleymane Cissé made the same decision at the same time. After completing a series of ethnographic shorts with *Les chanteurs traditionnels des Îles Seychelles* (Traditional singers of the Seychelles Islands, 1978), Cissé switched to feature fiction in *Baara* (1978), *Finye* (1982), and *Yeelen* (1987). Cissé described *Yeelen*, his most widely acclaimed film, as a response to European ethnographic films, "to a foreign gaze that had sometimes tended to mistake Africans for objects, for animals to be shown performing their exotic rituals."[31]

In its delicate balance between documentary and fictional narration and goals, Cheikh Ngaïdo Ba's *Rewo Daande Maayo* (The other side of the river, 1978) bears a strong resemblance to *Tiyabu-biru*. Bathily's compatriot, Ba returned to Dakar after training at the INA in France. He worked at the Senegalese Office of Radio and Television, directing Senegal's first television news broadcast, and assisted on films by Tidiane Aw, Ababacar Samb Makaram, and Momar Thiam, while shooting several short fictions of his own. Ba would go on to serve as president of the Association of Senegalese Cineastes (CINESEAS), a role in which he advocated for Africa-based production and distribution networks, and as secretary general of FEPACI. The Senegalese National Agency for Rural Development (SO.NA.DER) commissioned his first film, on the topic of irrigation and the cultivation of rice, just as it had Abikanlou's documentary about the mechanization of farming in Dahomey several years earlier. Like for Moustapha Alassane, Timité Bassori, and Moussa Kemoko Diakité in the 1960s, commissioned documentaries in the '70s and '80s provided on-the-job training, income, and, in some cases, the occasion for narrative experiments.

Paulin Vieyra characterized *Rewo Daande Maayo* as a "research film" employing "social anthropology," noting its fictional narrative strategies, while Mbye Cham called it "semi-fictional and semi-documentary" and Françoise

Pfaff simply "documentary."[32] Several acted roles serve as scaffolding for the sharing of information that is both ethnographic and propagandistic; the livelihood of members of a struggling family is preserved by equipment and expertise provided by the government. Shot in Mauritania, across the Senegal River, the film is almost entirely in Pulaar. A shepherd and his wife and children leave their drought-stricken village with a donkey and a few possessions to relocate near the river. Ba shows scenes of their daily lives in both contexts, with the man's thoughts presented as voice-over narration; he states in accented French that he fought in France during World War I, then wonders in Pulaar whether he will die at home or survive by going abroad. After evoking the specters of past colonial oppression and contemporary emigration, the film concludes with the arrival of SO.NA.DER representatives and a European adviser. Promoting a technological advance that Maïga would film again a decade later, they have brought machinery to enable villagers to pump water from the river to their fields. Given the last word, the government representatives announce that the project, which will also involve the allotment of land parcels to families, is "apolitical," and they urge village elders to agree to participate.

The documentary efforts to film Africa with an African point of view traced above accorded with calls from artists, intellectuals, and administrators for the representation of African cultures for African audiences. This goal was judged more urgent than the formal experimentation of the 1960s, which had been controversial. In 1961, encouraging newly independent filmmakers to show Africa to Africans, Blaise Senghor insisted that they must reject "the intellectual flights of fancy of the 'New Wave.'"[33] Abikanlou, Bathily, and Ba signaled a corresponding aversion to European ethnographic documentary, even to Rouch's innovations. Fiction filmmakers felt this antipathy as well, as evidenced by the career trajectory of Gaston Kaboré, another luminary of African cinema whose career began in the 1970s. Kaboré left Burkina Faso in 1972 to study history at the Sorbonne in Paris, where he prepared a master's thesis on the representation of sub-Saharan Africa in late nineteenth-century French illustrated magazines, specifically *Le petit journal illustré* (Little illustrated newspaper). Kaboré began a doctoral program, which he abandoned to pursue filmmaking. After a screening of Sembene's *Xala*, Kaboré had come to a similar realization as Vieyra two decades earlier: cinema could be used to represent African realities.[34] A familiarity with colonial-era French claims to represent an Africa caught *sur le vif* heightened his awareness that, in his words, "we only knew Africa through the gaze of others . . . and it was primordial that Africa reclaim its own gaze on its history, on its life."[35] After returning to Ouagadougou in 1976, Kaboré taught at the INAFEC and a year later became the director of Upper Volta's CNC, making a few commissioned documentaries before his remarkable historical fictions *Wend Kuuni* (1982) and *Zan Boko* (1988).

Even as sub-Saharan African cinema was becoming known for time-lessly traditional stories Manthia Diawara called "return to the source" films, however, the politically and culturally dynamic period of the 1970s and '80s launched the careers of two Senegalese filmmakers who would become Paulin Vieyra's first true documentarist heirs.[36] Through their documentary focus, Samba Félix Ndiaye and Safi Faye became among the most important sub-Saharan African directors. Ndiaye's extraordinary career in documentary cinema spanned four decades, from 1974 until his untimely death in 2009. Born in March 1945, mere months before the end of World War II and the reinvigorated African independence movements that followed, Ndiaye grew up in a milieu he described as both Christian and Muslim but primarily animist, strongly anchored in the traditions of southern Casamance.[37] His interest in cinema came after independence, when he participated in the French Cultural Center's ciné-club in Dakar. Movie marathons were followed by passionate debates, Ndiaye recounted, during which "the provocateurs who supported *Intolerance* were angry at the *Battleship Potemkin* fanatics, and the devotees of German expressionism felt the same way toward the disciples of Italian neorealism."[38] In 1969, Ndiaye left for Europe to study filmmaking at the University of Paris VIII, a less hierarchical and more experimentally oriented program than the IDHEC, receiving additional training at the Louis Lumière School.[39] Although he was based in Paris for over thirty years, virtually all of Ndiaye's films were shot in West Africa, almost exclusively in Senegal.

Toward the end of his time in France, Ndiaye situated his work in a tradition that began with Vieyra's *Afrique sur Seine*, explaining that he understood the West African films that preceded his to be "principally documentaries."[40] All of Ndiaye's own films are documentaries, and they showcase his varied and international education, always rooted in Africa, always reaching outward to explore a range of stylistic approaches. After four years in Paris, Ndiaye returned to Dakar to shoot a short film as the final project for his master's degree. Funded by the short-lived Senegalese National Cinema Company, *Perantal: L'éducation du nourisson* (Perantal: Infant education, 1974) demonstrates and defends traditional practices of baby massage and baby carrying, *damp* and *boot* in Wolof. The film begins in Wolof, although what follows, most notably an interview with a Senegalese woman physician accompanied by images of a mother massaging her baby and women working while carrying their babies, is narrated by Ndiaye's voice-over in French. This commentary summarizes the benefits of massage, said to be both relaxing and stimulating for the baby, and of *portage*, which provides close contact with the mother and sets the child's legs into the correct position. Portraying traditions practiced by women in both villages and city hospitals, *Perantal* not only affirms their value but also suggests that Europe could learn from African child-rearing practices. Too many young people in Senegal are conforming to European models, Ndiaye concludes; his film joins a "global struggle for the revalorization of our heritage."

Ndiaye's second film, *Geti tey* (Fishing today, 1978), documents, hour by hour, a day in the life of Cayar, the same Senegalese fishing village featured in Vieyra's *Môl*. Coproduced by his own company, Samba et Compagnie Films, later renamed Almadies Films, and the French International Audiovisual Consortium (CAI), it received additional funding from the ACCT. Ndiaye drops the explanatory French-language voice-over that *Perantal* inherited from colonial and early African ethnographic documentaries, using opening text on screen to provide basic information about Cayar. In winter and spring, it has a population of three thousand, spectators read, a number that doubles in summer and fall, when it becomes "the most important fishing village in Senegal, if not in all of West Africa." This importance is both local and global, with local resources far inferior to global ones. Fishermen from the region converge on a town that even in summer has a single clinic and one nurse, whereas "all of the big oil companies are represented."

The first quarter of *Geti tey* is silent aside from ambient noise, as fishermen put out their boats in the morning, then bring them in with fish that are prepared, dried, and sold by women on the beach. As the day continues, spectators hear from village inhabitants, who speak for themselves in Lebu Wolof. Men work and joke about how to repair their boats, and, ten minutes into the film, the head of Cayar, Abdoulaye Ndoye, begins to tell the history of its fishing practices. Precolonial traditions of fishing with nets and using small fish to catch larger ones were displaced by the French colonial administration's imposition of motorized boats, he explains, and now European trawlers idle off the coast, overfishing and forcing local fishermen to risk their lives by going farther and farther out in their pirogues. "Soon," Ndoye concludes, "our children will not find a single fish in the sea." He adds that the Senegalese government does not support local fishermen's efforts to compete even in the internal market, refusing to supply Cayar with a freezer to store fish to be transported and sold in the western part of the country.

Africa and Africans had been "de-cultured" in colonial films that showed "a stereotyped Africa: elephants, the jungle, dancing, things like that," Ndiaye stated in an interview with Ghanaian director Nii Kwate Owoo in the late 1970s. These films denigrated African civilization and denied an African "way of seeing, of understanding each other."[41] In his first films, therefore, Ndiaye—like Vieyra, Senghor, Alassane, and their colleagues discussed above—affirmed the contemporary importance of long-standing West African traditions. His dual interest in filmmaking and ethnography led Ndiaye to begin a doctoral program with Jean Rouch, a project he abandoned after a falling out with his renowned thesis director.[42] Mindful that African documentarists were working against a colonial ethnographic model epitomized in its later stages by Rouch's work, Ndiaye argued that "this exclusive and reductive form with grand scientific pretensions" did not account for complex social structures with which he was intimately familiar.[43] His earliest filmic training, as he understood it, had come from listening to his grandmother tell stories to the children in his neighborhood. Her lessons informed his sense of identity as well as his narrative style and technical aspects of his filmmaking, all three crucial to the representation of cultural realities he wished to portray rather than explicate. "She told us that if you need to go learn from someone," Ndiaye told film scholar Françoise Pfaff, "you should sit humbly, lower than this person, and not look at them from above, which would be aggressive." Thanks to his grandmother, he continued, he used low-angle shots.[44]

Like Samba Félix Ndiaye, Safi Faye worked with Jean Rouch early in her cinematic career, but their collaboration was less conflictual and longer lasting. Faye met Rouch while working at the 1966 Dakar World Festival of Negro Arts. He invited her to costar in his ciné-fiction *Petit à petit* (Little by little, 1969/1971), for which she, Damouré Zika, and Ibrahim Dia acted the experiences of a trio of West Africans in Europe. Damouré's character, planning to build a high-rise in Ayorou, leaves Niger for France to learn "how people live in multi-story buildings." In a reversal of the route of French *chasseurs d'images* from Machin to Rouch, he is on a mission to learn habits and customs. Rouch was still directing, however, and Faye later judged the film and her role in it inconsequential. Faye stayed in Paris and eventually studied ethnology with Rouch, writing a doctoral thesis on Serer religion at the School of Advanced Studies in the Social Sciences (EHESS) while taking filmmaking classes at the Louis Lumière School. She shot the short *La passante* (The passerby, 1972) along the banks of the Seine; her next two works, both ethnographic documentaries, were filmed in her native Serer region of Senegal, between the towns of Mbour and Djiffer on what is known as the Petite Côte. In her doctoral research and her early films, Faye wanted to "do ethnology," by which she meant work on her "real culture" and "real traditions." "Until now," she stated, "only foreigners who did not speak a word of our language have written about African culture."[45] In ethnographic films, Faye argued, Europeans had "deformed" Africans.[46]

Faye's *Kaddu Beykat* (1975) is widely recognized as the first feature-length film made by a Black African woman. Acclaimed upon its release, it was screened at Cannes and won both the 1975 Georges Sadoul Prize and the 1976 International Federation of Film Critics' (FIPRESCI) Prize, awarded at the Berlin International Film Festival. Faye shot the documentary as part of the fieldwork for her graduate studies, thus on a tiny budget, in black and white, and during vacation trips to her familial village; her crew included a French cameraman and her uncle as sound technician.[47] *Kaddu Beykat* addresses a series of linked topics that arose from Faye's research and in conversation with family members, topics brought together under a title in Serer that the film's conclusion defines as *la parole du paysan*—"the peasant's voice" or "the farmer's words." Faye later said the title signifies "the famine people's words," complaining that Europeans had mistranslated it as "peasant letter" or "letter from the village" simply because there is a letter in the film.[48]

Faye herself, however, did describe *Kaddu Beykat* as "testimony in the form of a letter."[49] This letter is spoken instead of written, and the film begins with Faye's first-person voice-over narration in French, inviting the spectator to meet her extended family. The credits bear a dedication to her grandfather, who appears in the film and died eleven days after shooting concluded. "As for me," Faye's commentary states, "I am in good health, thank God. This is how our letters begin when we write." This *our*, like those of Alassane and de Medeiros, situates and implicates Faye as belonging to the place and culture she is filming. As village inhabitants emerge from their houses and begin to work, Faye addresses viewers: "Here is my village, my relatives who are farmers and raise livestock.... You will live with me for a little while."

Faye notes in her voice-over that her relatives believe they will be mocked by the film's eventual spectators for being "badly dressed" and "always working." And much of the film is, in fact, made up of images of villagers working; they prepare their fields, gather wood, herd and milk goats, fish, gather salt, and cook. Using a mostly fixed camera, Faye observes and listens.[50] Like Ndiaye in *Geti Tey*, she allows her subjects to speak about their lived reality in their own language, their words translated in subtitles for non-Serer speakers. Faye's commentary provides occasional descriptions and sociological, geographical, and anthropological explanations: typical yearly incomes, weather patterns, and the division of labor. An elderly man plants roots in a field, for example, and in Serer tells the boys who accompany him to ask God for what they want so it will grow. Faye in French tells viewers that village residents bury certain roots to fertilize the earth and sacrifice animals to "the deities, the *pangols*," showing

Safi Faye, *Kaddu Beykat*, 1975.

men and boys hoeing the dry earth. She explains that, according to custom, young girls help older women who have lost their strength to farm, then shows girls singing as they till a field.

Although *Kaddu Beykat* is framed to give spectators the impression of witnessing village life, it becomes evident that the villagers are performing for the camera. In the first part of the film, for example, a man calls to his sons in the early morning; they come out of their house, exaggeratedly miming having just woken up. Faye then teaches spectators a proverb used by the father to encourage his children to eat their breakfast: "An empty bag cannot hold itself upright." In a more crafted fiction, Faye weaves into her film the story of Ngor and Koumba, who have been waiting for two years to get married. Whereas Mariam and Garba in Moustapha Alassane's *Aouré* demonstrate traditional marriage rites, Faye's young couple enacts the sociological problems standing in the way of traditional marriage. Although the names of Assane Faye and Maguette Gueye appear in the concluding credits, they are never identified as actors. There were no actors in her film, Faye insisted; she had not wanted any, since peasants could best address their own situation.[51] If the scenes featuring Ngor and Koumba were fictional in the sense that they "were not happening at that moment in the village," she asserted, it was at the same time true that "they could very easily have happened."[52]

Kaddu Beykat is documentary for the ethnographic information it provides, and, like Abikanlou's *Sous le signe du Vodun*, the film also offers a complex economic, social, and historical analysis of rural life in postcolonial Senegal. The men of the village discuss drought and economic problems under the *arbre à palabres*, or talking tree. They are trapped in a system in which they buy equipment and seeds on credit, they explain, and must repay with peanuts. This forced, export-based monoculture dates to the colonial era but is maintained by the Senegalese government, which will not allow farmers to return to the precolonial practice of growing rice and millet for their families and neighbors to eat. "Peanuts exhaust us," one man says, "but allow us to pay taxes," concluding that "our ancestors didn't have so many problems." Children also gather around the talking tree, where they act out the roles of tax collector and villagers after a bad harvest. "Pay the state or we will take you away!" one threatens. Faye's commentary summarizes: the government buys peanuts grown by village farmers, then resells them at a higher price and owes them a rebate, which it keeps in payment of their debts.

Ngor's parents discuss at length how he might raise money for Koumba's dowry and their wedding expenses by working an additional field his mother has rented. With the granaries empty, however, Ngor decides that his only hope of earning enough to marry is to leave the village to work in Dakar. Once there, he is deceived and exploited, like many other struggling farmers who arrive in the capital city. When Ngor returns home with ideas about planting trees, fertilizing the soil, and diversifying crops to improve harvests, an elder speaks directly to Faye's camera to suggest a rebellion against peanut monoculture. Extending Faye's voice-over critique, he points out that the money the government uses to buy peanuts comes from the European Development Fund. *Kaddu Beykat* is at the antipodes of Ba's commissioned *Rewo Daande Maayo*, in which government initiatives promise to bring peasants into the modern world while preserving traditional ways of life. Seven years after its release, Paulin Vieyra noted, Faye's film had still not been authorized for exhibition in Senegal, proof of the "piercing truth" of Faye's analysis.[53] Faye herself related that government censors had demanded she remove two scenes from the film—the first of village children playacting the cruelty of tax collectors and the second of a farmer accusing the government of having paid him less than the amount promised. She refused to do so.[54]

Only a few people in *Kaddu Beykat*'s village speak and read French: a teacher the others call "Director," who reads newspaper articles about current politics out loud for other residents, and young men back from the city who discuss the diplomas for which they are preparing. Concluding her film, Faye acknowledges her role as translator and transcriber, not onto paper but onto film. "The letter is from me," she states. "All the rest is from my farmer relatives. I thank them." Faye had used notes from her conversations with villagers to write a script that allowed farmers to "express themselves." "I have never made a fiction film," she declared, noting that she was interested in film "as a research tool."[55] As much a learning process as the creation of a finished product, her ethnographic and sociological filmmaking arose from a desire to know more about her country and culture.[56] And Faye characterized what she had learned through her research as reality. "I tried to put reality on film," she said in an interview published the year of *Kaddu Beykat*'s release, "a reality that I described and into which I mixed a fictional story around which the film is centered."[57]

Like *Kaddu Beykat*, Safi Faye's next film, *Fad'jal* (1979), was shot in her familial village and its environs. In Serer with French-language voice-over commentary, the documentary appeared the same year Faye earned her doctoral degree. With funding from the French Ministry of Cooperation, the INA, and the Bureau of Cinema, she was able to shoot in color. In recognition of the bureau's support of her work, which the Senegalese government refused to fund, Faye dedicated the film to Jean-René Debrix. In what might at first seem like a further nod to Senegal's former colonizer, she begins *Fad'jal* with images of African children in a Catholic church classroom; they recite, one after the other, a text about Louis XIV, "the greatest French king." Yet this scene is immediately juxtaposed with on-screen text of a famous citation from Senegalese historian, ethnographer, and autobiographer Amadou Hampaté Bâ: "In Africa, when an old man dies, a library has burned." Hampaté Bâ's assertion of an authentically African oral archive stands in stark contrast to the colonial formal education children shown in the film are receiving almost two decades after independence. Ten minutes into *Fad'jal*, Faye's first voice-over narration announces the end of the harvest and the arrival of the time of wrestling matches, with nothing further about Louis XIV. "A young Serer man must know how to work, dance, and wrestle," she explains, preparing spectators for what they will see.

Fad'jal is more technically accomplished and adventurous than *Kaddu Beykat*, with more camera movement and a wider range of shooting angles. Like Faye's earlier film, it is an ethnographic documentary, made up in large part of long scenes of daily life in the village of Fadjal. But Faye in her second work retreats, though not completely, from explanatory narration. Her voice is heard less frequently, with most ethnographic information conveyed by villagers' actions and words. Spectators witness two women helping a third give birth and the rituals that follow; the griot whispers the baby's name, a griotte sings, and a goat is sacrificed. In the burial and mourning rites featured later in the film, women ululate, a man strikes the ground with a staff while praising the dead, and a bull is sacrificed. A conflict breaks out between different factions of a family about the division of money given in the dead man's honor. Faye did not stage these events for the film; her father informed her about upcoming ceremonies, and she attended them with him and a cameraman.[58] As in *Kaddu Beykat*, Faye recorded not just customs and traditions but the reality of hard work, work that was taken for granted in colonial-era French documentaries. Villagers farm peanuts and millet, fetch water, weave baskets, work iron, gather salt, fish with spears and nets, and prepare meals. When elder Iba Ndong gathers children around him under the talking tree, he repeats that in Fadjal, "if you work, you are happy. If you don't work, they'll laugh at you." The name of the village, in fact, derives from the Serer words for "come" and "work."

Whereas *Kaddu Beykat* incorporates sociological and political analyses into ethnographic cinema, *Fad'jal* introduces a historical—specifically oral historical—dimension. The children gathered under the talking tree ask their elder to tell the story of their village. Another man arrives, sits down, and begins: "Our village was founded by a woman. She was named Mbang Fadjal." As the storytelling continues, both viewers and the astonished children hear drumming. Craning their necks, the children peer around the tree to find the source of the sound, and a cut takes viewers to footage of women dancing in the village square. An acted narrative thread then depicts the precolonial past as recounted in the oral tradition of the region. A blurry image transitions to a shot of a man on horseback; he is identified as King Latsouk Fagname in the story being told to the children, which continues in Serer in the voice-over. The king was jealous of the powerful village of Fadjal and swore to take it over. Inhabitants, forced to leave, suffered through drought and famine before returning from the Sine-Saloum delta. Faye's montage takes spectators back and forth between the present storytelling and the past of the story, sometimes but not always signaling shifts with a visual transition.

As *Fad'jal* progresses, the film foregrounds the contemporary political struggles of inhabitants of Fadjal. A village discussion of the matrilineal nature of traditional land inheritance leads into another about the government's plan to divide and reallocate land. All the villagers oppose this project except for one, whom the others accuse of wanting to construct a house for tourists. In the past, the elder explains to assembled children, families owned land in the village and could farm and distribute it as they wished; Faye's commentary quickly adds that a 1964 law had transferred ownership of all land to the state. In the last ten minutes of the film, Faye narrates something she did not film, the arrival in October 1977 of developers. "They had iron rulers, hammers, and stakes," she recounts, and were confronted by "the resistance of the peasants." This resistance was successful, viewers learn while watching a debate among villagers about what their representative should say during a meeting with regional officials. Although land reallocation has been suspended, the representative notes, the village is in desperate need of a doctor for its clinic, of farming machines, and of a road. *Fad' jal* draws to a close at the talking tree, where the children demonstrate what they have learned. One repeats the lesson about Fadjal and work, and another repeats the genealogy of the village in reverse chronological order back to founder Mbang Fadjal.

Understanding Vieyra's *Afrique sur Seine* to be docufiction, Loftus considers Faye's films to be *ethno-fictions*, a term often used to refer to works by Jean Rouch that he himself called *ciné-fictions*.[59] Faye, who acted for and then trained with Rouch, was very familiar with the French tradition of ostensibly objective ethnographic realism as well as the innovations introduced by Rouch. She stated in a 1979 interview that her artistic goal was to film "things which relate to our civilization . . . a typically African culture." "I make films," she repeated, "about reality"—a reality she knew as a member of African society, unlike the typical European filmmaker, "who arrives, observes, and goes away." When asked to comment on the mixing of documentary and fiction in *Kaddu Beykat* and *Fad' jal*, Faye suggested that the term *mise en scène* was more apt than *fiction*. "For me all these words—fiction, documentary, ethnology—have no sense," Faye continued; "I base what I do in reality."[60] This philosophy traversed her entire career, and in a master class recorded two decades later, Faye described her films as *documentaires rejoués* (reperformed documentaries).[61] Her performance-based nonfictions situate Faye in a lineage of African films going back to Vieyra's *Afrique sur Seine* and Alassane's *Aouré*, a tradition that refashioned the *grands documentaires* inspired by *Nanook of the North*.

In 1979, Safi Faye moved to Berlin, where she studied video production and made commissioned films financed by German television. *Goob Na Nu* (The harvest is done, 1979) and *Selbe et tant d'autres* (Selbe and so many others, 1982) continue the ethnographic themes of her first documentaries, if with a less innovative narrative structure and less detailed socioeconomic analysis. Coproduced by UNICEF, *Selbe et tant d'autres* addresses the situation of women in a West African village, with a range of women's issues focalized through a central character named Selbe Diouf. The village is not named, but the work that occupies its women resembles that performed by the women of *Kaddu Beykat* and *Fad'jal*. Spectators hear almost exclusively Selbe's voice, with occasional interventions by other inhabitants of the village and voice-over commentary.[62] Faye's last documentary, *Tesito* (Seize your destiny, 1989), was commissioned by the Catholic Committee Against Hunger and for Development and filmed in Casamance, the southernmost region of Senegal. The film is devoted to women working with a development project called PAMEZ, which fosters women's participation in the fishing industry. Like *Kaddu Beykat*, *Tesito* is structured like a letter, this one spoken by a thirteen-year-old girl named Zeïba, who explains, for example, that "fishing is reserved for men, while women buy the fish to transform it. . . . This is the custom." Women affiliated with the project introduce themselves and speak about their families' financial difficulties, providing context for their meeting with a French representative of the Catholic committee. Footage of this meeting confirms the women's commitment to self-reliance; they request financing to purchase fish to preserve and resell, a boat and nets to collect oysters, and a car to transport their products.

Over the course of the 1980s, a new group of African ethnographic filmmakers joined Samba Félix Ndiaye and Safi Faye to address precolonial traditions as well as contemporary cultural activities that bear their legacies. Along with Oumarou Ganda and Inoussa Ousseini, Mariama Hima learned about filmmaking from Jean Rouch and Serge Moati at the Niamey cultural center in the years just after independence.[63] After studying in France, Hima returned to Niger, where, in addition to making films, she became director of the National Museum. First broadcast on Nigerien television, Hima's *Baabu Banza* (Nothing is thrown away, 1984) won prizes at the Cinéma du Réel documentary film festival in Paris, the Venice Film Festival, and FESPACO.[64] While in Venice, Hima and Damouré Zika acted in Rouch's *Cousin, cousine* (1985), a short subject that recalls the reverse ethnography of *Petit à petit*. Rouch filmed Hima and Zika touring the city, where they visited a boatyard to compare gondola construction to that of West African pirogues.

At the start of *Baabu Banza*, Hima's commentary describes the growth of Niamey's shanty towns, where anything and everything is bought and sold in open-air markets. Focusing on the creative recycling of tires, she films the work of a man who, for ten years, has been using them to make sandals. He describes each step of the transformation in Hausa, his words paraphrased in the French-language voice-over. Another man demonstrates his use of inner tubes to make rubber containers that women use to fetch water from the well. Children play with old tires, rolling each other around and making slingshots out of pieces of rubber. Noting the professionalism of these independent artisans, Hima concludes that "they are working hard in an economy that they themselves have created." Returning to the theme of recuperation in *Badile* (Aluminum, 1985), Hima repeats the assertion that nothing is thrown away. Men working in a Niamey market are shown disassembling automobile carcasses, then purchasing a typewriter and aluminum cans that children have rescued from a load of trash delivered by a dump truck. They melt down the aluminum they have collected to pour into molds for cooking pots; Hima's voice-over shares that they can make up to twenty-five pots every day. Both artistry and industry, she notes, the process provides work for twenty people. Along with the other short films in her series, Hima hoped that these tributes to the ingenuity of traditional artisans working with very modern materials would find their place in a media center dedicated to "African values." Never created, it would have represented important figures of the independence era as well as African perspectives on a range of topics in history, politics, science, agriculture, and the arts.[65]

As filmmakers worked to valorize African cultures, they documented events that did so. Timité Bassori's *Akati et danses de Côte d'Ivoire* (Akati and dances from Ivory Coast, 1974), an ethnographic short produced by the Ivorian Cinema Company, linked precolonial tradition and contemporary performance. Opting not to use voice-over commentary, Bassori intercut footage of dancing in a village square with scenes of the daily life of village residents, accompanied by a soundtrack of singing, kora music, and drumming. A striking cut then connects images of dancers and musicians to an Air Afrique plane taking off, the camera panning to follow its path; a second cut transports the spectator to a Paris performance of Ivorian musicians and dancing masks. Oumarou Ganda undertook a parallel project—a feature-length documentary following the travels of dancers from the Niger Ballet—two decades after he starred in Rouch's *Moi, un noir*. The voice-over narration of *Cock cock cock* (1977) is simultaneously ethnographic and intimate, evocative as much as informative. Addressing performers on screen, it simultaneously implicates the film's spectators in its ethnographic enterprise: "The songs and dances that you will see today will perhaps be forgotten." The commentary continues, first formally then informally, "The film we are going to shoot with you will thus attest to the oral tradition that is disappearing. Are you ready?" *Cock cock cock* follows a group of professional musicians and dancers that visits a village, where local inhabitants sing to greet them, then leaves for Paris. They see the Eiffel Tower and eat ice cream in Montmartre, the narrator describing the trip as "fraternal salutations from the Black man." From France, the troupe travels to Canada and back to Niger. The commentary also concludes with a return to the local, promising to honor the farmers, shepherds, and blacksmiths who preserve the performers' traditions.

The Central African Republic first came to cinema through documentaries about cultural festivals. Director Joseph Akouissonne left Bangui in the mid-1960s for Paris, where he studied filmmaking at the University of Paris X and, like Ndiaye, Faye, and Hima, ethnology with Jean Rouch. Akouissonne made several documentary shorts, including *Festival des arts et cultures de Royan* (Royan Festival of Arts and Cultures, 1977). Commissioned by the French Ministry of Cooperation, the film shows music and dance troupes from Upper Volta, Mali, and Mauritania that have traveled to southwestern France for an international festival. Twenty years after Akouissonne went to France, Central African Léonie Yangba-Zowe enrolled at the EHESS in Paris, where she combined her interests in ethnography and African cinema in a thesis on marriage and the role of women in the films of Oumarou Ganda. Yangba-Zowe, who in her thesis thanked Mariama Hima for help and support, made three ethnographic documentaries on traditional dance, all filmed in Super 8 and blown up to 16mm.

Yangba-Zowe described her filmic trilogy, composed of *Nzalé*, *Lengue*, and *Yangba-Bolo*, as a "cultural testimony of the Central African people."[66] Produced with funding from the French Ministry of Foreign Relations, Rouch's Committee for Ethnographic Film, and the Central African Republic's National Educational Radio-Television, *Nzalé* (Buffalo, 1985) begins with a drumming performance. A painted sign identifies the Nzalé Folkloric Group, founded in Bangui in 1979, and a voice-over explains that the group's dance, which brings together several central African ethnic groups, illustrates confrontation. *Nzalé* is a new name for a dance inherited from Mbaka ancestors, viewers are told; the rest of the film consists of extended scenes of dancing without further commentary, whether explanatory or participatory. Long shots of the group, medium shots of individuals, and close-ups of feet, hands, and faces are set to sounds of drumming, singing, and whistling. Each of the dancers wears a skin and tail that represent an animal he or she embodies, and some have metal whistles in their mouths. The contrast between these costumes and the European-style clothing worn by most members of the African audience—the men in pants and button-up shirts and the children in shorts or dresses—accentuates the ethnographic nature of the spectacle.

In a progressive widening of documentary testimony to the wealth and persistence of African cultures, films about past and present customs and traditions were joined by biographical films about important figures. Paulin Vieyra's cinematic portraits of Senegalese storyteller and writer Birago Diop

Léonie Yangba-Zowe, *Nzalé*, 1985.

and painter Iba Ndiaye were produced by Vieyra's company, PSV Films, with support from the French Ministry of Foreign Relations. *Birago Diop: Poète-conteur* (Birago Diop: Poet-storyteller, 1982) features a series of interviews in which Diop discusses his life and illustrious literary career. These were shot in black and white in Diop's veterinary office, in the outdoor spaces of his youth in Dakar and Saint-Louis, in a bookstore where his works are sold, and in a classroom where his works are taught. The film closes with a voice-over reading of Diop's poem "Sympathy," followed by an on-screen citation in which fellow Negritude writer Léon Gontran Damas praises Diop as "an authentic value of traditional and modern Africa." Shot in color, *Iba Ndiaye: Portrait d'un peintre* (Iba Ndiaye: Portrait of a painter, 1983) begins with footage of Senegalese president Léopold Sédar Senghor touring a museum retrospective of the acclaimed artist's work. These images are interwoven with interviews conducted in Ndiaye's Dakar and Paris studios. The artist recounts his career and interprets several of his paintings, shown on screen, while additional information is provided by alternating male and female voice-over narrators.

David Ika Diop received funding from the Senegalese Ministry of Culture to make *David Mandessi Diop: Poète de l'amour* (David Mandessi Diop: Poet of love, 1986), a documentary testament to his father that was screened at FES-PACO. A celebrated poet associated with the Negritude movement and an activist for West African independence, Mandessi Diop died in a plane crash in 1960 at the age of thirty-three. Information about his family and career is provided in recorded interviews with those who knew and loved him, notably Maria Diop, the poet's mother and filmmaker's grandmother, and Léopold Sédar Senghor, who had been his teacher. Sharing on film what he had been too young to know, Ika Diop also includes readings of his father's poems; these are accompanied by archival photographs as well as contemporary footage of the places where Mandessi Diop lived and places and people about which he wrote.

In its reflective rather than ethnographic approach, David Ika Diop's poetic biography joins a rare avant-garde film of the period: Moussa Bathily's West African city symphony *Ndakkaru, impressions matinales* (Dakar, morning impressions, 1975), funded by the Senegalese cinema bureau. Bathily's film begins with early morning images of Dakar as it awakens. Panning shots of the city are accompanied by calls to prayer that become gradually more audible on the soundtrack; there is no voice-over narration. Situating his film within global documentary tradition as an heir to Dziga Vertov's *Man with a Movie Camera*, Bathily simultaneously insists on the Africanness of his work, whose title includes the name of Senegal's capital city in Wolof. *Ndakkaru, impressions matinales* is dedicated "in homage to silent cinema" but also to Henriette Bathily, who had danced in Paulin Vieyra's *Une nation est née* almost fifteen years prior. Intercut sequences filmed in the city's African and European neighborhoods follow these dedications, and a familiar shot of an Air Afrique jet on the airport tarmac signals the modernity of independence. Bathily shows restaurants opening for business, children going to school, women hanging up laundry, and performers at the Sorano National Theater dancing to both classical ballet and African music. Into these images of the city's contrasts, he incorporates the barest outline of a short, acted fiction. An older couple sits on a bench; when the woman catches the man staring at young women walking by, she gets angry and leaves. Shifting focus to display more of the city, including the train station and a second look at the airport, Bathily later returns to the couple, the man in pursuit, struggling to keep up.[67]

Successors not to *Une nation est née* or *Môl* but to Vieyra's *Afrique sur Seine*, a series of important documentaries of the 1970s and '80s took as their subject sub-Saharan African immigration to Europe. After Safi Faye moved to West Germany, television network ZDF funded *Man Sa Yaye* (I, your mother, 1980), about a young Senegalese man studying in Berlin. Faye again refused to use third-person omniscient voice-over commentary, here fragmenting the narration into the words of friends and family members quoted from letters read aloud by the central character and fellow students. The tenuousness of their position is revealed in scenes filmed in cafés, where Germans inevitably ask African students and workers, "How long are you going to be here?"[68] Mauritanian-born director Med Hondo had arrived in Europe almost two decades earlier, after completing a degree in hospitality studies in Morocco. He worked in the theater in both Marseille and Paris, then taught himself to make films. Hondo stunned audiences and critics with his 1968 *Soleil Ô*, an experimental, militant film that represents the historical and psychological effects of colonialism through the experiences of a Black African living in Europe. Selected for the Cannes Film Festival's Semaine de la Critique, it was also featured at the Carthage Film Festival.

Hondo's next feature, *Les Bicots-nègres, vos voisins* (Arab-Negroes, your neighbors, 1973), depicts the situation of immigrant workers living in hostels via the "graft," in his words, of a fictional narrative onto nonfictional footage of workers and the places where they live.[69] Hondo therefore characterized it as an *avant-garde* or *research* film, in terms similar to those used by Paulin Vieyra to describe Cheikh Ngaïdo Ba's *Rewo Daande Maayo*.[70] In a bitterly sarcastic prologue, actor Bachir Touré retraces the history of cinema in Africa to assert the need for African cinema. He notes what was all too evident in the first half of this book—the effort put forth in colonial films "to really give the impression that everything was 'true' and full of real local colour," giving European spectators "the sensation that the story was undoubtedly taking place in Africa."[71] Having challenged the truth and value of colonial films shot in Africa, Hondo worked to transform part of his hybrid film into an easily recognizable documentary. The original release of almost three hours was cut to half the length and reedited in the early 1980s. The excised material, consisting almost exclusively of nonfictional footage, became *Mes voisins* (My neighbors), which archivist Annabelle Aventurin has determined was then backdated to 1971, the year the footage was shot.[72]

Mes voisins, in which the possessive of the earlier film's title changes from a plural, spectatorial *your* to a singular *my,* begins with a shot of a Black man sitting in a café in Paris, speaking in Mauritanian Arabic. After a zoom to an extreme close-up and then a freeze frame, a French-language voice-over translates his story, still in the first person. Introducing himself as Sidna, the man provides his work history in France over the previous ten years, first as a street sweeper and then in Renault's automobile factories. We hear Sidna tell his story

Med Hondo, *Mes voisins*, 1971.

in his own words, the shot length periodically shifting, while the commentary continues to provide translation over freeze frames. Describing in detail his struggles with racism on the job as well as the miserable hostel in which he has to live, Sidna says that although he wants to return home, "I remember what happened to me in Mauritania." He had refused a transfer away from Nouadhibou, was fired by a European foreman as a result, and decided to leave for Europe.

Having identified his protagonist as a worker struggling to survive neocolonial capitalism first in Africa and then in Europe, Hondo over close-ups of Sidna's hands and face introduces the song that gives the film its title and which becomes its structuring principle and motif. Written and sung by Catherine Le Forestier, the song begins by contrasting the suffering abroad acknowledged by French spectators—"far-away countries, where people die of poverty and hunger"—with the suffering they prefer to ignore, that of immigrants from those very countries who have come to live in France. "Go see them," Le Forestier continues; they live "a stone's throw away from me" and are "my neighbors." As Hondo cuts between medium shots of men from North and sub-Saharan Africa, the song identifies "Moussa, Mohamed, and Salem" and warns viewers that it might be difficult to find the seemingly abandoned two-story building with broken windows that one of the men is entering. "Go see my neighbors," Le Forestier sings, as we see footage of African immigrants in a narrow, dilapidated hallway, standing together outside, then washing their faces at an outdoor faucet. She challenges the words of a xenophobic concierge, who states that the men are "good for nothing" and "breathe our air and eat our bread," by sarcastically retorting that "our grandparents were good people . . . when they took African land from Africans" and made those men into road workers and infantrymen. Linking New Delhi, Calcutta, and Harlem to Africa, Le Forestier encourages solidarity by changing the possessive *my* back to *your*: "If you want to talk about these faraway lands, then go see your neighbors, a stone's throw away from you."

The rest of *Mes voisins* forces viewers to see their neighbors in images that directly and precisely address the lives of immigrant workers in a Paris hostel. These immigrants, as one resident takes care to specify, are of a range of nationalities: Mauritanian, Malian, Senegalese, and Ivorian. Sidna recounts for Hondo's camera the story of a French man who promised to lodge him and other members of a group of African immigrants, then stole their money. They now must pay the property owner monthly to inhabit the dilapidated building on screen; pointing to the toilets—two for sixty men—Sidna says that when they clog, residents must use toilets at a nearby café. The roof leaks, the showers do not work, and broken bed frames hold torn mattresses. Another hostel resident, who recently arrived in France and is still looking for work, shares both his personal story and that of the residents' collective battle for adequate housing. Other men join him to protest the municipality's unsatisfactory response to their demands and ultimate closure of the hostel, as Hondo films a social and political analysis of France's failure to address the realities of immigrant labor. Coming to a conclusion, *Mes voisins* transitions abruptly to a one-and-a-half-minute animated sequence that extends this analysis. Cut-out photographs of North American, African, and European political leaders set against brightly painted backgrounds are accompanied by discordant marching band music; these images are intercut with pictures of flags, bills, and bombs, the quick montage indicating criminal complicity. Hondo's cartoon manifesto accelerates in tempo as photographs of starving Biafran children give way to images of representatives of the Catholic Church. The sounds of "La Marseillaise" lead to the film's final credits: "*Mes Voisins*, shot with the participation of immigrant workers."

Also born and raised in Mauritania, Sidney Sokhona emigrated to France at the age of fifteen. Once in Paris, Sokhona worked while studying photography

Med Hondo, *Mes voisins*, 1971.

and filmmaking, eventually volunteering on the sets of both Rouch's *Petit à petit* and Hondo's *Les Bicots-nègres, vos voisins*. Planning to make a fiction film about immigration in France, he changed course after participating in a strike at the Riquet Hostel for immigrant workers.[73] Over several years, on whatever film stock he could afford, Sokhona accumulated footage of workers' organizing efforts and his miserable living accommodations in order to make his first film, the seventy-minute *Nationalité immigré* (Nationality: Immigrant, 1975). Rouch provided the assistance of his editor Danièle Tessier as well as the use of editing equipment and space at the Cinémathèque Française, and Sokhona's extremely low-budget film went on to win the Georges Sadoul Prize, a special jury prize at FESPACO, and the Bronze Tanit at Carthage. *Nationalité immigré* was such a critical success in France that it was reviewed in *Le Monde* and featured in a special dossier in *Cahiers du cinéma*. Like Hondo, however, Sokhona understood his work within the model of militant cinema, maintaining that his target audience was not French film critics but African immigrant workers.[74]

To convey his message about France's politics of immigration, Sokhona both recorded and staged the experiences of these workers. Attempting to account for a combination of scenes that are difficult to categorize even individually, film historian Patrick Ilboudo describes *Nationalité immigré* as "half-reenacted reportage."[75] As the central character of the film, Sokhona uses his birth name, Sidi. In an avant-garde opening reminiscent of *Soleil Ô*, for which a poster appears halfway through the film, two white men sit at a small table in the center of a velodrome. Three men—one Black, one Arab, one white—come before them to receive lodging assignments; Sidi's reads "Slum Hostel." After the credits, a sociological and political voice-over narration begins over images of Sidi walking through busy city streets, providing statistics on the growing number of immigrant workers in France and noting the desperation not of workers to immigrate but of French companies to benefit from almost-free labor. The film's only images shot in Africa follow, showing peasants harvesting crops; the commentary explains how colonial-era taxation created the need for money that now drives rural Africans first to African cities and then to Europe.

Returning to Sidi, a newly arrived African immigrant looking for work in Paris, *Nationalité immigré* shows him talking to two other hostel residents. Acting out the effects of colonial and neocolonial cinema policy, he tells them he is eager to visit the Arc de Triomphe and the Eiffel Tower, which he saw several times during free film screenings at the French embassy in Dakar. Changing perspective, Sokhona then speaks from behind the camera, filming interviews during which he asks men on the street questions about immigration. A concluding voice-over announces that Sidi was arrested but has been freed from prison, and the workers have won their demand for new housing. "No longer the well-behaved children of days gone by," Sokhona proclaims, immigrant workers are ready for "economic and political battles." He would return to similar themes in *Safrana ou le droit à la parole* (Safrana or the right to speak, 1978), a fiction inspired by the true story of a group of factory workers from Mali who left Paris to farm in rural France, then decided to farm in Africa.

Despite the economic and political turmoil of the 1970s and '80s in sub-Saharan Africa, many more ethnographic than political documentaries were shot on the continent. From the Senegalese government's refusal to approve Safi Faye's *Kaddu Beykat* for screening, we may glean a sense of why. Richard de Medeiros noted in 1980 that those in power were "extremely suspicious" of cinema, leaving African filmmakers a choice between obsequiousness or circumvention.[76] From his base in Paris, however, Med Hondo traveled to the disputed territory of Western Sahara, spending four months living in camps set up by Sahrawi freedom fighters to make *Nous aurons toute la mort pour dormir* (We will have all our death for sleeping, 1976) and *Polisario, un peuple en armes* (Polisario, a people takes up arms, 1979). Both films foreground the Sahrawi people's political and military struggle for independence rather than their customs and traditions and, like *Mes voisins*, credit their participants as coproducers. Activist propaganda in support of the Polisario Front's fight to create the Sahrawi Arab Democratic Republic, *Nous aurons toute la mort pour dormir* is stylistically very different from *Mes voisins*. Two voices narrate—Hondo's and that of an unnamed woman—providing background information, war slogans, and translations from Arabic of answers given by fighters and refugees to questions asked by an off-camera interviewer. Hondo biographer Ibrahim Signaté describes the film, which screened at the Berlin Film Festival, as "raw," made up primarily of wide shots and long takes.[77]

Hondo presents Polisario's mission as an anticolonial one, focusing on the Sahrawi refusal of domination by outsiders, whether they be Spanish, Moroccan, or Mauritanian.[78] Joseph Akouissonne's *Zo Kwe Zo* (All men are human beings, 1982), an analysis and critique of French colonialism, was less threatening to postindependence leadership. The film's title is the Central African Republic's Sango-language motto, attributed to Barthélemy Boganda. Boganda died in a suspicious plane crash a year before independence, while he was serving as prime minister and working to draft a constitution for the future nation. To investigate, Akouissonne begins in the late nineteenth century and works his way forward to the present via interviews intercut with photographs and newsreel footage. *Zo Kwe Zo* was the country's first film to be screened at FESPACO, where it won three prizes including Best Cinematography, as well as the first presented at Cannes, where it won an award named for Debrix.

Twenty years after *Une nation est née* celebrated the anniversary of Senegalese independence, Paulin Vieyra completed *L'envers du décor* (Behind the scenes, 1981), a film about the making of Sembene's *Ceddo*. One of Vieyra's last films, it was the first of a series of sub-Saharan African documentaries to celebrate African cinema itself. After *Contras' City*, Djibril Diop Mambety returned to documentary only once, with *Parlons, grand-mère* (Let's talk, grandmother, 1989), a similar "making-of" about Idrissa Ouédraogo's *Yaaba*. In *Caméra d'Afrique, vingt ans du cinéma africain* (African camera: Twenty years of African cinema, 1983), which the Cannes festival featured in its Un Certain Regard section, Férid Boughedir provided a broad overview of the history of African filmmaking. Cofunded by French and Tunisian governmental agencies, the film consists of interviews with directors and clips from their works, featuring Safi Faye with *Kaddu Beykat* and Med Hondo with *Les Bicots-nègres, vos voisins*, among many others. Asked whether African films are understood in Europe, Ousmane Sembene responds to Boughedir that "Europe is not my center. Europe is a periphery of Africa. They stayed in Africa for one hundred years and they didn't speak my language." Reasserting this focus on an African center for African cinema a few years later, Akouissonne returned to the festival documentary with *Burkina cinéma* (Burkina cinema, 1986), a film about FESPACO shot in Ouagadougou.[79]

As the 1980s began, Dakar's African Cultural Institute (ICA) decided to endow a prize for Best Documentary Film at FESPACO, the festival's first recognition of documentary as such. The ICA sought to spur an increase in the production of documentaries by African directors, specifically "documentary films about the cultural reality of their countries of origin." The institute's guidelines made this ethnographic focus more explicit, stipulating that "the following themes are of particular interest: traditional ceremonies, natural and cultural heritage (museums, monuments, historical sites, etc.); traditional clothing, arts, and architecture, ancient and/or contemporary African artistic creation, educational and recreational activities etc."[80] Also in 1981, and at FESPACO, a group of young filmmakers led by Cheikh Ngaïdo Ba called for the transformation of filmmaking in Africa, forming a collective they named L'Oeil Vert (Green Eye) to indicate a fresh perspective. Frustrated by FEPACI's lack of activity, members demanded more concrete action on behalf of African cinema, particularly South–South cooperation to replace North–South aid.[81] They also wished to break away from a slow and, in their view, provincial film style often characterized as *calebasse* or gourd cinema, which they criticized for presenting an unchanging and even exoticized Africa belonging only to the past. L'Oeil Vert spoke out against even the label of "African cinema," considering it both limiting and overly general, "a fictitious unity that is scornful of cultural diversity and sensibility."[82]

This conjunction of the first institutional recognition of African documentary and the rebellion of a second generation of African filmmakers is significant. L'Oeil Vert members recognized the accomplishments of their predecessors but were ready to move forward, an attitude reflected in the ethnographic films produced through the end of the decade. In the 1960s and '70s, an awareness of the colonial origins of ethnography had led African documentarists to fracture conventional monovocal voice-over narration and experiment with reenactments and acted scenes. These interlocking strategies served to displace authoritative French-language commentary while forging a distinctively African version of ethnographic documentary, one that African audiences would find both informative and entertaining. Both tactics increase the presence of African languages, allowing participants to speak or act their own realities in their own words. And the use of *social actors* in documentary, to take another term from Bill Nichols, fosters a mode of ethnographic explanation that favors narrative instead of exposition.[83] In the 1980s, documentarists sought to innovate further, relinquishing voice-over commentary and the French associated with it.

Joseph Gaï Ramaka, a Senegalese director known for reflexive and genre-bending fiction films, began his career with ethnographic documentary. Raised in Saint-Louis and educated in Dakar, Ramaka studied in Paris—visual anthropology at the EHESS and filmmaking at the IDHEC. His film *Baw-Naan* (1984), about a traditional Lebu ceremony to bring rain, manifests this dual training in all of its aspects. Coproduced by Senegalese television with additional funding from Dakar's IFAN museum and the French Ministries for Foreign Relations and Agriculture, the film won awards at ethnographic film festivals in France and Italy.[84] "For an entire day," French text on screen begins, "men and women, made up and in costume, sing, dance, and tell funny stories in order to make God cry with laughter." Ramaka then presents the ritual, shot in a Lebu village, without commentary or subtitles. The film closes with two children who look up to the sky to feel raindrops on their faces, a sign of the ceremony's success. Often overlooked in Ramaka's filmography, *Baw-Naan* is notable not just for its form but also for its crew, which included Samba Félix Ndiaye, beginning documentarist Ousmane William Mbaye, and future documentarist and fiction filmmaker Moussa Touré. Ramaka pursued a similar topic a few years later in the feature-length *Nitt ... Ndoxx* (Those who make rain, 1987), which addresses the Lebu fight against drought in northern Senegal.

Idrissa Ouedraogo, with whose work the second half of this book began, is renowned for his career in feature fiction, which began with *Yam Daabo* (The choice, 1986) and *Yaaba* (Grandmother, 1986), both set in rural Burkina Faso. After graduating from the IDHEC, Ouedraogo, like Ndiaye, began but never finished a doctoral dissertation with Jean Rouch.[85] And his filmmaking career in fact began with a series of ethnographic short documentaries: *Les écuelles* (Bowls, 1983), *Issa le tisserand* (Issa the weaver, 1984), and *Ouagadougou, Ouaga deux roues* (Ouagadougou, Ouaga on two wheels, 1986). All three are in Mooré, with very little dialogue and no voice-over commentary or subtitles; Ouedraogo composed the films to be understandable to every spectator without translation. Tracing how wooden bowls are made, *Les écuelles* begins when two men leave their village to cut down a tree. With kora music on the soundtrack, the men reach out to the tree, touch it, then speak to each other. The setting shifts as viewers watch balls of wood being split in half, hollowed out, and scraped; the bowls are cured using a bellows and scraped again. Local

Idrissa Ouédraogo, *Issa le tisserand*, 1984.

women fill some of the finished bowls with food for a meal, while others are taken by a trader to be sold at market.

Like Ouedraogo's feature fictions, *Les écuelles* highlights a rural setting in which traditions have been maintained. *Issa le tisserand*, which won the ICA documentary prize at FESPACO, focuses instead on the disappearance of traditional artisanry in an urban setting. The film depicts the experiences of a weaver without local customers, his work of interest only to a visiting white ethnographic photographer. To earn money, the weaver has to abandon his work to sell secondhand T-shirts made abroad. In a similarly urban and contemporary milieu, *Ouagadougou, Ouaga deux roues* is composed primarily of shots of men, women, and children riding bicycles and motorbikes in the capital city, images taken in a variety of locations and from multiple angles. Used to transport everything from sacks to chickens to goats, the ubiquitous two-wheeled vehicles are also shown being constructed, repaired, and sold. A story lasting less than a minute illustrates the consequence of any mistake in the choreography of police officers directing traffic: a man and a woman lie on the ground injured after their motorbikes collide.

David Murphy and Patrick Williams, who characterize Mambety's *Contras' City* as "pseudo-documentary," describe *Les écuelles* as "'documentary,'" in scare quotes, and "docu-fiction" because the film's assistant director appears in the role of the trader taking the bowls to market.[86] This disinclination to recognize documentary in the first decades of African cinema ignores the ways in which typification and other forms of reenactment shaped global documentary filmmaking from its beginnings. A more systematic use of reenactment structures Burkinabé director Issiaka Konaté's first film, *Yiri Kan* (The voice in the wood, 1989), which, like *Issa le tisserand*, won the ICA documentary prize at FESPACO. *Yiri Kan*, however, is optimistic about the persistence of the traditions it represents. Konaté's objective, he said, was to show that "in Africa, there is no gap between art and people's everyday lives, which together make a coherent whole."[87] *Yiri Kan* depicts the initiation of the son of a famed Burkinabé balafonist into the culture of the instrument, which in Mooré is called *balan*. Father and son play themselves as they together make a balafon, splitting the wood, curing it in an oven, cooling it overnight, building the frame, adding slats, and hollowing out and adding the gourds. The boy asks questions at every stage, about the construction of the instrument as well as its cultural uses, then walks with his father to a distant village where an elder has died. Along the way, the father shares additional lessons, now in the form of legends of the instrument's origin and proverbs such as "A village chief without a *balan* player is a king without a crown." Konaté explained his strategy: layering a script onto cultural and historical research, the story of father and son allowed a question-and-answer structure to replace voice-over commentary.[88]

Samba Félix Ndiaye, who had minimized his voice-over commentary between *Perantal* and *Geti tey*, a decade later abandoned ethnographic narration in the five short documentaries of *Trésors des poubelles* (Treasures from garbage, 1989). The films show Senegalese artisans working with very local materials, and Ndiaye said that he approached each as a stylistic exercise "constructed in relationship to a filmic idea I had or a film that I liked."[89] In *Diplomate à la tomate* (Tomato diplomat), a group of men transforms discarded wood and soda cans into decorated briefcases to be sold in Senegal and abroad. Although we hear Ndiaye ask a few questions and glimpse the back of his head, the men speak for themselves, with no mediating narrator. The film begins with several wordless minutes, after which one of the artisans begins to describe, in Wolof, his technique. In *Les chutes de Ngalam* (Ngalam Falls), Ndiaye similarly asks questions, whereas the artisans of *Teug* (The art of metalwork) speak first to each other and then to the camera as they relate their struggle to find adequate work space. In *Les malles* (Suitcases), not a single word is spoken. Instead, Ndiaye's sound engineer worked to create a "symphony" of wind and hammers on

Samba Félix Ndiaye, *Les malles*, 1989.

metal, which together with the images would create a ballet.[90] All five shorts are edited such that the end product remains a mystery to the spectator until the final moments.

"How many times have we seen films about the harvesting of coffee, cacao, and rubber, or about small trades and native celebrations," wrote Paulin Vieyra in 1957, just two years after shooting his first documentary.[91] Working to valorize African artisanry, Ndiaye followed in Vieyra's footsteps to reject a tradition of nonfiction dating back to Pathé's *Métiers, types, et coutumes* and the SCA's *Vers le Tchad*, films that salute France's exploitation of African workers and condescend to African *petits métiers*. *Trésors des poubelles* constitutes a beautifully succinct response to French colonial documentary's simultaneous dismissiveness of African labor and obsessive ethnographizing about it. The strategic adaptations of African ethnographic filmmaking in the 1970s and 80s foretell a more dramatic change in the next decade. As the twenty-first century approached, formal innovation in documentary would continue without ethnography.

Notes

1. Férid Boughedir, "1982–83: De Carthage IX à Ouagadougou VIII: Nouvelle génération, nouveaux espoirs," *L'Afrique littéraire*, no. 68–69 (1983): 185.

2. Jean-R. Debrix, "Situation du cinéma en Afrique francophone," *Afrique contemporaine*, no. 81 (1975): 3.

3. Vieyra, *Réflexions d'un cineaste africain*, 63.

4. Manthia Diawara argues that the closing of the Bureau of Cinema was due less to the absence of Debrix, who died in 1978, than to pressure exerted by African leaders fearful of the political influence of African films on Africans. Diawara, *African Cinema*, 27.

5. Diawara, *African Cinema*, 29.

6. See Olivier Barlet, "The Ambivalence of French Funding," *Black Camera* 3, no. 2 (2012): 209, and for an immensity of detail about Davanture and ATRIA's commitment to African cinema, Claude Forest, *Andrée Davanture: La passion du montage* (L'Harmattan, 2021). ATRIA's archives can be consulted at the Departmental Archives of Seine-Saint-Denis, Sous-série 257J.

7. Férid Boughedir, *Le cinéma africain de A à Z* (Editions OCIC, 1987), 15.

8. Victor Bachy, *La Haute-Volta et le cinéma* (OCIC, 1983), 11–14, 24.

9. Vieyra, *Le cinéma au Sénégal*, 42. Mahama Traoré claimed just over a decade later that every Senegalese film made since the founding of the SNC had received some type of governmental support. Diawara, *African Cinema*, 57.

10. Boughedir, *Le cinéma africain de A à Z*, 19.

11. Mbye-Boubacar Cham, "Film Production in West Africa: 1979–1981," *Présence Africaine*, no. 124 (1982): 168.

12. Philippe Maarek, ed., *Afrique noire: Quel cinéma?* (Association du Ciné-Club de l'Université de Paris X, 1983), 34–35, 43.

13. English translations of these manifestos are collected in Imruh Bakari and Mbye Cham, eds., *African Experiences of Cinema* (British Film Institute, 1996); Scott MacKenzie, ed., *Film Manifestos and Global Cinema Cultures: A Critical Anthology* (University of California Press, 2014).

14. Bakari and Cham, *African Experiences of Cinema*, 20, 22.

15. Bakari and Cham, *African Experiences of Cinema*, 25.

16. Haffner and Vieyra, "Propos sur le cinéma africain," 44.

17. Françoise Pfaff, "Paulin Soumanou Vieyra pionnier de la critique et de la théorie du cinéma africain," *Présence Africaine*, no. 170 (2004): 33.

18. "Séminaire sur 'le rôle du cinéaste africain dans l'éveil d'une conscience de civilisation noire,'" *Présence Africaine*, no. 90 (1974): 125.

19. "Séminaire sur 'le rôle du cinéaste africain,'" 128–29, 177.

20. Hennebelle, "Jean Rouch et l'éthique du cinéma ethnographique," 49.

21. See Bouchard, "African Documentaries, Critical Interventions," 219.

22. Haffner, "Jean Rouch jugé par six cinéastes d'Afrique noire," 71.

23. "Ousseini Inoussa," *L'Afrique littéraire et artistique*, no. 49 (1978): 103.

24. Haffner, "Jean Rouch jugé par six cinéastes d'Afrique noire," 73.

25. Cited in Pfaff, *Twenty-Five Black African Filmmakers*, 47.

26. Djib Diedhiou, "Moussa Bathily au 'Soleil': 'Tiyabu Biru' n'est pas un film ethnographique," *Le soleil* (June 2–3, 1979): 2. Bathily later expressed discomfort with the documentary aspect of the film, claiming that it had been imposed on him in response to a request for funding. Haffner, "Jean Rouch jugé par six cinéastes d'Afrique noire," 69.

27. Nichols, *Representing Reality*, 38. For an overview of the latter, see Anna Grimshaw and Amanda Ravetz, *Observational Cinema: Anthropology, Film, and the Exploration of Social Life* (Indiana University Press, 2009).

28. "Séminaire sur 'le rôle du cinéaste africain,'" 11, 128.

29. Bakari and Cham, *African Experiences of Cinema*, 19.

30. Vieyra, *Le cinéma au Sénégal*, 151.

31. Charles Tesson, "L'Afrique dans la lumière: Propos de Souleymane Cissé," *Cahiers du cinéma*, no. 402 (1987): 29–30.

32. Vieyra, *Le cinéma au Sénégal*, 97. Cham, "Film Production in West Africa," 184. Pfaff, *Á l'écoute du cinéma sénégalais*, 47.

33. Senghor, "Le point de vue d'un futur producteur africain," 39.

34. Frank Ukadike, *Questioning African Cinema: Conversations with Filmmakers* (University of Minnesota Press, 2002), 110. Pfaff, *Twenty-Five Black African Film-makers*, 173.

35. "Emission spéciale avec le cinéaste Gaston Kaboré," *Tous les cinémas du monde*, podcast hosted by Elisabeth Lequeret and produced by Radio France Internationale, October 29, 2022.

36. Manthia Diawara, "African Cinema Today," *SVA Review* 6, no. 1 (1990): 72.

37. Henri-François Imbert, *Samba Félix Ndiaye: Cinéaste documentariste africain* (L'Harmattan, 2007), 304. The only published work to devote sustained attention to Ndiaye's work, filmmaker Imbert's unevenly reworked doctoral dissertation includes a survey of French ethnographic films shot in West and central Africa in the 1940s and '50s, an introduction to postindependence West African documentary, and an overview of Ndiaye's filmmaking career accompanied by a lengthy interview and complete filmography.

38. Samba Félix Ndiaye, "Le temps des grands frères," in *18ème Festival international de films ethnographiques et sociologiques: Cinéma du réel* (Centre National Georges Pompidou, 1996), 49.

39. Pfaff, *À l'écoute du cinéma sénégalais*, 166.

40. Ndiaye, "Le temps des grands frères," 49, 52.

41. Angela Martin, "Four Film Makers from West Africa," *Framework*, no. 11 (1979): 19.

42. Imbert, *Samba Félix Ndiaye*, 307.

43. Ndiaye, "Le temps des grands frères," 52.

44. Pfaff, *À l'écoute du cinéma sénégalais*, 165.

45. François Maupin, "Entretien avec Safi Faye," *La revue du cinéma*, no. 303 (February 1976): 80.

46. Vieyra, *Le cinéma au Sénégal*, 150.

47. Maupin, "Entretien avec Safi Faye," 76.

48. Joram ten Brink, "*Petit à petit*: Safi Faye," in *Building Bridges: The Cinema of Jean Rouch*, ed. Joram ten Brink (Wallflower Press, 2007), 160.

49. Vieyra, *Le cinéma au Sénégal*, 147.

50. Maupin, "Entretien avec Safi Faye," 78.

51. Vieyra, *Le cinéma au Sénégal*, 149.

52. Maupin, "Entretien avec Safi Faye," 77.

53. Vieyra, *Le cinéma au Sénégal*, 94.

54. Ukadike, *Questioning African Cinema*, 32.

55. Pfaff, *Twenty-Five Black African Filmmakers*, 117.

56. Vieyra, *Le cinéma au Sénégal*, 149. For a detailed reading of *Kaddu Beykat* as a departure from ethnographic conventions, see Melissa Thackway, "Challenging Documentary Practice," in *Francophone African Women Documentary Filmmakers: Beyond Representation*, ed. Suzanne Crosta, Sada Niang, and Alexie Tcheuyap (Bloomington: Indiana University Press, 2023), 50–64.

57. "Entretien avec Safi Faye," *Le soleil* (December 5, 1975): 12.

58. Nicholas Elliott, "Safi Faye: L'Afrique universelle," *Cahiers du cinéma*, no. 747 (2018): 92.

59. Loftus, "Appeal of Hybrid Documentary Forms in West Africa," 38.

60. Martin, "Four Film Makers from West Africa," 18. Faye created confusion among spectators with her single feature fiction film, *Mossane* (1996), for which she invented a culture and all of its rituals. See Beti Ellerson, "Africa Through a Woman's Eyes: Safi Faye's Cinema," in *Focus on African Films*, ed. Françoise Pfaff (Indiana University Press, 2004), 190.

61. Safi Faye, "Leçon de cinéma," 1998, http://www.dailymotion.com/video /xcmkn9_la-lecon-de-cinema-de-safi-faye_creation.

62. *Selbe* has recently been restored to its original Serer language version after circulating for decades in a dubbed version released by Women Make Movies. The dubbed version uses a single female voice for Selbe's first-person narrative and the third-person voice-over.

63. Nouri Bouzid and Mariama Hima, "Respondents," in *Symbolic Narratives/African Cinema: Audiences, Theory and the Moving Image*, ed. June Givanni (BFI, 2000), 104–5.

64. Assiatou Diallo, "Mariama Hima, la championne du cinéma pieds nus," *Amina: Le magazine de la femme*, no. 225 (January 1989): 28.

65. Diallo, "Mariama Hima," 30.

66. Nancy J. Schmidt, "Sub-Saharan African Women Filmmakers: Agendas for Research with a Filmography," in *With Open Eyes: Women and African Cinema*, ed. Kenneth Harrow (Rodopi, 1997), 170, 179; Ilboudo, *Le Fespaco, 1969–1989*, 435.

67. These roles were played by Haitian actors Jacqueline and Lucien Lemoine. Pfaff, *Twenty-Five Black African Filmmakers*, 46.

68. Mario Relich, "Chronicle of a Student," *West Africa*, no. 3393 (August 16, 1982): 2112.

69. Ibrahima Signaté, *Med Hondo, un cinéaste rebelle* (Présence Africaine, 1994), 23.

70. Signaté, *Med Hondo*, 105–6.

71. Abid Med Hondo, "*Les Bricot* (sic) *Nègres* Prologue," *Framework*, no. 7/8 (1978): 21. For a close reading of this prologue, see Aboubakar Sanogo, "The Indocile Image: Cinema and History in Med Hondo's *Soleil O* and *Les Bicots-Nègres, Vos Voisins*," *Rethinking History* 19, no. 4 (2015): 559–63.

72. Annabelle Aventurin, Léa Morin, and Nour Ouayda, "Non-aligned Film Archives," *Journal of Film Preservation*, no. 106 (2022): 35.

73. S. Daney et al., "Entretien avec Sidney Sokhona," *Cahiers du cinéma*, no. 265 (1976): 26.

74. Daney et al., "Entretien avec Sidney Sokhona," 32.

75. Ilboudo, *Le Fespaco, 1969–1989*, 397. Maria Loftus includes *Nationalité immigré* with Vieyra's *Afrique sur Seine* and Faye's *Kaddu Beykat* in the category of *docu-fiction*. Loftus, "Appeal of Hybrid Documentary Forms in West Africa," 51.

76. Richard de Madeiros (*sic*), "L'heure des bilans," *Le monde diplomatique* (September 1980): 12.

77. Signaté, *Med Hondo*, 104. A 1978 interview with Hondo makes reference to two animated sequences that were not included in the print I consulted. Don Ranvaud, "Interview with Med Hondo," *Framework*, no. 7/8 (1978): 30.

78. For a first-person narrative of Hondo's experience in Western Sahara along with his political analysis of the history of the region, see Abid Med Hondo, "Nous aurons toute la mort," *Framework*, no. 7/8 (1978): 23–25.

79. Ilboudo, *Le Fespaco, 1969–1989*, 177.

80. "Prix ICA du meilleur film documentaire," *ICA information: Revue trimestrielle de l'Institut Culturel Africain*, no. 13 (January–March 1981): 16. The award appears in FESPACO records as simply the ICA Prize. Ouedraogo, *Naissance et évolution du FESPACO*, 199–204.

81. Ba later claimed that the group had as many as eighty members, with the completion of a short film the only requirement for membership. Pfaff, *À l'écoute du cinéma sénégalais*, 50.

82. Emmanuel Bilé, "L'Oeil Vert," in *African Films: The Context of Production*, ed. Angela Martin (BFI, 1982), 78.

83. Bill Nichols, *Ideology and the Image: Social Representation in the Cinema and Other Media* (Indiana University Press, 1981), 184, 267.

84. Pfaff, *À l'écoute du cinéma sénégalais*, 130.

85. Françoise Pfaff, "Africa Through African Eyes: An Interview with Idrissa Ouedraogo," *Black Film Review* 4, no. 1 (1987–88): 11.

86. David Murphy and Patrick Williams, *Postcolonial African Cinema: Ten Directors* (Manchester University Press, 2007), 92, 151.

87. Cheick Kolla Maiga, "Issaka Konate: 'The Documentary Film Has Its Place in the African Cinema,'" *FEPACI News*, no. 6 (1991): 13.

88. "Entretien avec Issiaka Konaté," *Issiaka Konaté, deux films*, DVD p.o.m. Films Montréal.

89. Pfaff, *À l'écoute du cinéma sénégalais*, 171.

90. Claude Haffner, "'Dites simplement la vérité': Une leçon de cinéma de Samba Félix Ndiaye (Fespaco 2005)," *Africiné*, 2009, http://www.africine.org/analyse /dites-simplement-la-verite/9001.

91. Vieyra, *Le cinéma et l'Afrique*, 71.

6

DIALOGUE

Introspection and Interaction

Following the creation of the irregularly attributed ICA documentary prize, FESPACO gave several prizes of its own for nonfiction in the 1990s, starting with Issiaka Konaté's *Yiri Kan* in 1991. Konaté told interviewer Cheick Kolla Maiga that, although it had taken decades for FESPACO to "make room" for documentary, the festival was finally beginning to realize its value.[1] The same year, however, Samba Félix Ndiaye contrasted the dynamism of documentary cinema in England and France with its relative rarity in sub-Saharan Africa. Although African filmmakers sought to represent the reality of their place and time, he observed, most "prefer the artifice of fiction." Ndiaye argued that directors who insisted on a strict distinction between fiction and nonfiction rather than acknowledging the "passageways" between the two were imped-ing the development of "true documentary cinema" in Africa.[2] Prescient as always, Ndiaye articulated a transformation as it began, one that would result in a dramatic acceleration of African documentary filmmaking and its belated recognition both in Africa and internationally.

Paradoxically, Ndiaye held that he had come to documentary through dissatisfaction with the superficially nonfictional quality of many African feature films. "When I went to see African fictions," he maintained, "what I was left with at the end of the film was that these were documents about the locations, the landscapes, the people . . . but there was no mise en scène."[3] Frustrated with fictions that were not artful enough, Ndiaye, like Safi Faye, saw no inherent incompatibility between certain techniques of fiction and documentary. "Documentary allows me to capture a moment of life," he

244

explained, "and then to stage it."[4] In numerous interviews over the course of his career, Ndiaye identified kindred filmmaking spirits around the world who shared his interest in negotiating the border between documentary and fiction, an eclectic mix that included Italian and Indian neorealist directors such as Roberto Rossellini, Satyajit Ray, and Guru Dutt but also Glauber Rocha, Nelson Pereira dos Santos, Robert Flaherty, Orson Welles, Joris Ivens, Luis Buñuel, Chris Marker, Alain Resnais, Jean-Luc Godard, Eric Rohmer, Andrei Tarkovsky, Abbas Kiarostami, and Ousmane Sembene. In a strikingly unusual pairing of French directors, Ndiaye claimed as two of his most important influences ethnographic documentarist Jean Rouch and New Wave *confrère* turned improvisational experimentalist Jacques Rivette. "The first, I argued with him until just before his death," Ndiaye revealed; "Rouch taught me an enormous amount through my opposition to him [*en étant contre*]. And Jacques Rivette taught me gently."[5]

In his idiosyncratic theory of the novel, mid-twentieth-century Soviet philosopher and literary scholar Mikhail Bakhtin contrasted Socratic dialogue and the dialogic novel with what he called "*official* monologism, which pretends to *possess a ready-made truth*." An apt characterization of the colonial-era films discussed in the first half of this book, aside from a few exceptions, such monologism reflects what Bakhtin described as "the naïve self-confidence" of those persuaded that they possess the truth. In Bakhtin's understanding of literary narrative, truth cannot come from a singular source but is rather "born *between people* collectively searching for truth, in the process of their dialogic interaction."[6] Ndiaye's sense of learning in dialogue with both Rouch and Rivette models a contemporary sub-Saharan African documentary tradition no longer burdened by the task of creating regional and national cinemas in the wake of Europe's malign half-century head start. Earlier nonfiction filmmakers, as we have seen, were of necessity working against a recent colonial mode that had insisted on its sole access to the truth of Africa, even as they had to rely on the neocolonial funding France called "cooperation." Ndiaye and his colleagues in the '90s were able to build on this prior work at the same time as France widened its support structure first to filmmakers from the Global South (the Fonds Sud) and then the entire world (Aide aux Cinémas du Monde) and as new funding and coproduction opportunities became available with a number of governmental and private partners. Scholar Alexie Tcheuyap deems this new reality postnationalist in the sense of "thematically beyond the mode of resistance."[7]

At the very turn of the twenty-first century, Cameroonian documentarist Jean-Marie Teno cofounded and became president of the Paris-based African Guild of Directors and Producers. In addition to Teno's partners—filmmakers

Balufu Bakupa-Kanyinda from the Democratic Republic of Congo (DRC) and Fanta Régina Nacro from Burkina Faso—the guild's membership included full- and part-time documentarists Mahamat-Saleh Haroun from Chad, François Woukoache from Cameroon, Abderrahmane Sissako from Mali and Mauritania, Jihan El-Tahri from Egypt, and Imunga Ivanga from Gabon. Creating an exilic, pan-African alternative to FEPACI, guild members, like the members of L'Oeil Vert in the early 1980s, repudiated what they judged to be an outdated model of African filmmaking. In a 2001 manifesto, they reminded readers that "the first images of us were shot by a cinema that looked down on us." Different from the films of Africa's first postindependence decades, however, their "new cinema" would be affiliated with nomadism and travel rather than local self-knowledge. "Far from an ethnographic cinema that records habits and customs," the manifesto insisted, theirs would reach toward Africa's rightful place within world cinema. Asserting a need for films that ask difficult questions about contemporary African problems, guild filmmakers called for more *documentaires de création*, or creative documentaries.[8] Their approach paralleled that of the Black British cinema of the '80s, characterized by art historian and cultural critic Kobena Mercer as a "critical dialogism," in contrast to conventional and monologic documentary realism.[9]

The monologism of French colonial documentarists was from the earliest years of the twentieth century centered on an ethnographic showing and explaining of sub-Saharan Africa. If through the 1980s the most common response of African documentarists was to seek a way to represent Africa ethnographically from an African perspective, in the '90s ethnography was no longer a primary interest or goal. As the new millennium approached, filmmakers such as Ndiaye, Teno, Haroun, Woukoache, and Sissako instead crafted complex visual analyses of African historical, social, and political realities. This last chapter of *Documentary Objectives* presents their work as aligned with two dialogic approaches to nonfiction that unfolded as the number of sub-Saharan African documentaries and documentarists increased radically. Never completely distinct from one other, the first approach foregrounds internal dialogue within reflective, reflexive, and autobiographically framed narrative, whereas the second is anchored in artfully edited exchanges about topics with which the director may or may not have a personal connection. The films discussed here have been more widely seen than those of earlier decades, if more often in festivals than in theaters or on major streaming platforms. Many are available to purchase or rent on DVD or video-on-demand, sometimes through established distributors and sometimes from filmmakers themselves.

The increase in African documentary production becomes exponential, in fact, when we consider the new venues and platforms made possible by technological advances in digital video. I can therefore not come close to a comprehensive accounting and hope instead to provide a representative sense of both range and depth by focusing not just on documentaries but on documentarists, on filmmakers who have built a career in nonfiction, while also mentioning more films and directors than I can address in detail. I do so not to lessen the importance of any single documentary—and in some cases, these are too important to omit—but to reduce enormous breadth into a single chapter, the triumphal if provisional conclusion to the cinema history I have tracked across a century. I have made other arguably artificial choices, including that of maintaining the distinction between former imperial nation-states. The dominance of French funding, distribution, and educational networks through the 1980s made it reasonable to limit my corpus in chapters 4 and 5 to films with origins in countries that replaced France's colonies in West and central Africa. The subsequent globalization of production and coproduction as well as the increased mobility of media creators make this distinction less relevant. Given the use of French by filmmakers who still for the most part train and remain based in Western Europe, for example, it makes little sense to draw a dividing line between documentaries made by directors from the DRC and Senegal unless these reference a specific colonial history. In the interest of symmetry with part 1 of this book, however, I only allude to the extraordinary list of late twentieth and early twenty-first century documentarists from the DRC, which includes Mweze Ngangura, Monique Phoba, Balufu Bakupa-Kanyinda, and Dieudo Hamadi, and only mention briefly talents from countries without an established documentary tradition, such as Eddy Munyaneza from Burundi.

In 2006, thirty-two years after *Perantal* and the year Samba Félix Ndiaye's last film was released, Françoise Pfaff asked Ndiaye, "Do you often use your camera to explore socio-cultural traditions, as did director Safi Faye?" Despite his early focus on traditional practices, Ndiaye responded simply, and a bit abruptly, "No." He continued without responding in Pfaff's terms; "My primary intention is to talk about what pleases me, what moves me, what keeps me from sleeping, and to understand what is under the surface."[10] Speaking with Senegalese journalist and film critic Baba Diop around the same time, Ndiaye again evoked the enigmatic nature of any cinematic representation of reality, repeating his interest in "that little thing located at the exact juncture of fiction and documentary."[11] He tirelessly investigated this point of articulation in all his films, particularly, as we will see, after *Trésors des poubelles*. Having dropped the ethnographic voice-over, Ndiaye would go on to drop ethnography altogether while continuing to experiment with language, narrative voice, and generic boundaries in work he came to understand as both individual and shared. "The documentary approach necessarily requires personal involvement," Ndiaye argued, "and self-revelation with the protagonists."[12]

Ndiaye's *Dakar-Bamako* (1992) is the first of three films released in the early 1990s to herald a surge and a shift in West and central African documentary film production. Returning to the use of voice-over commentary, now in the first instead of third person, Ndiaye announces that he had planned to film a train trip from Dakar, Senegal, to Bamako, Mali, with his son. His son refused to join him, so he is traveling with a friend from school whom he has not seen in many years. Ndiaye narrates the film but does not appear on screen; his friend Gorgui as surrogate character focalizes the story, which becomes one of the history and importance of the Dakar-Niger Railway. Gorgui speaks with workers on the train, asking for information: How old is the railroad? Why was it built? Who constructed the track? Through these dialogues, spectators learn that the French relied on the forced labor of both West and North Africans to build the track and designed the railroad for colonial military conquest as well as economic exploitation. Products imported from Europe through the port of Dakar were transported to the interior, with agricultural products moving in the other direction. Ndiaye via Gorgui expressly shares information about African resistance, notably the railroad workers' strike of 1947, and brings contemporary social issues to the fore, as when Gorgui discusses polygamy with a woman passenger.

As smoothly as *Dakar-Bamako* tackles crucial historical, political, and social issues while the train moves along the tracks, the seemingly informal trip is carefully plotted and staged, filmed and edited. Images of people and landscapes taken through the train's windows by a handheld camera are accompanied by fixed shots, some from above, of the train approaching and leaving various stations. Gorgui's conversations are supplemented and commented by Ndiaye's voice-over narration, in which he points out, for example, that the Sahel is green in the rainy season, unlike the images of cracked soil and animal skeletons we are used to seeing on television: "Voyages destroy clichés." This voice-over is as personal as it is analytical. To accompany twilight shots of villages alongside the tracks, Ndiaye tells spectators that as a child, he was told that "this time is the realm of evil spirits." When the train crosses the unmarked border between Senegal and Mali, he remembers that "when Kayes was mentioned, it was the end of the world." Ndiaye also recalls how, when he departed for longer voyages, his mother would ask him to kneel while she sprinkled several drops of water at the threshold of the house: "Now I do this for my son when he leaves." In the same testy interview during which Ndiaye denied an interest in investigating customs and traditions on film, Pfaff asked if the use of first-person commentary negatively affects documentary objectivity. Ndiaye responded by challenging the objectivity of any artistic creation, and when Pfaff retorted that some documentarists pride themselves on being objective, he exclaimed, "They are not objective when speaking of objectivity!"[13]

Born a decade after Ndiaye and just six years before independence, Jean-Marie Teno similarly identifies the origins of sub-Saharan African cinema as documentary, situating his work in a tradition that began with Paulin Vieyra and continued through Richard de Medeiros to Samba Félix Ndiaye.[14] Born and raised in Cameroon, Teno studied first in England and then in France, where he trained at the INA and in Valenciennes. Still based in France, he has returned to Cameroon to shoot most of his films. Teno's career began with the autobiographical short *Hommage* (Homage, 1985), dedicated to his late father. More evocative than narrative, neither objective nor speaking of objectivity, the film centers on a character's return to his village. Things have changed, he notes in voice-over narration, but artisans are still doing "small jobs, but the work that they love." This contemporary color footage is intercut with still photographs and black-and-white clips from French-language newsreels, the montage structured by a soundtrack and conversational commentary. Stripped of its original sound, archival footage of official ceremonies of Cameroonian independence is accompanied by laughter and sarcasm. Disappointment and frustration at the continuity between colonial and postcolonial eras traverses Teno's oeuvre, and idiosyncratic first-person narration has become his hallmark.[15]

Teno is one of Africa's most prolific and skilled documentarists, with over a dozen films to his name, yet his first feature-length effort, *Afrique, je te plumerai* (Africa, I will fleece you, 1992), remains perhaps the best known. Whereas the voice-over narration of *Hommage* was written by Teno and read by others, here and going forward Teno's own voice has shaped and provided continuity to his body of work. Opening the film, he states, "My project was to make a film about writing, in order to propose a reading of the history of Cameroon from my point of view as a native [*indigène*]." Reclaiming a word used condescendingly in colonial productions, if also using it somewhat sarcastically, Teno links contemporary and colonial-era Cameroon in a historical analysis supported by a series of interviews. Remaining off screen, he interviews journalist and newspaper editor Pius Njawe and a range of Cameroonian scholars and elders; he also films his friend Marie, with whom he visits German, British, and French cultural centers and the outdoor book market in the capital city of Yaoundé. He speaks by and of himself, with and of others, and about Africa's past and present in an autobiographical first-person voice that Melissa Thackway, coauthor with Teno of a book on his work, understands as a response to the colonial-era silencing of African subjectivity.[16]

Escalating the reflexivity of Ndiaye's personal narration in *Dakar-Bamako*, Teno intertwines multiple categories of film footage, in color and in black and white, some shot for the film, some drawn from archives. A brief history of postcolonial Cameroon is combined with a critique of the current government's repression of journalists as well as an exposé of the country's continuing dependence on French schoolbooks, prompting scholar Kenneth Harrow to describe *Afrique, je te plumerai* as a "reconstituted history of Cameroon" that reveals what both colonial and neocolonial governments wish to hide.[17] Additional narrative strands stand in stark contrast to one other—clips from colonial and early independence-era films and fictional reenactments in black and white of Teno's childhood memories of reading. Teno recounts that this approach to documentary drew criticism after early screenings: "They said this was collage, it was not cinema."[18] An assemblage of perspectives as well as images, the film's constant questioning of genre, mode, and voice challenges the very idea of monologic and objective nonfictional narrative.

Less than two minutes into *Afrique, je te plumerai* and still before the credits, Teno cuts from scenes of 1991 demonstrations against President Paul Biya to newsreel footage of Cameroonian independence celebrations. Like *Hommage*, the film describes the optimism of the early days of independence, dashed by the single-party system of President Amadou Ahidjo and Biya's corrupt regime. An unusual interview attests to this corruption; an actor playing the role of director of Cameroonian National Television tells the truth the real director would not, asking Teno how much he will pay to get his film shown alongside popular shows like *Dallas*. In the colonial newsreel clip that follows, over an outline of the African continent, a triumphant voice-over declares that European colonizers in the mid-nineteenth century were "peaceful . . . selfless, eager only for knowledge." The map is gradually filled in as a series of dates marks the triple colonization of Cameroon by the Germans, British, and French. The pairing of this dated paean to the glory of colonization with the programming choices made for independent Cameroonian television provides a starting point for Teno's analysis of the cultural colonization of his home country. Instead of stories with an African frame of reference, like *Afrique, je te plumerai* itself, the viewing public is subjected to non-African narratives, while children learn from imported European textbooks.

Teno conveys his understanding of Africa's past via many such ironic juxtapositions of contemporary and colonial footage, exposing the hypocrisy and paternalism of European colonialism in Africa and, more specifically, European colonial documentaries shot in Africa. *Afrique, je te plumerai* includes a lengthy presentation of the Shumom language, whose orthography was developed by Sultan Njoya just before the arrival of German colonizers. A clip from a colonial documentary praising France's education of African children follows, as does the information that French colonial administrators mandated the closure of Shumom schools to force attendance at French schools. Describing African children learning the French language, a colonial-era voice-over narrator proclaims that "we strive to make France known and loved." This strategy of juxtaposition also exposes the cruelty of the profitable African work foregrounded in films from *Au Congo* to *La machine à écrire l'histoire* to *Okoumé*. To depict what these documentaries had refused to acknowledge, Teno filmed reenactments of the violent recruitment of Africans for forced labor, adding footage of working Africans taken from films made by the SCA's successor, the Photographic and Cinematographic Establishment of the Armies (ECPA). He detached this footage from the ideological commentary of its voice-over, replacing it first by drumming and next by the voices of contemporary Cameroonian analysts. More and more often imposing African commentary onto colonial European moving images, Teno derides the idea of third-world debt, noting the overwhelming contributions made by Africa to European economies and war efforts.

Afrique, je te plumerai closes with a skit performed by comedian Essindi Mindja, who mocks postcolonial African autocrats like Biya. In what are almost the last words of the film, Mindja sings a promise to return to the movie theater "when there are films that are really our own." In another reflexive moment, we grasp that this is what we have watched, a documentary *bien de chez nous* substantially different not only in substance but in style from the colonial documentaries with which Teno has familiarized us. Recounting his beginnings in the cinema, Teno described observing bored Cameroonian audiences watch documentaries that had "a monotonous, authoritarian voice." This experience led him to believe that the goal of documentary is not to present raw reality, but to retain the interest of spectators via "the reconstruction of this reality."[19] He sought to accomplish this reconstruction by means of montage and a complex, personal voice-over, through political, historical, and film historical analysis rather than the recovery and portrayal of ethnographic information.

It was in a comparison of *Afrique, je te plumerai* with another first, reflexive film, David Achkar's *Allah Tantou* (God's will, 1991), that African cinema scholar Frank Ukadike in the mid-1990s identified an emerging sub-Saharan African documentary trend.[20] Born in New York City in 1960 while his father was serving as United Nations ambassador of newly independent Guinea,

Jean-Marie Teno, *Afrique, je te plumerai,* 1992.

Achkar spent most of his life outside of his father's native country. After attending the School of Advanced Cinematographic Studies (ESEC) in Paris, he stayed to work as an actor and then undertook a career as a filmmaker. *Allah Tantou* begins with 8mm home movie footage of a family decorating a Christmas tree. Narrating additional footage of a father holding his young son, David Achkar states in a first-person voice-over, "I hardly knew my father. What I know of him, I know from what my mother or his friends have told me. But also from what he wrote to us." The title credits quickly follow, as a man writes while sitting on the floor of a prison cell. Spectators gather from the credits and subsequent narration that this is an actor, Michel Montanary, playing the role of the filmmaker's father, Marof Achkar, who died in 1971.

Doubly dedicated "to my father, and to all of the prisoners of Camp Boiro and elsewhere," *Allah Tantou*'s next images are of the letters Marof Achkar wrote to his family from prison, which are then replaced by more 8mm footage, now of a government ceremony. Viewers hear another voice-over commentary, but this time it is the actor playing the role of David Achkar's father who speaks in the present tense to announce his arrest. These first three minutes of

Allah Tantou are emblematic of the film's fragmented and polyphonic nature. Marof Achkar's son, David, speaks in a first-person autobiographical commentary, sometimes addressing spectators and other times addressing his father. Montanary also speaks in the first person, both in voice-overs and in diegetic dialogue in scenes that reenact Marof Achkar's time in prison. Third-person narration within David Achkar's voice-over and incorporated newsreel footage occasionally join the two first-person voices. These layered voices tell the story of Marof Achkar's political career; the son provides personal and historical information, supported by photographs, newspapers, and newsreel footage, and the acted father tells his personal, political, and prison experiences. Along with this story of an individual is told the national horror of Guinean president Sekou Touré's government purges, whose victims were tortured at the notorious Camp Boiro prison.

Like Teno, Achkar reflexively manipulates the visual media—documentary evidence and fictional reenactments—that make up *Allah Tantou*, linking the varied image fragments through both conjunctive and disjunctive uses of sound. Dialogues and voice-overs often overlap or bleed from one type of image into another, continuing over a cut, for example, from a reenactment to 8mm footage. The conjunction of a reenactment narration with images from home movies produces an effect of focalization such that the footage seems to constitute the memories of the character of his father. Yet Achkar consistently juxtaposes archival photographs and footage of Marof Achkar with shots of the character in the reenactments, making no attempt to convince the spectator that the two are the same. Achkar explained that "I shot [the film] with my cousin. He doesn't really look like my father—he's my mother's nephew. He didn't even see the home movies."[21] At the same time, the transitions back from reenactment to footage clearly marked as documentary remind us that Marof Achkar and his son had off-camera lives. Five years after the intricately constructed *Allah Tantou*, Achkar made a second documentary, *Kiti: Justice en Guinée* (Kiti: Justice in Guinea, 1996), this time using a first-person voice-over to introduce the post-Touré democratization of Guinea's justice system. "I reconnect with my own history, which blends with that of Guinea," Achkar declares in the commentary, noting that like his father, he had traveled with a Super 8 camera. Unlike Ndiaye and Teno, however, Achkar never built a documentary career, his life cut tragically short by leukemia at the age of thirty-eight.

The films released by Samba Félix Ndiaye, Jean-Marie Teno, and David Achkar in 1991 and 1992 are proof that Ndiaye was both heir to Vieyra and elder statesman of a younger generation of filmmakers. We find ourselves at a turning point in the history of African documentary cinema, at the start of a series of works that in French are most often called *documentaires de création*, the category invoked by the African Guild of Directors and Producers. Beyond this appellation, they also fit the more specific description of *essay film*. The idea of a filmic essay goes back at least as far as the late 1920s, when German documentarist Hans Richter suggested the importance of nonfiction films that portray concepts rather than just the stages of an event or process or, in vocabulary we now recognize, "scenery and quaint customs." Such films, Richter argued, construct an argument out of both "directly recorded actualities" and "acted scenes."[22] French expedition and French and African ethnographic documentaries made strategic use of acted scenes for purposes of illustration and entertainment, and African documentarists now supplemented direct recordings to different ends.

In the late 1970s, film scholar Jay Ruby distinguished between reference, reflection, and reflexivity in documentary, concluding that "to be reflexive is to reveal that films . . . are created, structured articulations of the filmmaker and not authentic, truthful, objective records."[23] Within two decades, Bill Nichols had expanded the question of reflexivity in documentary into a reflexive mode of documentary, one that engages in "metacommentary" and addresses "the process of representation itself." Such films, according to Nichols, interrogate "*how* we talk about the historical world."[24] A subset of reflexive documentary, the essay film as it has been understood since the early 1990s incorporates a personal voice that Michael Renov and Timothy Corrigan trace to the literary essay. Renov outlines a history of the essay from Michel de Montaigne in the late sixteenth century to Roland Barthes and then Jonas Mekas in the twentieth, arguing that the essay film, "a mode of autobiographical practice that combines self-examination with a deeply engaged outward gaze," is thus doubly reflexive.[25] Nora Alter likewise points to the hybrid nature of essay films, emphasizing the ways they combine fictional and nonfictional narrative strategies and "self-reflexively offer their own film criticism."[26]

African cinema has been notably absent from these British and North American discussions of the essay film, which began at the same time that African essay films started to appear. Jury members at the tenth edition of FESPACO in 1987, recognizing Teno's *Hommage* for having "the personal style of a cinematographic essay," recommended that the festival create a Grand Prize for documentary.[27] The only films about Africa cited in theoretical studies of either reflexive documentary or the essay film—Trinh Minh-ha's *Reassemblage* (1982) and Chris Marker's *Sans soleil* (Sunless, 1982)—are now over four decades old, both shot only partially on the continent and neither by an African director.[28] Catherine Russell addresses them in her 1999 *Experimental Ethnography*, an impressive analysis of how reflexive films question the colonial realism of the documentary enterprise that does not mention a single African work.[29] African films are equally missing from Hamid Naficy's 2001 *An Accented Cinema*, an overview of reflexive films made by postcolonial directors in exile that includes Trinh and Marker.[30] Even a 2019 edited collection with a promising title, *World Cinema and the Essay Film: Transnational Perspectives on a Global Practice*, accounts for Africa only in a text coauthored by a Polish-British director who shot a documentary in Zimbabwe.[31]

As a subgenre of documentary, the category of essay film designates non-fiction films that highlight their createdness rather than any purely indexical relationship to reality. The term brings from the French *essayer* a sense of trying, trying out, and experimenting; it reminds us once again that terms such as *pseudo-documentary, quasi-documentary, docufiction,* and *fictionalized documentary* have held African films to more limited aesthetic and interpretative standards than those made within dominant cinematic traditions. Well-versed in international cinema, their narrative voices intimate, individual, and sharply analytical, Ndiaye, Teno, and Achkar replaced ethnography with essay, telling and retelling colonial and postcolonial African history while exploring their place within contemporary Africa and its diaspora. Their shift from an ethnographic to a historico-political axis is significant in the context of Africa's long-standing relegation to the status of "ethnographiable" rather than "historifiable," as noted by Fatimah Tobing Rony, drawing on Lévi-Strauss.[32] African documentarists bring to the essay film particular subject positions, particular regional and film histories, and a particular matrix of local and global aesthetic and narrative traditions. Unlike reportage, Jean-Marie Teno affirms, documentary is not "the capturing of reality" but instead "reality from a clearly defined point of view."[33]

Cameroonian director François Woukoache's *Asientos* (1995), difficult to summarize, is most aptly characterized as an essay film. Woukoache set himself the task of making a documentary about the transatlantic slave trade from an African viewpoint, and he did so by means of a multivocal, poetic voice-over narration accompanied by carefully edited images. A documentary film that contains little documentary evidence of the past, it has several characters and speaking voices but lacks a coherent story. Born in Yaoundé in the mid-1960s, Woukoache studied math and physics in France, then attended Belgium's National Institute for the Advanced Study of the Arts of Performance (INSAS) for a master's degree in film production. He shot his first film, *Melina* (1991), while back in Cameroon for ceremonies marking the end of the mourning period for his father. *Asientos* followed, bringing Woukoache to international attention when it won the documentary prize at FESPACO in 1997. Ndiaye cited it as a successful documentary and a film he greatly admired. "If you don't know precisely both the topic and the point of view on which you will base your story," Ndiaye asserted, "there is no reason to make a documentary."[34]

Thackway avoids calling *Asientos* a documentary, placing the film instead in a group of "memory-history films" that includes Faye's *Fad'jal*, Teno's *Afrique, je te plumerai*, and Achkar's *Allah Tantou*. These works "restore a specifically African perspective as they strive to give space and voice to episodes hitherto ignored by 'official history,'" Thackway argues, an assessment echoed by scholar Jude Akudinobi in slightly different terms. For Akudinobi, *Asientos* is a nonfiction film that foregrounds "the tension between lived experience, imagination and historical memory."[35] Woukoache himself consciously engaged the history of French documentary cinema. The pressbook circulated upon his film's release featured a quote from Chris Marker's iconic and canonical essay film *Sans soleil*, a portion of which was shot in Guinea-Bissau and the Cape Verde Islands less than ten years after their independence from Portugal: "History moves forward, plugging its memory like one plugs one's ears."[36] In the wake of *Les statues meurent aussi*, Marker had become an acclaimed experimental documentarist and multimedia artist, and *Sans soleil* is considered by many critics to be his masterpiece. Almost overwhelmingly reflexive, the film persistently interrogates the functioning of memory and forgetting as well as the representation of reality in still and moving images. A female voice-over narrator recounts the travels of a male friend, paraphrasing and quoting from his letters. Given the name Sandor Krasna in the closing credits, he has sent her film footage of people and customs that fascinate him. Most of *Sans soleil* is set in Japan, with West Africa, Iceland, and the United States figuring briefly, but it is from the section of the film addressing Bissauan anticolonial philosopher and fighter Amilcar Cabral that Woukoache excerpted the quote about history stifling memory.

Of his task in *Asientos*, which was shot in Senegal, France, and Belgium, Woukoache wrote that "to make a film about the slave trade is to confront the absence of images" while working to "cross the border of time."[37] Only a few African films have represented the trade in Africa, before the Atlantic crossing, and these have been historical fictions. Very little documentary evidence remains, a few writings and a few drawings, noted Woukoache, and among these "nothing from the African side."[38] He decided therefore not to make an expository overview. Presenting the history he interrogates as his own, Woukoache works not to show what the slave trade was like but rather to explore what we remember of it and how. He brings the trauma of this memory, moreover, into contact with violence in contemporary Africa.

François Woukoache, *Asientos*, 1995.

Asientos begins with several screens of text explaining that in the early sixteenth century, an *asiento* was a license via which the king of Spain promised to deliver a certain number of enslaved African people to a contracting company to be taken to the colonies. The text gives way to a polyphonic voice-over, split among one female voice identified as European and two male voices identified as African, neither of which belongs to Woukoache. Before the opening credits, the female voice speaks, like the female narrator in *Sans soleil*, of friendship with a man. Unlike Marker's Krasna, he is allied with Africa, not Europe. "The first time we met," she begins, "I didn't understand what he wanted. I have never been to Africa. I don't know what Africa and Africans look like. I listen to him speak. . . . Too many images here in Europe, he says. Too many impotent images. The absence of images over there. And the difficulty of filling in the empty space of his memory." Over the course of the film, the identity of this "he" is never quite resolved, resonating with both Woukoache as director of the film and an unnamed young Black male character.

The film's opening minutes include different kinds of images edited together. The central thread, shot on 35mm, is set on a quiet beach near Popenguine, Senegal, where three characters—a young man, a young woman, and an elderly man—appear and disappear, sometimes sitting together, sometimes looking out across the waves. Jerky, handheld, black-and-white images shot on Super 8 show a young boy running on a beach. As performative as it is reflexive, *Asientos* recalls Edouard Sailly's evocative *Le troisième jour*; no explicit connection is made between Woukoache and the young man on screen, nor between the young man and the boy. The two male voice-over narrators tell the history of the slave trade, alternating between an intimate, emotional first-person perspective and a more neutral and formal third person. One speaks immediately after the opening credits, whispering insistently, "So much blood in my memory." This voice becomes associated with the older man on the beach and seems to be addressing both the young man and viewers, speaking of "these centuries that separate me from you." The other male voice and the female voice join to add historical information, which accompanies images of maps of Africa, the young man on the beach, and the young woman in a village amid broken pottery and hanging fabric. "This isn't reenactment," Woukoache said of his use of characters in documentary; "it's imagined reality."[39]

Woukoache opted to depict the experience of Africans on slave ships via drawings by Belgian musician and graphic artist Louis Joos, known for his illustrations of American jazz greats John Coltrane and Thelonious Monk. He also included images of material evidence, first a skull and then shackles and chains, filmed on exhibit in museums in Nantes, France, and Brussels, Belgium. The historical remnant at the heart of *Asientos* is the "House of Slaves" on Senegal's Gorée Island, to which Woukoache returns again and again, his camera traveling back and forth along the walls, scanning the ceilings, returning repeatedly to the famous "door of no return." Close-ups of the walls are intercut with extreme close-ups of the skin of the elderly man, who as the film progresses comes to represent a formerly enslaved person. Spectators are then shown a seemingly abandoned television, askew in a cluttered room, airing news footage of white photographers snapping images of an African man holding a dying child. These are both realities that we prefer to forget, *Asientos* argues: the historic slave trade, of which there are no photographic or filmic images, and contemporary African suffering, of which there are countless images, produced primarily by non-Africans.

Asientos addresses the circulation of memory, and in this sense, it is an essay film like *Sans soleil*. But Marker used fragmentation and reflexivity to portray the experience of a European adventurer, abstracting history and context in favor of reflections on visiting and filming one foreign place and culture after another. Jean-Michel Frodon notes that one of the film's best known images is of a woman in the Bissau market, yet despite Marker's active and long-standing attention to the relationship between filmer and filmed, she does not speak.[40] Her thoughts and actions are narrated by a third-person voice-over that, quite jarringly given Marker's knowledge of colonial history and cinema history, describes the "equal gaze" of a "ritual of seduction." Even more unsettling, perhaps, these images attributed to Marker were shot not by him nor even his Bissauan collaborators Sana Na N'Hada and Flora Gomes but by pan-Africanist performer and filmmaker Sarah Maldoror. Although she was a close friend of Marker, her name does not appear in the film's credits.[41] Woukoache's approach, on the contrary, is anchored and specific, tying the past very tightly to the present. Toward the end of *Asientos*, he provides some sense of resolution, of successful, if painful, remembering, through a traveling shot of a multiracial group posing in front of Gorée's staircase and door. In the last images of the film, the young man on the beach is joined by more and more people holding torches as night falls; they sit together and look out to sea.

Samba Félix Ndiaye's documentary trajectory continued with a short subject that like *Asientos* reflexively addresses the production of images, in this case in the context of African filmmaking. *Lettre à l'oeil* (Free letter, 1993) is also a reflection on the situation of a director who lives, voice-over narration explains, "between two continents, as if on a bridge between Africa and Europe." The only film Ndiaye shot in France, it opens with outdoor images of rain falling on streetlamps, then cuts to a man standing at a pay phone inside a hospital. The first words are ostensibly his, spoken to an unnamed interlocutor on the other end of the line: "One day, I called you from the hallway of the hospital in Vincennes and, while talking to you about African cinema, I had the idea of creating a parallel between this medical check-up and an assessment of the current state of our cinema." The first-person voice-over continues as Ndiaye claims a place in global film history for both African cinema as a whole and himself as an individual filmmaker. Referencing his favorite films, including Satyajit Ray's *Pather Pachali* (1955), he also cites his favorite long takes, like the one that famously opens Orson Welles's *Touch of Evil* (1958). Just as Woukoache fashioned an encounter with Marker, Ndiaye connects himself to Welles, extracting a clip from the Hollywood classic to cut seamlessly from the US–Mexico border road to his own Paris street, Welles's music and a few words of dialogue bleeding over from one location to the next.

In *Lettre à Senghor* (Letter to Senghor, 1998), Ndiaye reflects not on African cinema but on the life and legacy of Léopold Sédar Senghor as poet, founding father of the Negritude movement, first president of independent Senegal, and member of the Académie Française. Yet the film is neither biopic nor conventional biographical documentary.[42] A complex first-person commentary, written but not read by Ndiaye, addresses Ndiaye's individual and Senegal's national experiences of Senghor as much as Senghor's own life story. And the voice-over narrator speaks directly to Senghor, using the informal second person *tu* to challenge and praise this absent addressee. The resulting film is autobiographical, biographical, and historical, a critical and poetic interrogation of postindependence African identity and politics.

In 1960, viewers learn, Samba Félix Ndiaye was a teenager in Dakar, and Senghor had just taken office. The young Ndiaye was critical of Senghor for imposing the French language on his people: "I told myself that in truth I was much more African than he was." Juxtaposing newsreel images of 1968 student demonstrations in the capital with a recording of Senghor reading his poem "Elegy to the Saudades," Ndiaye shares his adolescent annoyance at Senghor claiming Portuguese blood rather than his Serer heritage. The narrator then asks and answers a fundamental question: "Why didn't I understand you? It was because we didn't know anything about your roots." The film's project therefore becomes the rediscovery of Senghor, uncovering the Serer origins in southern Senegal of the ninety-one-year-old retired African president living in France. To accomplish this, Ndiaye adds to his personal, reflective commentary documentary evidence of the past in the form of black-and-white photographs and newsreel footage of Senghor the statesman, as well as color footage of contemporary interviews.

The central dialogue of *Lettre à Senghor* is staged; Ndiaye's questions to Senghor, who did not participate in the making of the documentary, are all either rhetorical or answered by Ndiaye himself. The bulk of the film takes place in the villages of Senghor's childhood, where Ndiaye interviews the chiefs of Djilor and Fadiouth; poet, playwright, and Senghor's former cultural advisor Abdou Anta Ka; and Senghor's former majordomo Jean Ndiaye. He also records a performance by Senghor's griotte Yande Codou Sène. Several interviewees talk about Senghor's family and his early years, attesting to how he was shaped by the traditions of his birthplace, while others, including ethnologist Pierre Dlokh, supply more general information about the people and customs of the region. Toward the end of the film, Ndiaye appears on screen for the first time, visiting the grave of Senghor's mother with Ka. Echoing Ndiaye's project, Ka wonders if any connection remains between Senghor and his ancestral village. "He's in Normandy," Ka states, sending a message to Senghor via Ndiaye: "What I have to say to him is, don't satisfy the French, who don't know him, don't die with them! Come back and die with us." Senghor would die in Normandy just three years later, his body flown to Dakar for a state funeral and burial.

Ndiaye told Baba Diop that he felt himself to be in a "no man's land" in relation to African cinema, "someone who tills too personal a field while affiliating myself with documentary."[43] Inhabiting this limbo, Ndiaye both embraced and resisted the personal, rejecting the easy objectivity of the outsider in favor of reflexive questioning by a local. The deft counterpoint between image and commentary in his filmic essays relies on voices that are both individual and shared; Ndiaye narrates while Gorgui converses in *Dakar-Bamako*, and he speaks to an absent Senghor about himself and Senghor in *Lettre à Senghor*. Abderrahmane Sissako has embraced a similar documentary philosophy, contending that to approach others, a director must "talk about oneself or around oneself."[44] Born in Kiffa, Mauritania, home to his mother's family, Sissako spent most of his childhood with his father in Mali. He returned to Mauritania to finish high school, then left again at the age of nineteen to study filmmaking at the VGIK in Moscow. His student project *Le jeu* (The game, 1989) was shot in Turkmenistan, which doubles for Mauritania in a story about children who play at war in the midst of war. In *Rostov-Luanda* (1997), his first feature-length film, first documentary, and first film shot on the African continent, Sissako records his return to the village of his birth and then departure for Luanda, Angola, in search of Afonso Baribanga, an Angolan with whom he had studied Russian in Rostov-on-the-Don. Spectators are introduced to Sissako's project not by an omniscient authorial commentary but by the voice of his cousin, who situates Sissako in Kiffa and praises him for being there. "There are some who leave for France to study and who never return home, who never even think about returning home," he declares, characterizing Sissako's return as "an act of honor."

Sissako takes over the narration as spectators watch him leave Kiffa. The voice-over becomes historical; traveling shots shift almost seamlessly from desert sands to snow as his search for Baribanga takes the director from Mauritania to Russia to Angola, the landscapes of these countries linked by his life story and that of his old friend. Traveling across Angola, a country devastated by seventeen years of civil war, Sissako conducts interviews in Portuguese and Creole with the aid of a translator, occasionally communicating directly in French or Russian. After each conversation, Sissako shows a photograph of Baribanga, one of very few pieces of documentary evidence from the past that appear in the film. But these people met along the way become the ultimate object of his quest, more so than Baribanga, whom Sissako finally locates in the film's final minutes not in Angola but in Germany.

Rostov-Luanda ends with a brief scene in Europe, and Sissako's *La vie sur terre* (Life on Earth, 1998) begins with one. Amid the overflowing shelves of a Super Monoprix in Paris, Sissako rides up an escalator carrying an enormous, stuffed polar bear. This shot gives way to images of Sissako's father in Sokolo, Mali, reading a letter announcing his son's imminent visit to film Sokolo on the eve of the year 2000. As Sissako enters his father's compound, the filmmaker's voice-over quotes from Aimé Césaire's *Notebook of a Return to My Native Land* (1939), famous lines that may seem paradoxical coming from a documentary filmmaker. "Hold back from crossing your arms in the sterile attitude of the spectator," Césaire and Sissako warn, "because life is not a spectacle . . . because a man who screams is not a dancing bear." Living in exile, Sissako refuses the role of documentarist as adventurer, refuses to watch from behind the camera instead of engaging directly with others. He is both off-screen voice-over narrator and on-screen character, a strategy he explained to journalist Alessandra Speciale: "As I am filming you, I will be filmed in turn. . . . I am one of you despite everything."[45]

I have called *La vie sur terre* a documentary, yet the film was released before the time period it depicts. The men of Sokolo are shown listening to Radio France International reporting on New Year's Eve activities around the world, its journalists counting down to a new millennium that was still two years away when Sissako was shooting. Sissako did not record New Year's Eve in Sokolo, but all the actors in his drama play themselves; the credits at the end of the film identify him, his father, his uncle, and so on. Destabilizing the boundaries between fiction and documentary, Sissako intentionally places himself in Sokolo at a crucial moment in the future, filming and being filmed in an Africa that is both set against and intimately connected to the Europe heard on the radio. Commissioned by Franco-German television network ARTE as the sole African film in a series about the upcoming millennium, *La vie sur terre* was originally intended to be purely fictional, but Sissako came to feel that this would constitute an "abdication of responsibility" and "an escape to avoid reality."[46] It would be his last documentary, however; now one of the most widely known African filmmakers, Sissako has since made only feature fictions.

Like Sissako, Mahamat-Saleh Haroun chose to appear on screen in his first feature-length documentary, *Bye Bye Africa* (1998), which was also the first feature-length film from Chad. Born in 1961 in Abéché, Haroun was wounded during the civil war and in his late teens escaped first to Cameroon, then to China, and finally to Europe. He went on to study both filmmaking and journalism in France, where he has remained while retaining his Chadian citizenship and filming almost exclusively in Africa. After beginning his career in cinema with several short fictions, Haroun switched to documentary for *Bord'Africa* (1995), a profile of Senegalese musicians in Bordeaux, and *Sotigui Kouyaté: Un griot moderne* (Sotigui Kouyaté: A modern griot, 1996), a tribute to the great Burkinabé griot and actor. Variously deemed documentary, documentary fiction, fictional documentary, docu-fiction, and docu-drama by reviewers and critics, *Bye Bye Africa* was the first of his films to win global acclaim, including best first film at the Venice Film Festival. Haroun has described it as moving "constantly back and forth between fiction and reality"; an uneasy relationship between film and reality is not just one of its characteristics but also one of its primary themes.[47]

In *Bye Bye Africa*, Haroun acts, narrates, and films the return to Chad, after ten years in France, of a central character named Mahamat-Saleh Haroun, who is a filmmaker. Most of the film is made up of scenes in color in which Haroun is on screen. Other scenes consist of black-and-white images ostensibly filmed by his character's video camera. When spectators first see Haroun, however, he is asleep in his bed in France, waking up to the ringing of a telephone call that will announce the death of his mother. He leaves Paris to attend her funeral in N'Djamena, where he spends time with his father, grandmother, and nephew; reunites with an old friend; and starts the preparations for a film to be titled "Bye Bye Africa." Upon his arrival in Chad, Haroun demonstrates how years of exile have distanced his character from the reality of his native land, asking his taxi driver, "So, how is this country doing?" One of the film's goals is to answer this question. Haroun and the driver commiserate about the heat and the price of gas, then encounter a roadblock staffed by the military, a sign of Chad's long-standing civil war. Over the course of both "Bye Bye Africa" and *Bye Bye Africa*, Haroun portrays the varied landscapes of the city and provides glimpses of the lives of its inhabitants but without any ethnographic explanation of the actions on screen.

Recorded and staged, autobiographical and political, avowedly reflexive from the start, *Bye Bye Africa* is also a commentary on moviegoing in Chad and the state of African cinema. Few Chadians understand or approve of Haroun's chosen career; his father watches him pick up his video camera to record boys playing soccer in the streets and complains, speaking in Chadian Arabic, "Cinema! Cinema! We don't understand what you do." During the first of what will be many motorbike rides around the city, Haroun's old friend Garba, who used to work as a projectionist at N'Djamena's Normandy movie theater, tells Haroun that African films are not shown in Africa. Instead of responding to Garba, Haroun addresses viewers in a voice-over: "Yes, I know. Nobody sees my films here. I ask myself, then, for whom I make them." Engaging the question of how and why to make films in and for Africa by examining the current state of film exhibition, Haroun and Garba ride to the Normandy, transformed from the lively social center of Haroun's childhood to a scarred, dilapidated symbol of neglect. Haroun then takes spectators on a tour of N'Djamena's other crumbling movie theaters—the Shéhérazade, the

Rio, the Vog, and the Etoile—all destroyed by decades of war and emptied of their audiences.

While Haroun is standing in front of the Shéhérazade, a man grabs his video camera, yelling, "He's stealing our image! Thief! Why film us? He's a foreigner!" Garba attempts to explain the man's reaction, which he believes Haroun has been abroad for too long to understand: "Here people don't trust the camera. We have a huge problem with images. We can't distinguish between fiction and reality." As proof, Garba offers the case of Isabelle, an actress who played the role of a woman with AIDS in one of Haroun's earlier films and is now a pariah because people believe that she, like her character, is sick. Mixing layers of narrative, Haroun uses the multiple reflexive strategies of *Bye Bye Africa* to push his audience to wonder whether and where, in the words of Safi Faye, there is mise en scène. A bit of research reveals that the character of Garba, like that of Isabelle, was invented for the film. Actor Garba Issa was not a former projectionist and went on to play very different roles in Haroun's later fictions *Abouna* (2002) and *Daratt* (2006). The role of Haroun's father was played not by Haroun's father but by Khayar Oumar Defallah, who would also go on to act in *Daratt*, and that of his mother, as seen in home movie footage, by actress Hadje Fatima N'Goua, also of *Daratt* and *Un homme qui crie* (A screaming man, 2010). The only major characters playing themselves are African filmmakers: Mahamat-Saleh Haroun, his sole Chadian colleague Issa Serge Coelo, and David-Pierre Fila from the Republic of the Congo.

Discussing his decision to cite the same Aimé Césaire verse in the title of *Un homme qui crie* that Sissako had selected for *La vie sur terre*, Haroun explained that "the original sin comes from the fact that Africa was first filmed by others." Colonial cinema created what Haroun deemed a "distorted" representation of Africa, one that African filmmakers must work to "counteract."[48] Listening to the radio, Haroun's character hears a speech given ten years earlier by popular leader of Burkina Faso and supporter of FESPACO Thomas Sankara, who decried Africa's neocolonial reliance on imported food as well as imported cultural products. The urgent need for self-reliance is echoed later in the film as the need for a cinema produced by Africans, a message that arrives in a letter sent from Brazzaville, another city damaged by war, and spoken in voice-over by Haroun's friend and fellow documentarist Fila. Yet Haroun invokes both African and non-African cinematic influences. He has described *Bye Bye Africa* as drawing from an African narrative tradition: "There is a structure in the screenplay, but I wanted a story told in the oral tradition . . . counting the seconds and then moving in another direction."[49] In the penultimate scene of the film, Haroun in voice-over says of his on-screen grandmother, "This is the woman who taught me how to tell stories." When the character of Haroun's father is amazed to see home movie footage of his wife after her death, however, Haroun switches to French to respond that "a great man named Jean-Luc Godard said, 'Cinema makes memories.'" A large poster for Clint Eastwood's *Pale Rider* (1985), a film in which the director plays the role of a clearly fictional protagonist, is visible behind Haroun when he discovers Isabelle's body after her suicide. In interviews with *Cahiers du cinéma*, Haroun discussed the Indian and Charlie Chaplin films he watched as a child and his adolescent discovery of Roberto Rossellini and Wim Wenders; the list of directors he most admires includes Ousmane Sembene, François Truffaut, Robert Bresson, Yasujiro Ozu, and Akira Kurosawa.[50] And, as noted by film scholar Yifen Beus, the reflexive trope of a film about a man filming a city goes back to Vertov's *Man with a Movie Camera*, often identified as the first essay film.[51]

Like Haroun, Cameroonian documentarist Rosine Mbakam has gained international recognition as an accomplished director with personal and professional ties to Africa and Europe. A generation younger, she received her first media production training at an Italian NGO in Yaoundé, then in 2007 left a position with Cameroonian national television to study filmmaking at Belgium's INSAS. Mbakam has since filmed in her countries of birth and of adoption, opting to appear on screen in all her documentaries, if in different ways. Her first film, *Les deux visages d'une femme Bamiléké* (The two faces of a Bamileke woman, 2016), is among the rare essay films made by an African woman. Employing a French-language voice-over to address questions of exile, tradition, identity, and African cinema, Mbakam also plays a central role.

Mbakam's narration begins over traveling shots at night from the passenger seat of a vehicle: "I missed this darkness where you can't see anything. . . . I grew up with it. It's a part of me and my family." She announces her return to Cameroon after seven years, accompanied by her husband, her son, and also *le cinéma*. After a cut to daylight, Mbakam speaks in Bamileke to her mother, asking from behind the camera what she thinks of her daughter's work. Framed in a medium shot, Mbakam's mother recounts that she went once to a movie theater and saw a film about people fighting. "I thought it was real," she continues, "but they said it wasn't. They said it was cinema, that what you see isn't real." In this reflexive introduction, Mbakam asks spectators to consider the relationship between cinematic representation and reality, implicitly contrasting the documentary they are about to see to the films most often programmed in African theaters.

Mbakam travels with her mother to their familial village of Tonga, her place of origin and where she learned her traditions, she states in her voice-over commentary. We watch her mother clear off her late husband's tomb, and Mbakam

Rosine Mbakam, *Les deux visages d'une femme Bamiléké*, 2016.

steps in front of the camera for the first time, holding her son, Malick, to show him where his grandfather is buried. Then, filming her mother as she walks through the house where they lived before moving to Yaoundé, Mbakam asks a series of questions, prompting details about family history but also the period called the Cameroon War or the Bamileke War, the five years during which the Cameroonian People's Union (UPC) fought for independence from French colonists. Mbakam's mother later becomes a source of information about postindependence politics as well. At the market in Yaoundé, Mbakam remembers reading the old newspapers in which her mother wrapped the fish she sold from a stall. Her mother remembers first president Ahidjo positively but refuses to name Biya, who gets elected "every time no matter what."

Although Mbakam's mother shares information about her late husband's childhood and adult career, showing photographs and documents she has kept in a suitcase since his death, *Les deux visages d'une femme Bamiléké* is particularly focused on the experiences of women. Discussing her husband's second marriage, she reveals to her daughter that she did not get along with her cowife. Arranged marriage and polygamy are also the topic of a gathering of women from Mbakam's extended family, who prepare a meal while sharing their experiences of constraining and harmful traditions. Mbakam then engages with the Bamileke traditions that have nourished these women, those surrounding marriage and childbirth. Since she was married and gave birth in Europe, Mbakam herself has not performed them; her mother now gives her grandson the bath and her daughter the hot towel massage they would have received had he been born in Africa. On camera, Mbakam asks questions throughout the process, this time gathering ethnographic rather than historical information. A sequence shot during a meeting of her mother's tontine, a group of women who meet regularly and make financial contributions to be disbursed to members in need, highlights another tradition fostering solidarity among women. Mbakam then returns to the cinema, filming her mother and a friend watching Sembene's *La Noire de . . . .* As she ties her own work to this foundational classic about an African woman's tragic experience working in Europe, we see clips from the film as well as shots of the older women reacting to them, speaking to protagonist Diouana and laughing when her French employer flees at the end. Mbakam closes the film with a voice-over reflection on exile, cutting from a sequence of old family photographs to footage in which she teaches her son to say "I love you" to his grandmother in Bamileke.

Jean-Marie Teno has continued his documentary career since *Afrique, je te plumerai*, maintaining a distinctive first-person voice-over style. His voice-over narration in *La tête dans les nuages* (Head in the clouds, 1994), *Chef!* (Chief!, 1999), and *Vacances au pays* (Vacation at home, 2000) is instantly recognizable: autobiographically anchored, informal yet carefully crafted, humorous, impassioned, and analytical. It so unifies his films, in fact, that Harrow refers to it as the "Teno-narrator."[52] Producer, director, and editor as well as narrator, Teno like Haroun remains overwhelmingly identified with his work, although he is never visible on screen. Thackway deems his voice "extrospective," arguing that Teno uses his life story as an example of issues faced by all Africans.[53] Yet his commentary remains just as individual as representative while making meaning of the footage he has assembled.

La tête dans les nuages opens by quoting artist Pascale Martine Tayou, who defines *slum art* as a reflection of the misery of slum dwellings. Teno's commentary introduces a recurrent verbal and visual motif of the film, piles of trash in the streets of Yaoundé, which he links to simmering urban violence triggered by desperation. Reminding viewers of his personal connection to a city he left sixteen years prior, Teno recalls friends telling him not to stay in Europe, since he would risk Cameroon moving forward without him. These same friends, he says, now tell him he was right to have emigrated. The central theme of the film is the unrewarded hard work of ordinary Cameroonians, particularly those with university diplomas who are nonetheless unemployed, underemployed, or underpaid. Teno follows Jacky Ketcha, a recent law graduate, as he prepares application letters, which prove unsuccessful. Irène Pesonka has a job in the Ministry of Education but does not earn enough to support her children; she sells beignets on the street and works a plot of land to make ends meet. Both Ketcha and Pesonka survive thanks to the local tradition of the tontine. When Ketcha attempts to borrow money from a bank, Teno's voice-over tells viewers that such institutions lend only to politicians. Vianney Ombe Ndzana, an economist fired by the government for having expressed critical opinions, argues that Cameroon's bureaucratic class must be eliminated so that entrepreneurs can thrive. Alongside images of Tayou's recuperation art, Teno concludes that Cameroon's European-style educational system serves only to distance citizens from their African culture and identity.

Chef! and *Vacances au pays* portray Teno's successive returns to Cameroon, returning also to themes of education, modernity, and violence. *Chef!* resulted from an invitation to film the festivities surrounding the inauguration of a monument to King Kamga Joseph II in Bandjoun. In a mocking voice-over commentary, Teno addresses images of a group of men walking through a street overhung by a banner welcoming the greater chiefdom of the region: "O great men! Your faithful people are grateful." Informing us that the king being honored has been a friend to French colonizers and the regime that succeeded them, he provides context about the event's political and cultural valence as well as his personal connection to it—his uncle, a chief, is in attendance. But even if Teno shows spectators the dancing masks, his film is not ethnographic. Shooting without a specific plan, he finds his story the next morning when he discovers a group of villagers gathered around a teenage boy who has been caught stealing chickens. Teno shifts to an observational mode for several minutes, as we listen to the crowd, which debates a course of action. When several men begin to beat the accused thief, the screen goes black; the director announces that he stopped filming to intervene.

Chef! becomes an analysis of more than mob punishment as the film confronts, through an interlacing of recorded dialogues and voice-over, themes and languages, the same violence born of life under a corrupt dictatorship that Teno exposes in *La tête dans les nuages*. In a country full of chiefs, he observes, every man is a chief within his family, leaving little room to address gender inequality and violence against women. Footage of marriage ceremonies in Douala is intercut with interviews with activists for women's rights and against Biya's regime. "Country of chiefs, country of inequality," pronounces Teno, returning to images of the 1991 demonstrations seen in *Afrique, je te plumerai* and the continued failure of the Cameroonian state to help its people. He also returns to journalist Pius Njawe, who in the years since Teno's first film has been jailed for wondering in print whether President Biya might be ill. Interviewing other journalists at *Le messager*, Njawe's wife, and Njawe himself after his release from prison, Teno follows a final thread about the horrific conditions in Cameroon's prisons back to shots of the dancing chiefs in Bandjoun.

Vacances au pays, like *Afrique, je te plumerai* and *La tête dans les nuages*, begins in the crowded streets of Yaoundé, with Teno's commentary recounting both his recent arrival from France and his arrival in the city at the age of eleven from a small town in southern Cameroon. Teno's alternately humorous and accusatory narration is more autobiographically focused than in *Chef!*, mocking and condemning governmental corruption as well as misconceptions about the nature of African modernity. And footage of Teno's high school, once prestigious but now dilapidated, is accompanied by narration that repeats the harmful consequences of Africa's adoption of a European educational model. Leaving Yaoundé, Teno films a road trip to Mbieng, the familial village where he used to spend school vacations. Along the way, he reveals "toll booths" set up to extort money from drivers and passengers and interviews rural Cameroonians stuck in poverty, their hard physical labor unaided by modern machinery or state-sponsored infrastructure. Nostalgic for the summers of his childhood, Teno shares the traditional tales that he remembers. But the corruption he discovers even within Mbieng's annual Development Congress leaves him and his viewers with a sense of a "dead end," desperate for progress that might sustain more than just the country's chiefs and con men.

Soon after the release of *Vacances au pays*, Teno and his company, Les Films du Raphia, produced and distributed a film by a West African filmmaker who also wished to film a return home. Born in northern Benin in 1967, Idrissou Mora-Kpai moved to the capital of Cotonou for middle school and sought to study in Europe after high school. Unable to afford a plane ticket, he took a route now familiar to many emigrating Africans—across the Sahara to Algeria, then to Italy—and eventually to Film University Babelsberg in Potsdam, Germany. After making several short fiction films in the mid to late 1990s, Mora-Kpai moved to France and from there traveled back to Benin to shoot *Si-Gueriki, la reine mère* (Si-Gueriki, queen mother, 2002). Funded by Benin, France, Germany, and the European Union, the film was screened in major festivals in Africa, including FESPACO; in Europe, including International Film Festival Rotterdam and French documentary festival Cinéma du Réel; and in North America, including Montreal's Vues d'Afrique and the New York African Film Festival.

In his first feature, Mora-Kpai takes an autobiographical approach to the transformation of traditional family structures in his home country. He opens *Si-Gueriki, la reine mère* with French-language commentary over footage of the streets of Cotonou, remembering his arrival in the capital city twenty years prior. Then, as when he later left for Europe, Mora-Kpai continues, he traveled with the imposing image of his father, a descendant of royal Wasangari warriors, whom he shows in a series of still photographs. The director begins to appear on screen: in front of a hotel, carrying suitcases, then traveling north in a train toward his native village of Borgu. *Si-Gueriki*'s carefully crafted voice-over narration, focalized by a close-up of Mora-Kpai's face as he provides information about his voyage, is matched by equally intentional camerawork. As in Ndiaye's *Dakar-Bamako*, for example, viewers see landscapes through train windows from Mora-Kpai's perspective but also shots of the train from outside, from different angles and at various distances.

Mora-Kpai's father died while he was in Europe, and the first shots of his childhood home are accompanied by an evocation of this absence. He had planned to make a film about his late father, the director reveals, but ended up filming his mother and her closest cowife, neither of whom he knew well as a child; according to tradition, the family compound was divided by gender for both adults and children. Mora-Kpai records his mother speaking about work, family, and the young girl she is raising, just as his sisters were raised away from their nuclear family to prepare them to be good wives. Rather than pursue an ethnographic investigation of this cultural practice, Mora-Kpai asks his mother how she had felt when her own daughters left at a young age, then talks to his sister about her reaction to having been sent away to be raised by an aunt. These conversations, unlike the voice-over narration, are in Bariba. In this counterpoint of languages and between interviews and commentary, Mora-Kpai addresses both the history of colonial French schooling that led him to Europe and the access of girls in his family to Quranic and secular schools. His mother and her cowife become more talkative in response to his probing, discussing the ways in which they resisted the unreasonable expectations of his father, their husband, in a relationship based uniquely on work. Only as it approaches its conclusion does *Si-Gueriki, la reine mère* disclose that Mora-Kpai's mother is Queen Mother, a title she inherited from a patrilineal relative while her son was living in Europe. Wasangari royalty, she has a more prominent social position than did her late husband. Closing images of her official travel to an annual festival attest to the strength and power of West African women, not just in domestic but also in public, political spaces.

Most of the turn-of-the-century films discussed thus far were made while their directors were based in Europe, and Manthia Diawara locates Haroun's and Sissako's work within an "ARTE wave," referring to European television funding from which both benefited.[54] Given the diversity of funding sources and cinematic reference points of the filmmakers who made up this wave, however, we must go beyond such shorthand to understand their documentary choices and goals. Hamid Naficy suggests that an "exilic, diasporic, and ethnic" subjectivity created by "displacement from the margins to the centers" occasions the reflexive style he dubs "accented cinema."[55] And with a specific focus on feature fictions by African directors who trained and are still living in Europe, Lindiwe Dovey similarly argues that "alienation" in exile enables new ways of looking at one's native culture and society.[56] From Samba Félix Ndiaye to François Woukoache to Idrissou Mora-Kpai, these characterizations hold. An alliterative pairing of words chosen by journalist and film scholar Akin Adesokan to describe Abderrahmane Sissako's documentary positioning perhaps best encapsulates the spirit of the African essay films I have discussed thus far: "engaged expatriation."[57] Yet this stance is not unique to essay filmmakers.

Documentary filmmaking worldwide has grown and expanded with the ease and low cost of digital video, recently complemented by a host of inexpensive or free and easily accessible distribution networks. These have allowed directors from sub-Saharan Africa to deemphasize if not replace European laboratories and festivals. This transformation underway, nonfiction film gained a higher profile at FESPACO when in 2003 Jean-Marie Teno worked with colleagues to create the Côté Doc, a section of the festival dedicated to the production and distribution of African documentaries. A series of events and a special prize were sponsored by the African Guild of Directors and Producers, which declared in the program of the first edition that "it is via documentary that we access reality."[58] The commitment of participants to the craft of nonfiction as well as their interest in its global content and forms were highlighted in a master class given by Abderrahmane Sissako as well as in screenings of films by directors from around the African continent along with American Lee Hirsch's *Amandla!* (2002) and Thierry Michel's *Iran, sous le voile des apparences* (Iran, veiled appearances, 2002) from France. FESPACO canceled the Côté Doc when it created its own documentary section in 2007, with a distinct jury and two documentary prizes added two years later.

Although it is still the case that filmmakers working in Europe have better access to resources and the prestigious festivals that lead to international distribution and funding for future projects, twenty-first-century directors have the option of submitting their work to multiple sub-Saharan African documentary festivals. These are not always long lived, but the list has included Stlouis' Docs in Senegal, Benindocs in Benin, Koudougou Doc in Burkina Faso, Escales Documentaires (Documentary stage) in Gabon, and the Blitta Documentary Film Festival in Togo. Opportunities for training in documentary filmmaking have also appeared on the continent, many organized by

Le Côté Doc, FESPACO, 2003.

Africadoc, a program founded in 2002 by Ardèche Images in Lussas, France, that in 2012 became a division of the global Docmonde network. In addition to offering workshops and internships in France, Africadoc has created satellite programs in nine West and central African nations—Benin, Burkina Faso, Cameroon, Congo-Brazzaville, Mali, Mauritania, Niger, Senegal, and Togo—resulting in the annual production of dozens of documentaries of varying lengths. It was also instrumental in the development of a master's program in *documentaire de création* at Senegal's Gaston Berger University in Saint-Louis.[59] In a comparable effort, the BERTHA Foundation, established by South African pharmaceutical titan Anthony Tabatznik, expanded its support of global documentary to Africa in 2014 with the creation of the African Documentary Film Fund (ADFF).

As contemporary African documentary production has expanded, so has its range. A second and increasingly predominant strand of documentaries has turned away from the introspection and reflective commentary of the essay films with which this chapter began. No less powerful for their decentering of authorial experience and perspective, these films are equally—if differently—dialogic. In a final recourse to Nichols's classificatory system, we might characterize them as *interactive documentaries*, works in which "textual authority shifts toward the social actors recruited." Such films, Nichols explains, may or may not have voice-over narration, but with "a sense of situated presence and local knowledge that derives from the actual encounter of filmmaker and other," they almost always construct their arguments through interviews.[60] Scripts may be more or less prepared in advance and films shot on digital video, 16 mm, or the occasional 35mm; the art common to interactive documentaries is that of montage. This format allows for a continued displacement of French, no longer sole interpretative guide but one language among many.

Returning to the filmography of Samba Félix Ndiaye, we discover works that hearken back to the narratorial reticence of *Trésors des poubelles*, in which Ndiaye is virtually unseen as well as virtually unheard. To shoot *Ngor, l'esprit des lieux* (Ngor, the spirit of place, 1994), Ndiaye returned to Senegal and his childhood home in Ngor's Medina neighborhood. Like *Dakar-Bamako*, the film begins with first-person voice-over commentary. After sharing what Ngor represents for him, however, Ndiaye disappears from the soundtrack, leaving contemporary inhabitants of Ngor to speak about their lives. A group of men discusses the five-centuries-long history of the Lebu and Serer village and describes the workings of its council. Men and women recount the strenuousness of their work, and Ndiaye shows them fishing, collecting shellfish, and raising livestock. Viewers learn that Ngor has been invaded by hotels patronized by

Americans and wealthy Senegalese; ignoring the ocean heritage of residents, these establishments bar their access to the beach. Representing local Ngor, Ndiaye includes a *n'doep* ceremony that was intimately familiar to him, since his grandmother hosted such rituals in her living room.[61] Ndiaye insisted that the film is neither anthropological nor observational, contrasting his work to French ethnographies and echoing Sembene's criticism of Rouch; "I do not dissect people to put them in boxes and classify them to see if they have evolved or not. I only talk about the people whom I have met and trusted, who have given me words that I have tried to gather in the greatest humility."[62]

In *Un fleuve dans la tête* (A river in your head, 1998), Ndiaye traces the voyage along the Niger River to Niamey of a group of twenty European and African artists and musicians. He begins by acknowledging his own presence not in voice-over commentary but indirectly: a colleague approaches the camera to say, "Hello Samba," and he replies, "Hello." Just a few years after Ndiaye's film was released, François Woukoache spoke with journalist and critic Olivier Barlet about a "radicalization" of his own film style. Similarly choosing to displace his narrative voice, Woukoache moved away from the reflexivity of *Asientos* and toward low-budget films aligned with "daily life and the real."[63] Affiliated with Fest'Africa's Writing as Commitment to Memory project in Rwanda, Woukoache completed a feature-length documentary about the genocide titled *Nous ne sommes plus morts* (We are no longer dead, 2000); coproduced by Ndiaye's Almadies Films, it was selected for the Berlin International Film Festival.

After shooting the film, Woukoache stayed in Rwanda, making films for Rwandan television, teaching film production at the National University of Rwanda, and running his NGO Kemit Productions, founded to support the local creation of visual media. He began a series of short and medium-length interview-based documentaries about the Rwandan genocide and its aftermath with *Humura* (2004) and *Icyizere* (Hope, 2006); *Ntarabana* (2017) has been the most widely seen. Also a Fest'Africa participant, Ndiaye shot footage that became *Rwanda, pour mémoire* (Rwanda, for memory, 2003). In 2004, after thirty-five years in France, he returned to live in Senegal, where he continued to make documentary films and established the Dakar Media Center to train aspiring videographers and filmmakers. Ndiaye envisioned a school that would resemble Rome's celebrated Centro Sperimentale, "where students came with their projects, they were given a camera, and told 'go show us what you know how to do,' after which they were advised." In addition to giving practical guidance, he hoped to inspire a focus on film theory, history, and criticism.[64]

In what was to be his last film, *Questions à la terre natale* (Questions to the native land, 2006), Ndiaye again minimized his voice-over narration, this time in favor of an edited interplay of images of contemporary Senegal and interviews with West African economists, scientists, and social leaders. Forty-five minutes into a fifty-two-minute film, viewers see a brief image of Ndiaye on screen, discussing the concept behind his documentary in progress with Mouride Serigne Babacar Mbow, who was working to develop his grandfather's village in terms that refuse globalization as defined by international banks and NGOs. "There is a character, who is meant to be me," Ndiaye explains: "You return home, plus the rumors you hear are so disastrous, and you come to confirm what is real. Because you know that the solutions are here, there are people who have proven that the solutions are here." The moment is in a sense a red herring, since although Ndiaye shows himself introducing this premise, the film we have almost finished watching does not match it. The discrepancy is meaningful. A returning exile, Ndiaye ultimately kept his own story behind the scenes, instead seeking answers to the fundamental questions facing Senegal from those who have been working on-site.

Recalling conversations with Samba Félix Ndiaye about documentary filmmaking, Jean-Marie Teno noted both their differences of opinion and their mutual respect. Ndiaye had criticized the use of voice-over commentary as an easy narrative solution, Teno observed, before returning to a partial voice-over in *Questions à la terre natale*. In the wake of these exchanges, Teno decided to work toward less sustained if still "poetic and forceful" voice-overs in his own films.[65] We can perhaps locate the origins of this gradual transformation in *Le mariage d'Alex* (Alex's wedding, 2002), for which Teno accepted an old friend's request to film his wedding. He discovered that the wedding would be to Alex's second wife; the film, shot in an afternoon, becomes an exploration of polygamy in contemporary Cameroon. Despite Teno's direct involvement, he described his role as that of "witness."[66] In the more historical than sociological *Le malentendu colonial* (The colonial misunderstanding, 2004), commissioned by the same German television station as Safi Faye's *Man Sa Yaye* a quarter of a century earlier, Teno bears witness to events to which he does not have a personal connection.[67] One hundred years after the genocide of the Herero people in what is now Namibia, Teno edits together interviews conducted in Germany and Namibia to elucidate the historical ties between Christian missionaries and colonialism.

Minimizing introspection without abandoning a first-person voice—still reflective if not always reflexive—Teno returns to the subject of African cinema in *Lieux saints* (Sacred places, 2009), musing in the opening voice-over about how much has changed. The film centers on a popular ciné-club in the Saint Léon neighborhood of Ouagadougou, Burkina Faso, far from the hotels and restaurants frequented by FESPACO attendees. Interviewed by Teno, the club's owner, Bouba, insists that his clients want to see African films. Compared to Hollywood, Bollywood, or karate movies, however, they are too expensive to acquire. This revelation leads Teno to discuss with fellow filmmaker Idrissa Ouedraogo the intricate calculus of reaching African audiences without allowing one's films to be pirated; he also facilitates a screening of *Chef!* at Bouba's club. Other featured Saint Léon figures include Abbo, a public writer who composes on walls in chalk, and djembe maker Jules César, who builds an instrument in a long, unnarrated scene that comes close to ethnographic attention. Jules César also announces the ciné-club's programming; speaking for himself and on Teno's behalf, it seems, he contends that music and cinema are associated rather than opposed forms of entertainment.

Teno's *Une feuille dans le vent* (A leaf in the wind, 2013) is a single conversation rather than a series of interviews—in his words, a "dual first-person narrative."[68] Like *Lieux saints*, the film retains a commentary, though neither about Teno himself nor about African cinema. And like *Afrique, je te plumerai*, it addresses the corruption of politics in Cameroon and incorporates footage from colonial documentaries, if to different ends. In the first minute of *Une feuille dans le vent*, before the opening credits, the shots of African laborers felling trees in French Equatorial Africa that appeared in Teno's first feature-length documentary return, this time intercut with contemporary color images of trees with full canopies. "How do you expect a leaf without a stalk to live," central character Ernestine Ouandié asks in a voice-over before introducing herself on screen in footage from an extended interview with Teno. Teno informs viewers that Ernestine, the daughter of assassinated Cameroonian freedom fighter Ernest Ouandié and a Ghanaian mother, has since committed suicide. In images that now appear ghostly, Ernestine recounts that she left Ghana for Cameroon to learn more about her father but has been unsuccessful. She faces Teno's camera, a leaf seeking its stalk, to maintain that the French still control African history. Indicating where Ouandié and other rebels were killed by the government of Amadou Ahidjo and their heads put on display, a spot not marked even by a plaque, Teno like Ernestine points to a criminal silence, evidence that African leaders have taken over the role of their former colonizers.

After two very successful feature fictions, Mahamat-Saleh Haroun returned to documentary, retreating from the essay format as had Ndiaye and to a lesser extent Teno. The medium-length *Kalala* (2005) begins with a reflexive wink as a white pickup truck carries a man with a megaphone through the streets of N'Djamena, announcing a screening of *Bye Bye Africa* by Mahamat-Saleh Haroun. We discover that this is old footage in which Haroun appears with his

Mahamat-Saleh Haroun, *Hissein Habré: Une tragédie tchadienne*, 2016.

late coworker and friend Kalala; in the present of filming, Haroun is back in N'Djamena to shoot a film about Kalala's death from AIDS at the age of forty. Interviews with both Kalala's and Haroun's family members are intercut with shots of Haroun and Kalala working together as well as photos of Kalala with other African filmmakers. Despite a deep personal connection to the subject of the documentary, Haroun's voice-over narration is minimal, his voice heard primarily asking questions to interviewees. As he investigates Kalala's illness, the film becomes not just about Kalala but about the tendency of Chadians to deny the existence of AIDS. "I made this film," Haroun tells Kalala's former neighbor, "to say what he died from . . . to help people be vigilant against this illness."

It is in Haroun's documentary masterpiece *Hissein Habré: Une tragédie tchadienne* (Hissein Habré: A Chadian tragedy, 2016), however, that we best grasp the tension between competing nonfictional narrative strategies. Like *Bye Bye Africa* and *Kalala*, the film begins as a reflexive personal narrative. Shot in vivid 35mm, spiraling images of the sky give way to a close-up of a hand scribbling in a notebook. "Hissène Habré," the hand writes, then stops, taps the pen, crosses this out, then writes, "In my childhood," then crosses that out as well. A long shot of Haroun sitting at a table in a grassy courtyard with pen and notebook is followed by a close-up of his face, accompanied by an authorial voice-over in French: "The first time I heard of Hissein Habré, I must have been thirteen years old." Haroun stages himself as an essayist, hesitating between writing about Habré and writing about himself. The choice made, his voice-over turns toward the informational, providing background information about Habré accompanied by archival images. Among other details, Haroun shares a perfect anecdote for our history of documentary filmmaking in sub-Saharan Africa; Habré made his name known in 1974 when, as the leader of an armed rebel group, he took a French ethnographer hostage.

Linking his own adolescent flight from Chad to Habré's crimes, Haroun deplores the world's refusal to address them and provides historical context. Just a few minutes into the film, we see more close-ups, this time not of Haroun but of the scars on different parts of a man's body. These terrible images transition to the main focus of *Hissein Habré: Une tragédie tchadienne*, the testimonies of survivors of the torture inflicted by Habré's secret police, the Documentation and Security Directorate (DDS). Most often framed in medium close-up, these survivors bear witness in interviews conducted by the film's central character, Dohkot Clément Abaïfouta, himself a survivor and the founder of a local support association. Most interviews are conducted in Chadian Arabic, and a few in French; both languages are also heard in scenes shot at the association's headquarters. In an astonishing conversation that ends with formal forgiveness, Abaïfouta sits on a bench between a victim and his former torturer, who pleads that he was just following orders. Haroun periodically appears on screen, no longer reflecting on his cinematic process but, for example, showing Abaïfouta drawings of torture techniques reproduced in a book about the DDS. The film approaches a conclusion as Abaïfouta's association and the lawyer representing its members prepare for a long-awaited trial to bring Habré to justice. The last images of *Hissein Habré* were shot in a courtroom in Dakar twenty-three years after Habré fled into exile in Senegal, and the last words, heard in voice-over, are from the lawyer's closing argument. Text on screen announces Habré's sentence to life in prison.

After the release of *Si-Guériki*, Idrissou Mora-Kpai founded a production company and began to distribute his own films, becoming internationally recognized as an almost exclusively documentary filmmaker. In a transition more abrupt than Haroun's, Mora-Kpai's second film differs significantly in both content and style from his first. When he left Benin to study in Algeria in the 1980s, the director stopped in Arlit, Niger, to see an old friend, Issa. From Algeria, Mora-Kpai moved to France; when he returned to Benin to shoot *Si-Guériki*, he saw Issa again.[69] The two decided to shoot a film in Arlit about the catastrophic situation that had led Issa to return home, but Mora-Kpai chose not to include the story of their personal connection in the resulting *Arlit: Deuxième Paris* (Arlit: Second Paris, 2005). The film has no authorial narration, reflective or expository.

Arlit: Deuxième Paris communicates the history and present reality of exploitative uranium mining in Niger. Without voice-over commentary to guide them, viewers gather and synthesize information from intercut images and interviews, coming to understand the bitter irony of the film's subtitle. After uranium was discovered in northern Niger in 1968, European companies dug large mines in both Arlit and Agadez. In the 1970s, the Arlit mine employed up to twenty-five thousand workers, and the town was known locally as "the second Paris." When the price of uranium collapsed, this economy also collapsed. In a series of fixed introductory shots, Mora-Kpai displays the mine's cavernous pit and machinery set against a desert background, and buses transporting workers appear throughout the film. Images of the desolate landscape alternate with interviews with mine workers and other residents of Arlit, who testify in Hausa and French to how the mines have impacted their lives.[70] Some are directly affected by both the economic crash that led to less work and the deadly illnesses caused by the work still available. Others, such as a Tuareg man who claims to have no idea what goes on in the mining facilities, participate in Arlit's other economy—the smuggling of migrants across the desert—about which men and women in transit from multiple West African nations provide additional testimony. It is for this witnessing of the dual agonies of mining's toxic legacy and the lethal risks faced by migrants en route to Europe that scholar Cajetan Iheka deems the film an example of "ecotrauma cinema."[71]

Mora-Kpai's *Indochine: Sur les traces d'une mère* (Indochina: Traces of a mother, 2011), a prize-winner at FESPACO, similarly requires that the spectator work to make sense of documentary narrative. Like *Arlit*, the film connects Mora-Kpai's native country to another, this one in East Asia and this time via the history of the *tirailleurs sénégalais*. From 1946 to 1954, more than sixty thousand Africans were conscripted and sent to French Indochina to fight against the Viet Minh, which was fighting for independence from France, one colonized people set against another. Mora-Kpai focuses on members of a subsequent generation that resulted from this conflict, the children African soldiers had with Vietnamese women. Many of these "Africasians" were forcibly separated from their mothers and sent to West Africa, where they were isolated and rejected.

Mora-Kpai does not tell this history in chronological order. Returning to the use of a voice-over, he cedes the narration to his central character, who was one of these children. First seen from afar walking through Vietnamese streets, he introduces himself in French by his Vietnamese name, Duc, explaining that it means *virtuous*. In medium close-up, he explains that he learned the meaning of his name only after fifty years of living in Africa and thanks to a visiting Vietnamese delegation. To discover the name itself, he had needed to consult archival documents, since the African officer who adopted him and took him from Vietnam to Benin had renamed him Christophe Soglo. While Duc recounts the few memories he has of his mother, expressing anguish at having been forced to leave her behind, his testimony is both situated and heightened by intercut Vietnamese-language newsreel footage of retreating French troops.

Mora-Kpai met Soglo when eating in his restaurant in Cotonou and felt compelled to travel with him to Vietnam to make a film. *Indochine: Sur les traces d'une mère* juxtaposes interviews shot in Benin and Vietnam with contemporary images of the places described in this testimony to past events. Former Vietnamese officers analyze their war against France, and former African soldiers relate their experiences of conscription and battle as well as their relationships with Vietnamese women. Another child of such a union tells his story, as does a Vietnamese woman who was allowed to leave for Africa with her child. Through these intertwined narratives, Mora-Kpai forces viewers to confront the incongruity between the mutually proclaimed sympathy between Vietnamese and African soldiers and the alacrity with which African soldiers abandoned the Vietnamese mothers of their children, and sometimes their children as well. Those Africans who refuse to accept Africasians become proof of the discrimination that exists even within a context of shared colonial-era oppression.

The themes and structure of *Arlit: Deuxième Paris* are echoed in Burkinabé director Michel Zongo's equally interactive *Pas d'or pour Kalsaka* (No gold for Kalsaka, 2019). The documentary addresses the consequences of mining for a town in northern Burkina Faso, Zongo's ironic title reflecting the same lesson learned and taught by Mora-Kpai; the wealth extracted from mining is of little or no benefit to those laboring or those who live nearby. If gold, unlike uranium, is not itself lethal, mining in Kalsaka injures workers, contaminates water sources, reduces the availability of farmable land, and damages historically important sites. The largest mine in the area, moreover, was open for only four years, and neither the company that operated it nor the national government have helped residents recover from the damage it caused. Instead of an expository voice-over, an opening clip from Burkinabé national television announcing a deal between the government and a private mining company provides context, and Zongo allows the film's story to be told by those he interviews. A participant, however, if never on screen, the director can be heard on the soundtrack arranging water testing as evidence for future litigation.

Like many of the filmmakers I discuss in this chapter, Michel Zongo is a career documentarist. A workshop at Burkina Faso's CNC led him from a career in the hospitality industry to a job as a cameraman for national television. After more extensive training in France, Zongo shot *Sibi, l'âme du violon* (Sibi, the soul of the violin, 2010) in his hometown of Koudougou. The short subject features his brother, blind musician and griot Sibi Zongo, whose primary instrument is the single-string violin. A performance in a courtyard is followed by interviews with neighborhood residents who have known Sibi since he was a child. Throughout the film, Zongo highlights the contemporary relevance of Sibi's traditional music, most notably in a joint recording session with Burkinabé rap superstar Serge Bambara, better known as Smockey. *Espoir voyage* (Hope-voyage, 2011) was inspired by another of Zongo's brothers, Joanny, who left for Côte d'Ivoire at the age of fourteen, when the director was only five years old. After eighteen years without news, the family was informed of Joanny's death. Following his late brother's path, Zongo records his attempt to understand Joanny's motivations and experiences. His voyage, and particularly the interviews conducted with migrants met along the way, becomes a work exploring the intra-African emigration overshadowed by perilous crossings of the Mediterranean.

In *La sirène de Faso Fani* (The siren of Faso Fani, 2014), Zongo tells the economic, political, and social story of Koudougou's Faso Fani textile factory, established by the government of Upper Volta in the 1970s and supported and promoted by Thomas Sankara's Burkina Faso. Unlike Kalsaka's mining company, Faso Fani sustained its local community, and its closure is shown to have been both a local tragedy and a national embarrassment. More heavily plotted than Zongo's previous documentaries, *La sirène de Faso Fani* begins with voice-over narration in both the first and third persons. Explaining that the siren of the film's title woke factory workers for their morning shift, Zongo acknowledges his personal connection to the story. "I was born and raised in this city," he begins; "The factory was very important during my childhood." He remembers peering through the factory gate to watch workers on their lunch break and dreaming of joining them one day, then shows viewers the same gate in the present; a boy peers at the dilapidated, empty shell of a factory.

Zongo builds his film around a series of interviews with former factory employees, all of whom share the pride they took in working with high-grade machinery and earning salaries that enabled their families to live well. Archival marketing footage proclaims strong consumer demand for a superior product featuring patterns inspired by African culture, whereas contemporary handheld shots of Koudougou's market reveal only cheap cloth made in China. Both interviewees and archival radio broadcasts recount the factory's closure and the protests that attempted to convince the government to change course. To supplement his narrative with details that Blaise Compaoré's regime forbade national stations from announcing at the time, Zongo recorded new radio broadcasts. Simultaneously fictional and factual, present and past, these explain that structural adjustment programs introduced by global financial institutions required the

Michel Zongo, *La sirène de Faso Fani*, 2014.

factory's privatization, in a nation where no private individuals or companies were in a position to take over. To repay its financial backers, the factory was liquidated.

The environmental and social traumas of mining reappear in two films made by young West African women. Amina Weira's *La colère dans le vent* (Anger in the wind, 2016) is centered on her father, who worked at Arlit's Areva mine for thirty-five years.[72] Chloé Aïcha Boro takes a more observational approach in *Le loup d'or de Balolé* (The golden wolf of Balolé, 2019), filming entire families from a poor Ouagadougou neighborhood who work, unofficially, in the pit of the Balolé granite quarry. Safi Faye, Mariama Hima, and Léonie Yangba-Zowe stood alone as sub-Saharan women documentarists in the 1970s and '80s; all three studied in Paris and made ethnographic films, and Faye and Hima worked with Jean Rouch. In the 1990s, however, with more opportunities for training and less expensive filmmaking technology, documentary became a mode of choice for African women filmmakers, so much so that their work has been recognized in two of the very few existing scholarly studies of African documentary cinema.[73]

A turn-of-the-century shift away from ethnography is equally pronounced in the documentary work of African women, the transition evident in the trajectory of director Anne Laure Folly. Originally from Togo, Folly began a career as an international human rights lawyer with UNESCO in 1981. Back for a work assignment, she attended her grandmother's funeral, an experience that led to *Le gardien des forces* (Guardian of the forces, 1992), a comparative reflection on African and

European understandings of death and the supernatural and the first Togolese film. Self-trained and shooting on Betacam video, Folly recorded a Vodun religious ceremony, which the practitioner narrated for the camera. Initiated before witnessing the rites, Folly was careful to avoid any hint of exoticism, using close-ups, for example, to bring spectators in proximity to the people on screen. She considered the final version of the film to be "a reportage on reality with a female sensibility."[74]

Folly's next documentaries, shot across West and central Africa in a variety of languages, share a focus on women. The best known of them, *Femmes aux yeux ouverts* (Women with open eyes, 1993) features women from Burkina Faso, Côte d'Ivoire, Mali, Senegal, and Benin. The film is divided into sections on excision, forced marriage, AIDS, combat, survival, and politics, each combining voice-over narration and interviews. Addressing female genital mutilation, for example, Folly contrasts the testimony of women who have had painful and damaging experiences with that of an elderly woman who performs clitoridectomies. Her presentation of forced marriage similarly reveals both its dire consequences and its cultural functioning. The film concludes on an optimistic note, portraying the strength and potential of African women. Scenes of hard work—cleaning and drying fish, selling gas on the side of the road, repairing cars—culminate with the impact of women's associations in the political realm. And in the wake of the Malian army's attacks on student demonstrators in 1991, Folly documents the women's marches that led to the overthrow of the government.

Folly pursued these themes further in *Femmes du Niger: Entre intégrisme et démocratie* (Women of Niger: Between fundamentalism and democracy, 1993). Nigerien women testify to the effects of forced marriage and polygamy, and, examining how religion is used to keep women out of the political process, the film also shows their successful activism. *Deposez les lames* (Put down the razor blades, 1999) returns to the topic of excision, with an expository commentary detailing the practice supported by lengthy interviews with two Senegalese women who are fighting against it. And to make *Les oubliées* (The forgotten women, 1997), Folly traveled to Angola to speak with female victims of the thirty-year-long civil war, explaining in voice-over narration that she had been inspired by Sarah Maldoror's film *Sambizanga* (1972). In Luanda, Folly stayed with Maldoror's daughter Henda, a moment marked by a brief shot of the two together. The subsequent *Sarah Maldoror ou la nostalgie de l'utopie* (Sarah Maldoror or nostalgia for utopia, 1998) combines clips from Maldoror's films with footage from interviews with Maldoror and her collaborators.

Folly's work has influenced a number of important women directors who opt to focus on stories of women, including one of Senegal's youngest documentarists, Angèle Diabang Brener. After studying law at Cheikh Anta Diop University,

Diabang Brener trained at Samba Félix Ndiaye's Media Center in Dakar. In her first film, the mid-length, interview-based *Sénégalaises et Islam* (Senegalese women and Islam, 2007), a group of women share what prove to be very different relationships with their religion. For *Yande Codou: Le griot de Senghor* (Yande Codou: Senghor's griot, 2008), Diabang Brener entered into a more direct filmic relationship with her elderly subject, who had appeared in Ndiaye's *Lettre à Senghor* ten years prior. Her difficulties working with Yande Codou disappeared once Diabang Brener left her position with the crew to be on camera, she recounted, leading her to reconceive the film as a discussion between them.[75] And *Congo, un medecin pour sauver les femmes* (Congo, a doctor who saves women, 2014) presents the work of Dr. Dennis Mukegwe, founder of a hospital that treats rape victims in Kivu, DRC. Diabang Brener's production company, Karoninka, produces and coproduces her films as well as documentaries by other West African directors.

Senegalese documentarist Katy Léna Ndiaye began her career as a television journalist for France's TV5. Like Folly never formally trained in filmmaking, she has similarly focused on African women's lived experiences. Both *Traces: Empreintes de femmes* (Traces: Imprints of women, 2003) and *En attendant les hommes* (Waiting for the men, 2007) were shot across Senegal's borders, the first in Tiébélé, Burkina Faso, and the second in Oualata, Mauritania, a connection inspired by a book of photographs taken in these towns by Namibian visual artist Margaret Courtney-Clarke.[76] Transforming still into moving images, Ndiaye intercuts interview footage with shots of landscapes in which women live and create. The first of the films centers on the character of Anetina, a single mother who works as a guide to murals women in her town have painted for generations. Also anchored in traditional wall art by women, *En attendant les hommes* tells the stories of Khady, Massouda, and Tycha, grandmothers waiting for their husbands and sons to return home from months of work. Ndiaye's fixed camera grants the spectator time to "meet and understand" her subjects, she asserts, her work not that of an ethnographer but of a documentarist who "recreates the real."[77]

Rosine Mbakam has continued to film Cameroonian women, but her second and third feature-length documentaries are very different from her first. Whereas Mbakam's reflective commentary overlaid and punctuated the recorded conversations of *Les deux visages d'une femme Bamiléké*, her voice is heard almost exclusively in dialogue with the women filmed in *Chez Jolie Coiffure* (2018) and *Les prières de Delphine* (Delphine's prayers, 2021). Mbakam developed personal relationships with Sabine and Delphine, both of whom live in Belgium, and asked them to participate in framing how their stories would be told. Contextualizing this need for collaboration, Mbakam contrasts her work to neocolonial documentaries that deny Africans the freedom to set the terms of their depiction on screen.[78] Moving portrayals of immigrant life in a former colonial metropole, her films have been screened at festivals on three continents, including FESPACO, Cinéma du Réel, True/False, and AFI Docs.

Chez Jolie Coiffure begins in the hallway of an indoor shopping mall in Brussels's Matonge neighborhood, outside the hair salon where Sabine works, but only in these opening images do spectators get an external perspective on the salon. Sweeping up piles of hair, Sabine calls into the hallway, telling Rosine to come in; Mbakam joltingly films her way through the doorway. The rest of the documentary is shot inside, where over the course of a year Mbakam spent extended periods of time watching, listening, and talking to Sabine and her colleagues and clients. Filming, she uses the salon's multiple mirrors to add depth to the small space and reflect the warmth and complexity of the relationships. Thanks to carefully calculated angles, Mbakam and her camera are never visible, and her documentary has no voice-over narration. Her perspective is firmly allied with that of her interlocutors: African women in Europe who discuss life, love, and work; the damage done to Black women's skin by lightening products; the white men who pursue them; and the monthly meetings of Sabine's tontine. The impossible expense of traveling home comes up again and again, and even a client with papers and a good job must ask for donations to send her mother's body back for burial.

Visible through the windows of the salon, groups of white Europeans walk through the mall, touring African Brussels. Referencing the "human zoos" of late nineteenth- and early twentieth-century Europe where the earliest filmed images of Africans were shot, Sabine comments, "Move along, white people. If you go to the zoo, you pay. When we go to your zoos, we pay." When tourists and school groups pass by, Sabine says with a big smile, "Rosine, you need to film them. Film them!" Doing so, Mbakam turns the tables; at the same time as they peer in at the African women they consider exotic foreigners, they themselves are put on display. Although Mbakam does not appear on screen in this film, she regularly converses with her main character from behind the camera. Sabine tells the story of a young woman's emigration odyssey from Cameroon to Lebanon to Belgium in the third person and then again, more intimately, in the first. The experience was so difficult, she says, that she would not do it again. But women who leave Cameroon encourage others to leave, and Lebanese agents pay for their tickets and arrange their employment. "You do it because you want to get to Europe," Sabine concludes, and Mbakam takes over: "And then you get to Europe, and it doesn't stop."

Sabine is undocumented, having tried and failed twice to obtain asylum in Belgium. In the last ten minutes of *Chez Jolie Coiffure*, a commotion in the mall signals a police raid. Sabine turns off the lights and moves off camera while

Mbakam keeps filming the dark salon. Alone, she answers a call from Sabine and, implicating herself directly in the action, asks what to do should the police come in. Recounting the raid the next day, Sabine expresses her frustration with the unending pursuit: "This little Matonge is where we earn a living, and they want to take it away." Mbakam reminds us of the price paid to earn this living as Sabine speaks the last words of the film, responding to a client who asks if she will go home this year. Braiding, Sabine shakes her head, "I don't know."

In *Les prières de Delphine* (Delphine's prayers, 2021), Mbakam goes even farther toward codirection with her film's main character. Before the opening credits, a woman sitting on a bed asks in Cameroonian English if it is time to start. Mbakam, from behind the camera, answers yes, adding in English, "But don't worry, I will do montage, don't worry," continuing that they can pause whenever necessary. The woman on the bed is Delphine; she tells Mbakam where to sit, then begins to tell her story as Mbakam films. Whereas *Chez Jolie Coiffure* is shot in the two rooms of Sabine's hair salon, the ninety minutes of *Les prières de Delphine* take place in a single room of Delphine's apartment, with only two characters present. Mbakam's questions and prompts indicate that she knows Delphine's story and is giving her the chance to retell it on camera, and Delphine herself says that it is her testimony: "Nobody will stop this story from being told." Narrating her life, Delphine is sometimes calm and joking, sometimes angry and almost crying, and almost always smoking a cigarette. Only when she requests a break does the frame change, with shots of a window or pictures on the walls replacing the view of the bed.

Like Haroun at the start of *Hissein Habré*, Mbakam gives her film a reflexive frame, choosing not to cut Delphine's early comments through montage but retaining her promise to do so. She periodically reminds viewers that documentaries, and even documentary interviews, are staged, shot, and edited. These reminders happen neither in voice-over nor through reenactment but in dialogue between Mbakam and Delphine. At one such moment, Delphine asks Mbakam what is in the journal for today, making evident that they have planned a schedule for a sequence of topics. And toward the end of the film, Delphine holds a piece of white paper in front of her face as she and Mbakam discuss balance and background, comparing the color filming of white and Black subjects. Mbakam would return to the theme of white skin as the default for color calibration in *Prism* (2021), a COVID-19 lockdown production made in collaboration with documentarists Eléonore Yaméogo from Burkina Faso and An van Dienderen from Belgium.

Delphine's story starts with her childhood in Douala: her mother dead, her father cruel or absent, and her family poor and hungry. Raped at a young age, she, like her older sister, earned money through prostitution, eventually marrying the Belgian man with whom she came to Brussels. Delphine angrily continues that she does not love her husband, who does not respect her culture or appreciate her intelligence. In a sad and furious prayer for forgiveness, she begs for her life to change. After this emotional turning point, the conversation between Delphine and Mbakam reveals that they have known each other since Mbakam's own arrival in Brussels. In the film's sole voice-over, Mbakam remembers their shared past braiding hair in a salon. Praising Delphine for her courage in speaking the struggles and pain of women, she notes that they would never have met in Cameroon, their friendship possible only in a West that defines them solely as Black and African despite the difference of social class between them. In the film's final images, Mbakam appears on screen as Delphine braids extensions into her hair.

Women documentarists, of course, do not only tell women's stories. In her more recent work, Katy Léna Ndiaye has returned to her journalistic roots. *On a le temps pour nous* (Time is on our side, 2019) follows Burkinabé rapper Smockey in his role as cofounder and leader of the 2014 *Balai citoyen* movement that chased Blaise Compaoré from power. And Ndiaye's breakthrough *L'argent, la liberté, une histoire du franc CFA* (Money, freedom, a story of the CFA Franc, 2022), selected for both the FESPACO and Cinéma du Réel festivals, presents a critical history of the neocolonial West African currency, originally pegged to the French franc and now to the euro. Like Ndiaye, Cameroonian director Osvalde Lewat came to documentary from a background in journalism. Born and raised in Yaoundé, Lewat studied filmmaking first at Montreal's National Institute of Image and Sound (INIS) and then at Paris' La Fémis, formerly the IDHEC. Returning to work for the daily *Cameroon Tribune*, she at the same time began to make politically motivated and formally innovative documentaries. Lewat later returned to Paris to study at the famed Sciences Po in search of better academic preparation to tackle the subjects that interest her.[79]

Lewat's career as a documentarist began with a short subject, *Au-delà de la peine* (The forgotten man, 2002), about Pierre Owono, at the time the oldest prisoner in Cameroon. Sentenced to four years of prison in 1969, Owono's scheduled release was postponed until 2028 because of three escape attempts. With the help of several human rights organizations, and thanks to Lewat's film as well as a legal battle she organized, he was released after thirty-three years behind bars. *Une affaire de nègres* (Black business, 2008), Lewat's first feature-length film, examines the repressive nature of the Cameroonian government via a question posed by Nigerian Nobel Prize winner Wole Soyinka: "They say Africans are not ready for democracy. So, I wonder, have they ever been ready for dictatorship?" After the opening credits, spectators watch a group of people, mostly women, prepare a burial in silence. The grave, we discover, will contain not a body but a leafy branch cut from a nearby tree, the symbolic representation of a young man who disappeared years earlier and is presumed dead. In voice-over commentary, Lewat describes the creation at the turn of the twenty-first century of a special unit called the Commandement Opérationnel, charged with controlling crime. In a single year and mostly in secret, its policemen and soldiers killed over one thousand people. Over the course of many years, Lewat met with families who had lost loved ones; they showed her photographs as well as notes and letters they had received asking for money and medicine. She wanted to forget them but could not, Lewat says in the first person and present tense: "I know that I have no other choice but to make this film."

Although Lewat narrates the film, viewers see her only once, and then only from the back. Since the people she met had been denied the right to speak, she explained, she did not want to take away from their on-screen space.[80] Lewat interviews family members of men killed by the Commandement, legal and political representatives who speak out against its actions, and rare survivors of a jail that prisoners call "Kosovo." In between these recorded discussions, her voice-over expresses the desire to understand their experiences, something she can only do by "trying to imagine." Lewat films crime scenes, the different neighborhoods and villages from which men were taken, a fish market, and the dirt roads where their dead bodies were found. In several of her conversations, the past comes to life. Farmer Richard Nzamyo recounts how he witnessed his son's death, showing exactly where everything happened, pointing here and there with his machete. And in an astounding performance, former member of the Commandement Rigobert Kouyang describes his work in detail, holding a stick like a gun and making shooting noises as he remembers killing prisoners. Describing her horror at this unprompted reenactment, Lewat recalled that, when editing the film, she had to decide whether to keep the footage. The example of Rithy Panh's *S21* (2003), in which a Khmer Rouge torturer repeats his own past gestures, convinced her to do so.[81]

Tcheuyap argues that the close-ups of living bodies in *Une affaire de nègres* accentuate their fragility and future decomposition in a corrupt Cameroon that matches Achille Mbembe's postcolony.[82] This was a dangerous film to make, and Lewat had to convince families to speak with her on camera. Journalist Séverin Tchounkeu testifies to the role of the Cameroonian press in revealing the extent of the Commandement's crimes. But he and other interviewees equally stress the contemporary relevance of this tragic piece of recent history, since the Cameroonian government continues to keep its citizens in a state of fear. Lawyer Jean de Dieu Momo wonders aloud who can comprehend a country in which policemen can kill without ever appearing in court, giving the film its title: "In Europe, do people understand what I am saying? . . . As long as it's Black business, Negro business, people don't care." And it is with Cameroon's political future that Lewat ends her film, interspersing the closing credits with the responses of passers-by to the question of whether they would be for or against the reestablishment of the Commandement. Almost all answer that they would support it, shocking viewers who have endured what Lewat has shown us. The very last reaction and the film's last words are "never again."

From Jean-Marie Teno to Rosine Mbakam and Osvalde Lewat, Cameroon is the central African country most associated with documentary filmmaking. In West Africa, it is Senegal, the homeland of Paulin Soumanou Vieyra, Samba Félix Ndiaye, Katy Léna Ndiaye, and others I have not had the space to discuss here, including Moussa Touré, Alassane Diago, and Cheikh Ndiaye. To begin to conclude this chapter, which is both far too long and not nearly long enough, I therefore turn to the work of two documentarists with long careers who, unlike the directors in exile with whom I began, have remained locally based. After making a series of fiction films, Joseph Gaï Ramaka returned to documentary with *Et si Latif avait raison!* (And if Latif was right!, 2006), a self-financed activist intervention rushed to an unofficial release in the run-up to the 2006 elections. President Abdoulaye Wade had jailed his former prime minister and opponent Idrissa Seck in what would prove a preview of his 2008 push to amend the constitution and run for a third term. Ramaka based his film on a book by journalist Abdou Latif Coulibaly, who had investigated Wade's connection to the 1993 murder of Babacar Seye, at the time president of Senegal's Constitutional Council. *Et si Latif avait raison!* has a double dedication: to Seye and to the victims of the sinking of the Joola ferry, another tragedy connected to Wade's presidency.

An unidentified voice-over narrator opens the film, asking, with a question mark that is not in the title, "What if Latif was right?" and answering that he will investigate the desire for power. A black-and-white reenactment of Seye's murder follows, accompanied by a voice-over reading of a confession that implicates Wade. A cut to color footage then shows a figure who reappears periodically throughout the film—smoking, reflecting on the case, and asking rhetorical questions. Like the so-called witnesses who indirectly answer these questions, he is positioned in front of a screen onto which are projected large-scale images and newsreel footage of the relevant political actors. Unlike the smoking figure, the witnesses in Ramaka's filmic trial are identified by their names and roles in Senegalese civil and political society. They describe and analyze the events in question, not just the murder of Seye but the whole of Abdoulaye Wade's first campaign and subsequent presidency, considering the

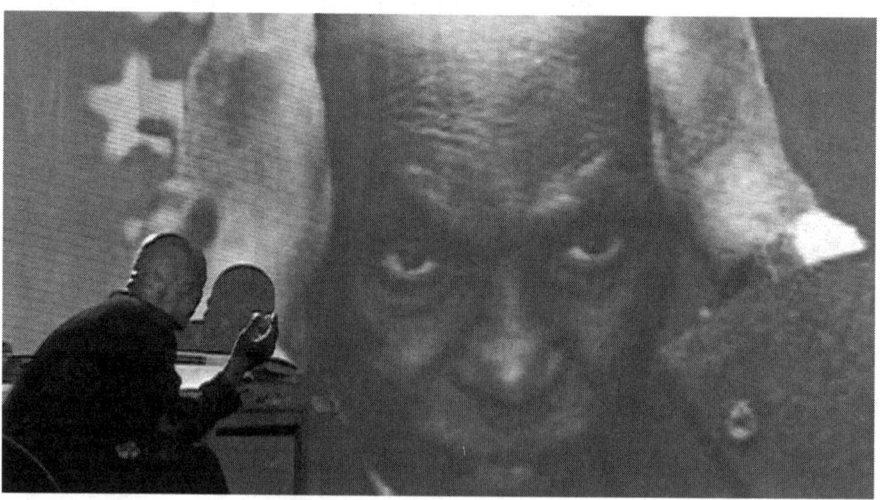

Joseph Gaï Ramaka, *Et si Latif avait raison!*, 2006.

longer history of Senegalese politics going back to inaugural president Léopold Sédar Senghor.

Like Lewat's *Une affaire de nègres*, *Et si Latif avait raison!* was dangerous to make, and the final credits indicate that some crew members wished to remain anonymous. Ramaka emphasized that his role in the enterprise was that of filmmaker, not witness or judge, by which he meant the organizer of testimony into a coherent argument.[83] Led by witness testimony to pursue his story beyond the investigation of Seye's murder, Ramaka includes digital video footage of mass street protests against Wade, joining Katy Léna Ndiaye's *On a le temps pour nous* and a constellation of activist media linked to *Balai citoyen* in Burkina Faso and partner social movement *Y en a marre* in Senegal.[84] He continued his documentary work with *Plan Jaxaay* (2009), a short film exposing the failures of the Wade government's plan to address flooding in a suburban neighborhood of Dakar. Senegalese director Rama Thiaw began her career as a documentarist with *Boul fallé* (2009), about the youth movement of the film's title, whose members bring together hip hop music and traditional wrestling. In *The Revolution Will Not Be Televised* (2016), Thiaw follows the three members of rap group Kër Gui to explore their artistic and political activism within *Y en a marre*, which built opposition to Wade toward the end of his second term.[85]

Like Ramaka, Ousmane William Mbaye was born in the decade prior to independence. The son of Senegalese journalist Annette d'Erneville Mbaye, founder of the Dakar Cinematographic Conference (RECIDAK) and the magazine *Ciné*

Culture Afrique, he studied filmmaking at the University of Paris VII. Inspired by both his mother and Samba Félix Ndiaye, whom he met in Paris, Mbaye made a short film after returning to Senegal and in 1981 joined L'Oeil Vert. Over the course of the decade, he was a crew member for documentaries made by Bathily, Ba, Ramaka, and others. Mbaye's own career as a documentarist began in the twenty-first century, with several films commissioned by Ndiaye's Almadies Films and two cultural documentaries, *Xalima la plume* (Xalima the quill, 2003) and *Fer et verre* (Iron and glass, 2005), about a Senegalese musician and artist, respectively.

Like many other directors I have discussed in this concluding chapter, Mbaye has described his documentary work as grounded in dialogue: "I want to show that I have a bond with the character."[86] He chose characters from among important figures in Senegalese history, starting with a biographical portrait of his mother in *Mère bi* (The mother, 2008). D'Erneville Mbaye's position in cultural and independence circles in Paris and then governing circles in Dakar makes the film not just biographical but historical and political, with a transnational scope. Her family history goes back, D'Erneville Mbaye explains in an interview illustrated by documents and photographs, to an ancestor named Charles Jean-Baptiste d'Erneville from Maubuisson, France, who arrived in West Africa in the eighteenth century. Her description of the stages of her illustrious career is similarly enriched by archival sources, in this case clips from Senegalese radio and television programs. Mbaye's parents together recount the 1962 conflict between Léopold Sédar Senghor and Mamadou Dia, during which Senghor had Dia, Valdiodio Ndiaye, and Mbaye's uncle Joseph Mbaye arrested and sentenced to twenty years in prison. This political crisis of early independence is the focus of Mbaye's second feature-length documentary, *Président Dia* (2012), in which the director remembers in a personal voice-over his childhood confusion about the course of events. To clarify the story for himself and his future spectators, Mbaye again excerpts radio broadcasts and video footage, which are narrated in voice-over by Dia and intercut with interviews with D'Erneville Mbaye, author and former minister Cheikh Hamidou Kane, former president of Senegal Abdou Diouf, and others.

In *Kemtiyu: Séex Anta* (Black lands: Cheikh Anta, 2016), Mbaye turns to the biography of a towering figure of Senegalese intellectual history, philosopher Cheikh Anta Diop, with whom he also has a family connection. The film takes him from Dakar to Paris to Atlanta and back to Dakar, seeking again to join archival evidence to contemporary interviews. In Paris, where Diop spent the fourteen years prior to independence, Mbaye speaks with Christiane Diop, wife of *Présence Africaine* founder Alioune Diop, who first published

Diop's *Nations nègres et culture* (The African origin of civilization, 1954). He also discusses Diop's controversial conclusions about the Blackness of ancient Egyptians with French historians and Egyptologists. To acknowledge Diop's insistence on the use of African rather than colonial languages, Mbaye used the Wolof spelling of *Cheikh* in his film's title and released versions subtitled in Wolof and dubbed in Swahili. In testimony to Diop's global impact, Mbaye includes footage from an interview with Atlanta mayor Andrew Young, who arranged for Diop to receive an honorary degree from Georgia's Morehouse College in 1985. Calling for similar recognition within Senegal, *Kemtiyu: Séex Anta* concludes with a montage of pleas that Diop's work be included in school curricula in his native country.[87]

I have already listed several Senegalese filmmakers whose work is missing here, and other sub-Saharan African documentarists would be featured were this final chapter an entire book: Burkina Faso's Eléonore Yaméogo, Côte d'Ivoire's Idriss Diabaté and Joël Akafou, Niger's Rahmatou Keïta and Aïcha Macky, and the Central African Republic's Rafiki Fariala, to name a few of the most interesting and prolific. David-Pierre Fila from the Republic of the Congo, who reads a letter about African cinema in Mahamat-Saleh Haroun's *Bye Bye Africa*, is also on this list. Fila's work spans four decades of the exciting story of African documentary cinema; trained in anthropology in France and filmmaking in the Soviet Union, he began his career in the 1980s with ethnographic shorts, retaining aspects of ethnography in his work through the early '90s. *Le dernier des Babingas* (The last of the Babinga, 1990) was shot in the Central African Republic, south of Bangui, its voice-over narration shared between Fila and Mangala, a member of the Babinga ethnic group that Léon Poirier found so repugnant and Jacques Dupont so fascinating.

Fila has made over a dozen nonfiction films since *Le dernier des Babingas*, with recent topics ranging from the logging of the equatorial forest in *Territoires* (Territories, 2011); to biographical portraits of musician and griot Casimir Zoba and filmmaker Mweze Ngangura in *Zao* (2009) and *Mweze* (2020); to transnational histories of Cuban music and Congolese fashion in *Sur les chemins de la rumba* (Following the routes of rumba, 2014) and *Le sapeur* (2019). Born in the Central African Republic the year that Fila made his first film, Elvis Sabin Ngaïbino brought the story of threatened Babinga traditions into the twenty-first century with *Makongo* (Caterpillars, 2020). Focusing on the transformative effect not of logging but of schooling, the film also shows the contempt in which Aka people are held not by the French but by contemporary residents of Bangui, the city where they sell the caterpillars they harvest and roast in the forest. The pessimism of Fila and Ngaïbino is warranted, yet

Thierno Souleymane Diallo, *Au cimetière de la pellicule*, 2023.

Ngaïbino's deliberate and innovative filmmaking assures the forward trajectory of African documentary. His work has continued with *Le fardeau* (The burden, 2023), which addresses the consequences of church-based taboos around AIDS through the story of Ngaïbino's cousin and his wife. Like Samba Félix Ndiaye a generation earlier, Ngaïbino has established a local ciné-club with a group of fellow fans as well as his own production company.

If Ngaïbino joins a circle opened by Fila, Guinean filmmaker Thierno Souleymane Diallo links the present of sub-Saharan African documentary to the very origins of sub-Saharan African cinema, his story of a loss at the heart of African film history a vibrant contribution to its future. On screen in *Au cimetière de la pellicule* (The cemetery of cinema, 2023), Diallo travels around his home country and as far as France in search of Mamadou Touré's *Mouramani*, the mythic, missing African film that predates Paulin Vieyra's *Afrique sur Seine*. In the same year and exactly twenty years after the Côté Doc, the 2023 edition of FESPACO saw the creation of Doc Day, cofounded by Michel Zongo's Koudougou Doc, Jean-Marie Teno's Bandjoun Film Studio, and Docmonde, organizations based in Burkina Faso, Cameroon, and France. Offering master classes and the opportunity to network with filmmakers, producers, sponsors, exhibitors, and streaming platforms, the program suggests that Ngaïbino, Diallo, and their current and future colleagues will have support for their careers, while festivals like Koudougou Doc work to foster what Zongo calls the "documentary cinephilia" of African spectators.[88]

Notes

1. Kolla Maiga, "Issaka Konate," 13–14.

2. Samba Félix Ndiaye, "L'Afrique et le documentaire," *Le film africain*, no. 3 (1991): 7.

3. Haffner, "'Dites simplement la vérité.'"

4. Jean-Pierre Garcia, "Rencontre avec Samba Félix Ndiaye, réalisateur," *Le film africain & Le film du sud*, nos. 35–36 (2001): 90.

5. Aboubacar Demba Cissokho, "Samba Félix Ndiaye: 'Dites simplement la vérité,'" *Senciné*, no. 3 (2015): 68.

6. Mikhail Bakhtin, *Problems of Dostoevsky's Poetics*, trans. Caryl Emerson (University of Minnesota Press, 1984), 110. On rethinkings of ethnography influenced by Bakhtin's concepts of heteroglossia and dialogism, see Christopher Miller, *Theories of Africans: Francophone Literature and Anthropology in Africa* (University of Chicago Press, 1990), 25–29.

7. Tcheuyap, *Postnationalist African Cinemas*, 30.

8. La Guilde, "Pour un nouveau cinéma africain," in *Afriques 50: Singularités d'un cinéma pluriel*, ed. Catherine Ruelle (L'Harmattan, 2005), 269–70.

9. Kobena Mercer, *Welcome to the Jungle: New Positions in Black Cultural Studies* (Routledge, 1994), 65.

10. Pfaff, *À l'écoute du cinéma sénégalais*, 167.

11. Diop, "Il est parti Mister Doc . . . ."

12. Garcia, "Rencontre avec Samba Félix Ndiaye, réalisateur," 90.

13. Pfaff, *À l'écoute du cinéma sénégalais*, 169.

14. Teno, "Writing on Walls," 89–90.

15. For a discussion of Teno's films as analyses of postcolonial Cameroonian society and history, see Patrice Nganang, "Deconstructing Authority in Cinema: Jean-Marie Teno," in *Cinema and Social Discourse in Cameroon*, ed. Alexie Tcheuyap (Thielmann and Breitinger, 2005), 139–56.

16. Melissa Thackway and Jean-Marie Teno, *Reel Resistance: The Cinema of Jean-Marie Teno* (James Currey, 2020), 57.

17. Kenneth Harrow, *Postcolonial African Cinema: From Political Engagement to Postmodernism* (Indiana University Press, 2007), 79–80.

18. Jean-Marie Teno with Jonathan Nossiter, "I Want to Retrace My Steps," in *Through African Eyes: Dialogues with the Directors* (African Film Festival, 2003), 58.

19. Melissa Thackway, "Filmer le réel: Une conversation avec Jean-Marie Teno," in *Figuration et mémoire dans les cinémas africains*, ed. Jean Ouédraogo (L'Harmattan, 2010), 133.

20. Ukadike, "African Cinematic Reality," 88–96. For an extended analysis of *Allah Tantou*, see Rachel Gabara, *From Split to Screened Selves: French and Francophone Autobiography in the Third Person* (Stanford University Press, 2006), 132–42.

21. Pat Aufderheide, "Memory and History in Subsaharan African Cinema: An Interview with David Achkar," *Visual Anthropology Review* 9, no. 2 (1993): 112.

22. Jay Leyda, *Films Beget Films: A Study of the Compilation Film* (Hill and Wang, 1964), 30–31.

23. Jay Ruby, "The Image Mirrored: Reflexivity and the Documentary Film," in *New Challenges for Documentary*, ed. Alan Rosenthal (University of California Press, 1988), 75.

24. Nichols, *Representing Reality*, 56–57.

25. Michael Renov, *The Subject of Documentary* (University of Minnesota Press, 2004), 69; Timothy Corrigan, *The Essay Film: From Montaigne, After Marker* (Oxford University Press, 2011). Corrigan, who also begins with Montaigne, makes the case for Soviet montage and French New Wave films as the precursors of an eclectic selection of contemporary works in which subjectivity is shifting and multiple.

26. Nora Alter, "Translating the Essay into Film and Installation," *Visual Culture* 6, no. 1 (2007): 44.

27. "Lecture du palmarès du Grand Prix FESPACO 87," *Présence Africaine*, no. 143 (1987): 196.

28. For a strong critique of *Reassemblage*'s approach to West Africa, see Ukadike, *Black African Cinema*, 54–56, and for a critique of this critique, Steven Zacks, "A Problematic Sign of African Difference in Trinh T. Minh-Ha's *Reassemblage*," in *African Cinema: Post-colonial and Feminist Readings*, ed. Kenneth Harrow (Africa World Press, 1999), 75–87.

29. Russell, *Experimental Ethnography*. The same is true of Laura Rascaroli's *The Personal Camera: Subjective Cinema and the Essay Film* (Wallflower Press, 2009) and *How the Essay Film Thinks* (Oxford University Press, 2017), the latter of which reads the African "ethnolandscape" of Werner Herzog's *Fata Morgana*, shot in the late 1960s during travels through a half-dozen African countries (82–83).

30. Hamid Naficy, *An Accented Cinema: Exilic and Diasporic Filmmaking* (Princeton University Press, 2001).

31. Brenda Hollweg and Igor Krstić, eds., *World Cinema and the Essay Film: Transnational Perspectives on a Global Practice* (Edinburgh University Press, 2019), 138–55.

32. Tobing Rony, *Third Eye*, 7.

33. Ilham Lamouri, "'Toute la notion de développement reste pour moi une fumisterie': Jean-Marie Teno," *Ciné-Bulles* 18, no. 4 (2000): 22.

34. Samba Félix Ndiaye, "Le documentaire pour témoigner de l'Afrique," *Ecrans d'Afrique*, no. 16 (1996): 56.

35. Thackway, *Africa Shoots Back*, 97; Jude Akudinobi, "Reco(r)ding Reality: Representation and Paradigms in Nonfiction African Cinema," *Social Identities* 6, no. 3 (2000): 347. See also Tcheuyap, *African Documentary Cinema*, 164–70.

36. Thackway, *Africa Shoots Back*, 109.

37. Didier Coureau, "*Asientos* (1995) de François L. Woukoache," *Recherches et travaux*, no. 84 (2014): 202.

38. Olivier Barlet, "Entretien avec François Woukoache," *Africultures*, 1997, http://africultures.com/entretien-dolivier-barlet-avec-francois-woukoache-306/.

39. Barlet, "Entretien avec François Woukoache."

40. Frodon, *Le cinéma à l'épreuve du divers*, 165–67.

41. Private conversation with Annouchka de Andrade, daughter of Sarah Maldoror. Russell addresses Marker's essentializing of Japanese and African cultural otherness by asserting the film's modernism, arguing that it also explains his gendered gaze. Russell, *Experimental Ethnography*, 301–2.

42. Tcheuyap places *Lettre à Senghor* in a category of African "biodocumentaries," which includes twenty-first-century documentaries made by both European and African directors. Tcheuyap, *African Documentary Cinema*, 39–71.

43. Diop, "Il est parti Mister Doc . . . ."

44. Olivier Barlet, "À propos de *La vie sur terre*: Entretien avec Abderrahmane Sissako," *Africultures*, 1998, http://www.africultures.com/php/index.php?nav=article&no=469.

45. Alessandra Speciale, "Abderrahmane Sissako: Pour l'amour du hasard, il faut partir," *Ecrans d'Afrique*, no. 23 (1998): 29. For an extended discussion of authorship in Sissako's oeuvre, see Rachel Gabara, "Abderrahmane Sissako: On the Politics of African Auteurs," in *The Global Auteur: The Politics of Authorship in 21st Century Cinema*, ed. Seung-hoon Jeong and Jeremi Szaniawski (Bloomsbury Publishing, 2016), 43–60.

46. "Entretien avec Abderrahmane Sissako," *Le film africain*, no. 28 (1998): 2.

47. Olivier Barlet, "Une relation d'amour avec le spectateur: Entretien avec Mahamat Saleh Haroun," *Africultures*, no. 45 (2002): 22.

48. Olivier Barlet, "'Plus l'Afrique est oubliée, plus il faut la ramener au souvenir du monde,'" *Africultures*, 2010, http://www.africultures.com/php/index.php?nav=article&no=9501.

49. A. O. Scott, "Taking What You Need to Refresh," in *Through African Eyes*, 90.

50. Erwan Higuinen, "Rencontre/Mahamat-Saleh Haroun," *Cahiers du cinéma*, no. 577 (2003): 85; Vincent Malausa, "Un cinéaste tchadien: Entretien avec Mahamat-Saleh Haroun," *Cahiers du cinéma*, no. 660 (2010): 45.

51. See Yifen Beus, "Authorship and Criticism in Self-Reflexive African Cinema," *Journal of African Cultural Studies* 23, no. 2 (2011): 142.

52. Harrow, *Postcolonial African Cinema*, 77.

53. Thackway and Teno, *Reel Resistance*, 63.

54. Manthia Diawara, *African Film: New Forms of Aesthetics and Politics* (Prestel, 2010), 100.

55. Naficy, *An Accented Cinema*, 11. See also Manthia Diawara, "The 'I' Narrator in Black Diaspora Documentary," in *Struggles for Representation: African American Documentary Film and Video*, ed. Phyllis R. Klotman and Janet K. Cutler (Indiana University Press, 1999), 315–28.

56. Lindiwe Dovey, "Subjects of Exile: Alienation in Francophone West African Cinema," *International Journal of Francophone Studies* 12, no. 1 (2009): 58.

57. Akin Adesokan, "Abderrahmane Sissako and the Poetics of Engaged Expatriation," *Screen* 51, no. 2 (2010): 143–60.

58. "Le Côté Doc du FESPACO: Le programme," 2003.

59. For more information on this program and the work of its graduates, see Gora Seck, "Les défis d'une génération de cinéastes documentaristes," in *Dix films d'Afrique*, ed. François Fronty (L'Harmattan, 2019), 159–76.

60. Nichols, *Representing Reality*, 44. Nichols a decade later renamed this interactive mode the *participatory mode* of documentary, its directorial intervention sometimes off and sometimes on camera. Nichols, *Introduction to Documentary*, 115–23.

61. Imbert, *Samba Félix Ndiaye*, 304.

62. Pfaff, *À l'écoute du cinéma sénégalais*, 173.

63. Olivier Barlet, "Il faut oublier les sunlights: Entretien avec François Woukoache," *Africultures*, no. 45 (2002): 13–14.

64. Imbert, *Samba Félix Ndiaye*, 295.

65. Thackway and Teno, *Reel Resistance*, 146.

66. "Le mariage d'Alex," *Le film africain & Le film du sud*, no. 43 (2003): 46.

67. Thackway and Teno, *Reel Resistance*, 77.

68. Thackway and Teno, *Reel Resistance*, 61.

69. Olivier Barlet, "Un témoignage plus large que prévu: Entretien avec Idrissou Mora Kpai," *Africultures*, 2005, http://africultures.com/un-temoignage-plus-large-que-prevu-3708/.

70. Sheila Petty argues that connections between scenes are built via landscape shots in "*Sacred Places* and *Arlit: Deuxième Paris*: Reterritorialization in African Documentary," *Nka, Journal of Contemporary African Art*, no. 32 (2013): 75.

71. Cajetan Iheka, *African Ecomedia: Network Form, Planetary Politics* (Duke University Press, 2021), 142. Moussa Sow similarly reads Ndiaye's *Trésors des poubelles* and *Ngor* through the lens of ecocinema in "Ecocinema in Senegalese Documentary Film," *Journal of African Cinemas* 5, no. 1 (2013): 3–17. For a reading of Mora-Kpai's film as a chronicle of the "slow violence" of uranium mining, see Carmela Garritano, "Waiting on the Past: African Uranium Futures in *Arlit, Deuxième Paris*," *Modern Fiction Studies* 66, no. 1 (2020): 122–40.

72. Weira describes making the film in Sada Niang, "*La colère dans le vent*: Entretien avec Amina Weira," *International Journal of Francophone Studies* 23, nos. 3–4 (2020): 309–12.

73. See Sonia Lee and Irène Assiba d'Almeida, *Essais et documentaires des africaines francophones* (L'Harmattan, 2015); Crosta, Niang, and Tcheuyap, eds., *Francophone African Women Documentary Filmmakers*.

74. Olivier Barlet, "'Quel est le regard d'une femme cinéaste?,'" *Africultures*, 1997, http://africultures.com/quel-est-le-regard-dune-femme-cineaste/; C. T., "Nouveaux visages: Anne Laure Folly," *Écrans d'Afrique* 1, no. 2 (1992): 36.

75. Daniela Ricci and Thierno Ibrahima Dia, "Angèle Diabang: L'art du montage et l'écriture documentaire pour dire sa vision du monde," in *Regards sur les migrations: Mobilités africaines entre écrit et écran*, ed. Véronique Corinus and Daniela Ricci (L'Harmattan, 2021), 90–91. For an overview of Diabang Brener's oeuvre, see

Daniela Ricci, "La voix des femmes dans les documentaires d'Angèle Diabang," *Nouvelles Études Francophones* 33, no. 1 (2018): 73–87.

76. Albertine Fox, "Collaborative Listening, Collaborative Pedagogy," *Screen-Worlds*, 2022, https://screenworlds.org/publications/collaborative-listening -collaborative-pedagogy/.

77. Albertine Fox, "Voir et écouter autrement: Un échange avec la cinéaste documentariste, Katy Léna Ndiaye," *ScreenWorlds*, 2022, https://screenworlds.org /publications/voir-et-ecouter-autrement-un-echange-avec-la-cineaste -documentariste-katy-lena-ndiaye/.

78. Yasmina Price, "Unfinished Stories: A Conversation with Rosine Mbakam," Criterion, 2022, https://www.criterion.com/current/posts/7735-unfinished -stories-a-conversation-with-rosine-mbakam.

79. Aurélien Bodinaux, "Three-Ring Cinema Verité," in *Through African Eyes*, 2:114. For a lengthy interview with Lewat, see Michelle Chilcoat and Cheikh Ndiaye, "Entretien avec Osvalde Lewat-Hallade, jeune réalisatrice d'origine camerounaise," *French Review* 83, no. 2 (2009): 388–96.

80. "Entretien avec Osvalde Lewat," *Une affaire de nègres*, Les Films du Paradoxe.

81. Assiba d'Almeida and Lee, *Essais et documentaires des africaines francophones*, 97. Haroun's *Hissein Habré* and Lewat's *Une affaire de nègres* share aspects of what Raya Morag, in a study of Cambodian documentary that relies on Panh's work, calls "perpetrator cinema." Raya Morag, *Perpetrator Cinema: Confronting Genocide in Cambodian Documentary* (Wallflower Press, 2020).

82. Alexie Tcheuyap, "Cinéma documentaire et expériences féminines en Afrique francophone," *French Forum* 35, nos. 2–3 (2010): 72–73.

83. Pfaff, *À l'écoute du cinéma sénégalais*, 140.

84. For an overview of the media production associated with these movements, see Carina Yervasi, "Youth and *Média-engagé*: Is This West Africa's Heterolinguistic Cinéma-monde?," in *Cinéma-monde: Decentred Perspectives on Global Filmmaking in French*, ed. Michael Gott and Thibaut Schilt (Edinburgh University Press, 2018), 304–20.

85. For a reading of Thiaw's second film in the context of Senegalese film history, see Sada Niang, "Looping the Loop: Rama Thiaw's *The Revolution Won't Be Televised*," in Crosta, Niang, and Tcheuyap, *Francophone African Women Documentary Filmmakers*, 161–74.

86. Pfaff, *À l'écoute du cinéma sénégalais*, 152.

87. See Sheila Petty, "Unsilencing History: Reclaiming African Cultural Heritage in *Kemtiyu-Séex Anta*," *Black Camera* 9, no. 2 (2018): 414–26.

88. Pélagie Ng'onana, "Michel Zongo: 'Créer un public cinéphile documentaire,'" *Africiné*, 2024, http://www.africine.org/entretien/michel-zongo-creer-un -public-cinephile-documentaire/16115.

CONCLUSION

Each half of *Documentary Objectives* has its own set of theses, which come together to form a film historical narrative spanning two continents and over a hundred years. As a whole, the book relies on a capacious understanding of documentary to include works that are European and African, canonical and noncanonical, familiar and forgotten. The French colonial documentary tradition of films shot in sub-Saharan Africa elaborated here is likely more familiar to readers than the sub-Saharan African documentary film tradition that began with independence, and even a bit before. My goal has been to enrich and connect existing scholarship of the former while helping to develop a scholarship of the latter—identifying, contextualizing, and interpreting nonfiction films in a number of modes and across decades. Doing so, it becomes evident that African documentary cinema exists, with its own historical trajectory and aesthetic, social, and political concerns. This corpus established, it can be recognized alongside others from around the world, both dominant and younger industries.

Within the broader field of global cinema studies, the range of forms and styles of film I examine is consistent with Bill Nichols's widely accepted taxonomy of documentary. I have used Nichols's simultaneously structured and elastic framework only loosely, however; it was fashioned without African case studies, and classification is not my primary interest. Given the long-standing exclusion of African cinema from documentary studies, I have refrained from relying on field-defined geographical boundaries and historical periodization. And given the nature of my project, I have also refrained from comparative analyses with other regional traditions, be they European, North or South American, East or South Asian. This work needs to be done, but my aim has been the establishment of an underrecognized tradition on its own terms.

Writing this critical history of a mode of filmmaking in distinct spaces, I have used the word *postcolonial* in its simplest sense of after political independence, but I have not yet invoked the term *decolonial* or the correlated concept of *decolonization*. If sometimes too easily deployed, both illuminate the enormity of the task undertaken by African documentarists, especially considering that the first discussions of decoloniality within Latin American studies note its inseparability from coloniality. Literary scholar Walter Mignolo, having summarized both Anibal Quijano's and his own earlier work on the topic, describes decolonial thinking as "a relentless analytic effort to understand, in order to overcome, the logic of coloniality underneath the rhetoric of modernity."[1] If not a perfect analogy for the situation of African filmmakers and spectators and scholars of their work, a fuller understanding of French documentary—an analysis of colonial logic within a certain model of nonfiction—enables a fuller appreciation of sub-Saharan African documentary's decolonial project, from its anticolonial to independent but neocolonial contexts.

At the same time, philosopher Achille Mbembe's assertion that "colonialism rhymes with monolingualism" helps us understand why a dialogic and multivocal approach has been crucial to decolonizing documentary. Mbembe continues, citing both Ngugi wa Thiong'o and W. E. B. Dubois, that an Africa-based project of decolonization must have a global scope, extending beyond any single nation or even continent. For the future of the South African university, the subject of Mbembe's 2016 essay, this means creating "new diasporic intellectual networks," strengthening "new spaces of transnational engagement," and developing "our understanding of our own situatedness in Africa and the world."[2] For documentarists, it has meant filming one's place in Africa from a position rooted in local cultural, historical, and political knowledge while also reaching outward, toward other African spaces and those beyond Africa.

I noted in the opening pages of this book that it originated with what became its final chapter, contemporary sub-Saharan African documentary film. In 2003, I had the privilege of attending the Côté Doc organized at FESPACO by the African Guild of Directors and Producers, an experience that inspired my project. Having followed a film historical thread from colonial beginnings to postcolonial present via a heritage that has impelled nonfiction filmmakers to interrogate and transform the content and form of documentary, what next? To whom is this narrative useful, and how? How can the connections it draws contribute to the decolonization not just of the academic field of documentary studies but also of documentary films themselves?

The inaccessibility of most of the films discussed here, particularly those in the first five of the book's six chapters, made the project difficult to accomplish. The French colonial documentaries that remain are for the most part held by governmental media archives such as the INA and the CNC, scientific archives like the CNRS, and the ECPAD army archive, as well as by private image archives, primarily Gaumont Pathé. Access to these often embarrassing relics is restricted and extremely difficult to obtain, and one might wonder who would want to watch such productions, which manage to be simultaneously boring and painful. Over time, and perhaps surprisingly, the answer to this question has included both African intellectuals and African filmmakers. Alice Gallois discovered in the archives of Jean Rouch's Committee for Ethnographic Film that a group of Africans had attended its screenings in the 1950s. The minutes of the committee's governing board note that, as a result, postscreening discussions were not just about ethnography but also about "the essential problem of the context of the contacts between colonized and colonizers."[3] And director Abderrahmane Sissako a generation later acknowledged the importance of a retrospective of colonial films organized by FESPACO in 1995 on the occasion of the centenary of cinema. Although he knew that these films existed, seeing how Africa had been filmed—seeing, Sissako explained, the expression of a Babinga man who did not understand what it meant to be filmed—led him to the realization that "there are different ways of violating people . . . and the images are there to prove this permanent violation."[4]

Writing about his work preparing voice-over commentary for a feature-length documentary about World War I, historian Marc Ferro described the importance of archival film footage, but he was also attentive to the dilemmas created by the incompleteness of archives.[5] This "documentation problem," in Ferro's words, refers both to the loss of footage that was once available and the absence of footage that was never shot. Scholars and filmmakers seeking to discover or author an African perspective on the colonial period are confronted by incompleteness on both fronts, since colonial Europe—France even more so than Belgium and Great Britain—was determined to keep cameras out of the hands of Africans. The French archive is therefore of vital interest to documentarists who, beyond gaining a greater understanding of colonialism's many impacts, may wish to use images from colonial films to make independent anticolonial and decolonial films.

However labyrinthine the required procedures, access to archival images, whether publicly or privately held, does not guarantee the right to use them. The

CNRS provides free online access to watermarked versions of ethnographic films shot in Africa before independence but charges 450 euros for five-year rights to thirty seconds of footage for a French television documentary. For ten-year worldwide theater and video-on-demand rights, those thirty seconds cost 1,500 euros for a documentary film and 3,000 euros for a feature fiction. The INA has an even more complex fee chart, charging extra to include the soundtrack to newsreel footage from its collections. Gaumont Pathé restricts online access even to watermarked, low-resolution versions of its holdings to moving image professionals who might pay for the right to use them, then charges 3,000 euros per minute of footage for ten-year worldwide TV rights, plus an additional 700 euros per minute for streaming or DVD releases. It is prohibitively expensive for African directors to acquire and use archival material shot on their home continent. And it is bitterly ironic that they are asked to pay a premium for worldwide rights to include footage in a film to be shown in this home continent, a premium most often paid to an organ of the colonial power that exploited their lands and people.[6]

In the French mediascape, on the other hand, it is easier to reuse images from once popular colonial films, with no need to pay for worldwide rights and little attention given to the perspective of the source. In 2013, sixty years after the completion of *Les statues meurent aussi*, national television station France 3's popular science series *C'est pas sorcier* (It's not rocket science) broadcast an episode about central African "Pygmies" that staged an arrival in the equatorial forest very similar to that of Jacques Dupont and his crew. To do so, the show included archival footage from Georges Manue's 1941 *Français, vous avez un empire* in the same way Marker and Resnais had reused Dupont's footage, as if an objective recording and with no commentary on its age, origin, or colonialist status. The shooting of film, as we have amply seen, was an extractive enterprise of images instead of coffee, gold, or palm oil, and European archives and media structures continue to profit from it. Black British installation artist and filmmaker Isaac Julien, who only uses colonial archival footage without its authoritative voice-over, also employs what he calls "deconstructive approaches" like slowing down and refocusing images.[7] But only filmmakers with an international profile and production funding from European and North American companies and governmental agencies can afford to pay high fees to use such material against the grain, as Rithy Panh was able to do in his experimental and reflective *La France est notre patrie* (France is our fatherland, 2018).

The African Film Library in Ouagadougou, associated with FESPACO, held as of 2020 a collection of twenty colonial films because, according to an institutional statement, "the films of this period . . . are the only images of Africa in the first half of the twentieth century."[8] As we saw in the first half of this book, this is but a tiny fraction of the many hundreds of films shot by European and North American cameramen and directors in colonized sub-Saharan Africa. These twenty films, moreover, are available only for consultation, not for reproduction, reediting, or redistribution. The question I am approaching, of course, is that of restitution, one that was publicly and comprehensively addressed in Felwine Sarr's and Bénédicte Savoy's commissioned report to French president Emmanuel Macron, released the same year as Panh's film. The report for the most part focuses on objects belonging to an "African cultural heritage" held in museums and other art and ethnographic collections. Sarr and Savoy also assert, however, that archival materials such as sound recordings, photographs, and documentary films constitute a crucial "source of memory" for African nations. They call for the "digital sharing" of colonial photographs and films—not only free access but also free use.[9]

With still and moving images liberated from European archives and their fee structures, Africans, and African filmmakers in particular, would be free to do what they want with them. This critical and creative freedom, as Jean-Marie Teno's example has shown, would allow for more projects anchored in what literary scholar and cultural historian Saidiya Hartman calls "close narration": a method that "elaborates, augments, transposes, and breaks open archival documents so they might yield a richer picture."[10] Beyond the awareness and use of colonial-era films, moreover, the question of restitution is equally relevant to the majority of the African films from the 1960s, '70s, and '80s I have discussed in these pages. Those made with French funding have been conserved in French governmental archives whose names have changed as France's official relationship to her former colonies has evolved. In another bitter irony, they circulate only via a network of agencies charged with the global promotion of French culture. Mahamat-Saleh Haroun became a Chadian filmmaker without having been able to see Edouard Sailly's films.[11]

Teno notes the paradox of European funded and led training programs for young, twenty-first-century African filmmakers like those sponsored by Africadoc, arguing that "Europeans are back to train our youth to look at and represent themselves, often taking as examples and references the ethnographic images they are familiar with, rather than the works of other African filmmakers."[12] With more limited resources, Teno established in 2017 the no-cost three-month training program Patrimoines-Héritages (Inheritance-heritage) and in 2018 the Bandjoun Film Studio, both in the region of his birth. In 2023, he began a crowdfunding campaign to support the creation of La'a Lom—The House of Documentary—a cultural center in Bandjoun that would host workshops and film screenings while also housing a print library and film archive. With access to African films, aspiring documentarists could look to an African documentary tradition while developing their craft.

In a remarkable speech delivered in Paris in 1978, Senegalese director-general of UNESCO Amadou Mahtar M'Bow called for the restitution of "cultural property" to Africa, Asia, Latin America, and Oceania. Restitution for M'Bow signified "the return to those who created it of an irreplaceable cultural heritage," and he stressed that such a return was essential for true independence as well as for the development of national identity.[13] He did not understand an object's place of origin to be its final resting place, instead proposing a circulation that would allow newly independent nations to participate fully in global cultural exchange. Following in M'Bow's footsteps, Sarr and Savoy explain the process of restitution not as a strict dividing up and repatriating of objects but as an opening up of their meaning, an idea reflected in their report's subtitle, "Toward a New Relational Ethics." We might then consider both French colonial documentaries and independent African documentaries shot in sub-Saharan Africa to be part of both European and African cultural heritages. More importantly, and as is the fundamental conclusion of this book, to do so requires that African documentary, originating in spaces that were once only captured on film, be acknowledged as an equal cinematic partner.

Notes

1. Walter Mignolo, *The Darker Side of Western Modernity: Global Futures, Decolonial Options* (Duke University Press, 2011), 10.

2. Achille Joseph Mbembe, "Decolonizing the University: New Directions," *Arts and Humanities in Higher Education* 151, no. 1 (2016): 41.

3. Alice Gallois, "Le cinéma au Musée de l'homme: La construction d'un patrimoine, l'invention d'une culture? Deuxième partie: 1953–1960," *Journal des anthropologues*, nos. 136–37 (2014): 376.

4. Thackway, *Africa Shoots Back*, 200. Film scholar Priya Jaikumar describes being "startled" by a "sense of visual familiarity and intimacy" while viewing colonial British films shot in India, an experience that prompted her to seek out non-filmic records of the colonized spaces represented. Priya Jaikumar, "An 'accurate imagination': Place, Map and Archive as Spatial Objects of Film History," in *Empire and Film*, ed. Lee Grieveson and Colin MacCabe (Palgrave Macmillan, 2011), 177.

5. Marc Ferro, "1917: History and Cinema," *Journal of Contemporary History* 3, no. 4 (1968): 45, 46.

6. For a discussion of this problem and the British Film Institute's solution with respect to colonial-era films shot in India, see Grazia Ingravalle, "Indian or British

Film Heritage? The Material Life of Britain's Colonial Film Archive," *JCMS: Journal of Cinema and Media Studies* 61, no. 2 (2022): 63–87.

7. Isaac Julien, "Undoing the Colonial Archive," in *Film and the End of Empire*, ed. Lee Grieveson and Colin MacCabe (Palgrave Macmillan, 2011), 273.

8. "The African Film Library of Ouagadougou," *Black Camera* 12, no. 1 (2020): 507.

9. Felwine Sarr and Bénédicte Savoy, "Rapport sur la restitution du patrimoine culturel africain: Vers une nouvelle éthique relationnelle," Ministère de la Culture and Institut des sciences sociales du politique, 2018, http://restitutionreport2018.com/sarr_savoy_fr.pdf, 35, 38, 57–58. See also Rachel Gabara, "*Restituer*: Sharing Colonial Films," *Contemporary French Civilization* 48, no. 1 (2023): 7–26.

10. Saidiya Hartman, *Wayward Lives, Beautiful Experiments: Intimate Histories of Riotous Black Girls, Troublesome Women, and Queer Radicals* (W. W. Norton, 2019), xiii–xiv.

11. Patrick Ndiltah, "Mahamat-Saleh Haroun face à la presse tchadienne," *Africultures*, 2010, http://africultures.com/mahamat-saleh-haroun-face-a-la-presse-tchadienne-rien-de-grand-ne-sobtient-sans-passion-9711/.

12. Teno, "Writing on Walls," 91. See also Olivier Barlet, *Contemporary African Cinema*, trans. Melissa Thackway (Michigan State University Press, 2016): 301–2.

13. Amadou-Mahtar M'Bow, "Pour le retour à ceux qui l'ont créé d'un patrimoine culturel irremplaçable," *Le courrier de l'UNESCO* 31 (1978): 4–5.

Abel, Richard. *The Ciné Goes to Town: French Cinema, 1896–1914.* University of California Press, 1994.

Abel, Richard. *French Film Theory and Criticism.* Vol. I, *1907–1939.* Princeton University Press, 1988.

Abel, Richard. *French Film Theory and Criticism.* Vol. II, *1929–1939.* Princeton University Press, 1988.

Adesokan, Akin. "Abderrahmane Sissako and the Poetics of Engaged Expatriation." *Screen* 51, no. 2 (2010): 143–60.

Akudinobi, Jude. "Reco(r)ding Reality: Representation and Paradigms in Nonfiction African Cinema." *Social Identities* 6, no. 3 (2000): 345–67.

Andrade-Watkins, Claire. "France's Bureau of Cinema: Financial and Technical Assistance Between 1961 & 1977." *Visual Anthropology Review* 6, no. 2 (1990): 80–93.

Andrew, Dudley. "Praying Mantis: Enchantment and Violence in French Cinema of the Exotic." In *Visions of the East: Orientalism in Film,* edited by Matthew Bernstein and Gaylyn Studlar, 232–52. Rutgers University Press, 1997.

Astourian, Laure. *The Ethnographic Optic.* Indiana University Press, 2024.

Aubert, Michelle, and Jean-Claude Seguin, eds. *La production cinématographique des Frères Lumière.* Bibliothèque du Film, 1996.

Aufderheide, Pat. "Memory and History in Subsaharan African Cinema: An Interview with David Achkar." *Visual Anthropology Review* 9, no. 2 (1993): 107–13.

Babin, Gustave. "Les grandes chasses africaines." *L'illustration,* no. 3425 (October 17, 1908): 254–9.

Bachy, Victor. *Le cinéma au Gabon.* OCIC, 1986.

Bachy, Victor. *Le cinéma au Mali*. OCIC, 1983.

Bachy, Victor. *La Haute-Volta et le cinéma*. OCIC, 1983.

Bakari, Imruh, and Mbye Cham, eds. *African Experiences of Cinema*. British Film Institute, 1996.

Bakhtin, Mikhail. *Problems of Dostoevsky's Poetics*. Translated by Caryl Emerson. University of Minnesota Press, 1984.

Ballif, Noël. *Les danseurs de Dieu*. Hachette, 1954.

Barlet, Olivier. *Contemporary African Cinema*. Translated by Melissa Thackway. Michigan State University Press, 2016.

Barlet, Olivier. "Entretien avec François Woukoache." *Africultures*, 1997, http://africultures.com/entretien-dolivier-barlet-avec-francois-woukoache-306/.

Barnouw, Erik. *Documentary: A History of the Non-fiction Film*. 2nd ed. Oxford University Press, 1993.

Bassori, Timité. "Un cinéma mort-né?" *Présence Africaine*, no. 49 (1964): 111–15.

Bazin, André. "Le cinéma et l'exploration." In *Qu'est-ce que le cinéma?*, 25–34. Éditions du Cerf, 1999 [1958].

Benali, Abdelkader. *Le cinéma colonial au Maghreb: L'imaginaire en trompe-l'oeil*. Éditions du Cerf, 1998.

Beus, Yifen. "Authorship and Criticism in Self-Reflexive African Cinema." *Journal of African Cultural Studies* 23, no. 2 (2011): 133–52.

Bhely-Quenum, Olympe. "Interview exclusive de Blaise Senghor." *L'Afrique actuelle*, no. 19 (1967): 8–15.

Blanchard, Pascal, Nicolas Bancel, Gilles Boëtsch, Éric Deroo, Sandrine Lemaire, and Charles Forsdick, eds. *Human Zoos: Science and Spectacle in the Age of Colonial Empires*. Liverpool University Press, 2008.

Bloom, Peter. *French Colonial Documentary: Mythologies of Humanitarianism*. University of Minnesota Press, 2008.

Bloom, Peter. "Trans-Saharan Automotive Cinema." In *Virtual Voyages: Cinema and Travel*, edited by Jeffrey Ruoff, 139–56. Duke University Press, 2006.

Bonetti, Mahen, and Morgan Seag, eds. *Through African Eyes: Conversations with the Directors*, 2. African Film Festival, 2010.

Bottomore, Stephen. "Rediscovering Early Non-fiction Film." *Film History* 13, no. 2 (2001): 160–73.

Bouchard, Vincent. "African Documentaries, Critical Interventions: The Non-fiction Film Production at the Origins of Francophone West African Film Production." *Critical Interventions* 11, no. 3 (2017): 214–27.

Boughedir, Férid. *Le cinéma africain de A à Z*. Editions OCIC, 1987.

Boulanger, Pierre. *Le cinéma colonial, de "l'Atlantide" à "Lawrence d'Arabie."* Seghers, 1975.

Bousquet, Henri. *Catalogue Pathé: Des années 1896 à 1914*. Henri Bousquet, 1996.

Burch, Noël. *Life to Those Shadows*. Translated by Ben Brewster. British Film Institute, 1990.

C., R. "Le cinema à l'Exposition coloniale." *La critique cinématographique*, no. 226 (1931), 45–46.

Carné, Marcel. "Le cinéma à la conquête du monde." *Cinémagazine*, no. 9, October 1930, 9–11.

Carné, Marcel. "L'exotisme au cinéma, en marge de l'Exposition coloniale." *Cinémagazine*, no. 7, July 1931, 15–20.

Cervoni, Albert. "Une confrontation historique en 1965 entre Jean Rouch et Sembene Ousmane." *L'Afrique littéraire*, no. 61–62 (1981): 77–78.

Cham, Mbye-Boubacar. "Film Production in West Africa: 1979–1981." *Présence africaine*, no. 124 (1982): 168–69.

Chilcoat, Michelle, and Cheikh Ndiaye. "Entretien avec Osvalde Lewat-Hallade, jeune réalisatrice d'origine camerounaise." *French Review* 83, no. 2 (2009): 388–96.

Cissokho, Aboubacar Demba. "Samba Félix Ndiaye: 'Dites simplement la verité.'" *Senciné*, no. 3 (2015): 67–69.

Clifford, James. *The Predicament of Culture: Twentieth-Century Ethnography, Literature, and Art*. Harvard University Press, 1988.

Coissac, G.-Michel. "Le cinéma au service de la civilisation et de la propagande." *Tout-cinéma*, 1931, 53–80.

Coissac, G.-Michel. "Le cinéma et la propagande coloniale." *Cinéopse*, no. 103, March 1, 1928, 259.

Coissac, G.-Michel. "Le cinématographe utilisé comme propagande aux colonies." *Cinéopse*, no. 14, October 1920, 414.

Coissac, G.-Michel. *Histoire du cinématographe: De ses origines jusqu'à nos jours*. Éditions du Cinéopse, 1925.

Colleyn, Jean-Paul, ed. *Jean Rouch: Cinéma et anthropologie*. Cahiers du cinéma/ INA, 2009.

Conklin, Alice. *In the Museum of Man: Race, Anthropology, and Empire in France, 1850–1950*. Cornell University Press, 2013.

Conklin, Alice. *A Mission to Civilize: The Republican Idea of Empire in France and West Africa, 1895–1930*. Stanford University Press, 1997.

Convents, Guido. "Africa: French Colonies." In *Encyclopedia of Early Cinema*, edited by Richard Abel, 13. Routledge, 2005.

Convents, Guido. *À la recherche des images oubliées: Préhistoire du cinéma en Afrique, 1897–1918*. Éditions OCIC, 1986.

Convents, Guido. "Documentaries and Propaganda Before 1914: A View on Early Cinema and Colonial History." *Framework*, no. 35 (1988): 104–13.

Corrigan, Timothy. *The Essay Film: From Montaigne, After Marker*. Oxford University Press, 2011.

Cosandey, Roland. "Some Thoughts on 'Early Documentary.'" In *Uncharted Territory*, edited by Daan Hertogs and Nico de Klerk, 37–50. Stichting Nederlands Filmmuseum, 1997.

Coureau, Didier. "*Asientos* (1995) de François L. Woukoache." *Recherches et travaux*, no. 84 (2014): 201–13.

Cousin, Jeanne. *Histoire du cinéma en Guinée depuis 1958*. L'Harmattan, 2017.

Crosta, Suzanne, Sada Niang, and Alexie Tcheuyap, eds. *Francophone African Women Documentary Filmmakers: Beyond Representation*. Indiana University Press, 2023.

D'dée. "Enfin du vrai cinéma africain." *La vie africaine*, no. 29 (1962): 47.

D'dée. "Jeune cinéma d'Afrique noire." *L'Afrique actuelle*, no. 15 (1967): 3–40.

Debrix, Jean-R. "Le cinéma africain." *Afrique contemporaine*, no. 40 (1968): 2–12.

Debrix, Jean-R. "Situation du cinéma en Afrique francophone." *Afrique contemporaine*, no. 81 (1975): 2–8.

Delmeulle, Frédéric. "Production et distribution du documentaire en France (1909–1929)." *1895, revue d'histoire du cinéma*, no. 18 (1995): 200–15.

Dia-Moukori, Urbain. "Intuition d'un langage cinématographique africain." *Présence africaine*, no. 61 (1967): 206–18.

Diawara, Manthia. *African Cinema: Politics and Culture*. Indiana University Press, 1992.

Diawara, Manthia. "African Cinema Today." *SVA Review* 6, no. 1 (1990): 65–74.

Diawara, Manthia. *African Film: New Forms of Aesthetics and Politics*. Prestel, 2010.

Di Iorio, Sam. "Les vivants et les morts: Marker, Resnais et *Les statues meurent aussi*." *Trafic*, no. 105 (2018): 52–62.

Diop, Baba. "Il est parti Mister Doc . . ." *Africiné*, 2009, http://www.africine.org/?menu=art&no=9003.

Dovey, Lindiwe. *Curating Africa in the Age of Film Festivals*. Palgrave Macmillan, 2015.

Dovey, Lindiwe. "Subjects of Exile: Alienation in Francophone West African Cinema." *International Journal of Francophone Studies* 12, no. 1 (2009): 55–75.

Dunn, Kevin. "Lights . . . Camera . . . Africa: Images of Africa and Africans in Western Popular Films of the 1930s." *African Studies Review* 39, no. 1 (1996): 149–75.

Dupont, Jacques. *Profession: Cinéaste, politiquement incorrect!* Italiques, 2013.

Dureau, G. "La cinématographie coloniale." *Ciné-Journal*, no. 257, 1913, 3.

Edwards, Brent Hayes. *The Practice of Diaspora: Literature, Translation, and the Rise of Black Internationalism*. Harvard University Press, 2003.

Ferro, Marc. "1917: History and Cinema." *Journal of Contemporary History* 3, no. 4 (1968): 45–61.

Frodon, Jean-Michel. *Le cinéma à l'épreuve du divers*. CNRS Éditions, 2021.

Fronval, George. "Films documentaires." *Ciné-Comoedia*, August 30, 1928, 1.

Fronval, George. "Haut les masques!" *Cinémonde*, March 17, 1938, 213.

Gabara, Rachel. *From Split to Screened Selves: French and Francophone Autobiography in the Third Person*. Stanford University Press, 2006.

Gabara, Rachel. "*Restituer*: Sharing Colonial Films." *Contemporary French Civilization* 48, no. 1 (2023): 7–26.

Gallois, Alice. "Le cinéma au Musée de l'homme: La construction d'un patrimoine, l'invention d'une culture? Première partie: 1937–1960." *Journal des anthropologues*, nos. 134–35 (2013): 375–92.

Gallois, Alice. "Le cinéma au Musée de l'homme: La construction d'un patrimoine, l'invention d'une culture? Deuxième partie: 1953–1960." *Journal des anthropologues*, nos. 136–37 (2014): 373–87.

Gallois, Alice. "Le cinéma ethnographique en France: Le Comité du Film Ethnographique, instrument de son institutionnalisation? (1950–1970)." *1895, revue d'histoire du cinéma*, no. 58 (2009): 80–108.

Garcia, Jean-Pierre. "Rencontre avec Samba Félix Ndiaye, réalisateur." *Le film africain & Le film du sud*, nos. 35–36 (2001): 90–95.

Garritano, Carmela. "Waiting on the Past: African Uranium Futures in *Arlit, Deuxième Paris*." *Modern Fiction Studies* 66, no. 1 (2020): 122–40.

Gauthier, Guy. *Un siècle de documentaires français: Des tourneurs de manivelle aux voltigeurs du multimédia*. Armand Colin, 2004.

Genova, James. *Cinema and Development in West Africa*. Indiana University Press, 2013.

Girardet, Raoul. *L'idée coloniale en France de 1871 à 1962*. La Table Ronde, 1972.

Givanni, June, ed. *Symbolic Narratives/African Cinema: Audiences, Theory and the Moving Image*. BFI, 2000.

Godard, Jean-Luc. "L'Afrique vous parle de la fin et des moyens." *Cahiers du cinéma*, no. 94 (1959): 21–22.

Goerg, Odile. *Tropical Dream Palaces: Cinema in Colonial West Africa*. Translated by Melissa Thackway. Hurst, 2020.

Griaule, Marcel. *Les grands explorateurs*. Presses universitaires de France [Que sais-je?], 1945.

Grieveson, Lee, and Colin MacCabe, eds. *Empire and Film*. Palgrave Macmillan, 2011.

Grieveson, Lee, and Colin MacCabe, eds. *Film and the End of Empire*. Palgrave Macmillan, 2011.

Griffiths, Alison. "'To the World the World We Show': Early Travelogues as Filmed Ethnography." *Film History* 11, no. 3 (1999): 282–307.

Griffiths, Alison. *Wondrous Difference: Cinema, Anthropology, and Turn-of-the-Century Visual Culture*. Columbia University Press, 2002.

Grimshaw, Anna. "Who Has the Last Laugh? *Nanook of the North* and Some New Thoughts on an Old Classic." *Visual Anthropology*, no. 27 (2014): 421–35.

Groo, Katherine. *Bad Film Histories: Ethnography and the Early Archive*. University of Minnesota Press, 2019.

Gunning, Tom. "The Cinema of Attractions: Early Film, Its Spectator and the Avant-Garde." In *Early Cinema: Space, France, Narrative*, edited by Thomas Elsaesser and Adam Barker, 56–62. BFI, 1990.

Haffner, Claude. "'Dites simplement la vérité': Une leçon de cinéma de Samba Félix Ndiaye (Fespaco 2005)." *Africiné*, 2009. http://www.africine.org/analyse /dites-simplement-la-verite/9001.

Haffner, Pierre. "L'esthétique des films." *L'Afrique littéraire*, no. 68–69 (1983): 58–71.

Haffner, Pierre. "Jean Rouch jugé par six cinéastes d'Afrique noire." *L'Afrique littéraire*, no. 61–62 (1981): 62–76.

Haffner, Pierre. "Nations nègres et cinéma." *Les cahiers de médiologie* 1, no. 3 (1997): 147–55.

Haffner, Pierre. *Palabres sur le cinématographe: Initiation au cinéma*. Les Presses Africaines, 1978.

Haffner, Pierre, and Paulin Soumanou Vieyra. "Propos sur le cinéma africain." *Présence africaine*, no. 170 (2004): 43–54.

Harrow, Kenneth. *Postcolonial African Cinema: From Political Engagement to Postmodernism*. Indiana University Press, 2007.

Heider, Karl G. *Ethnographic Film*. Rev. ed. University of Texas Press, 2006 [1976].

Henley, Paul. *The Adventure of the Real: Jean Rouch and the Craft of Ethnographic Cinema*. University of Chicago Press, 2009.

Henley, Paul. *Beyond Observation: A History of Authorship in Ethnographic Film*. Manchester University Press, 2020.

Henley, Paul. "From *Vues* to Ethnofiction: French Ethnographic Filmmaking in Africa Before Jean Rouch." *Visual Anthropology* 33, no. 1 (2020): 32–80.

Hennebelle, Guy. *Les cinémas africains en 1972*. Société Africaine d'Edition, 1972.

Hertogs, Daan, and Nico De Klerk, eds. *Nonfiction Film from the Teens*. Stichting Nederlands Filmmuseum, 1994.

Hertogs, Daan, and Nico De Klerk, eds. *Uncharted Territory: Essays on Early Nonfiction*. Stichting Nederlands Filmmuseum, 1997.

Hoefert de Turégano, Teresa. *African Cinema and Europe: Close-Up on Burkina Faso*. European Press Academic, 2004.

Huret, Marcel. *Ciné actualités: Histoire de la presse filmée 1895–1980*. Henri Veyrier, 1984.

Ichac, Pierre. "Notes d'un chasseur d'images: Cinéma et colonies." *Cinéma*, no. 35, January 1931, n.p.

Iheka, Cajetan. *African Ecomedia: Network Form, Planetary Politics*. Duke University Press, 2021.

Ilboudo, Patrick. *Le FESPACO, 1969–1989: Les cinéastes africains et leurs oeuvres*. Éditions La Mante, 1988.

Imbert, Henri-François. *Samba Félix Ndiaye: Cinéaste documentariste africain*. L'Harmattan, 2007.

Jacobs, Lewis, ed. *The Documentary Tradition.* 2nd ed. W. W. Norton, 1979.

James, Alison. *The Documentary Imagination in Twentieth-Century French Literature.* Oxford University Press, 2020.

Jeantet, Claude. "Opinion sur les documentaires." *Cinémonde,* no. 77, April 10, 1930, 227.

Jolly, Eric. "Démasquer la société dogon: Sahara-Soudan, janvier–avril 1935." *Les carnets de Bérose,* no. 4 (2014): 96–100.

Jolly, Eric. "Les missions Griaule et le cinéma ethnographique." In *À la naissance de l'ethnologie française: Les missions ethnographique en Afrique subsaharienne (1928–1939),* 2016. http://naissanceethnologie.fr/files/pdf/43.pdf.

Kahana, Jonathan, ed. *The Documentary Film Reader.* Oxford University Press, 2016.

Kala-Lobe, Iwiyè. "Alioune Diop et le cinéma africain." *Présence Africaine,* no. 125 (1983): 329–50.

Kodjo, François. "Les cinéastes africains face à l'avenir du cinéma en Afrique." *Tiers-monde* 20, no. 79 (1979): 605–14.

Lacassin, Francis. *Alfred Machin, 1877–1929.* Anthologie du Cinéma, 1968.

Lacassin, Francis. *Alfred Machin: De la jungle à l'écran.* Dreamland Éditeur, 2001.

Landau, Paul, and Deborah Kaspin, eds. *Images and Empires: Visuality in Colonial and Postcolonial Africa.* University of California Press, 2002.

Landay, Maurice. "Propagande et cinéma: Le film colonial." *La dépêche coloniale,* September 6, 1918, 1.

Landay, Maurice. "Propagande et cinéma: Les leçons cinématographiques coloniales." *La dépêche coloniale,* September 3, 1918, 1–2.

Landry, Lionel. "Documentaires." *Cinémagazine,* no. 4, January 26, 1923, 154.

Laubriet, P. "L'outre-mer vu par le cinéma." *Mer outre-mer,* no. 1 (1947): 12–14.

Lee, Sonia, and Irène Assiba d'Almeida. *Essais et documentaires des africaines francophones.* L'Harmattan, 2015.

Lefebvre, T., and L. Mannoni, eds. *Cinéma des premiers temps: Nouvelles contributions françaises.* Presses de la Sorbonne nouvelle, 1996.

Leprohon, Pierre. *Chasseurs d'images.* Éditions André Bonne, 1960.

Leprohon, Pierre. "L'exotisme au cinéma." *Cinémonde,* no. 45, August 29, 1929, 792.

Leprohon, Pierre. *L'exotisme et le cinéma: Les 'chasseurs d'images' à la conquête du monde.* Éditions J. Susse, 1945.

Leroi-Gourhan, André. "Cinéma et sciences humaines: Le film ethnologique existe-t-il?" *Revue de géographie humaine et d'ethnologie,* no. 3 (July–September 1948): 42–50.

Le Roy, Eric. "Le fonds cinématographique colonial aux Archives du film et du dépôt légal du CNC." *Journal of Film Preservation,* no. 63 (October 2001): 55–59.

Letorey, Pierre. "Le cinéma colonial." *Le film,* February 27, 1914, 7.

Leyda, Jay. *Films Beget Films: A Study of the Compilation Film.* Hill and Wang, 1964.

Liotard, André, Samivel, and Jean Thévenot. *Cinéma d'exploration, cinéma au long cours.* Chavane, 1950.

Loftus, Maria. "The Appeal of Hybrid Documentary Forms in West Africa." *French Forum* 35, no. 2–3 (2010): 37–55.

Lotman, Jurij. *Semiotics of Cinema.* Michigan Slavic Contributions, 1976.

Lourdou, Philippe. "The Dawning Commentary in Ethnographic Film: Marcel Griaule's Cinematographic Work." *Visual Anthropology,* no. 6 (1993): 65–84.

Maarek, Philippe, ed. *Afrique noire: Quel cinéma?* Association du Ciné-Club de l'Université de Paris X, 1983.

Machin, Alfred. "Le cinématographe dans le désert: Comment s'organise une expédition cinématographique." *Ciné-Journal,* no. 37, April 29–May 5, 1909, 6, 8.

Machin, Alfred. "Le cinématographe et la conquête du monde." *Ciné-Journal,* no. 36, April 23–28, 1909, 9.

Malausa, Vincent. "Un cinéaste tchadien: Entretien avec Mahamat-Saleh Haroun." *Cahiers du cinéma,* no. 660 (2010): 43–46.

Marguet, Jean. "La France, puissance coloniale, possède-t-elle un cinéma colonial?" *Cinémonde,* no. 95, August 14, 1930, 519.

Martin, Angela, ed. *African Films: The Context of Production.* BFI, 1982.

Martin, Angela. "Four Film Makers from West Africa." *Framework,* no. 11 (1979): 16–21.

Mbembe, Achille Joseph. "Decolonizing the University: New Directions." *Arts and Humanities in Higher Education* 151, no. 1 (2016): 29–45.

M'Bow, Amadou-Mahtar. "Pour le retour à ceux qui l'ont créé d'un patrimoine culturel irremplaçable." *Le courrier de l'UNESCO* 31 (1978): 4–5.

Mesguich, Félix. *Tours de manivelle: Souvenirs d'un chasseur d'images.* Grasset, 1933.

Mignolo, Walter. *The Darker Side of Western Modernity: Global Futures, Decolonial Options.* Duke University Press, 2011.

Mottier, Damien. "Jean Rouch au rendez-vous de juillet: Métamorphose d'un ethnologue cinéaste." *Journal des Africanistes* 87, no. 1–2 (2017): 64–93.

Mottier, Damien. "*Voyage au Congo*: Cinéma, littérature et ethnographie." In *Ciné-Expéditions, Une zone de contact cinématographique,* edited by Caroline Damiens, 187–209. AFRHC, 2022.

Moussinac, Léon. *Naissance du cinéma.* J. Povolozky et Cie, 1925.

Mudimbe, V. Y. *The Idea of Africa.* Indiana University Press, 1994.

Mudimbe, V. Y. *The Invention of Africa: Gnosis, Philosophy, and the Order of Knowledge.* Indiana University Press, 1988.

Murphy, David. "Francophone West African Cinema, 1955–1969: False Starts and New Beginnings." In *Africa's Lost Classics: New Histories of African Cinema,* edited by Lizelle Bisschoff and David Murphy, 50–62. Legenda, 2014.

Murphy, David, and Patrick Williams. *Postcolonial African Cinema: Ten Directors.* Manchester University Press, 2007.

Murray, Alison. "Documentary Fiction: Images of Sub-Saharan Africa in Colonial Film Between the Wars." In *Proceedings of the Western Society for French History: Selected Papers of the Annual Meeting*, edited by Barry Rothaus, 186–95. University Press of Colorado, 1998.

Murray Levine, Alison. "Film, Propaganda, and Politics: *La France est un empire*, 1939–1943." *Contemporary French Civilization* 40, no. 1 (2015): 71–90.

Murray Levine, Alison. *Framing the Nation: Documentary Film in Interwar France*. Continuum, 2010.

Musser, Charles. "Problems in Historiography: The Documentary Tradition Before *Nanook of the North*." In *The Documentary Film Book*, edited by Brian Winston, 119–28. British Film Institute, 2013.

Musser, Charles. "The Travel Genre in 1903–1904: Moving Towards Fictional Narrative." In *Early Cinema: Space, France, Narrative*, edited by Thomas Elsaesser and Adam Barker, 123–32. BFI, 1990.

Naficy, Hamid. *An Accented Cinema: Exilic and Diasporic Filmmaking*. Princeton University Press, 2001.

Nagib, Lúcia. *World Cinema and the Ethics of Realism*. Continuum, 2011.

Ndiaye, Pap. "Présence africaine avant 'Présence africaine': La subjectivation politique noire en France dans l'entre-deux-guerres." *Gradhiva*, no. 10 (2009): 65–79.

Ndiaye, Samba Félix. "L'Afrique et le documentaire." *Le film africain*, no. 3 (1991): 7.

Niang, Sada. *Djibril Diop Mambety: Un cinéaste à contre-courant*. L'Harmattan, 2002.

Niang, Sada. *Nationalist African Cinema: Legacy and Transformations*. Lexington Books, 2014.

Nichols, Bill. *Blurred Boundaries: Questions of Meaning in Contemporary Culture*. Indiana University Press, 1994.

Nichols, Bill. *Ideology and the Image: Social Representation in the Cinema and Other Media*. Indiana University Press, 1981.

Nichols, Bill. *Introduction to Documentary*. Indiana University Press, 2001.

Nichols, Bill. *Representing Reality: Issues and Concepts in Documentary*. Indiana University Press, 1991.

Nichols, Bill. *Speaking Truths with Film: Evidence, Ethics, Politics in Documentary*. University of California Press, 2016.

Norindr, Panivong. "Enlisting Early Cinema in the Service of 'La Plus Grande France.'" In *Early Cinema and the "National,"* edited by Richard Abel, Giorgio Bertellini, and Rob King, 109–17. Indiana University Press, 2008.

Ouedraogo, Hamidou. *Naissance et évolution du FESPACO de 1969 à 1973*. Imprimerie Nationale du Burkina, 1995.

Parsons, Neil. *Black and White Bioscope: Making Movies in Africa 1899–1925*. Intellect, 2018.

Peterson, Jennifer Lynn. *Education in the School of Dreams: Travelogues and Early Nonfiction Film*. Duke University Press, 2013.

Petty, Sheila. "*Sacred Places* and *Arlit: Deuxième Paris*: Reterritorialization in African Documentary." *Nka, Journal of Contemporary African Art*, no. 32 (2013): 70–79.

Petty, Sheila. "Unsilencing History: Reclaiming African Cultural Heritage in *Kemtiyu-Séex Anta*." *Black Camera* 9, no. 2 (2018): 414–26.

Pfaff, Françoise. *À l'écoute du cinéma sénégalais*. L'Harmattan, 2010.

Pfaff, Françoise, ed. *Focus on African Films*. Indiana University Press, 2004.

Pfaff, Françoise. *Twenty-Five Black African Filmmakers*. Greenwood Press, 1988.

Piault, Marc Henri. *Anthropologie & Cinéma: Passage à l'image, passage par l'image*. 2nd ed. Téraèdre, 2016 [2000].

Piault, Marc Henri. "L'exotisme et le cinéma ethnographique: La rupture de *La croisière noire*." *Journal of Film Preservation*, no. 63 (October 2001): 6–16.

Poirier, Léon. "Le cinéma exotique." *Ciné-Miroir*, no. 101, July 1, 1926, 195.

Poirier, Léon. *La croisière noire: Journal cinégraphique de l'expédition Citroën-Centre-Afrique*. Imprimerie Draeger, 1926.

Prabhu, Anjali. *Contemporary Cinema of Africa and the Diaspora*. Wiley-Blackwell, 2014.

Pratt, Mary Louise. "Transculturation and Autoethnography: Peru, 1615/1980." In *Colonial Discourse / Postcolonial Theory*, edited by Francis Barker, Peter Hulme, and Margaret Iversen, 24–46. Manchester University Press, 1994.

Ramirez, Francis, and Christian Rolot. *Histoire du cinéma colonial au Zaire, au Rwanda, et au Burundi*. Musée Royal de l'Afrique Centrale, 1985.

Raymond-Millet, J.-K. "Le film de voyage documentaire ou reportage cinématographique a une valeur . . ." *Comoedia*, June 22, 1930, 1.

Raymond-Millet, J.-K. "Les nègres sont-ils photogéniques?" *Ciné-Miroir*, no. 227, August 9, 1929, 503.

Regnault, Félix. "Le rôle du cinéma en ethnographie." *La nature*, no. 2866 (1931): 304–6.

Renov, Michael. *The Subject of Documentary*. University of Minnesota Press, 2004.

Renov, Michael, ed. *Theorizing Documentary*. Routledge, 1993.

Reynolds, Glenn. *Colonial Cinema in Africa: Origins, Images, Audiences*. McFarland, 2015.

Ricci, Daniela. "La voix des femmes dans les documentaires d'Angèle Diabang." *Nouvelles Études Francophones* 33, no. 1 (2018): 73–87.

Rice, Tom. *Films for the Colonies: Cinema and the Preservation of the British Empire*. University of California Press, 2019.

Rotha, Paul. *Documentary Film: The Use of the Film Medium to Interpret Creatively and in Social Terms the Life of the People as It Exists in Reality*. Hastings House, 1952.

Rouch, Jean. *Alors le Noir et le Blanc seront amis*. Mille et une nuits, 2008.

Rouch, Jean. *Ciné-Ethnography*. Translated and edited by Steven Feld. University of Minnesota Press, 2003.

Rouch, Jean. *Connaissance de l'Afrique noire*. Le Livre de Paris, 1957.

Rouch, Jean. "Le film ethnographique." In *Ethnologie Générale*, edited by Jean Poirier, 429–71. Gallimard, 1968.

Ruby, Jay. "The Image Mirrored: Reflexivity and the Documentary Film." In *New Challenges for Documentary*, edited by Alan Rosenthal, 64–77. University of California Press, 1988.

Ruelle, Catherine, ed. *Afriques 50: Singularités d'un cinéma pluriel*. L'Harmattan, 2005.

Russell, Catherine. *Experimental Ethnography: The Work of Film in the Age of Video*. Duke University Press, 1999.

Sadoul, Georges. *Le cinéma français*. Flammarion, 1962.

Sadoul, Georges. *Histoire du cinéma mondial, des origines à nos jours*. 7th ed. Flammarion, 1963.

Sadoul, Georges. *Histoire d'un art: Le cinéma, des origines à nos jours*. Flammarion, 1949.

Sanogo, Aboubakar. "The Indocile Image: Cinema and History in Med Hondo's *Soleil O* and *Les Bicots-Nègres, Vos Voisins*." *Rethinking History* 19, no. 4 (2015): 559–63.

Sarr, Felwine, and Bénédicte Savoy. "Rapport sur la restitution du patrimoine culturel africain: Vers une nouvelle éthique relationnelle." Ministère de la Culture and Institut des sciences sociales du politique, 2018. http://restitutionreport2018.com/sarr_savoy_fr.pdf.

Saving Bruce Lee: African and Arab Cinema in the Era of Soviet Cultural Diplomacy. Haus der Kulturen der Welt, 2018.

Schmidt, Nancy J. "Sub-Saharan African Women Filmmakers: Agendas for Research with a Filmography." In *With Open Eyes: Women and African Cinema*, edited by Kenneth Harrow, 163–90. Rodopi, 1997.

Seck, Gora. "Les défis d'une génération de cinéastes documentaristes." In *Dix films d'Afrique*, edited by François Fronty, 159–76. L'Harmattan, 2019.

"Séminaire sur 'le rôle du cinéaste africain dans l'éveil d'une conscience de civilisation noire.'" *Présence africaine*, no. 90 (1974): 3–203.

Shaka, Femi Okiremuete. *Modernity and the African Cinema*. Africa World Press, 2004.

Shaka, Femi Okiremuete. "Politics of Cultural Conversion in Colonialist African Cinema." *Black Camera* 12, no. 2 (2021): 61–90.

Sichel, Kim. "Germaine Krull and *L'Amitié Noire*." In *Colonialist Photography: Imag(in)ing Race and Place*, edited by Eleanor Hight and Gary Sampson, 257–80. Routledge, 2002.

Signaté, Ibrahima. *Med Hondo, un cinéaste rebelle*. Présence Africaine, 1994.

Slavin, David. *Colonial Cinema and Imperial France, 1919–1939*. Johns Hopkins University Press, 2001.

Sow, Moussa. "Ecocinema in Senegalese Documentary Film." *Journal of African Cinemas* 5, no. 1 (2013): 3–17.

Stoller, Paul. *The Cinematic Griot: The Ethnography of Jean Rouch*. University of Chicago Press, 1992.

Stoller, Paul. "Regarding Rouch: The Recasting of West African Colonial Culture." In *Cinema, Colonialism, Postcolonialism*, edited by Dina Sherzer, 65–79. University of Texas Press, 1996.

Tapsoba, Clément. "Filmer l'Afrique." *Ecrans d'Afrique*, no. 16 (1996): 45–54.

Tcheuyap, Alexie. *African Documentary Cinema*. Routledge, 2024.

Tcheuyap, Alexie. "Cinéma documentaire et expériences féminines en Afrique francophone." *French Forum* 35, nos. 2–3 (2010): 57–77.

Tcheuyap, Alexie. "Documenter l'Afrique: Enjeux théoriques et politiques." *Nouvelles études francophones* 33, no. 1 (2018): 18–37.

Tcheuyap, Alexie. *Postnationalist African Cinemas*. Manchester University Press, 2011.

Thackway, Melissa. *Africa Shoots Back: Alternative Perspectives in Sub-Saharan Francophone African Film*. Indiana University Press, 2003.

Thackway, Melissa. "Filmer le réel: Une conversation avec Jean-Marie Teno." In *Figuration et mémoire dans les cinémas africains*, edited by Jean Ouédraogo, 131–46. L'Harmattan, 2010.

Thackway, Melissa, and Jean-Marie Teno. *Reel Resistance: The Cinema of Jean-Marie Teno*. James Currey, 2020.

Tobing Rony, Fatimah. *The Third Eye: Race, Cinema, and Ethnographic Spectacle*. Duke University Press, 1996.

Toulet, Emmanuelle. "Le cinéma à l'Exposition universelle de 1900." *Revue d'histoire moderne et contemporaine* 33, no. 2 (1986): 179–209.

Ukadike, Frank. "African Cinematic Reality: The Documentary Tradition as an Emerging Trend." *Research in African Literatures* 26, no. 3 (1995): 88–96.

Ukadike, Frank. *Black African Cinema*. University of California Press, 1994.

Ukadike, Frank. *Questioning African Cinema: Conversations with Filmmakers*. University of Minnesota Press, 2002.

UNESCO. *Premier catalogue sélectif international de films ethnographiques sur l'Afrique noire*. 1967.

Ungar, Steven. *Critical Mass: Social Documentary in France from the Silent Era to the New Wave*. University of Minnesota Press, 2018.

Ungar, Steven. "Making Waves: René Vautier's *Afrique 50* and the Emergence of Anti-colonial Cinema." *L'esprit créateur* 51, no. 3 (2011): 34–46.

Van Bever, L. *Le cinéma pour africains*. G. Van Campenhout, 1952.

Vautier, René. *Caméra citoyenne: Mémoires*. Éditions Apogée, 1998.

Veray, Laurent. "Fiction et 'non-fiction' dans les films sur la Grande Guerre de 1914 à 1928." *1895, revue d'histoire du cinéma*, no. 18 (1995): 234–55.

Verhylle, A. "Les coulisses du cinématographe: La confection d'un film." *La science et la vie*, February 1914, 183–99.

Vienna Symposium. "The Documentary Film in Africa and Asia." Vienna Institute for Development, 1966.

Vieyra, Paulin Soumanou. *Le cinéma africain: Des origines à 1973*. Présence africaine, 1975.

Vieyra, Paulin Soumanou. *Le cinéma au Sénégal*. OCIC, 1983.

Vieyra, Paulin Soumanou. *Le cinéma et l'Afrique*. Présence africaine, 1969.

Vieyra, Paulin Soumanou. "Le cinéma et la révolution africaine." *Présence Africaine*, no. 34/35 (1960): 92–103.

Vieyra, Paulin Soumanou. "Le film africain d'expression française." *African Arts* 1, no. 3 (1968): 60–69.

Vieyra, Paulin Soumanou. "Quand le cinéma français parle au nom de l'Afrique noire." *Présence Africaine*, no. 11 (1956): 142–45.

Vieyra, Paulin Soumanou. *Réflexions d'un cineaste africain*. OCIC, 1990.

Vieyra, Paulin Soumanou. "Responsabilités du cinéma dans la formation d'une conscience nationale africaine." *Présence Africaine*, no. 27/28 (1959): 303–13.

Vieyra, Paulin Soumanou. *Sembène Ousmane, cineaste*. Présence Africaine, 1972.

Wilder, Gary. "Framing Greater France Between the Wars." *Journal of Historical Sociology* 14, no. 2 (2001): 198–225.

Williams, Alan. "The Lumière Organization and 'Documentary Realism.'" In *Film Before Griffith*, edited by John Fell, 153–61. University of California Press, 1983.

Williams, Alan. *Republic of Images: A History of French Filmmaking*. Harvard University Press, 1992.

Williams, James S. *Ethics and Aesthetics in Contemporary African Cinema: The Politics of Beauty*. Bloomsbury, 2019.

Williams, James S. "A Thousand Suns: Traversing the Archive and Transforming Documentary in Mari Diop's *Mille Soleils*." *Film Quarterly* 70, no. 1 (2016): 85–95.

Yervasi, Carina. "Youth and *Média-engagé*: Is This West Africa's Heterolinguistic Cinéma-monde?" In *Cinéma-monde: Decentred Perspectives on Global Filmmaking in French*, edited by Michael Gott and Thibaut Schilt, 304–20. Edinburgh University Press, 2018.

INDEX

Man Sa Yaye [I, your mother] (Faye, 1980), 227–28, 275

Manue, Georges, 114, 302

Man with a Movie Camera (Vertov, 1929), 5, 227

Maran, René, 87

Marchand, Colonel Jean-Baptiste, 27–28, 44, 45–46, 52n3

Marche vers le soleil, La [March toward the sun] (Le Somptier, 1930), 79, 86

Marey, Étienne-Jules, 20–21

Marguet, Jean, 61, 67

Mariage d'Alex, Le [Alex's wedding] (Teno, 2002), 275

Marie, Michel, 29

Marker, Chris, 136, 137, 154, 176, 254, 255, 258–59, 302

Mauritania, 89, 90, 141–42, 211, 213, 261

Mbakam, Rosine, 265–67, 284–87, 289

Mbaye, Ousmane William, 235, 290–92

Mbembe, Achille, 288, 300

Mbigou, poésie du Gabon [Mbigou, Gabonese poetry] (Augé, 1976), 191

M'Bow, Amadou Mahtar, 304

Mbow, Mouride Serigne Babacar, 275

Meignant, Michel, 183

Mekas, Jonas, 254

Melina (Woukoache, 1991), 255

Mercer, Kobena, 246

Mère bi [The mother] (Mbaye, 2008), 291

Mesguich, Félix, 4, 33, 38, 42, 86, 94

Mes voisins [My neighbors] (Hondo, 1971), 228–30, 229, 231, 233

Métiers, types, et coutumes [Trades, types, and customs] (Pathé, 1913), 46, 238

Michel, Thierry, 271

Mignolo, Walter, 300

Mille soleils [A thousand suns] (Diop, 2013), 197

Mirages de Paris [Parisian mirages] (Socé, 1937), 88

Mission Gradis au Sahara [Gradis mission to the Sahara] (Gaumont, 1924), 72

Moana (Flaherty, 1926), 5, 67, 91, 94

Moati, Serge, 223

Moeurs et coutumes des Chillouks [Habits and customs of the Shilluk] (Machin, 1910), 44, 45

Moi, un noir [I, a Black man] (Rouch, 1958), 140–41, 163, 224

Moignon, Pierre, 123

Môl [Fisherman] (Vieyra, 1966), 176–78, 215, 227

Momo, Jean de Dieu, 288–89

Mongita, Albert, 159

Mora-Kpai, Idrissou, 269–70, 271, 278–80

Moreau, René, 38, 88, 93, 104

Morocco, 23, 49, 62, 132

Mory, Philippe, 163, 191, 193

Mouly, Georges, 106–7

Mouramani (Touré), 160, 293

Mourlan, Roger, 109

Moussinac, Léon, 67, 74

Mozambique, 7, 155

Mudimbe, V. Y., 3, 112

Munyaneza, Eddy, 247

Murphy, David, 236

Museum of Mankind (Musée de l'Homme), 109, 121, 124, 130, 136; CFE (Committee for Ethnographic Film), 134; Ethnographic Film Committee, 163; Griaule and, 130; opening of, 105; reopening after World War II, 119; Rouch and, 131, 133. *See also* Trocadero Museum of Ethnography (Paris)

Musser, Charles, 6, 31

Mvet, Le (Zé, 1965/1972), 181

Mweze (Fila, 2020), 292

Mystères du continent noir, Les [Mysteries of the Black continent] (Aubert, 1926), 72–73

Nacro, Fanta Régina, 246

Naficy, Hamid, 255, 271

Nagib, Lúcia, 6

Nanook of the North (Flaherty, 1922), 5, 44, 67, 77, 91, 94, 132, 177

Nationalité immigré [Nationality: Immigrant] (Sokhona, 1975), 231

National Museum of Natural History, 19, 88, 105, 106

Nation est née, Une: La république du Sénégal [A nation was born: The Republic of Senegal] (Vieyra, 1961), 167–68, 177, 186, 227, 233

Nations nègres et culture [The African origin of civilization] (Diop, 1954), 292

Rachel Gabara is Nancy Gillespie Brinning Professor in French at the University of Georgia. She is author of *From Split to Screened Selves: French and Francophone Autobiography in the Third Person.*

For Indiana University Press

Sabrina Black, Editorial Assistant

Tony Brewer, Artist and Book Designer

Allison Chaplin, Acquisitions Editor

Anna Garnai, Production Coordinator

Sophia Hebert, Assistant Acquisitions Editor

Samantha Heffner, Marketing Production Manager

Katie Huggins, Production Manager

Gigi Lamm, Director of Sales and Marketing

Nancy Lightfoot, Project Manager/Editor

Alyssa Nicole Lucas, Marketing and Publicity Manager

Annie L. Martin, Editorial Director

Pamela Rude, Senior Artist and Book Designer

Dan Pyle, Online Publishing Manager

Michael Regoli, Director of Publishing Operations